16-34

THE PROTESTANT CHURCHES OF AMERICA is a comprehensive survey of the more than two hundred Protestant denominations in the United States today. It was written by John A. Hardon, one of the leading authorities on comparative religion, and the author of RELIGIONS OF THE WORLD, a presentation of the history, beliefs, and practices of the world's major religions.

In the present volume, Fr. Hardon has separated the American Protestant Churches into two classes, the major and the minor, in the interest of thoroughness and clarity. The fourteen major denominations represent by actual count 90 per cent of the total Protestant affiliation in the United States. These are treated individually and include every denomination with a half a million or more members together with smaller groups which have had a recognized influence on our pluralistic society. The minor denominations have been grouped into distinct families to concentrate a maximum of significant detail without confusing the reader unnecessarily. For each Church or group of Churches, the author covers its history, doctrinal position, ritual practice, and organizational structure.

A careful and accurate scholar, Fr. Hardon has used only Protestant sources—formal doctrinal statements, official Church publications, and books and tracts by the leading spokesmen of the various bodies treated. The resulting objectivity makes this an indispensable source book for Christians of all denominations.

In THE PROTESTANT CHURCHES OF AMERICA, John A. Hardon has succeeded in presenting an accurate, concise picture of American Protestantism which is informative in its concentration of significant data, illuminating in its firm grasp of the distinctive spirit of each of the denominations as well as the similarities among them, and above all interesting in its clear and readable presentation of the beliefs and practices of those Christian denominations which have had such a great influence on the American tradition.

JOHN A. HARDON, a Jesuit priest, is a leading authority in the field of comparative religion and the author of RELIGIONS OF THE WORLD, published by Image Books in two volumes.

RELIGIONS OF THE WORLD: Volume one (Image D 241A) clearly presents the history, beliefs, and practices of the eight major Oriental religions and Judaism. This includes Hinduism, Buddhism, Jainism, Confucianism, Taoism, Zoroastrianism, Shinto, Sikhism, and Judaism. Volume two (Image D 241B) offers the same comprehensive treatment of the leading religions of Judaic origin, covering Early Christianity, Catholicism, Islam, Eastern Orthodoxy, Protestantism, and Old Catholic Churches.

John A. Hardon, S.J.

The Protestant Churches of America

REVISED EDITION

IMAGE BOOKS

A Division of Doubleday & Company, Inc.

Garden City, New York

Image Books edition 1969
by special arrangement with Paulist-Newman Press

Image Books edition published March 1969

CONTENTS

ACKNOWLEDGMENTS

The author and publishers are gratefully indebted to about fifty copyright holders for permission to use quotations from their books and periodicals. Special gratitude is due to the National Council of the Churches of Christ for its generous co-operation in furnishing the statistical data on the religious bodies in the United States.

Where publishers requested a certain wording in the acknowledgment, this has been followed in each case. However, specific permission was received for the use of quotations from all the publications here listed.

If any publisher was inadvertently omitted from the following list, the author acknowledges the source quoted in the reference section which follows at the end of the book.

ABINGDON PRESS, New York and Nashville:
William K. Anderson (editor), *Methodism*, 1947. 1967; *Protestantism, A Symposium*, 1945.
Doctrines and Discipline of the Methodist Church, 1952, 1964.
Methodist Hymnal, 1966. [1967]
Charles C. Selecman, *The Methodist Primer*, 1953.
William M. Sweet, *Methodism in American History*, 1933. [1967]

AUGSBURG PUBLISHING HOUSE, Minneapolis:
Hjalmar Lendroth, "Confession and Absolution," *The Encyclopedia of the Lutheran Church*.

BARNES HOPKINS, St. John, New Brunswick:
George E. Levy, *The Baptists of the Maritime Provinces, 1753–1946*. [1967]

BEACON HILL PRESS, Kansas City, Missouri:
Mendell Taylor, *Fifty Years of Nazarene Missions*, 1958. [1967]

BEACON PRESS, INC., Boston:
Ralph L. Roy, *Apostles of Discord*, 1953.
Harry B. Scholefield, *Pocket Guide to Unitarianism*, 1955. [1967]
Services of Religion, 1953. [1967]

THE BETHANY PRESS, St. Louis:

B. A. Abbott, *The Disciples, An Interpretation,* 1964. [1967]

Alonzo W. Fortune, *Origin and Development of the Disciples,* 1953. [1967]

Winfred E. Garrison and Alfred T. DeGroot, *The Disciples of Christ, A History,* 1954. [1967]

G. Edwin Osborn, *Christian Worship—A Service Book,* 1963. [1967]

Benjamin L. Smith, *Minister's Manual,* 1951. [1967]

THE BRETHREN PRESS, Elgin, Illinois:

Paul H. Bowman, *An Adventurous Future,* 1959. [1967]

LEROY BROWNLOW PUBLICATIONS, Fort Worth, Texas:

Leroy Brownlow, *Why I Am a Member of the Church of Christ,* 1945. [1967]

The author was requested by Mr. Brownlow to add the following clarification: "One of the basic and fundamental teachings of the church of Christ is that she is neither Roman Catholic nor Protestant, but Christian only, believing that such was true of the church in the first century. Yet, permission is granted to quote from the book *Why I Am a Member of the Church of Christ* in this volume on *The Protestant Churches of America,* understanding that the purpose of the volume is to acquaint Roman Catholics with the views and convictions of non-Roman Catholics."

CAMBRIDGE UNIVERSITY PRESS, New York:

John L. Nickalls, *Journal of George Fox,* 1952. [1967]

CAREY KINGSGATE PRESS, London:

Ernest A. Payne, *The Fellowship of Believers,* 1952.

CHRISTIAN BOARD OF PUBLICATION, St. Louis. (See THE BETHANY PRESS.)

THE CHRISTIAN CENTURY, Chicago:

Issues of Dec. 16, 1953; July 6, Sept. 7, Nov. 23, 1955; Feb. 8, 1956. Copyrighted by the Christian Century Foundation and reprinted by permission from *The Christian Century.*

CHRISTIAN EDUCATION PRESS, Philadelphia:

Oscar J. Rumpf, *Christian Faith and Life,* 1952. [1967]

The Constitution and By-Laws of the Evangelical and Reformed Church.

My Confirmation, 1955. [1967]

THE CHRISTIAN SCIENCE PUBLISHING SOCIETY, Boston:

The Christian Science Journal, passages reprinted from December 1954 issue.

THE CHURCH OF JESUS CHRIST OF LATTER-DAY SAINTS, Salt Lake City:

Book of Mormon, 1921. [1967]

Joseph F. Smith, *Essentials in Church History*, 1950. [1967]

James E. Talmage, *Articles of Faith*. [1967]

CONCORDIA PUBLISHING HOUSE, St. Louis:

Walter A. Baepler, *A Century of Grace*, 1947. [1967]

F. E. Mayer, *The Religious Bodies of America*, 1954. [1967]

John T. Mueller, *My Church and Others*, 1945.

Francis Pieper, *Christian Dogmatics*, Vol. III, 1953. [1967]

Arthur G. Piepkorn, *What the Symbolical Books Have to Say About Worship and the Sacraments*, 1952. [1967]

E. G. Schwiebert, *Luther and His Times*, 1950. [1967]

Dr. Martin Luther's Small Catechism, 1943. [1967]

The Lutheran Agenda. [1967]

The Lutheran Hymnal, 1941. [1967]

CONGREGATIONAL CHRISTIAN CHURCHES, New York:

A Book of Worship for Free Churches. Copyright 1948 by The Board of Home Missions of The Congregational and Christian Churches. All rights reserved.

The Congregational Christian Ministry, 1953. Quoted with permission from the Department of the Ministry.

CONSERVATIVE BAPTIST ASSOCIATION OF AMERICA, Chicago:

Declaration of Purpose, 1965. [1967]

COWLES MAGAZINES, INC., New York:

Leo Rosten (editor), *A Guide to the Religions of America*, 1955. [1967]

DUELL, SLOAN AND PEARCE, INC., New York:

Norman Beasley, *The Cross and the Crown*, 1952. By permission of Duell, Sloan and Pearce, Inc. [1967]

EDEN-HEIDELBERG BOOKSTORES, St. Louis:

James I. Good, *Aid to the Heidelberg Catechism*. [1967]

J. H. Horstmann and H. H. Wernecke, *Through Four Centuries*, 1938. [1967]

Book of Worship, 1947. [1967]

Evangelical Catechism, 1929. [1967]

EERDMANS, Grand Rapids:

Jesse Jai McNeil (editor), *Minister's Service Book of Pulpit and Parish*, 1961. [1967]

THE EVANGELICAL PRESS, Harrisburg, Pennsylvania:

Paul H. Eller, *These Evangelical United Brethren*, 1950. [1967]

Paul W. Milhouse, *Christian Worship in Symbol and Ritual,* 1953. [1967]

The Discipline of the Evangelical United Brethren, 1947, 1955. [1967]

THE FRANK GAVIN LITURGICAL FOUNDATION, INC., Mount Sinai, New York:

The People's Anglican Missal in the American Edition, 1961. [1967]

GENERAL COUNCIL OF THE ASSEMBLIES OF GOD:

Statement of Fundamental Truths, 1961. [1967]

GOSPEL ADVOCATE COMPANY, Nashville:

G. C. Brewer, *Is the Church of Christ a Denomination.* [1967]

Leslie G. Thomas, *Restoration Handbook,* 1954. [1967]

GOSPEL PUBLISHING HOUSE, Springfield, Missouri:

Klaude Kendreick, *The Promise Fulfilled: A History of the American Pentecostal Movement,* 1961. [1967]

GOSPEL TRACTS UNLIMITED, Hayward, California:

J. M. Stowell, *Background and History of the General Association of Regular Baptist Churches,* 1949.

HALF MOON PRESS, Grand Rapids, Michigan:

Constitution of the Reformed Church in America, 1950.

HARPER AND BROTHERS, New York:

Harry E. Fosdick, *The Man from Nazareth,* 1949.

Winfred E. Garrison, *Religion Follows the Frontier,* 1931. [1967]

Rufus M. Jones, *The Faith and Practice of the Quakers,* 1927.

Charles S. Morrison, *The Unfinished Reformation,* 1953. [1967]

Anson P. Stokes, *Church and State in the United States,* Vols. II, III, 1950. [1967]

Mark Twain, *Christian Science,* 1907. [1967]

J. Paul Williams, *What Americans Believe and How They Worship,* 1952. [1967]

HENRY HOLT, New York:

G. Bromley Oxnam, *Social Problems in America,* 1955. [1967]

W. L. JENKINS, Philadelphia:

Presbyterian Law for the Local Church, edited by Eugene Carson Blake. Copyright 1954 by W. L. Jenkins. Used by permission. [1967]

THE JUDSON PRESS, Philadelphia and Valley Forge:

A New Baptist Church Manual, 1966. [1967]

J. Newton Brown (editor), *The Baptist Church Manual,* 1965. [1967]

Edward T. Hiscox, *The New Directory for Baptist Churches.* [1967]

J. M. Pendleton, *Baptist Church Manual,* 1955. [1967]

Robert G. Torbet, *A History of the Baptists.* Copyright 1950 by The Judson Press. [1967]

JOHN KNOX PRESS, Richmond, Virginia:

Walter Lingle, *Presbyterians, Their History and Beliefs.* Copyright 1950 by John Knox Press, Richmond, Virginia. Used by permission. [1967]

LITTLEFIELD-ADAMS, Patterson:

Vergilius Ferm (editor), *Living Schools of Religion,* 1961. [1967]

THE LIVING CHURCH, Milwaukee:

Editorials from the issues of Apr. 29, 1951; Aug. 30, 1953; Nov. 6, 1955.

LONGMANS, GREEN AND CO., INC., New York:

Ernest W. Barnes, *The Rise of Christianity,* 1947. [1967]

William James, *The Varieties of Religious Experience,* 1902.

THE MACMILLAN COMPANY, New York:

Vergilius Ferm, *What Is Lutheranism?* 1930. [1967]

Rufus M. Jones, *A Call to What Is Vital,* 1948.

William A. Linn, *The Story of the Mormons,* 1923.

MENNONITE PUBLISHING HOUSE, Scottdale, Pennsylvania:

Mennonite Confession of Faith, 1963. [1967]

MOREHOUSE-GORHAM CO., INC., New York:

George P. Atwater, *The Episcopal Church, Its Message for Men of Today,* page 74. Copyright 1953 by Marie Carey Atwater. Used by permission of Morehouse-Gorham Co., New York. [1967]

George E. De Mille, *The Episcopal Church Since 1900,* pages 74, 85, and 118. Copyright 1955 by Morehouse-Gorham Co.

F. S. B. Gavin, *Liberal Catholicism and the Modern World,* Vol. I, page vii. Copyright 1934 by Morehouse-Gorham Co. [1967]

NATIONAL COUNCIL OF THE CHURCHES OF CHRIST, New York:

Preamble to the Constitution, 1950. [1967]

Yearbook of American Churches 1968. Copyright 1968 by The National Council of Churches. Used with permission.

NATIONAL SPIRITUALIST ASSOCIATION OF CHURCHES, U.S.A., Milwaukee:

Declaration of Principles. [1967]

NATIONAL SPIRITUALIST ASSOCIATION, Washington:
Spiritualist Manual. [1967]

NAZARENE PUBLISHING HOUSE, Kansas City, Missouri:
Constitution and Special Rules, Church of the Nazarene, 1966. [1967]

OUTLOOK PUBLISHERS, Richmond, Virginia:
Kenneth J. Foreman, *God's Will and Ours,* 1954.

OXFORD UNIVERSITY PRESS, INC., New York:
The Book of Common Prayer, 1944. Quotations used through the courtesy of Rev. John W. Suter, D.D., Custodian of the Standard Book of Common Prayer.

PACIFIC PRESS PUBLISHING ASSOCIATION, Mountain View, California:
Uriah Smith, *The Prophecies of Daniel and the Revelation,* 1951.

Ellen G. White, *The Desire of the Ages,* 1955 [1967]; *The Great Controversy Between Christ and Satan,* 1953 [1967].

THE PENTECOSTAL HOLINESS PUBLISHING HOUSE, Franklin Springs, Georgia:
Joseph Cambell, *The Pentecostal Holiness Church,* 1951. [1967]

PENTECOSTAL PUBLISHING HOUSE, St. Louis, Missouri:
Our Gospel Message. [1967]
Your Special Invitation. [1967]

PHILADELPHIA YEARLY MEETING OF THE RELIGIOUS SOCIETY OF FRIENDS:
Faith and Practice of the Philadelphia Yearly Meeting, 1955.

PHILOSOPHICAL LIBRARY, INC., New York:
Vergilius Ferm (editor), *The American Church,* 1953. [1967]
Henry W. Steiger, *Christian Science and Philosophy,* 1948.

PILGRIM PRESS, Boston:
G. G. Atkins and F. L. Fagley, *History of American Congregationalism,* 1941.
Richard H. Bennet, *Christian Faith and Purpose, A Catechism.*
L. Wendell Fifield, *What It Means to Be a Member of the Congregational Church.*
Oscar Maurer (editor), *Manual of the Congregational Christian Churches,* 1951. [1967]
Roy L. Minich, *What the Church Has to Offer.* [1967]
Albert W. Palmer, *I Believe in Baptism.*
Christian Teachings: A Manual for Those Preparing for Church Membership. [1967]
Manual for Church Members, 1952. [1967]

My Church: Pastor's Manual, 1944.

The Congregational Christian Churches, For What They Stand. [1967]

We Believe. [1967]

PRESBYTERIAN CHURCH IN THE U.S.A., Philadelphia:

The Book of Common Worship. Copyright 1946 by the Board of Christian Education of the Presbyterian Church in the U.S.A. Used by permission.

Confessional Documents of the Presbyterian Church in the U.S.A.

The Constitution of the Presbyterian Church in the U.S.A., Revised Edition. Copyright 1955 by the Board of Christian Education of the Presbyterian Church in the U.S.A. Used by permission.

C. McAfee and E. Porter, *Why A Presbyterian Church.* Copyright 1930 by the Board of Christian Education of the Presbyterian Church in the U.S.A. Used by permission. [1967]

PROTESTANT EPISCOPAL CHURCH IN THE U.S.A.:

Constitution and Canons for the Government of the Protestant Episcopal Church in the U.S.A., 1964. [1967]

REVIEW AND HERALD PUBLISHING ASSOCIATION, Washington, D.C.:

Leroy E. Froom, *The Prophetic Faith of Our Fathers,* Vol. IV, 1954. [1967]

Emma E. Howell, *The Great Advent Movement,* 1951. [1967]

Francis D. Nicol, *Answers to Objections,* 1952. [1967]

James White, *Sketches of the Christian Life and Public Labors of William Miller,* 1875.

Manual for Ministers, 1964. [1967]

Seventh-Day Adventist Yearbook, 1967.

SALVATIONIST PUBLISHING AND SUPPLIES, LTD., London:

William Booth, *In Darkest England and the Way Out,* 1942. [1967]

M. L. Carpenter, *Salvationists and the Sacraments,* 1945. [1967]

Alfred J. Gilliard, *The Faith of the Salvationist.*

Orders and Regulations for Officers of the Salvation Army, 1950. [1967]

Salvation Army Ceremonies, 1947. [1967]

Salvation Army Handbook of Doctrine, 1955. [1967]

Salvation Army Yearbook, 1956. [1967]

SCIENTIFIC AMERICAN, New York:

Issues of February and May 1952.

CHARLES SCRIBNER'S SONS, New York:

James T. Addison, *The Episcopal Church in the United States*, 1951. [1967]

William A. Brown, *Toward A United Church*, 1946. [1967]

Edwin F. Dakin, *Mrs. Eddy*, 1930.

Reinhold Niebuhr, *Beyond Tragedy*, 1937 [1967]; *Human Destiny*, 1935. [1967]

THE SEABURY PRESS, INC., Greenwich, Connecticut:

Powel Mills Dawley, *The Episcopal Church and Its Work*, 1955.

Greenwich: The Seabury Press. Used by permission of the publisher. [1967]

James A. Pike and W. Norman Pittenger, *The Faith of the Church*, 1951. Greenwich: The Seabury Press. Used by permission of the publisher. [1967]

Report of the Anglican Congress, 1954, Powel Mills Dawley, editor. Greenwich: The Seabury Press. Used by permission of the publisher. [1967]

W. J. Wolf (editor), *Protestant Churches and Reform Today*, 1964. [1967]

SIMON AND SCHUSTER, INC., New York. (See Cowles Magazines.)

SOCIETY FOR PROMOTING CHRISTIAN KNOWLEDGE, London:

Theodore Andrews, *The Polish National Catholic Church*, 1953. [1967]

Peter F. Anson, *The Call of the Cloister*, 1955. [1967]

Report of the Lambeth Conference, 1930. [1967]

SOCIETY FOR REFORMED PUBLICATIONS, Grand Rapids, Michigan:

Reformed Standards of Unity, 1957. [1967]

SOUTHERN BAPTIST CONVENTION (BROADMAN AND CONVENTION PRESS), Nashville:

Baptist Faith and Message. [1967]

James R. Hobbs, *The Pastor's Manual.*

Thomas B. McDormand, *The Art of Building Worship Services*, 1946. [1967]

THE STANDARD PUBLISHING FOUNDATION, Cincinnati:

Alexander Campbell, *The Christian System.* [1967]

James DeForest Murch, *Christian Minister's Manual*, 1937.

STUDENT CHRISTIAN MOVEMENT PRESS, LTD., London:

R. Newton Flew (editor), *The Nature of the Church: Papers Presented to the Theological Commission of the World Conference on Faith and Order*, 1952. [1967]

Stephen Neill, *Towards Church Union*, 1952. [1967]

Oliver S. Tomkins (editor), *Third World Conference on Faith and Order*, 1953.

TRUSTEES UNDER THE WILL OF MARY BAKER EDDY, Boston:
Mary Baker Eddy, *Science and Health with Key to the Scriptures*, 1934, 1967; *Message to the Mother Church*, 1900. [1967]
Manual of the Mother Church, the First Church of Christ, Scientist, 1895.

UNITARIAN UNIVERSALIST ASSOCIATION, Boston:
Constitution. [1967]
J. Mendelsohn, *Why I Am a Unitarian Universalist*, 1966. [1967]

UNITED LUTHERAN CHURCH OF AMERICA, Philadelphia:
Works of Martin Luther, Vols. III, VI, 1930–32. By permission of the Board of Publication of the United Lutheran Church. [1967]

UNITY SCHOOL OF CHRISTIANITY, Lee's Summit, Missouri:
Eric Butterworth, *The Word is Unity*, 1967.
Unity Statement of Faith, 1967.
What is Unity? 1967.

UNIVERSITY OF CHICAGO PRESS:
Paul Tillich, *The Protestant Era.* Copyright 1963 by the University of Chicago. [1967]

VANTAGE PRESS, INC., New York:
Marley Cole, *Jehovah's Witnesses*, 1955. [1967]
Owen D. Pelt and Ralph Lee Smith, *The Story of the National Baptists*, 1960. [1967]

VOLUNTEERS OF AMERICA:
Statement of Cardinal Principles of the Volunteers of America. Received from National Headquarters, June 30, 1967.

THE WESTMINSTER PRESS, Philadelphia:
The Book of Common Worship, 1964. [1967]
J. Fletcher, *Situation Ethics, The New Morality*, 1966. [1967]
L. A. Loetscher, *A Brief History of the Presbyterians.* Copyright 1938 by The Westminster Press. Used by permission. [1967]

INTRODUCTION

This volume is intended for the general non-specialist reader, to give him an up-to-date manual of information on the Protestant churches in the United States. The need for such a manual is obvious. Catholics and Protestants deal with one another on every level of human relationship, from the intimacy of family life to the less personal but very important associations in the professional and business world. Yet each of us has often only the vaguest notion of what our fellow Christians believe, how they worship, and what their religion means to them. It is the intent of the author of this volume to give a straightforward and objective account of these aspects of the various Protestant denominations in the United States.

Instead of trying to cover all two hundred denominations in the country, and as a consequence saying little about any one of them, it seemed preferable to separate the churches into two classes, the major and the minor, and treat the individual denominations in greater detail. The fourteen churches in the first class were chosen on the basis of their size or because of their recognized influence in American sectarian life. They include every denomination with a half million or more members, and smaller groups like the Unitarians and Quakers because of their historic impact on our pluralistic society. By actual count, these fourteen bodies represent 90 per cent of the total Protestant affiliation in the United States. The other 10 per cent, scattered through a bewildering variety of organizations, were conveniently grouped into distinctive families to make their treatment more intelligible. The major denominations are covered at greater length, going into the respective church histories, their doctrinal position, ritual practice, and organizational structure. But in every case, even for the smallest society, the aim was to concentrate a maximum of significant detail in order to give the reader a concise picture of American Protestantism in the present day.

The most serious problem that faces anyone who writes on Protestant beliefs and practices is where to find authentic information. When a cynic remarked that "trying to describe Protestantism is like trying to describe the United States, one can say almost anything about it," he was exaggerating. But the fact remains that Protestants have "no united voice with which to give authoritative answers" on what they believe and how their people worship. They are distinctive as denominations, and further divided as subdenominations, and still further as churches within the smaller divisions. The practical solution which the writer adopted was to limit his source of information in doctrinal and ritual matters to official publications of the various bodies and to writings by leaders within the denominations. It was assumed that in spite of the freedom of thought in American Protestantism, whatever common elements the churches profess may be found in these two sources. Moreover, even for historical data, only Protestant authorities were used in order to give as objective a presentation as the resources of time (several years) and material (several hundred books and tracts) would allow.

There is an obvious risk in reading about so many different bodies with such a variety of religious persuasions. It may be impossible to recognize the forest for the trees. Yet Protestantism in America is not an aggregation of conflicting opinions. It has features that are quite different from those of other religious bodies in the country, and even distinct from Protestantism outside the United States. The first may easily be traced to its Reformation ancestry. The second is more subtle, and may be partially explained as a transfer of American love of liberty to the sphere of religion, with consequent fragmentation of churches, and more recently with a growing ecumenical consciousness that is trying to correct this historical sectarianism.

Protestants deplore the multiplicity of churches in America. They confess that "denominationalism is scandalously wasteful of Protestant resources," by it "the missionary expansion of the Christian faith is seriously handicapped," it "robs Protestantism of its inherent strength in its inescapable competition with a formidable and aggressive Roman Catholicism," it "provincializes Protestant mentality" and "breeds a subtle and perilous moral insincerity among Protestant Christians."[1] The ecumenical movement has been remarkably successful in reuniting a divided Protestantism in the United States.

While the beginnings of the ecumenical movement in America go back more than a century, large-scale mergers of Protestant denominations have all taken place since 1900. By 1950, thirty religious bodies had merged into thirteen, and these by remerger were reduced to nine. Since then organic mergers have affected practically every major Protestant body in the country.

The most ambitious plan to date is the Consultation on Church Union, in which some ten denominations (excluding the Lutherans) are planning to join. This would be the largest Protestant body in America.

Besides denominational mergers in which the uniting elements fused into a new society or one element absorbed the others, there have been three other coalitions on a wider but less intensive scale, in which the product was not a new church but a co-operative organization. The three federations are closely related.

In 1908 came the Federal Council of Churches of Christ in America, when twenty-eight Reformed Churches were organized along structural lines which duplicated the federal union of the United States. It was difficult at first for the churches of the Federal Council to believe that their autonomy would not be jeopardized. This suspicion kept many from joining the union. Actually they had nothing to fear because the federation was most careful not to encroach on the independence of the member churches. One incident in the forty-year existence of the Federal Council may illustrate its character. For years the Unitarians had asked to be admitted and were always refused. Their creedal position was too liberal. They deny the Trinity and their concept of God is not far removed from monism. Ostensibly, therefore, the motive for refusing them admission was based on principle. But when the president of the Council was directly questioned, he admitted it was a matter of expediency. "If we let in the Unitarians, we let out the Lutherans."[2]

The second stage in federated unionism came in 1941, when ultraconservative Protestants formed an organization of their own in protest against the "libertarian" Federal Council. While the latter would have been happy to admit the Conservatists, "provided they came in a cooperative spirit," their opponents claimed that the leaders of the Federal Council were promoting a new denominational effort independently of the Word of God. The American Council of Christian Churches is therefore a rival organization, comprising about a dozen national constituent bodies together with independent congregations. However, because Fundamentalists are generally found among the poorer and less privileged classes, in rural areas and small towns, they are not generally taken seriously. Their aggressive dogmatism is said to be antiquarian, "frozen in the crudest form of orthodoxy known in Protestant history."[3]

Finally, in 1950 the Federal Council of Churches enlarged its scope of activities and changed its name to the National Council of the Churches of Christ, to become the largest federated union of Protestants in American history. It numbers most of America's Protestant denominations and the main Orthodox bodies in this country. Structurally the National Council is the same as its predecessor, with a notable difference. Three new agencies were added for co-operative effort: Christian Education, the Home, and Foreign Missions. Their inclusion in the National Council marked an appreciable deepening of the feeling of Protestant unity. For these three functions came nearer to being ecclesiastical than any which the denominations had ever committed to a federal responsibility.

However, the National Council is not a union of denominations; it is a merger of their common, external interests. In the preamble to its Constitution, the founders of the National Council gave the reasons for establishing this federation. "In the Providence of God," they declared, "the time has come when it seems fitting more fully to manifest oneness in Jesus Christ as Divine Lord and Savior, by the creation of an inclusive cooperating agency of the Christian churches of the United States . . . to continue and extend the . . . general agencies of the churches and to combine all their interests and functions."[4] Since the Constitution was adopted, the Council has firmly adhered to these principles, with great benefit not only to its affiliated members but to the whole cause of Christian unity.

There is a permanent and healthy tension in American Protestantism which it is hoped the following pages will clarify: a tension between the "Protestant" and "Catholic" elements in the denominations; between the spirit of independence and a strong sense of tradition; or, in Paul Tillich's phrase, between the autonomy which asserts that "man as the bearer of universal reason is the source and measure of culture and religion—that he is his own law," and the heteronomy which holds that man requires help from the outside, ultimately from God, but proximately "subjects the forms and laws of thinking and acting to authoritative criteria of an ecclesiastical religion."[5]

Certain denominations like the Episcopalians and Lutherans will be seen to emphasize the heteronomous side of Protestantism; others, like the Congregationalists, to stress autonomous self-sufficiency—but in every case the dialectic is somehow there. Once recognized, it becomes a frame of reference for making a proper estimate of any religious body. It helps to explain the ebb and flow of Protestant orthodoxy, the constant struggle between liberals and conservatives in every denomination, and the growing sense of urgency that has produced the ecumenical movement. It affords an insight into what seem to be paradoxes, but which Protestants prefer to call "an inclusive Christianity." Above all, it gives to all Christians a sympathetic understanding of what others believe and a desire to share their common loyalty to Jesus Christ.

PREFACE TO THE NEW EDITION

Since it was first published in the fall of 1956, *The Protestant Churches of America* has gone through nine printings. Its general acceptance by so many readers as an authentic description of American Protestantism is also its highest recommendation. Why, then, a new edition with the most extensive revision since the book was written as a concise manual on the Protestant churches based exclusively on Protestant sources?

The reason is not that the churches have essentially changed in the last decade. There have been mergers and realignments, and a much greater involvement in the ecumenical movement. But the churches themselves are substantially the same. This is not an a priori judgment but one based on a lifetime of study and constant association with Protestant leadership in the academic and ecclesiastical world.

Reflecting the stable character of American Protestantism is the keeping of all the principal ideas and interpretations from the first edition in the present volume. In that sense *The Protestant Churches of America* has not been revised.

What called for revision, however, were the myriad details of persons, events, and data that are associated with any growing movement such as Protestantism, and with any institution such as America's numerous denominations.

The nearest thing to a major revision was made in dealing with the United Methodists, the Pentecostals, and the United Presbyterians.

Coming into existence as a new religious body in 1968, the United Methodists typify the prevalent tendency to reduce the number of separated churches where previous history or current policy recommends organic union, in this case with the Evangelical United Brethren.

The Pentecostals now have a chapter of their own among the principal denominations. Recent developments warrant the more extensive treatment of what many consider the most significant feature of present-day American Protestantism, the rise of a "Third Force" in our religious culture that caters especially to the spiritually deprived among our people.

When the United Presbyterians in 1967 adopted a new confession of faith, they did not replace the classic Westminster Confession that is still standard for Protestants in the Anglo-Saxon Reformed tradition. Yet their willingness to produce a new witness of faith illustrates the general desire among the heirs of Luther and Calvin to express the genius of the Reformers in terms that are relevant to modern times.

Reference sources are now placed together at the end of the volume, instead of following each chapter. This was done in order to give the book more continuity. The whole reference section was brought up to date. Where ministers' manuals or official denominational sources are quoted, often two dates are given: the first is that of the latest printed edition, and the second is the most recent date that the work was issued by the denominational publishing house.

Moreover, the new edition could not have been done except for the generous and competent assistance of many persons, especially of Mrs. Warren Joyce and Joseph Radelet, whose many hours of research and secretarial assistance were indispensable.

A companion volume is being published under the title *The Origins and Spirit of American Protestantism,* as a comprehensive source book of the confessions of faith and creedal positions of all the major denominations stemming from the Reformation.

If we cannot predict the future we can at least guess how promising it must be for interfaith relations in the United States in the light of all that has happened since Pope John and the now famous passage in the *Decree on Ecumenism,* that "all who have been justified by faith in baptism . . . are accepted as brothers by the members of the Catholic Church."

The Protestant Churches of America has contributed its own modest share to improving these relations in the past. In Protestant circles, it was adopted as a textbook in colleges and seminaries. And the author was informed that it is regularly used by Vatican officials as a reference book in matters relating to American Protestantism. Hopefully the new edition will be just as acceptable and ecumenically profitable in the future.

PART ONE

MAJOR PROTESTANT
DENOMINATIONS

Adventists

The largest Adventist body in the United States, the Seventh-Day Adventists, in many ways reflects the spectrum of Protestant Christianity. Its emphasis on Old Testament practices as a corrective of the New Law has led to the adoption of the Jewish Sabbath in place of the Christian Sunday, and the acceptance of a rigid code of abstinence from forbidden food and drink. Its desire for release from the evils of this world has become crystallized in the doctrine of an early second coming of Christ and the consequent millennium. Its insistence on private interpretation of the Bible has developed into a theory of private inspiration beyond the sacred Scriptures, with visions and prophecies which amplify the Christian revelation.

At the same time, the Seventh-Day Adventists have gained a reputation as the most generous church-givers in America. Every member is carefully instructed on the duty of tithing. One tenth of his income, from whatever source, should be turned over to God. The tangible result has been a chain of publishing houses and sanatoriums, missions and educational institutions in more than twenty countries, including Soviet Russia—a tribute to Adventist zeal and often, as in Latin America, a challenge to Roman Catholicism.

HISTORY

While Adventism as a religious phenomenon has been found in every period of Christian history, the existing Adventist churches in America trace their origin to the preaching of William Miller, a Baptist minister, who predicted the end of the world in the early 1840s. Miller was a farmer whose studies of the Book of Daniel convinced him that the second coming of Christ to the earth would take place between March 21, 1843, and March 21, 1844. He preached his first Adventist sermon in 1831, and by 1844 an estimated fifty thousand followers anxiously awaited the imminent Parousia. When March 21, 1844, passed without anything happening, the Adventists were dismayed and Miller wrote, "I confess my error and acknowledge my disappointment." But he added, "I still believe that the day of the Lord is near, even at the door."[1] One of his disciples discovered that Miller had miscalculated by seven months. The real date was October 21, 1844. Enthusiasm flared up again; men planted no crops, gave away their money, and settled their debts in anticipation of the fateful day. When nothing happened a second time, the Millerite movement split into three main divisions. A small group remained faithful to Miller and organized as the American Millennial Association (later the Evangelical Adventists), but through internal dissensions was finally (1926) dissolved as a separate denomination.

Another segment was rallied by Jonathan Cummings, who advanced the coming of Christ to 1854. When nothing materialized, the society was reorganized along congregational lines, minus the specific millennium, and came to be known as the Advent Christian Church.

The Advent Christians split from the parent body over the doctrine of the immortality of the soul. Their new concept of conditional immortality explained that the dead are unconscious until the final resurrection, after which only the good will exist into eternity. A General Conference was organized at Salem, Massachusetts, in 1860. They adopted a creedal statement in 1900. Unlike the Seventh-Day body, the Advent Christians worship on Sundays.

A kindred group of Adventists, the Life and Advent Union, was organized in 1863. Its main grievance with the Millerites was over Sabbatarianism. They insisted that the Christian Sabbath is on the first day of the week. In 1964 they merged with the Advent Christian Church.

The headquarters of the Advent Christian Church is in Aurora, Illinois. Advent Christians conduct two prominent institutions of higher learning, in Aurora and Lenox, Massachusetts. Mission work began in 1891 and now extends to Mexico, Malaya, Japan, India, and the Philippine Islands.

Independent local groups of Adventists formed a small national organization in 1921 under the name of the Church of

God, Abrahamic Faith. The name symbolizes a literal belief that a second coming of Christ will start at Jerusalem in deference to the Jewish ancestors of the Savior. Their central authority is located in Oregon, Illinois.

The most important offshoot of the Millerites, the present Seventh-Day Adventists, owes its inception and remarkable development to the reputed mystical experiences of a woman disciple of William Miller, Ellen Harmon, later Mrs. James White. Her family joined the Miller followers in 1840. In December 1844, at the age of seventeen, she reported her first heavenly vision, predicting the growth of Adventism, to be followed by other communications which directed the Millerites to organize into an evangelistic body. After years of struggle, along with encouragement from Ellen White, the Adventists held their first General Conference, May 20–23, 1863, at Battle Creek, Michigan.

They elected Mrs. White's husband, James, as president, but he declined in favor of John Byington, although White later served three full terms as head of the Seventh-Day Adventists. Meantime his wife became the mainstay and guide of the young denomination, alternating between messages from God and communication to the Adventists by word of mouth and in published writings. Though she had never studied theology, her output of religious literature was monumental: twenty full-length volumes and upward of three thousand articles, dealing with every phase of Scripture exegesis, dogmatics, morals, and church organization and government. "Of myself," she wrote in 1905, "I could not have brought out the truths in these books, but the Lord has given me the help of His Holy Spirit. These books, giving instruction that the Lord has given me during the past sixty years, contain light from heaven, and will bear the test of investigation."[2]

Under her direction, the Adventists entered the publishing business on a scale unparalleled in any other denomination of like size. "You must begin to print a little paper," a vision told her. "From this small beginning it was shown to me to be like streams of light that went clear around the world."[3] At present, the Adventists have publishing houses in some forty countries, printing literature in two hundred languages and dialects, with Braille for the blind, and including several hundred periodicals. "These simple facts," the Adventists claim, "speak for themselves. The test of prediction [by Ellen White] seems fully met in this . . . literary production."[4]

In 1872 Mrs. White published a work on *Proper Education,* after "God had shown her . . . the plan upon which our denominational schools should be founded."[5] She urged the building of church schools, with special emphasis on combining mental training with physical exercise and the learning of mechanical skills. From a single academy in 1872, the Adventists now operate several thousand institutions, in addition to so-called Sabbath Schools, with more than a million pupils.

Parallel with institutional education, the Adventists have organized the Missionary Volunteer movement for the youth. The purpose is concisely expressed in its aim: "The Advent Message to All the World in This Generation." Its solemn pledge reflects the spirit of service that binds the members in fellowship in every land: "Loving the Lord Jesus, I promise to take an active part in the work of the Young Peoples Missionary Volunteer Society, doing what I can to help others and to finish the work of the gospel in all the world." Its source of inspiration is revealed in the motto: "The Love of Christ Constraineth Us."

Early in the beginnings of Adventism, some leaders urged the scriptural obligation of keeping the Sabbath instead of Sunday as the Lord's Day. The controversy which arose was finally settled by a vision of Mrs. White, in which she saw the tables of the Law and "the fourth [Catholic third] commandment with a soft halo of light encircling it." She was told by the angel in the vision that "It is the only one of the ten which defines the living God." And "if the true Sabbath had been kept, there would never have been an infidel or an atheist."[6] Further publicity ensured acceptance of the doctrine as coessential with the imminent second coming of Christ. The name "Seventh-Day Adventists" was officially adopted in 1860.

Another divine communication from Mrs. White confirmed the Adventists in the elaborate health program which is now part of their denominational character. First came "a message which pointed out the dangers of the use of such poisonous articles as tobacco, tea and coffee. A little later, further instruction was given on the importance of cleanliness, both of the person and of the surroundings." Finally, "there was opened up to Mrs. White, in a very comprehensive vision, the important relationship which exists between good health and godliness and efficiency in service. The causes of disease, its treatment through aiding nature in its work, and other phases of the health message, such as diet, rest, exercise and cleanliness, were all opened up to Mrs. White in this vision."[7] In response to these revelations, the Adventists went into the manufacture and distribution of vegetarian, non-stimulant, non-intoxicating foods. They have more than fifty food companies in various countries. They also began the construction of hospitals, sanatoria, and rest homes, with a concentration in the foreign mission field; for example, there are over forty hospitals and dispensaries directly controlled by the Seventh-Day Adventists in South Africa. The American Health and Temperance Association was formed in 1879, requiring its members to abstain from intoxicating beverages, tobacco, and all stimulants, including coffee and tea. During the presidential campaign of 1932, the American Temperance Society was organized "to preserve the cause of temperance," by education and propaganda.

Under pressure from their environment, the Adventists founded the National Religious Liberty Association, now a department of the General Conference. Its establishment in 1888 was occasioned by the introduction into Congress of a bill which provided for the proper observance of Sunday as a day of rest. Adventists opposed the bill in public congressional hearings because they considered "the whole principle of [civil] legislation in behalf of a religious institution as fundamentally wrong."[8] Twenty years later a series of similar bills was proposed for the District of Columbia, but defeated when the Adventists presented to Congress a lengthy memorial which has since become a classic statement of protest against Sunday legislation in America. The passage of such laws, it declared, "would mark the first step on the part of the national government in the path of religious legislation—a path which leads inevitably to religious persecution."[9] In practice, the Religious Liberty Department is mainly concerned with protecting the Adventists' right to observe the Sabbath in-

stead of Sunday as the Lord's Day. Behind this agitation lies
a principle delivered by Mrs. White, foretelling that "there
would arise in the United States a hierarchy similar to the
Papacy of the Middle Ages, which would use the civil power
of the government to accomplish its own ends."[10] By its
insistence on the observance of Sunday, Adventists are told,
the United States is promoting the world domination by Rome
which changed the Sabbath Day of Scripture in opposition
to the Law of God.

Evangelism outside the States began in 1874, when an
American Adventist "responded to a call" from a small group
of "Sabbath-keepers" in Switzerland. A year later the movement spread to Germany, and then through all the countries
of Europe. Spearheading the work on the continent was an
ex-priest, M. B. Czechowski, who "believed in the second
coming of Christ and in the seventh-day Sabbath," after
proper indoctrination in America. Currently Adventist periodicals are published in every country of Europe, including Iceland, Spain, and Italy. Oceania was opened to the Adventist
apostolate in 1885, after Mrs. White had a vision which specified Australia as the next object of evangelization. A newspaper criticism of the Adventists read by a man in Argentina
led to the introduction of the church into South America in
1890, which has since become the principal field of missionary activity, where some of the most powerful radio stations
are broadcasting the Adventist message. Missions in Asia and
Africa are operating in all the major countries, especially India and South Africa. No matter how thinly spread, the Adventists want to be represented in as many nations as possible,
on the conviction that even a handful of zealous workers can
affect a whole country because of the promised help of the
Holy Spirit.

DOCTRINE AND RITUAL

The Seventh-Day Adventists have no formally adopted creed.
They consider the Scriptures "all sufficient" and "the only
unerring rule of faith and practice."[11] Jesus Christ is accepted as "very God, being of the same nature and essence

as the Eternal Father." While remaining God, "He took upon Himself the nature of the human family, lived on earth as a man, exemplified in His life as our Example the principles of righteousness, attested His relationship to God by many mighty miracles, died for our sins on the cross, was raised from the dead, and ascended to the Father, where He lives to make intercession for us."[12]

As a church system, the Adventists refuse to "consider themselves . . . simply another in the maze of denominations, but rather are in the line of those dissentients of the centuries [like] the Waldenses, Wycliffites, Hussites, Reformers, Baptists and Wesleyans."[13] They claim that many innovations alien to apostolic Christianity were introduced, first by Rome and then by modernist Protestants. Above all, two principles of the ancient Church need to be recovered: Adventism and Sabbatarianism, from whose emphasis the Seventh-Day Adventists receive their distinctive name. As Adventists, they believe in "the imminent, personal, visible, and pre-millennial return of Jesus Christ to redeem His followers"; as Sabbatarians, they hold "the observance of the seventh day as the Sabbath in obedience to the changeless obligation of the moral law and the express example of Christ."[14] Both elements call for explanation.

Second Coming. Adventist teaching on the Parousia is based on a singular interpretation of the prophetic text in Daniel 8:14, foretelling that: "Unto evening and morning, two thousand three hundred days: and the sanctuary shall be cleansed." William Miller explained the text to mean that twenty-three hundred years from 457 B.C. (the reputed date of Daniel's vision), Christ would come to cleanse the sanctuary (earth) in final judgment at the end of the world. He projected twenty-three hundred years from 457 B.C. and concluded that the end of the world would come in A.D 1843–1844.

When the prediction failed, the Adventists reinterpreted the prophecy, retaining 1844 as a key date, but explaining that what actually happened in that year was not a purification of the earthly sanctuary but a cleansing process only began in 1844 and "its completion will close human probation." It is "a time of investigative judgment, first with reference to the dead, and secondly with reference to the living. This investigative judgment determines who of the myriads sleeping in the dust of the earth are worthy of a part of the first resurrection and who of its living multitudes are worthy of translation."[15]

To be stressed is the brevity of this investigative judgment, which is the present age. Once completed, there will be the second coming of Christ, accompanied by the resurrection of the just, to be followed by a thousand years (millennium) which are closed with the resurrection of the wicked. At the end of the millennium, "the finally impenitent, including Satan, the author of sin, will, by the fires of the last day be reduced to a state of non-existence, becoming as though they had not been, thus purging God's universe of sin and sinners."[16]

In their statement of *Fundamental Beliefs,* the Seventh-Day Adventists profess an eschatology that is often misunderstood.

> The Seventh-Day Adventists hold . . . that there shall be a resurrection both of the just and of the unjust. The resurrection of the just will take place at the second coming of Christ; the resurrection of the unjust will take place a thousand years later, at the close of the millennium (John 5:28, 29; I Thessalonians 4:13–18; Revelation 20:5–10).
>
> That God, in the time of the judgment and in accordance with His uniform dealing with the human family in warning them of coming events vitally affecting their destiny (Amos 3:6–7), sends forth a proclamation of the approach of the second advent of Christ; that this work is symbolized by the three angels of Revelation 14; and that their three-fold message brings to view a work of reform to prepare a people to meet Him at His coming.[17]

Seventh-Day Sabbath. Reverting to the Jewish custom of keeping Saturday as the day of rest, the Adventists acquired a logical basis for their attitude toward the Catholic Church, which they accuse of corrupting the Scriptures and usurping the place of God. They argue that since the Decalogue is unalterable, "the fourth commandment of this unchangeable law requires the observance of the seventh-day Sabbath."[18] No other pertinent argument is offered, except the immutability of God and His commandments. Adventists reinterpret the Acts of the Apostles, where the early Church is described as keeping holy the first day of the week. They explain that the text should read: "Paul abode at Troas 'seven days.' Then on Saturday night, the beginning of 'the first day of the week,' he 'preached unto them, ready to depart on the morrow.' "[19] There is no good reason to believe, they say, that Paul refrained from preaching during the "seven days," and then because "the first day of the week" had come, held the service.

The Adventists claim the change was made by the Roman papacy, through centuries of gradual innovation. "The archdeceiver," wrote Mrs. White, "was resolved . . . to exercise his power through his vicegerent, the proud pontiff, who claimed to be the representative of Christ . . . In nearly every council [of the Catholic Church] the Sabbath which God had instituted was pressed down a little lower, while the Sunday was correspondingly exalted. Thus the pagan festival [of Sunday] came finally to be honored as a divine institution, while the Bible Sabbath was pronounced a relic of Judaism."[20]

In common with most Protestants, the Adventists recognize only two sacraments, baptism and the Lord's Supper, but they have added ceremonies and interpretations which considerably modify both of these "ordinances of the Church."

Baptismal Service. No provision is made for the baptism of infants, since this ordinance "should follow repentance and forgiveness of sins. By its observance faith is shown in the death, burial and resurrection of Christ."[21] Before the administration of baptism, the candidate must answer a series of questions in the presence of the whole congregation, or at least of the local church board. He is asked about his belief in God, the atonement of Christ, the renunciation of Satan, the Bible as the only rule of faith, and the keeping of the Sabbath on the seventh day. Then more specifically:

Do you believe that your body is the temple of the Holy Spirit and that you are to honor God by caring for your body in abstaining from such things as alcoholic beverages tobacco in all its forms, and from unclean foods?

Do you accept the doctrine of spiritual gifts, and do you believe that the Spirit of prophecy is one of the identifying marks of the remnant church?

Is the soon coming of Jesus the blessed hope in your heart, and is it your settled determination to prepare to meet Him in peace, as well as to help others to get ready for His glorious appearing?

Do you believe in church organization, and is it your purpose to support the church by your tithes and offerings, your personal effort, and your influence?[22]

After satisfactorily answering these questions, the candidate is baptized by immersion. But *"before* the immersion takes place, the minister should raise his right hand and solemnly utter one of the following declarations:

'My brother, upon the profession of your faith in Jesus Christ as your personal Saviour, I now baptize you into the name of the Father, and of the Son, and of the Holy Spirit. Amen.'

'In harmony with the commandment of our Lord and Saviour, Jesus Christ, I now baptize you into the name of the Father, and of the Son, and of the Holy Spirit. Amen.' "[23]

Communion Service. The Seventh-Day Adventist Communion service begins with the ritual of foot washing. After an appropriate sermon, the men and women in the congregation go into separate rooms or cubicles where basins of water and towels have been prepared. "It is the practice, based on the example of Jesus, to wash both feet of those who participate."[24] Deacons and deaconesses assist in the process, which may be accompanied by hymns, "and such conversation as may be carried on is of a devotional and religious character and in a subdued voice."[25] According to Adventist belief, the washing of feet is a kind of sacrament of penance. "As baptism symbolizes the cleansing from sin at the beginning of the Christian experience, so the ordinance of foot washing

epresents the efficacy of the blood of Christ in washing away
n from the stained heart of one who, although a church
nember, has either knowingly or unintentionally committed
n after baptism. It also represents the progressive work of
race in the life of the Christian which is possible only by the
ontinuing experience of cleansing through the sacrifice of
Christ on the cross and the application of His blood in the
anctuary in heaven on our behalf."[26]

Following the washing of feet, the men and women reas-
emble for the celebration of the Lord's Supper. While the
eople are seated, the minister stands at the communion table
vhere he uncovers the plate on which unleavened bread has
een placed. After the words of institution from St. Paul and
ther prayers are recited, the bread is broken into small
vieces, during which time "the one officiating may repeat
uitable Scriptures or make timely remarks, or the organist
nay play suitable soft music."[27] Deacons distribute the bread
o the people, who hold it in their hands until the minister
s served. Then all partake together. A brief interlude of
ilent prayer introduces the same ritual for the wine, which
s received in individual glass cups. Like the Methodists, the
Adventists require that "only the unfermented juice of the
grape . . . should be used in the Lord's Supper."[28] They
also practice open Communion, allowing anyone who attends
he service to communicate. "Christ's example [in favor of
udas] forbids exclusiveness at the Lord's Supper . . . There
nay come into the company persons who are not in heart
ervants of truth and holiness, but who may wish to take part
n the service. They should not be forbidden."[29] This direc-
ive is taken verbally from a communication of Mrs. White.

Although the Eucharist is considered as only "symboliz-
ing Christ's broken body and spilled blood,"[30] the ritual demands that great reverence be shown for the elements after
the public Communion service is over. The deacons are instructed to "see that any unused bread that remains is dis-
posed of by burning. Any unused wine should be poured out
on the ground. In no case should either bread or wine be
distributed or consumed in private or at home." Moreover, "if
sickness has prevented members from attending the ordi-

nances, either the minister or the elder may take a sma
portion of the emblems to these sick ones and thus share wit
them the rich blessing of fellowship."[31]

GOVERNMENT AND ORGANIZATION

The Seventh-Day Adventist Church is at once hierarchica
and highly representative. On the global level, the Genera
(World) Conference meets every four years and has authori
ity to amend, repeal, or enact provisions which affect th
whole denomination. A two-thirds vote is required. Belov
the General Conference are Divisions with their own subordi
nate Conferences, which are "to operate within a specifie
territory, in harmony with the policy of the General Con
ference."[32] Next in authority, on an intracontinental basis
are Union Conferences which, at least in America, are furthe
divided into State Conferences, with immediate jurisdiction
over the local churches. It was Mrs. White's desire to have a
thoroughly democratic society. "Every member of th
church," she declared, "has a voice in choosing officers of th
church. The church chooses the officers of the State [or local
conferences. Delegates chosen by the State conference
choose the officers of the union conferences; and delegate
chosen by the union conferences choose the officers of th
General Conference. By this arrangement, every conference
every institution, every church, and every individual, eithe
directly or through representatives, has a voice in the election
of the men who bear the chief responsibilities of the Genera
Conference."[33]

In practice, however, the Adventist is fundamentally con
gregational. Each local body is largely independent in it
government, although subject to the State Conference o
which it is a member. Churches are started, as among th
Congregationalists, when a group of believers "desires to
unite in fellowship." Under the leadership of a minister, they
are duly baptized, elect officers and become incorporated in
the larger Adventist denomination. There is not the same
degree of "independency" among the local churches that is
found in other congregational denominations like the Bap-

tists. This is precluded by the two doctrinal "foci" of Adventism: the imminent second coming and the Saturday Sabbath, along with a uniform code of abstinence from tobacco and every kind of stimulant. What unites the Seventh-Day Adventists more than any other factor, however, is the common acceptance of their foundress as a messenger from God. "The spirit of prophecy as manifested through Mrs. White" is held to be "woven so intricately into the progress of our denominational history that the story of no work can be told without the feature of divine leadership standing out clearly and unmistakably."[34] For sixty years Mrs. White was the visible head of the Adventists, and after death she still consolidates their organization.

Baptists

The Baptists exemplify in a striking way the importance of a name in the genesis and development of a religious movement. It was almost an accident of history that they came to be called Baptists, as a term of opprobrium to describe their insistence on immersion and profession of believer's baptism. They accepted the title and capitalized on it as a synthesis of fifteen centuries of controversy over the sacrament of regeneration, and a mark of their ancestry from apostolic times. In common with the Donatists they hold that baptism is invalid unless conferred by one of their own group; with the Arians they deny that baptism removes the stain of original or actual sin; with the Waldenses and Albigenses they reject infant baptism as superstition and against the words of the Bible; with the Anabaptists they claim that no one can be validly baptized until after a personal confession of faith in Christ as his Savior, and consequently demand a rebaptism (anabaptism) of all those baptized in infancy; with the English Separatists they require immersion in water as the only mode of baptism allowed by the Sacred Scriptures.

Centering their specific difference as a religious society around these various phases of the first sacrament, the Baptists have acquired a spirit of unity that is difficult to reconcile with a denomination which is nominally the largest Protestant group in the country, but is also the most fragmented. Whatever their differences, however, in doctrine, ritual, and church organization, they are still united in a common preoccupation with the place of baptism in the Christian economy. It is the key to an understanding of this people, bound together by only "a rope of sand," yet the most flourishing Protestant body in the United States.

HISTORY

There are two views as to the origin of the Baptists: the domestic viewpoint of certain Baptist apologists, and the corresponding data of religious history. Baptists do not hesitate to trace their beginning to Christ Himself. "No man can put his finger," they claim, "upon any person or date this side of Jesus Christ and truthfully say, 'here is where and when Baptists began.'"[1] They appeal to the spirit of independence as a distinguishing mark of the church in apostolic times. Since "the New Testament shows that each church at that time was a free independent body, directing its own affairs, and that its officers were servants and not masters," any organization, like the Baptists, which has remained "loyal to this type, trusting the Holy Spirit," must go back to early Christianity.[2] Although their church was founded by Christ, the name "Baptist" is said to have "originated with John the Baptist, who was divinely sent to be the forerunner of Our Lord."[3] No serious effort, however, is made to defend this origin of the title. In tracing the church's lineage, some Baptist writers developed the theory of spiritual kinship with successive independents like the Novatians, Donatists, Waldenses, and the continental Anabaptists. But this theory is rejected by moderate Baptist scholars as violating "the principles of historical accuracy."[4]

As a matter of history, commonly recognized by Protestant writers, the Baptists were started by John Smyth, Cambridge graduate and ordained Anglican minister (1570–1612), who "approved himself a factitious man" by his non-conformism and had to flee to Holland.[5] At Amsterdam he organized the first Separatist Church, with some eighty parishioners. Technically he was not yet a Baptist, until about a year later, when he came under the influence of the Waterlander Mennonites and decided that "infants ought not to be baptized" because there is no precept or example of infant baptism in the New Testament, and because Christ told His disciples first to preach and only then to baptize.[6] Some of Smyth's followers returned to England and started another church in London. The English branch soon divided into three conflicting groups: the General Baptists, who believed in a general redemption of all men; the Particular Baptists, who followed Calvin's doctrine of selective predestination; and Immersion Baptists, who required baptism by immersion as of divine precept.

The Baptists migrated to America "to escape the restrictions which had been placed upon their religious practice and faith in the Old World."[7] Under the leadership of Roger Williams, founder of Rhode Island, the first Baptist Church in the colonies was established at Providence in 1639, and two years later the first Baptist Church of Newport was started by John Clarke. Both were Particular or Calvinist Baptists, and to this day their basic theology is the doctrinal standard of most Baptists in the country. A small group of General Six-Principle Baptists, still extant, also claim to have been the first Baptists in Rhode Island (1638). They take their name from the six basic principles expressed in the letter to the Hebrews 6:1–2, namely, ". . . a foundation of repentance from dead works and of faith towards God, of the doctrine of baptisms and the laying on of hands, of the resurrection of the dead and of eternal judgment."

During the next century and a half, American Baptists split into a number of factions that were temporarily united under the common foreign-missions crusade. The first Protestant Mission Society in America, the American Board, was originally made up of Baptists, Reformed, Congregationalists, and Presbyterians. In 1814, the Baptists withdrew to form a society of their own, the General Missionary Convention, which marked the first real denominational consciousness of American Baptists. Other organizations soon followed along national lines, but the unity was only transient. Between 1810 and 1830, Alexander Campbell initiated the defection which formed the Disciples of Christ; in 1845 William Miller, preacher in New York, was voted out of the Baptist ministry and took with him a group of followers who became the Adventists.

The most serious schism in Baptist ranks, however, was provoked by the slavery question. Two parties, the North and South, could not agree on whether slaves should be kept or not. "The southerners did not attempt to defend the evils of the slavery system, but described the institution as an inherited disease to be healed slowly; many justified its continuance on biblical grounds, pointing out that the Negroes' contacts with white masters brought them in touch with the gospel. Northern abolitionists also argued from the Scriptures, holding that they taught the inherent dignity and worth of every individual in the sight of God and the moral wrong of the enslavement of men by their fellows."[8] Unable to conciliate the two parties, leaders on both sides decided to effect a division—with the Southern slaveholding Baptists taking the initiative. In April 1845, the separation was voted on favorably by the American Baptist Home Missionary Society, and in the following month was born the Southern Baptist Convention, "a new type of Baptist organization, being a firmly centralized denominational body functioning through various boards," as it has remained substantially to this day.[9] At the time of the division, there were approximately 325,000 Baptists below, and 250,000 above the Mason-Dixon line.

Further dissension over doctrinal and ritual questions created a medley of groups, usually with names that expressed their characteristic differences. But the most deep-rooted division, besides the cleavage of the Northern and Southern Baptists, occurred along racial lines. With the Emancipation Proclamation arose a desire among the Negroes to establish their own churches, independently of the non-colored Baptist organizations. In 1895, therefore, the Negroes founded their own National Baptist Convention of America, which was to function through a Foreign Mission Board, a Board of Education, and a Board of Missions. Twenty years later a dispute arose over the control of property and publications, resulting in court action and a new schism. The larger segment became incorporated as the National Baptist Convention of the United States of America, Incorporated; the smaller section kept the original name. The two Conventions account for about one half the Negro population in the United States.

After the defection of the Southern Baptists in 1845, the Northerners were hard put to maintain their home and foreign mission work. So in 1907 they united in a loose corporation which absorbed the Free Baptists in two mergers, one in 1911, and another in 1950, when the expanded body changed its name to the American Baptist Convention. It is now fourth among the major Baptist associations in America.

The nearest competitor among the remaining Baptist bodies has less than half the membership of the American Convention.

Since American Baptists have long represented about nine tenths of the world total, they were the logical prime movers in organizing the Baptist World Alliance. Founded in London, England, in 1905, its object is "the more fully to show the essential oneness of the Baptist people in the Lord Jesus Christ, to impart inspiration to the brotherhood, and to promote the spirit of fellowship, service, and cooperation among its members, and serve as the nerve center and corporate will of Baptists throughout the world."[10] Headquarters are in Washington, D.C.

DOCTRINAL POSITION

I. MAJOR BAPTIST CONFESSIONS OF FAITH

Since there are more than twenty autonomous Baptist denominations in present-day America, it is clearly beyond the scope of this study to analyze their doctrinal positions in detail. However, a close approximation is possible if we first survey the basic points of faith which Baptists hold in common, and then review the principal differences among the larger denominational bodies. The common doctrinal element is agreed to exist in two great Baptist Confessions of faith: the Philadelphia Confession of 1688, and the New Hampshire Confession of 1833. The first is practically a redaction of the Presbyterian Westminster Confession, and strongly Calvinistic. Though always referred to in Baptist histories, it has been largely supplanted by the New Hampshire Confession, which is accepted, at least nominally, by all American Baptist communions.

Among the doctrines held in common with the Catholic Church are the Trinity, the divinity of Christ, original sin, and the need of redemption, salvation through Christ, everlasting heaven and hell. But the divergences are numerous.

Scripture is declared to be "divinely inspired, and is a perfect treasure of heavenly instruction." At the same time, tradition is implicitly outlawed, since the Bible alone is held to be "the supreme standard by which all human conduct, creeds and opinions should be tried."[11]

The Fall of Man is described in the tradition of the Reformers. As a consequence of Adam's sin, "all mankind are now sinners . . . being by nature utterly void of that holiness required by the law of God, positively inclined to evil and therefore under just condemnation to eternal ruin."[12]

Justification is a restatement of Luther's *sola fide,* since "it is bestowed, not in consideration of any works of righteousness which we have done, but solely through faith in the Redeemer's blood."[13] Correlative to this is the doctrine of distinction between the "truly regenerate" and the "superficial professors." The former alone, once converted, "will not utterly fall away and finally perish, but will endure unto the end"; whereas the latter fall back into sin and so are considered as never having been truly justified.[14]

The Church is nowhere described, explicitly, as invisible; which is a departure from the Philadelphia creed where the "Catholic or Universal Church" is called "invisible," and said to consist of "the whole number of the elect, that have been, are, or shall be gathered into one, under Christ."[15] In the more recent doctrinal formula, "a visible Church of Christ is a congregation of baptized believers, associated by a covenant in faith and fellowship of the Gospel; observing the ordinances of Christ; governed by His laws; and exercising the gifts, rights and privileges invested in them by His word."[16] Several items are worth noting: Since Baptist churches are built along Congregational lines, what constitutes a church in the visible order is the single local organization called a parish. The term "baptized believers" is technical. Mere baptism does not make a person a member of the church; faith plus baptism are required. Association by covenant is also redolent of Congregational polity, where a church is organized by the consent of a group of people, who agree to worship together under a common pastor of their choice. "The ordinances of Christ" is Baptist parlance for the sacraments, only two of which are admitted: baptism and the Lord's Supper.

Ecclesiastical Authority and Ministry are limited to two categories, as the Church's "only scriptural officers are bishops or pastors, and deacons, whose qualifications, claims and duties are defined in the Epistles to Timothy and Titus."[17] Baptists lay great stress on the identity of bishop, presbyter, and elder in the New Testament, in order to eliminate the episcopate as a distinct hierarchical office. "Only two orders of officers," it is claimed, "are known in the Church until near the close of the second century. Those of the first are styled either bishops or presbyters; of the second, deacons."[18] In defending this position, they rest their case on the textual interchange of *episcopos* and *presbyteros* in St. Paul, while ignoring the context which shows an exercise of episcopal authority superior to the presbyterate. Clement of Rome and Ignatius of Antioch (c. A.D. 100), who regarded the episcopate as essential, are naïvely described as "defenders of prelatical—as against episcopal—supremacy," but without quotation.[19]

Baptism is called an ordinance, not a sacrament, and defined as "the immersion in water of a believer in Christ, into the name of the Father, and Son, and Holy Ghost, to show forth, in a solemn and beautiful emblem, our faith in the crucified, buried and risen Savior, with its effect, in our death to sin and resurrection to a new life." It is considered "prerequisite to the privileges of a Church relation, and to the Lord's Supper."[20] Baptists are generally agreed that "Baptism does not provide salvation, or produce salvation, or procure salvation, or even perfect salvation." Their contention is that, no external physical act can produce a spiritual blessing upon the soul.

According to Baptist theology, the Bible recognizes only believer's baptism. What justifies a person is his faith and not the baptismal ritual.

Our Lord in his Great Commission enjoins baptism on only those who believe. Peter, on the day of Pentecost, said to the inquiring multitude, "Repent and be baptized." As a result, "they that gladly received his word" were baptized (Acts 2:41), thus showing that they had undergone a change of heart before baptism was administered. Thus also the Samaritans were baptized "when they believed" (Acts 8:12).

From all this it appears that faith and repentance must precede baptism; nor is there a single instance of, or declaration concerning, baptism in the New Testament that will admit of an opposite conclusion. It is upon the above understanding of the teaching of the New Testament that Baptists repudiate the doctrines of baptismal regeneration and infant baptism.[21]

With rare exception, immersion is regarded as essential for valid baptism; although not a few Northern Baptist congregations no longer insist upon the practice. Such liberties, however, are comparatively rare, and promptly branded as modernistic.

As taught by the Baptists, the efficacy of baptism does not correspond to the Catholic doctrine on infusion of sanctifying grace, *ex opere operato*. Baptism, they say, does not produce faith and a new heart. Regeneration is by the Holy Spirit alone and should precede baptism. Consequently infants are not baptized.

The Lord's Supper is conceived in the Zwinglian sense of a mere external sign, and declared to be "a provision of bread and wine as symbols of Christ's body and blood, partaken of by the members of the Church, in commemoration of the suffering and death of their Lord."[22] While denying the real presence, Baptists generally are rigid in their practice of "closed communion," which prohibits any but "immersed believers" from partaking of the Lord's Supper. Lengthy prescriptions are formulated to exclude the non-baptized, those baptized only in infancy, and those baptized as adults but not by immersion.

Faith is commonly associated with repentance in Baptist creedal statements. Thus, "We believe that Repentance and Faith are sacred duties, and also inseparable graces, wrought in our souls by the regenerating Spirit of God; whereby, being deeply convinced of our guilt, danger, and helplessness, and of the way of salvation by Christ, we turn to God with unfeigned contrition, confession, and supplication for mercy; at the same time heartily receiving the Lord Jesus Christ as our Prophet, Priest, and King, and relying on him alone as the only and all-sufficient Saviour."[23]

II. DIFFERENCES IN DOCTRINE AMONG BAPTIST GROUPS

Among the Baptist confessions of faith, none are binding on the conscience of any, and members are not required to subscribe to any. The New Testament alone is respected as authoritative. At most, these Confessions help to hold the minds of the people to the radical forms of evangelical truth. Consequent on this freedom, Baptist churches have, on their own initiative, added to the basic New Hampshire creed other doctrines and statements of religious principle. Thus the powerful Southern Baptist Convention has an article on religious liberty which declares that "Church and state should be separate . . . The Church should not resort to the civil power to carry on its work. The gospel of Christ contemplates spiritual means alone for the pursuit of its ends . . . The state has no right to impose taxes for the support of any form of religion."[24] Consistent with this principle, Louie D. Newton, then president of the Southern Baptist Convention, helped to found in 1948 the society of Protestants and Other Americans United for Separation of Church and State (P.O.A.U.), in order "to assure the maintenance of the American principle of separation of church and state upon which the Federal Constitution guarantees religious liberty to all people and all churches of this republic."[25] Surprisingly, though perhaps with an implied distinction between Catholic and Protestant churches, the Southern Baptist Confession insists that "the state owes the church protection . . . in the pursuit of its spiritual ends."[26]

Consistent with their freedom of confessional belief, the Baptists have experienced their share of doctrinal tension between denominations. A striking example is the General Association of Regular Baptist Churches, which was formed in 1932 as a protest against the alleged modernism in the policies and program of the Northern Baptist Convention. In a published indictment of the parent denomination, leaders of the new association summarized the charges against the Northern Baptists. The latter, they said, praise and reward persons who profess modernistic doctrines: that the Bible is only a human record of the best thoughts of men and not an inspired revelation from God; that Jesus Christ is a son of God like other men and not God Himself in human form; that Christ died as a martyr to give us an example, not to redeem us from sin, and that after death He did not rise from the grave in a physical body but only seemed to be risen as a sign that His spirit is immortal.

Comparable to the doctrinal liberties indulged by groups of Baptist churches is the liberalism of individual ministers in good standing in their denomination. In the mid-twenties, Harry Emerson Fosdick was accused of modernism by fundamental Baptists and his case was tried by church leaders. He was acquitted, and until his retirement in 1946 remained at the Riverside Church in New York City, as "America's most popular preacher." His thirty volumes of sermons, reflections, and essays are literary models built around the concept of an ethical religion whose founder, Jesus Christ, was just "The Man from Nazareth," with no such divine sonship "as Hellenistic Christianity later put into the Nicene Creed."[27] At the other extreme is a Baptist like Billy Graham, professing an uncompromising faith in Christ's divinity and in the Bible as the inspired word of God. According to Graham, "God gives a new nature to those that receive by faith His Son, Jesus Christ . . . Human nature can only be changed by a new birth that Jesus Christ offers. Respectability cannot be substituted for regeneration . . . God's supreme objective is to have a new man created in Christ Jesus, conformed to the image of His Son."[28] Graham's Christology has found a sympathetic hearing among Catholics and Protestants alike.

III. DISTINCTIVE FEATURES OF BAPTIST BELIEF

Historically the most striking feature of the Baptist churches is their doctrine and practice regarding baptism. They have consistently held that believers' or adult baptism was the only form sanctioned by the Scriptures, and for more than four hundred years this has been the single most characteristic aspect of their tradition. Unfortunately, this preoccupation has been misunderstood. It has been easy for religious historians, and even theologians, to take believers' baptism out of context and not see it as part of a larger issue that goes deep into the roots of the Christian religion.

The cardinal principle of the Baptist ethos is spiritual liberty: where the freedom professed and safeguarded covers the whole spectrum of man's personal and social existence as a religious being. In Baptist parlance, a man is free when he is not under the control of some person or arbitrary power, when he is able to think and act as a Christian without compulsion or restriction, according to the inner light and motivation that comes of the Spirit residing in the soul of every believer.

1. Consequently, his acceptance of Christ as Lord and Savior should not be predetermined, as happens where children are baptized in infancy; nor assumed to be present when they reach maturity. But each one must himself make a personal commitment to the Christian faith, and receive baptism only when he comes to the age of discretion and has been duly instructed in the gospel.

2. As he enters adulthood, the Christian should not be required to join a particular religious body, although conditioned by his environment or sanctioned by society. He ought to be free to enter into voluntary association with persons of kindred spirit, even though their number is small and their degree of agreement on religious matters may be limited. Implicit here is the idea that religion is part of the continuum of human existence. If a man is free to marry whom he wishes, live where he wants, associate with whom he pleases, and form whatever organizations he desires, he should be not less but more free to do the same in things of the spirit. Baptists have followed the principle of voluntary association with great fidelity and often at great sacrifice, as in their Separatist and Non-Conformist days in England.

3. Consistent with the freedom of religious association is the notion of liberty of ecclesiastical affiliation, where the stress is on the absence of church authoritarianism. Each local congregation has the right to its own autonomy. There must be no agency above the group of covenanted believers with a right to dictate policy or determine organizational structure. The local church, therefore, is regarded as a gathered

company of believers, which is itself a manifestation of the one church of God on earth and in heaven. But above this localized segment of Christianity, no earthly power may claim divine authorization to govern the members of the congregation. If larger groups are formed for reasons of efficiency or good order, they are at most federations of individually sovereign communities whose privilege of self-rule is a divine mandate.

4. In the same category is the absence of binding creeds. All the great statements of Baptist belief are carefully identified as "confessions of faith," no more and no less. When a group of believers join beliefs in fellowship to form a congregation, it is assumed they share certain beliefs and may verbalize their agreement. They may even concretize the agreement on a broad scale to include many congregational bodies. But the resulting statement is descriptive rather than prescriptive, and more a reflection of shared religious attitudes than a creedal profession of required articles of faith.

This kind of ecclesiastical non-creedalism should be carefully distinguished from personal libertarianism or disbelief. Baptists have been a remarkably believing people, and among Protestants some have been outstanding for orthodoxy. Yet they are poles apart from such bodies as the Lutherans, for whom the Confession of Augsburg and the Catechisms of Luther are normative of the faith, or the Presbyterians, whose recent approval of a restatement of doctrine after years of study and top-level discussion would be quite foreign to the Baptist mentality.

5. Along with congregationalism and non-creedalism is a preference for simple worship, or, put in another way, the avoidance of ritualism as practiced in other Protestant bodies, notably among the Anglicans and Lutherans. The Baptist interpretation of Christianity does not favor sacramental mediation in the strict sense. The primary accent is on the communion of the soul with God, which is of an inward and spiritual nature and is not brought about, even when greatly helped, by any sacraments or divine ordinances that effectuate the communication of grace. Thus, the ministry, though set apart with prayer and commonly with the laying on of hands, is regarded as functional rather than priestly. And the rites

of Christian worship, including baptism and the Lord's Supper, are not productive of grace *ex opere operato* by reason of any causality that is intrinsic to the rites themselves.

6. Finally, the Baptists have always insisted on complete separation of church and state in order to free the church from coercion by the civil government in religious matters of conscience. This concern is more than the familiar church and state issue so much publicized today. It means the practical exclusion of civil authority from entrance into questions of morality and, above all, of anything connected with an established church or preferential position of a single religious body as in England, Sweden, and Spain.

The one feature of Baptists' policy that best typifies them in the United States is their concept of separation of church from the state, where the phrase "from the state" is crucial. Their desire for preserving the church's integrity is so strong and their faith in its self-sufficiency so clear that they are willing to leave its future in the hands of God and not entrust it, even minimally, to the tender mercies of the state.[29]

RITUAL AND WORSHIP

Under suasion from Baptist liturgical reformers, numerous changes are being introduced in order to make public worship more meaningful to the people. The most significant innovation affects the administration of the ordinances of baptism and the Lord's Supper.

According to a leading Baptist liturgist, "the Ordinances of the Church are commands of our Lord Jesus Christ to His Church. They, therefore, concern the whole congregation and should be administered in the presence of the congregation as far as this is possible. Participation in the observance of these ordinances is a duty and a privilege of every believer. They are observed not only as an act of obedience to God in Christ but as a means of grace to all who share in these rites."[30]

A typical Lord's Supper service begins with an invocation, thanking God for His mercies and asking Him for the grace to benefit from the Eucharistic worship.

We bless Thy glorious name, O God, for the gift of Thy
Son for the redemption of the world, and for the changes
Thou, through the Holy Spirit, hast wrought in our heart.
Grant us Thy grace now that, as we worship Thy Holy
Name, we may do so with a true heart and a humble and
contrite spirit. May what we do in this Service meet with
Thine approval that Thou mayest be known to us in the
breaking of bread; through Jesus Christ our Lord. Amen.[31]

The invocation is followed by a hymn, and the reading of
the Ten Commandments or a summary of the Law from St.
Matthew. Another hymn followed by the Beatitudes and a
passage from St. Paul precede the next hymn, which introduces the sermon, the Offering, and the celebration of the
Eucharist. Very similar to the Preface of the Mass, the Prelude
to the words of Institution begs the heavenly Father "to
sanctify these elements of bread and wine and so bless Thine
Ordinance that we, in faith and love and obedience, may be
spiritually nourished and our souls preserved blameless unto
the Lord's Second Coming; through Jesus Christ our Lord.
Amen."[32]

The bread and wine are separately blessed and distributed
to the congregation after the words of Institution are pronounced. Significantly, all the people receive before the minister, who concludes with the words "Let us all now commune
together in remembrance of Him."[33] A benediction closes the
liturgy.

As further evidence of departure from their Calvinist origins, modern Baptists are urging the use of pictures and
symbols as aids to devotion in worship services. Symbols,
they are told, have played an important role in the history
of Christian liturgy. "The cross," for example, "has become
to all the world a symbol of the Christian faith." Consequently, "while recognizing that the use of symbols may
become too dominant a feature of worship, we nevertheless
emphasize the values to be derived from an intelligent use
of them."[34] Among the symbols suggested are IHS, incorrectly
interpreted to stand for the Latin, *Iesus Hominum Salvator;*
the triangle, signifying the Trinity; a seven-pointed star to
represent the seven gifts of the Holy Spirit; a six-pointed star

"to remind us of God, the Creator"; a single circle depicting eternity; and a triple circle representing the Trinity. The same five liturgical colors as in Catholic services are admitted and similarly explained, with the addition of blue as a symbol of loyalty, faith, heaven, and eternity. Object symbolism is practically limited to six items: the cross representing Christ, the Bible standing for the word of God, an anchor for hope, a banner for victory, a globe for authority, and a gate for protection and freedom. Religious pictures are used, but restricted to "heightening the spirit of worshipful devotion" during actual services.

The most solemn ritual among Baptists is the ordination of a pastor or elder, and the administration of the Lord's Supper. Ordination is basically congregational. The initiative comes from a local church requesting some person to become their pastor. If he is not yet ordained, but otherwise prepared by study in a seminary and approved by a committee drawn from several churches, the rite of ordination is duly performed by one of two bodies, a council or the presbytery. In the South, ordinations are generally done only by a presbytery, i.e., a group of ordained ministers under the authority of the Baptist denomination; elsewhere the laying on of hands is usually performed by a simple council, composed of ministers and unordained laymen. The ordination ceremony is very plain. There is a sermon, preceded by Scripture reading, song, and prayer, and followed by the laying on of hands. After the sermon has been preached, the candidate is asked to kneel, and some brother chosen for the purpose prays the ordination prayer; when the prayer is completed, the candidate remains on his knees while the members of the presbytery or council lay their hands on his head as a token of his full ordination to the Baptist ministry. No formula of prayers or method of imposition is prescribed. The effect of ordination, whether to eldership or the diaconate, is purely external and juridical. It does not endow the candidate "with any intellectual, moral or spiritual grace which he did not before possess."[35]

There is wide divergency among Baptists on the frequency of celebrating the Lord's Supper. Some churches celebrate it the first Sunday in each month, others the first Sunday in each quarter, others semiannually and still others but once a year. The rite of administration follows the general plan of an ordinary Baptist service, except for the addition of the Eucharistic ritual.

ORGANIZATION AND GOVERNMENT

While details of operation differ widely, Baptists are fairly agreed on certain principles of church government. These may be reduced to three:

1. The governing power of the church is vested ultimately in the people. "It resides with the people in contradistinction from bishops or elders—that is to say, bishops or elders can do nothing, strictly and properly ecclesiastic, without the concurrence of the people."[36]

2. Majority rule prevails in Baptist church polity, "in accordance with the law of Christ." So that "the will of the majority having been expressed, it becomes the minority to submit."[37]

3. Local church authority is inalienable and final in all matters of ecclesiastical law and doctrine. Thus "the power of a church cannot be delegated. There may be messengers of a church, but there cannot be delegates in the ordinary sense of the term."[38] Even Baptists have to be reminded occasionally that "in their letters to associations and councils," the church should "say messengers, not delegates," since "no church can empower any man, or body of men, to do anything which will impair its independency."[39]

On the basis of its strong congregationalism, Baptist church polity would seem to be incompatible with the ecumenical movement. Actually many Baptist churchmen believe that the time has come for a return to what they call the original Baptist concept of the Church. As they read their history they see that Baptist separatism was more an accident of the times than a conscious theological orientation. In the words of one of their leaders, "there remains a pulsing catholicity about the Baptist witness that needs to be articulated. The insistence upon the ministry of the people of God, obedient to the mission of Christ, having a visible,

historical being in this world, may well be fundamental to
the nature of the Christian Church."[40] These sentiments are
being implemented by Baptist church leaders through ecumenical contacts with other Christian brothers, including the
Roman Catholic Church.

BAPTIST DENOMINATIONS IN AMERICA

Although the Baptist bodies in the United States reflect a
common respect for the Scriptures and insistence on local
church autonomy, they are the most denominational Protestant
family in the country. It is impossible to do any more than
briefly describe the differences among the various American
Baptist groups. Some have more than a century of past history, while others are more recent creations. Together they
represent perhaps the most characteristic feature of American
Protestantism, which is the love of freedom.

No attempt will be made to cover all the Baptist societies
which generally avoid being called churches and prefer less
ecclesiastical terms like "Convention" or "Association."

1. *Southern Baptist Convention.* Founded in 1845, when
the Southern Baptists withdrew from the General Missionary
Convention over the question of slavery. It is the fastest-
growing Protestant body in the States, with a net increase
of a quarter million each year. Originally confined to the
southeastern states, the Southern Convention is rapidly developing in the North by the absorption of conservative groups
who are dissatisfied with the liberalizing tendency of Northern Baptist organizations.

It is not easy to describe the spirit of the Southern Convention. Yet certain lines of character can be identified.
Southern Baptists are highly centralized. Unlike their Northern confreres, where such centralization as exists evolved
gradually, the Southern Convention was formed deliberately
and its leaders were given comprehensive charge from the
start. Historians of Baptist polity believe that the Southern
Baptist Convention was actually a denomination from the very
beginning. In the same way, Southern Baptists are strongly
conscious of doctrinal positions and are theologically con-

servative, in marked contrast with their Northern counter-parts.

Friendly critics predict that Southern Baptists will have to examine and change themselves in the near future. It is said that perceptive leaders will arise among the younger sons of Dixie, deprovincialized and turned cosmopolitan, who will challenge the traditional religious teachings and defect from the Convention unless their demands are met. Southern churchmen, however, generally feel quite different. Most of them are convinced that centralization and doctrinal con-servatism are the main reasons for the remarkable growth of the Baptist tradition in the South. It is not coincidental, they point out, that their membership has more than sextupled since the turn of the century, whereas Baptist organizations in the rest of the country have not grown except where they became centralized and more concerned for creedal stability.

2. *National Baptist Convention, U.S.A., Inc.* and *National Baptist Convention of America*. Organized in 1895 and 1915, these two Conventions account for one third of the Negro population in the United States. Substantially alike in or-ganization and doctrinal profession, the old enmities between the two bodies seem to be waning, but there is no immedi-ate prospect of union. Generally more Calvinistic than white Baptists, the Negro churches are only poorly known outside their own denomination. All the evidence points to an unde-veloped condition. The large number of churches gives an average of less than two hundred persons to a congregation. Only a few scattered periodicals are listed officially for both Conventions.

As might be expected, Negro Baptists are deeply con-cerned about civil rights. Their denominational literature, sermons and public speeches, and even confessions of faith reflect the desire to achieve equal rights under the Consti-tution. A few provisions in the current Statement of Belief of the National Baptist Convention illustrate the attitude.

1. We believe that all citizens should take their full share of the responsibility in building a greater, stronger, and better America for the weal of man and to the glory of God.

II. We believe that segregation and discrimination based upon race, national origins, or religion are not only sins against the fundamental laws of the land but also against the Supreme Law Giver. We must continue to fight the sins against human freedom without apology, without compromise.

III. We believe that the battle for freedom is not only America's battle but also the battle of all humanity supported by the moral laws of the universe and by the God who made out of one blood all races of men to dwell in peace on the face of the earth. And the struggle must move forward to victory since right is right and God is God.[41]

Foreign mission work among Negro Baptists is emphasized, with Nigeria, Liberia, and South Africa as the principal outposts.

3. *National Baptist Evangelical Life and Soul-Saving Assembly of the U.S.A.* In 1937 this evangelical group separated from the National Baptist Convention to become an independent body. Its main efforts are devoted to revival and relief activity. The Assembly operates an Automatic Correspondence School with courses in "evangelology, deaconology, missionology, pastorology, and laymanology," conferring degrees in sixty to one hundred and twenty days. Strictly non-creedal, the Assembly professes to teach only "the Bible doctrine as announced by the founder of the Church, Jesus Christ." Its national center of operation is in Detroit, Michigan.

4. *Progressive National Baptist Convention, Inc.* Organized at Cincinnati in 1961, with a charter membership of more than half a million, the Progressive National Baptists seceded from the National Baptist Convention, Inc. over procedures in the election of convention officers. Its mainly Northern membership suggests a development similar to that which divided the Baptists geographically at the time of the Civil War.

5. *American Baptist Convention.* This competitor to the Southern Convention for Baptist leadership in America began as the Northern Baptist Convention in 1907, changing its name to the present form in 1950. "As we adopt the name

American Baptist Convention," the delegates affirmed, "we hold the name in trust for all Christians of like faith and mind who desire to bear witness to the historic Baptist convictions in a framework of cooperative Protestantism."[42] While adhering to the historic Baptist Confessions, the A.B.C. stands for a more liberal concept of Scripture and theology. It is also more ecumenical-minded, officially participating in the National and World Council of Churches, with delegates playing a leading role in the Assemblies at Edinburgh, Utrecht, and Evanston. The A.B.C. is actively promoting the union of all major Baptist bodies; in 1911 it was joined by the Free Baptists. But its free-lancing modernism has resulted in numerous defections, the most serious being the exodus of the General Association of Regular Baptists in 1932.

Highly organized and socially conscious, the American Baptist Convention is widely accepted as the most representative Baptist organization in the States. Besides maintaining some forty colleges, universities, and theological seminaries, and upward of fifty hospitals and welfare homes, it supports a large contingent of foreign missionaries, mostly in Latin America and the Far East. The A.B.C. has formed a cooperative union with the General Baptists, originally an anti-Calvinist segment which emigrated from England and Holland. Like the A.B.C., the Association of General Baptists professes to exist in order "to effect better relations and closer cooperation between various bodies of liberal Baptists."

Characteristic of the American Baptist Convention is their opening of negotiations with the Roman Catholic Church. Early in 1967, representatives of the A.B.C. met at DeWitt, Michigan, with Bishop Joseph Green of Reno, Nevada, and Catholic specialists to discuss the prospects of Christian unity. After two days of top-level discussion, a statement was issued declaring that three areas were projected for further study: 1) The relationship between believers' baptism and the sacrament of Confirmation, 2) The nature of Christian freedom in relation to ecclesiastical authority, and 3) The role of the congregation in the total life of the Church. It was recognized that there is real tension in these topics between Baptists and Roman Catholics but also a much wider agreement than might have been anticipated.

6. *Conservative Baptist Association of America.* As the name implies, the Conservative Baptists are critical of what they called the "liberal and modernistic" teachings of the American Baptist Convention from which they broke in 1947. Their concern was over the dilution of doctrine, as they saw it, among the missionaries belonging to the American Baptist Foreign Mission Society. They profess belief in the infallibility of the Scriptures, man's absolute need of grace, local church autonomy, and Christ's divinity. In their Declaration of Purpose they give the five reasons why they came into existence. They are also the reasons why they have grown with unprecedented appeal to like-minded Baptists above the Mason-Dixon line.

i. To provide a fellowship of churches and individuals upon a thoroughly Biblical and historically Baptistic basis, unmixed with liberalism and those who are content to walk in fellowship with unbelief and inclusivism;

ii. To encourage the spiritual and financial interest of local churches in sound and Biblical Baptist institutions and projects both at home and abroad;

iii. To encourage the creation of agencies and institutions wherever necessary and advisable to fulfill the commission of our Lord in the face of rising apostasy;

iv. To provide mutual assistance among conservative Baptist churches for the encouragement of the local church's activities, such as evangelism, missions, and Bible teaching; and

v. To present a positive testimony to the New Testament faith and historic Baptist principles as a body of churches before the world, religious and otherwise; and to oppose departure and deviation from the great foundational truths of the Word of God.[43]

Understandably critical of those who do not share their convictions, Conservative Baptists are convinced that "God's blessing will not fall on Baptist support of an affiliation with apostate ecumenical organizations, that is, organizations that would coercively combine the professed Christian religions of the world into one universal church."[44]

7. *Free-Will Baptists.* Of Welsh origin, they were founded

in 1780 by Benjamin Randall, son of a ship captain in New Hampshire. Randall's kindly nature rebelled against the harsh Calvinism of the Baptists of his time. In a reported mystical experience, he discovered "the universal love of God to man, the universal atonement in the work of redemption by Jesus Christ . . . the universal appearance of Grace to all men, and . . . the universal call of the Gospel."[45] True to the spirit of their founder, the Free-Will Baptists represent the right-wing opposition to Calvinist predestinarianism still prevalent among many Baptists. Since their partial absorption by the American Baptist Convention in the North, the Free-Will Baptists are now practically confined to the South. Their doctrinal position is Arminian.[46] They hold that all may be saved, and are one of the few Baptist groups which practice open Communion, i.e., giving the Lord's Supper to those baptized in infancy, or not by immersion, or in a non-Baptist church. Besides baptism and the Lord's Supper, they observe the rite of foot washing as an ordinance of Christ.

While numerically inferior, by their fidelity to Randall's universalism the Free-Will Baptists are credited with providing "a corrective which has influenced Baptists favorably by causing them to combine with their traditional point of view a warm evangelism." Their principles of "free grace, free salvation, free will and free communion have become increasingly acceptable to numerous Baptists, particularly in the Northern States."[47]

8. *United Free Will Baptist Church.* The Negro counterpart of the Free Baptists is organized as the United Free Will Baptist Church. Doctrinally similar to the white denomination, it separated from the parent body in 1901 for racial reasons. Its governmental structure gives less autonomy to the local church and is more hierarchical. Special provisions are made for presenting the settlement of doctrinal disputes up to the General Conference; District Conferences have the right to exclude unworthy members from fellowship—both of which practices are somewhat unique in Baptist church policy.

9. *American Baptist Association.* Also called Landmarkers, members of the American Baptist Association deny that other Baptists are faithful to the Scriptures. They profess a strict

fundamentalism: the verbal inspiration of the Bible, the Trinity, Virgin Birth, divinity of Christ and His substitutionary passion, the bodily resurrection of Christ and of all the saints. They also believe in a second coming of Christ, "physical and personal," which is to be premillennial.[48] Like the Southern Baptists, they are strongly opposed to any kind of union of church and state. Originally rural, the Association is rapidly shifting to an urban status. Because of their insistence on perfectly equal rights among local churches, adherents of the A.B.A. are sometimes called Church-Equality Baptists.

10. *North American Baptist Association.* In May 1950, a schism in the American Baptist Association produced an independent faction, legally entitled the North American Baptist Association, which withdrew over doctrinal differences.

In its Doctrinal Statement, the North American Baptist Association tersely expresses its position "to defend and promulgate the historic Missionary Baptist Faith and Practice." It further declares that it stands for: "The separation of the Lord's Church from all so-called churches or church alliances which advocate, practice, or uphold heresies and other human innovations which are not in harmony with the word of God. Open communion, alien baptism, pulpit affiliation with heretical churches, modernism, and all kindred evils arising from these practices are unscriptural."[49]

Organized at Little Rock, Arkansas, the denomination is still limited to the Midwestern and Southern states, but gradually expanding elsewhere. Titles of periodicals like *The Baptist Trumpet* and *The Advancer* illustrate the uncompromising character of this latest addition to the Baptist family.

11. *The General Association of Regular Baptist Churches.* This group severed connections with the Northern Baptist Convention in 1932 because the latter had become modernistic. A dozen years before the final break, conservatives drew up a protest resolution that was to become the doctrinal basis of the new denomination. "Within our own fold," they complained, "we hail as leaders men who deny the miraculous birth of Christ, the vicarious death of Christ, the triumphant resurrection of Christ, and the promised second coming of Christ. If one dares to raise his voice in protest,

some one immediately hauls up the banner of Christian charity and seeks to cover with its folds the teaching that denies our Lord, meanwhile saying, 'Yes, we have radical differences among us, but surely the Baptist denomination is big enough, generous enough, charitable enough to include men of all shades of opinion.' . . . This subtle appeal put forth in the name of tolerance and charity is utterly at variance with the admonition that we 'contend earnestly for the faith.'"[50] In 1932, when this protest cystallized into an autonomous denomination, its first avowed purpose was "to maintain a testimony to the supernaturalism of Christianity as opposed to the anti-supernaturalism of modernism."[51] Interestingly, the conservatives referred to the action of Rome which "put down the [modernist] views extended by the Abbé Loisy . . . by the Encyclical of Pius X," as a precedent for its condemnation of like errors in the Baptist communion.[52]

12. *Primitive Baptists.* They are concentrated in two denominations, the white, simply called Primitive Baptists, and the colored, organized in the National Primitive Baptist Convention of the U.S.A. More popular names for these groups are: Old School, Regular, Anti-mission, and Hard-Shell Baptists, which correspond to their reputation for being the most strictly orthodox of Baptist churches. Strongly predestinarian, they believe that Adam's fall completely vitiated human nature. All church societies are regarded as human inventions. Ministers must have a special call from God, which, even in the absence of theological training, is considered sufficient for ordination to the clergy. Most Primitive Baptists are opposed to the use of instrumental music in churches as unscriptural. Admission to a local church is conditioned on a doctrinal examination and favorable vote by the congregation.

13. *Baptist General Conference.* This body has operated as a Conference since 1879, although its first church was organized in 1852. The founder was a Swedish schoolteacher, Gustaf Palmquist. As counselor to his fellow immigrants, he baptized them as adult believers and received them into the Baptist faith. The Swedish Baptist General Conference of America, which he established, dropped the title "Swedish"

in 1945 when all church services became English. With the change of name and ritual language, Swedish membership suddenly declined. The enrollment, however, has continued to grow among native American Baptists who prefer a strong theological conservatism. Central offices are in Chicago.

14. *North American Baptist General Conference.* Another European group of Baptists came from Germany and formed a bilingual Conference with membership throughout the United States. Sometimes called the German Baptists, the North American Baptist General Conference follows the New Hampshire Confession in a Bible-focused faith. Strongly mission-minded, the Conference supports missionaries in the Cameroons, West Africa, and Japan. Their national headquarters are in Forest Park, Illinois, although their own divinity school is in South Dakota.

15. *Seventh-Day Baptists.* There are two national groups of Baptists who favor worship on Saturdays, as did some of the English Sabbatarian Baptists in pre-colonial days.

The earlier body was organized in Rhode Island in 1671. Their stress on civil liberty is closely associated with advocating strictly individual Bible interpretation. Local churches are completely independent and the Lord's Supper is given to anyone who wishes to receive. They are centered in Plainfield, New Jersey.

A later group of Baptist Sabbatarians were refugees from the Palatinate in Germany. Often called Brethren or Dunkers, they arrived in Philadelphia in 1720. Eight years later, they founded a community under the direction of John Conrad Beissel, who had been associated with Peter Becker, the Germantown mystic and founder of the Dunkards or German Baptist Brethren.

Leaving Becker, Beissel started a monastic community at Ephrata, Pennsylvania, for celibate religious life. Men and women formed their respective communities, but denominational membership steadily declined. Professing the usual Dunkard doctrines, members claim that the Ten Commandments are the only rule of life. Yet they immerse candidates for baptism three times in honor of the Trinity, practice Saturday worship, foot washing, and the blessing of infants.

16. *United Baptists.* The term "United Baptists" is a later

derivative coined to describe the reunion of those who divided over doctrinal differences in early Baptist history. Technically the United Baptists date from meetings of Regular and Separate Baptists held in Richmond, Virginia, in 1787 and a later meeting in Clark County, Kentucky, in 1801. Concentrated in these two states, they teach salvation through grace rather than good works and speak of man as having been born with a totally corrupt human nature. Yet they are sufficiently Arminian to say that everyone has a free choice of either repenting or rejecting the divine call. Foot washing is honored along with baptism and the Lord's Supper as a biblical ordinance.

Closely associated with the United Baptists are independent groups like the Regular Baptists, the Separate Baptists in Christ, and the Duck River Associations of Baptists. A word of explanation may clarify the difference. Regular Baptists, properly so called, claim to be the modern representatives of the original Baptists in England before they divided into Particular (Calvinist) and General (Arminian) factions. Originally the term "Regular" was applied to Baptists in the Northern, Southern, and National Conventions. The usage ended around 1890 and is now applied only to denominations that carry the name, largely the North Carolina, Virginia, West Virginia, and Kentucky denominations.

The Separate Baptists in Christ date back to an association formed in 1758 in North Carolina. They reject the "election, reprobation, and fatality" of Calvin and favor instead a mild Arminianism. Unlike other Baptists, they do not claim to be Protestants. The expression "Separate" recalls their ancestry in Elizabethan England. Their baptism of infants, though not general, is quite unique in the Baptist tradition.

The Duck River (and Kindred) Associations began as a protest movement in 1825. Doctrinally they are liberally Calvinistic and express their faith in the motto: "Christ tasted death for every man." Since they admit to close scriptural bond with Regular, Separate, and United Baptists, there is a growing sentiment in favor of merging. They are almost exclusively in the Southern states of Tennessee, Alabama, Georgia, Kentucky, and Mississippi.

17. *Smaller Baptist Organizations*. There are at least a

dozen lesser bodies that are not easy to classify. For example, the *Bethel Baptist Assembly* was originally the Evangelistic Ministerial Alliance, founded at Evansville, Indiana, in 1934. Its membership is practically limited to Indiana and Illinois.

The *Christian Unity Baptist Association* was organized in 1934. Formerly the Macedonian Baptist Association, its members believe in universal atonement and perseverance until death as a condition of salvation. Government is strictly congregational with only one association for advisory purposes. Home missions and prayer meetings are favored. Affiliation is mainly in the Deep South.

18. *Canadian Baptists.* There are four Canadian Baptist societies that correspond to denominations in the United States. The Baptist Convention of Ontario and Quebec is centered in Toronto and has a flourishing department of Canadian Missions and does extensive work in the mission field overseas. Its theology is based on the creedal position of the Baptist union of Great Britain and Ireland. Its spirit is remarkably "association," i.e., favoring a broader conception of the Church as the *Una Sancta* than is common among their coreligionists in the United States, as stated in their most recent Confession of Faith, which declares:

> Although Baptists have for so long held a position separate from that of other communions, they have always claimed to be part of the one holy catholic Church of our Lord Jesus Christ. They believe in the catholic Church as the holy society of believers in our Lord Jesus Christ, which He founded, of which He is the only Head, and in which He dwells by His Spirit, so that though manifested in many communions, organized in various modes, and scattered throughout the world, it is yet one in Him. The Church is the Body of Christ and a chosen instrument of the divine purpose in history.[53]

The Baptist Union of Western Canada is a smaller group, with headquarters in Edmonton, Alberta. The Western Baptists were organized in 1909, and from the beginning favored a more elaborate structure than was normal in the East, while safeguarding the autonomy of the local church.

The United Baptist Convention of the Atlantic Provinces

is the eastern counterpart to the Union of Western Canada. Practically all of its administration is concentrated in New Brunswick. A problem that has plagued the Baptists in the maritime provinces has been the rapid shift of population, compared to the relative stability of the Canadian West.

The Fellowship of the Evangelical Baptist Churches in Canada was formed in 1953. After years of negotiation the Union of Regular Baptist Churches of Ontario and Quebec merged with the Fellowship of Independent Baptist Churches of Canada. As the name implies, the stress is on evangelism and a more conservative creedal policy. The Fellowship is concentrated in Ontario and Quebec, with main offices in Toronto. Its membership is bilingual, as reflected in its two main periodicals, *The Evangelical Baptist* and *Le Phare*, published in Toronto and Quebec respectively.

Unlike the situation in the United States, Canadian Baptists are fairly well organized across denominational lines. In 1944 the Baptist Federation of Canada was established as a co-ordinating agency for the Baptist Convention of Ontario and Quebec, the Baptist Union of Western Canada, and the United Baptist Convention of the Maritime Provinces. It came into existence, as its founders declared, "To form a united front against the forces that endanger Christianity." It was not to be a superchurch but a federation, which "was not intended to supplant the executive functions of the different Conventions, or to prejudice in any way the autonomy of the local church."[54]

Christian Scientists

Probably no religious system in America has been more controversial than the Church of Christ, Scientist, popularly known as Christian Science. Its adherents are among the most devoted religionists in contemporary Western culture. They describe Christian Science as "a universal gospel designed to meet every human need and for the benefit of all mankind. It has permeated religious and philosophic thinking, medicine and literature, wherever such exists."[1] They accept without hesitation the prophecy of Mrs. Eddy that, "If the lives of Christian Scientists attest their fidelity to the Truth, I predict that in the twentieth century every Christian church in our land, and a few in far off lands, will approximate the understanding of Christian Science sufficiently to heal the sick in his name."[2]

At the other extreme critics like Mark Twain describe Christian Science as "a sovereignty more absolute than the Roman Papacy, more absolute than the Russian Czarship; it has not a single power, not a shred of authority, legislative or executive, which is not lodged in the sovereign; all its dreams, its functions, its energies, have a single object—to build the glory of the sovereign, and keep it bright to the end of time. Mrs. Eddy is the sovereign; she devised that great place for herself, she occupies that throne."[3]

Somewhere in between these estimates is the correct understanding of Mrs. Eddy's scientific system of divine healing. In the interest of truth, both sides of its history and theology should be given.

HISTORY

The history of Christian Science is the history of its founder, Mary Baker, born at Bow, New Hampshire, July 16, 1821. Her early life was marked by long periods of sickness, owing to her naturally delicate temperament and nervous disposition. At the age of twenty-two, she married George Washington Glover, a bricklayer, who died six months later, leaving his widow practically destitute among strangers. When, after her husband's death, her only child was born, she named him after his father.

In 1853 Mrs. Glover married a traveling dentist, Daniel Patterson. But by 1866 he declared that living with her was unbearable. His periodic sojourns at home were "made dreary . . . by the ills of a neurotic wife whose strange spells and fierce tempers became a byword over the whole neighborhood."[4] Meantime she had been visiting a Dr. Quimby, mesmerist faith healer, from whose notes she copied the principles and technique of faith healing. She later re-edited these notes as her own. The gist of Quimby's teaching, still operative in Christian Science, was a simple rule of autosuggestion: Disease is a matter of faith, and so is its cure.

Not coincidentally, less than a month after Quimby died, Mrs. Glover-Patterson initiated Christian Science. On January 30, 1866, she fell at her home and suffered an injury that required medical care. There are two versions of the accident and its sequel: Mrs. Patterson's and the doctor's who treated her. According to Mrs. Patterson, the physician said she was injured beyond recovery. Awaiting a clergyman who was to prepare her for death, she began to read the Bible and came upon the words of Christ in St. Matthew's Gospel, addressed to the man sick with palsy. As she read, "Arise, take up thy bed," she realized that death is only a figment of the mind, based on the error of duality in human nature. "This moment marked the end of any belief she might have had that God created man into parts—a body that rots and a soul that lives."[5] She was instantly cured.

This story, however, is challenged by Doctor Alvin M. Cushing, the attending physician, as witnessed by an affidavit.

There was, to my knowledge, no other physician in attendance upon Mrs. Patterson during this illness from the day of the accident, February 1, 1866, to my final visit on February 13th, and when I left her on the 13th day of February, she seemed to have recovered from the disturbance caused by the accident and to be, practically, in her normal condition. I did not at any time declare, or believe that there was no hope for Mrs. Patterson's recovery, or that she was in a critical condition, and did not at any time say, or believe, that she had but three or any other limited number of days to live. Mrs. Patterson did not suggest, or say, or pretend, or in any way whatever intimate, that on the third, or any other day, of her said illness, she had miraculously recovered or been healed, or that, discovering or perceiving the truth of the power employed by Christ to heal the sick, she had, by it, been restored to health."

Mrs. Patterson now divided her time between organizing the practice of healing, usually done by others, and teaching the principles of her new-found science. In 1875 she published the first edition of *Science and Health*, which she kept revising and practically rewriting till the end of her life. Each new edition was bought by faithful Christian Scientists, although the change might be as little as a single sentence. Two years after the first printing of *Science and Health*, Mrs. Patterson married a student, Asa Gilbert Eddy, who died five years later. She had divorced Patterson on grounds of infidelity.

In 1879, Mrs. Glover-Patterson-Eddy founded the Church of Christ, Scientist; the state charter authorizing the new organization was dated August 23. In 1881, at the age of sixty, she founded the Massachusetts Metaphysical College with herself as the entire faculty for most of the eight years of the school's existence. Courses were offered in "pathology, ontology, therapeutics, moral science, metaphysics, and their application to the treatment of diseases." On her own testimony, four thousand students took the twelve-lesson course, later reduced to seven lectures. Tuition was three hundred dollars for the elementary course, with an occasional charity student admitted; there were no discounts or scholarships in the higher courses.

As the number of her followers grew, dissatisfaction increased over the way Mrs. Eddy treated her disciples. She would give the lessons in Christian Science, but they had the burden of demonstrating it before the public, sometimes with tragic consequences. The most celebrated case was the unexpected death of mother and child when practitioner Mrs. Corner of Chicago attended her own daughter in childbirth. Instead of being defended, Mrs. Corner was denounced by her former teacher as a quack. A large percentage of Mrs. Eddy's disciples rebelled and were finally dismissed, which occasioned a complete ecclesiastical reorganization.

The foundress conceived the idea of making the society in Boston the Mother Church of Christian Science. She stipulated that branch churches in other cities or even countries must be not only affiliated with the Boston church but entirely dependent on its jurisdiction. Only members of the Mother Church could receive a degree C.S.B. (Bachelor of Christian Science) or C.S.D. (Doctor of Christian Science); only such members could teach and only they could be Readers in branch churches. Mrs. Eddy then placed herself as head of the Mother Church, with detailed provisions to exclude any interference with her authority. No conference of churches was permitted; officers in the church, from the president and board of directors down to local church managers, were to be chosen only with her approval; she abolished the office of pastors, substituting instead the Readers, who were allowed only to read from *Science and Health* and forbidden even to make explanatory remarks on the text; any Reader could be removed from office at the foundress' pleasure.

Evidence abounds for the high esteem in which Mrs. Eddy was held by her followers. Her deposed pastors submitted without complaint, like one who attributed his demotion to a divine communication received by Mrs. Eddy. "Did anyone suspect such a revelation," he wrote in the *Christian Science Journal*, "such a new departure would be given? No . . . Such disclosures are too high for us to receive. To One alone did the message come."[7] Not only were pronouns referring to Mrs. Eddy frequently capitalized, but, on occasion, the Mother of Christian Science herself encouraged such adulation.

In the *Journal* for June 1899, a certain Martha Sutton Thompson wrote to describe a visit she made in January of that year to the meeting of the Christian Science Board of Education in Boston.

When I decided to attend I also hoped to see our Mother . . . I saw that if I allowed the thought that I must see her personally to transcend the desire to obey and grow into the likeness of her teachings, this mistake would obscure my understanding of both the Revelator and the Revelation. After the members of the Board had retired they reappeared upon the rostrum and my heart beat quickly with the thought "perhaps *she* has come." But no, it was to read her message . . . She said God was with us and to give her love to all the class. It was so precious to get it directly from her.

I will not attempt to describe the Leader, nor can I say what this brief glimpse was and is to me. I can only say I wept and the tears start every time I think of it. Why do I weep? I think it is because I want to be like her and they are tears of repentance. I realize better now what it was that made Mary Magdalen weep when she came into the presence of the Nazarene.[8]

While consolidating her church, she met opposition on all sides. The worst was a fear that she called Malicious Animal Magnetism, by which absent enemies could mentally project their hatred and injure her. Out of this fear grew the attempted-murder charge against her husband, Asa Eddy, that he wished to dispose of one such mental tormentor of his wife. The case was later dismissed for want of evidence. More real, if less distressing, were the court proceedings by which her son and other prospective heirs tried, but failed, to get a legal declaration of her insanity. And only a year before her death, the whole control of Christian Science was in danger of falling into the hands of her rival, Mrs. Augusta Stetson—until the latter humbly submitted to being excommunicated from the church she helped to found.

In spite of her protestations against the reality of death, Mrs. Baker Eddy died of pneumonia, December 3, 1910. Unimpeachable testimony indicates that she freely used drugs all through life to quiet her nerves, and later on for physical pain, to the point of developing a "morphine habit."[9] When she died, her followers decided, "There will be no 'Leader' named to take the place of Mrs. Eddy. There is no need for any leader."[10]

Since her death, this prediction has been fairly verified because of the loyalty to her person which still unifies Christian Science, and because of the absolute control over every member exercised by the Mother Church of Boston. In a true sense, the Church of Christ, Scientist, has not changed since the death of its foundress. The numbers have increased; but the organizational structure, doctrine, and method of procedure are practically the same as when Mrs. Eddy wrote that "Exegesis on the prophetic Scriptures cites 1875 as the year of the second coming of Christ. In that year the Christian Science textbook, *Science and Health with Key to the Scriptures,* was first published."[11]

DOCTRINE AND PRINCIPLES

The principles of Christian Science are the teaching of Mrs. Baker Eddy, as found in her published books (seventeen volumes), and her contributions over a period of twenty-seven years to the four periodicals she founded, especially *The Christian Science Journal* (1883) and *The Christian Science Sentinel* (1898). In spite of a strange use of language that often seems like jargon to the uninitiated, there is much intelligibility in Mrs. Eddy's writings; therefore, it is possible to reconstruct the main outline of her teaching.

God. Although Mrs. Eddy wrote a short treatise in self-defense, *Christian Science vs. Pantheism,* it is certain that the deity of Christian Science is pantheistic. According to the author of *Science and Health,* we may speak of God as all substance, so that whatever is substantial is divine.[12] We may also describe Him as all real being, so that nothing is real except God.[13] Given these premises, the basic doctrine of Eddyism is the identification of God with all substance and reality. "Christian Science," says its founder, "reveals incontrovertibly that Mind is All-in-all, that the only realities are the divine Mind and idea."[14] If she seems to object to speaking of God as a person, it is only when the word "person" implies a real distinction between God and the human race. "As the word *person* and *personal* are commonly and ignorantly employed, they often lead, when applied to Deity, to confused and erroneous conceptions of divinity, and its distinction from humanity."[15] Provided no such distinction is inferred, God may be called a person.

When Mrs. Eddy denied that Christian Science was pantheistic, it was because she redefined pantheism as a kind of animism which claims that matter can think. Hers was rather "a spiritual pantheism, which holds that God is all in all, but that matter is only an appearance and not reality."[16] One of her favorite expressions in speaking of God was the compound term, "Father-Mother," which meant that as "Father [is] Eternal Life; the one Mind; the divine Principle, commonly called God,"[17] so "Mother [is] God; divine and eternal Principle; Life, Truth and Love."[18] As understood by one of her followers, "Mrs. Baker Eddy . . . has set forth clearly the idea of God not only as the wise Father, but also as the tender Mother."[19]

Man. Christian Science describes man in terms of God. He is "the compound idea of infinite Spirit; the spiritual image and likeness of God; the full representation of Mind."[20] Man's body is non-existent. Accordingly, "matter [is] mythology; mortality; another name for mortal mind; illusion"; it is often mistaken for "intelligence, substance, and life in non-intelligence and mortality; life resulting in death, and death in life"; but really it is "sensation in the sensationless; mind originating in matter; the opposite of Truth; the opposite of Spirit; the opposite of God; that of which immortal Mind takes no cognizance; that which mortal mind sees, feels, hears, tastes, and smells only in belief."[21] The human spirit is indeed real, but identical with God. We may not speak therefore of a multiplicity of souls. "The term *souls* or spirits is as improper as the term *gods*. Soul or Spirit signifies Deity and nothing else. There is no finite soul nor spirit. Soul or Spirit means only one Mind, and cannot be rendered in the plural."[22]

Sickness and Death. Logically there can be no sickness or pain if there is no body in which they can occur; and no death, because there is no body from which the divine Soul can be separated to make a person die. Thus "man is never sick, for Mind is not sick and matter cannot be [exist] . . . It is well to be calm in sickness; to be hopeful is still better; but to understand that sickness is not real and that Truth can destroy its seeming reality, is best of all, for this understanding is the universal and perfect remedy."[23] Moreover, since God is the only life, and He is immortal, death is an illusion.[24] The erroneous "belief that matter has life results, by the universal law of mortal mind, in a belief in death. So man, tree, and flower are supposed to die; but the fact remains that God's universe is spiritual and immortal."[25] Contrary to appearances, however, "In reality, man never dies."[26]

Christ and Christianity. Mrs. Eddy distinguishes between Christ and Jesus. The former is spiritual and divine; the latter is corporeal and human.[27] She explains that "the invisible Christ was imperceptible to the so-called personal senses, whereas Jesus appeared as a bodily existence. This dual personality of the unseen and the seen, the spiritual and material, the eternal Christ and the corporeal Jesus manifest in flesh, continued until the Master's ascension, when the human, material concept, or Jesus disappeared, while the spiritual self, or Christ, continues to exist in the eternal order of divine Science, taking away the sins of the world, as the Christ has always done, even before the human Jesus was incarnate to mortal eyes."[28]

According to Mrs. Eddy, "The Church is that institution which affords proof of its utility, and is found elevating the race, rousing the dormant understanding from material beliefs to the apprehension of spiritual ideas and the demonstration of divine Science, thereby casting out devils, or error, and healing the sick."[29] There is no question of a Church founded by Christ, no place for mysteries or creeds, no priesthood or sacraments; only a society of like-minded people who band together to be undeceived about the existence of matter, suffering, and death.

Essence of Christian Science. It was in 1866, Mrs. Eddy wrote, that "I discovered the Christ Science or divine laws of Life, Truth and Love, and named my discovery Christian Science. God had been graciously preparing me during many years for the reception of this final revelation of the absolute divine Principle or scientific mental healing."[30] Her discovery is called *Christian* because Christ first "demonstrated the power of Christian Science to heal mortal minds and bodies."[31] It was a *discovery*, because "this power was lost sight of, and must again be spiritually discerned, taught and demonstrated according to Christ's command, with 'signs following.'"[32] It is a *Science* in opposition to mere belief. In Mrs. Eddy's vocabulary, science is synonymous with understanding, as against belief, which means ignorance. The object of belief is the visible corporeal world and an apparent distinction among persons and things. The object of science is Spirit and Mind, or God, which alone has real existence animating the world of ostensible reality as the Soul of the Universe. "Science," then, "so reverses the evidence before the corporeal human senses as to make this Scriptural testimony true in our hearts, 'The last shall be first, and the first last,' so that God and His idea may be to us what divinity really is and must of necessity be—all inclusive."[33] It is a practical science, however; its purpose is not prayer or contemplation but the shedding of sickness, death, and sin by driving out the devil of belief in their existence.[34] Another name for this exorcism is Christian Science healing.

PRACTICE OF HEALING

The healing process of Christian Science covers three principal types of activities sponsored by the Church. Every Sunday and Thanksgiving Day, public services are held, which consist substantially of reading alternately from the Bible and from *Science and Health*, done by professional Readers, one man and one woman. The main part of the function is a Lesson-Sermon prepared by a committee from the Mother Church in Boston and issued quarterly by the Christian Science Publishing Society. On Wednesday evenings, the First Reader reads select passages from the Bible along with correlative sections from *Science and Health*, but the feature of these midweek services is the public testimonies from the congregation, telling about their healing from sickness and sin.

Besides public services, there is an elaborate system of private healing, performed by certified practitioners who are listed as such in the official catalogue of the Mother Church. A practitioner who had class instruction from an authorized teacher is indicated with a C.S. (Christian Scientist) after his name; if he took a course at the Massachusetts Metaphysical College or in the Christian Science Board of Education, he is designated as C.S.B. (Bachelor of Christian Science).

Practitioners are allowed to engage in healing on request from clients, whether members of the Church or not. Phone numbers and, in some cases, office hours are listed for all practitioners; up to one hundred and more in a single city like Chicago or New York.

In the early days, Mrs. Eddy favored manipulation as part of the practice of healing. She described this mesmerism in detail, explaining how her students should treat their patients:

> Wetting your hand in water, rise and rub their head. This rubbing has no virtue; only as we believe and others believe, we get nearer to them by contact, and now you would rub out a belief, and this belief is located in the brain. Therefore, as an M.D. lays a poultice where the pain is, so you lay your hands where the belief is, to rub it out forever.[35]

But in 1872, when one of her students (Richard Kennedy) left her fold, to repudiate him she accused him of pernicious mesmerism because he used manipulation. At the same time she changed her own method, dispensing with any physical handling of the subject. Current practice absolutely forbids manipulation; pure mental healing of mind to mind is alone permitted.

As described in case histories, the actual healing process is quite simple. The client listens to the practitioner, reading from Science literature or talking extempore, in order to undeceive the patient about his sickness by making him lose himself in the conviction of his identity with the infinite Mind which is God. If personal testimonies are to be believed, the method works even with children, as recently witnessed by a mother:

With the help of a practitioner our young son had a quick healing of enlarged tonsils. The public school authorities had said that he must have an operation because the tonsils were so large they feared the consequence should they become inflamed and additionally swollen. He was taken to a practitioner, who lovingly and firmly declared man's oneness, or unity, with his Father-Mother-God and the perfection of his being. The tonsils returned to their normal size after this one treatment.[36]

In most cases, however, the healing takes place without the help of a practitioner, and often involves the curing of a moral disease. A woman testified gratefully that she was estranged from a friend who had treated her, she felt, "most unjustly and cruelly." She began to reflect on Mrs. Eddy's words that, "In Science, Mind is *one*, including noumenor and phenomena, God and His thoughts." Suddenly came the cure:

> The absolute unity of divine Mind and its expression was revealed to me, and I saw that truth prohibits the misconception of two warring minds and the unpleasant results that go along with the belief. That realization wiped out the whole false picture, including the grief.
>
> My consciousness was filled with forgiveness and compassion for the other woman, for I saw that since we both had the same Mind, she in reality loved me as I loved her.[37]

The Christian Science Reading Rooms in every large city are intended to serve this purpose of "self-healing," where quiet reflection on the great truths of Eddyism dispels the error of mortal belief in physical sickness and mental pain.

ORGANIZATION AND AGENCIES

The organization of Christian Science is rigidly centralized. At the head stands the Mother Church in Boston. Branch churches in other cities are completely dependent on the Mother Church; a prospective branch church is called a

Christian Science Society. "When members of The Mother Church in a community believe the time has come for the organization of a Christian Science Society, or a branch Church of Christ, Scientist," they contact the Mother Church and request affiliation, conditioned on the observance of strict regulations laid down by Mrs. Eddy. Among Protestant bodies, Christian Science is unique in having two kinds of members: those associated immediately and only with the Mother Church, and those who also belong to a branch church of the denomination. Heading the Mother Church is the Board of Directors, including a president, Readers, a clerk and treasurer; comparable officers also direct the branch churches, which are called First, Second, etc., Church of Christ, Scientist, according to the order of erection in a given locality.

The evangelism of Christian Science is world-wide, and directed by a series of agencies, emanating from the Mother Church and outstanding for their efficiency.

The Christian Science Publishing Society publishes all the official writings of Mrs. Eddy and of the Mother Church of Boston. Five periodicals are printed: *The Christian Science Journal,* an English monthly; *Christian Science Sentinel,* an English weekly; *Herald of Christian Science,* monthly and quarterly, in French, German, Dutch, Danish, Norwegian, Swedish, Spanish, Portuguese, Italian, English, and Braille; *Christian Science Quarterly,* in eight languages; and *The Christian Science Monitor,* daily except Sunday and holidays, in English, with a religious article in one of twelve different translations. To ensure orthodox Scientism in its publications, "articles are accepted only from members of The Mother Church." Although "freshness, originality, naturalness, variety are prized," it is prescribed that "at least one quotation from the Bible and also one from our Leader's writings should be included."[38] In practice, the articles are either commentaries on Mrs. Eddy's doctrines, or personal testimonials (with appropriate quotations from the Leader) of how Christian Science has benefited the writer. Even a newspaper like the *Monitor* is written according to Christian Science prescription. For instance, the word "death" is never used when referring to persons, because, according to editorial policy, "We don't believe this happens to people; so we report the termination of this earthly residence of people in the news by saying that they have 'passed on,' which any Christian should admit is a more accurate description of what has happened."[39]

The Board of Lectureship, consisting of some thirty members, is appointed annually by the Board of Directors. Its function is to accept invitations for giving free lectures in branch churches throughout the world. Through the lecture program, even the most disparate units are assured conformity of doctrine with the Mother Church of Boston.

The Board of Education instructs authorized teachers of Christian Science. As prescribed in the *Church Manual,* a certified teacher is limited to thirty in the number of pupils he may instruct during any calendar year. Infraction of this rule makes the teacher liable to dismissal from the Church.

Less familiar is the Committee on Publication, whose creation by Mrs. Eddy was occasioned by the repeated attacks she suffered from newspapers and other molders of public opinion. With a home office in Boston, state committees were appointed by the Mother Church with the twofold purpose of furnishing censored news and policy releases to the press, and of watching the publications for any statement unacceptable to the Church of Christ, Scientist. Under the duties of this agency Mrs. Eddy prescribed a singular routine:

> This Committee on Publication shall be responsible for correcting or having corrected a false newspaper article which has not been replied to by other Scientists, or which has been forwarded to this Committee for the purpose of having him reply to it. If the correction by the Committee on Publication is not promptly published by the periodical in which it is desirable that this correction shall appear, this Committee shall immediately apply for aid to the Committee on Business.[40]

Calling for aid from the Committee on Business meant to contact the editor of a newspaper or periodical, e.g, through one of its advertisers, to avoid anything in the future which might offend the religious sentiments of Christian Scientists.

Proof of the Publication Committee's effectiveness is the practical absence of any controversial articles on Christian

Science in American magazines, popular or scientific. During a ten-year period, the writer could find only two full-length articles in the 120 magazines listed in the *Reader's Guide to Periodical Literature* that were critical of Christian Science. Both were later answered in the same publications. Moreover, the Church's vigilance extends into other areas. The *Scientific American* reported that the New York State Department of Education dropped all questions relating to bacteria and infection from the Regents' Examinations in biology. This was in accordance with a law which "the State Legislature, at the request of the Christian Science Church, had quietly passed . . . providing that 'a pupil may be excused from such study of health and hygiene as conflicts with the religion of his parents or guardian.' "[41] Three months later this news item was answered by a representative of the Mother Church, pointing out that "the Christian Science Committee on Publication for New York specifically asked that changes not be made in the examination questions because of certain legal exemptions available to Christian Scientists."[42] There was no suggestion, however, that these exemptions might have influenced the changes in the biology tests in order to avoid further conflict with the Scientists.

RELIGIOUS LIBERTY

As might be expected, the Christian Scientists are strong advocates of religious liberty. Although their main concern has been with individual cases, there is evidence that they are also interested in the larger aspects of social legislation.

As far back as 1938 their Board of Directors adopted a general statement that reflects this attitude. The growing success of Christian Science, the statement read, shows that the time is approaching when civil governments will realize that reliance on material means generally leads to failure and defeat. Slowly the civil authorities are coming to see that no state can long endure without the spiritual influence of the Christian churches. As students of Christian Science, the document said, the followers of Mary Baker Eddy have a definite responsibility to protect the civil rights of all people and ensure them freedom of speech, of the press, and of religious worship.

In pursuance of these principles, the Church of Christ, Scientist, has struggled for years to secure its right to treat patients by prayer rather than by medicine. Its members are law-abiding citizens whose conflict with the state has been due mainly to their insistence that spiritual healing be recognized by law as a legitimate method of curing disease. They want their "healers" to have all the rights of physicians without being bound by the rules imposed by civil statutes for medical practitioners, and they wish their followers to be exempt from such medical practices as vaccination, of which they disapprove.

A review of the laws of the states shows that Christian Scientists have been remarkably successful in obtaining freedom to practice their art of divine healing without liability to prosecution for failure to meet the ordinary requirements demanded of those who practice medicine.

Nothing in this chapter [defining and regulating the practice of medicine] shall inhibit service in an emergency, or the domestic administration of family remedies, nor the practice of religion or treatment by prayer [Arizona].

Provided, that nothing in this Order [defining and regulating the practice of medicine] shall be construed to prohibit the practice of the religious tenets of any church in the administration of the sick or suffering by mental or spiritual needs without the use of any drug or remedy, whether gratuitously or for compensation, provided that such sanitary laws, orders, rules, and regulations as now are or hereafter may be, in force in said Canal Zone are complied with [Canal Zone].

This law [defining and regulating the practice of medicine] shall not prohibit the practice of Christian Science or religious rules or ceremonies as a form of religious worship, devotion or healing [Louisiana].

This Act [defining and regulating the practice of medicine and surgery] shall not be construed to affect or prevent the practice of the religion of persons who endeavor to prevent or cure disease or suffering by prayer or other spiritual needs in accordance with the tenets of any church; nor shall anything in this Act be construed so as to interfere in any manner with the individual's right to select or employ the practitioner or mode of treatment of his choice, or to interfere with the right of the person so employed to give the treatment of his choice, or to interfere with the right of the person so employed to give the treatment so chosen; provided, however, that sanitary laws, rules and regulations are complied with [Oregon].[43]

Other special recognitions of Christian Science for its convictions are found scattered through the state laws. For example, in California "practitioners" and "readers" are exempt from jury duty. In Florida Christian Scientists and other healers "who pray for the recovery of the sick" are exempt from certain vocational taxes.

Not the least benefit of this promotion of religious liberty has been the recognition that other churches besides Christian Science have received from state legislatures and the civil courts. Not only Catholics and Protestants but even such little-known groups as the "I Am Movement" have profited from the efforts of Christian Science to ensure freedom of religious belief and practice. When the United States Court reversed the conviction against the Ballard family charged with using the mails to defraud, the court stated that: "Men may believe but cannot prove. They may not be put to the proof for religious doctrines or beliefs. Religious experiences which are as real as life to some may be incomprehensible to others . . . The miracles of the New Testament, the Divinity of Christ, life after death, the power of prayer are deep in the religious convictions of many. If one could be sent to jail because a jury in a hostile environment found these teachings false, little indeed would be left of religious freedom."[44] Years of strong representation by the Christian Scientists have much to do with evoking this wise decision of the nation's highest judiciary.

Disciples and Christians

The initial difficulty to be cleared in any study of the Disciples and Christians is the matter of names. Are they one group or two? And if two, how can we distinguish between them when they seem to use each other's names interchangeably?

There are two bodies, one called the Disciples, or Disciples of Christ, and the other Christians, or Churches of Christ. However, the Disciples also call themselves collectively the "Christian Church," especially in the Midwest and South, and local congregations with rare exception are named "Christian." The rival group, listed in the federal census as the "Churches of Christ," never speaks of itself as Disciples, but always uses the term "Christian" or "of Christ," either in denominating the whole body or when referring to a single congregation.

What further complicates the issue is the use of "Christian" to describe still other religious groups, whether existing or absorbed by another denomination. Among the defunct "Christian" bodies, the most important was an offshoot of the present-day Churches of Christ, which joined the Congregationalists in 1931. Among the still extant, but alien, Christian Churches the largest are the "Holiness Church of Christ," which is a Baptist derivative, and the "Christian and Missionary Alliance," specializing in evangelism.

A final source of confusion is the denominational status of the Disciples and Christians. Most Christians disclaim the title of denomination as unwarranted by reason of their amorphous ecclesiastical character; many Disciples also prefer to be considered interdenominational. Yet between them they constitute the largest purely indigenous religious movement in America.

HISTORY

The founder of the Disciples of Christ was Thomas Campbell, born in Ireland in 1763, of a Catholic father who left his faith. He began as an Anglican but withdrew from the English Church in protest against its ritualism. As a Presbyterian he worked for union in his own church and among other denominations. Discouraged by the opposition his efforts met in Ireland, he came to the States in 1807, beginning his ministry in Philadelphia as a Presbyterian. Within two years he was resisted by the presbyteries, especially after his now famous *Declaration and Address*, issued "to all that love our Lord Jesus Christ in all sincerity, throughout all the churches." Its main tenet was that the Church of Christ upon earth is one. The constitution of this Church of Christ, said Campbell, is not a creedal statement or confession of faith but the New Testament itself. Sectarian churches have no right to impose on their members as articles of faith anything not expressly taught in the Bible. Even inferences or deductions from the New Testament are not to be held binding on the conscience of individuals unless they are realized as true by the persons themselves.

In view of its importance, the *Declaration and Address* should be quoted in detail. The core of the Address is a series of thirteen propositions which, in condensed form, still remain the best expression of faith commonly professed by the Christians and Disciples.

1. The church of Christ upon earth is essentially, intentionally, and constitutionally one.

2. Congregations ought to be in close fellowship with one another though they are necessarily separate and often distant in location.

3. Nothing ought to be an article of faith, a term of communion, or an obligatory rule for the constitution and government of the church except what is expressly taught by Christ and his apostles.

4. The New Testament is as perfect a constitution for

the worship, discipline and government of the New Testament church, and as perfect a rule for the particular duties of its members; as the Old Testament was for . . . the Old Testament church.

5. No human authority can make new laws for the church where the Scriptures are silent. Nothing ought to be received into the faith or worship of the church; or be made a term of communion amongst Christians, that is not as old as the New Testament.

6. Inferences and deductions from Scripture may be true doctrine, but they are not binding upon the consciences of Christians further than they perceive them to be so. Hence no such deductions or inferential truths ought to have any place in the church's confession.

7. Doctrinal exhibitions of the great system of divine truths are highly expedient but must not be made terms of communion, because they are the product of human reasoning, contain many inferential truths, and are beyond the understanding of simple people and children.

8. Full knowledge of all revealed truth is not necessary to entitle persons to membership in the church, "neither should they, for this purpose, be required to make a profession more extensive than their knowledge." Realization of their need of salvation, faith in Christ as Savior, and obedience to him are all that is essential.

9. All who are thus qualified should love each other as brothers and be united as children of one family.

10. Division among Christians is a horrid evil, fraught with many evils.

11. Divisions have been caused in some cases by neglect of the expressly revealed will of God; in others, by assumed authority to make human opinions the test of fellowship or to introduce human inventions into the faith and practice of the church.

12. All that is needed for the purity and perfection of the church is that it receive those, and only those, who profess faith in Christ and obey him according to the Scriptures; that it retain them only so long as their conduct is in accord with their profession; that ministers teach only what is expressly revealed; and that all divine ordinances be ob-

served after the example of the primitive church, exhibited in the New Testament.

13. When the church is forced to adopt "expedients" in order to observe the divine ordinances, where the necessary means are not revealed, they should be recognized as what they are and should not be mistaken for divine commands, so that there may be no dissension or division over them if there is occasion to change them.[1]

In the same year (1809), Thomas Campbell was joined by his son, Alexander, who came to America to share and later carry on the work of his father. Together they organized (1810) the Christian Association of Washington, Pa., the first local church of the new denomination. Soon after, a crisis arose on the manner of administering baptism. Deciding that the ordinance must be by immersion, father and son had themselves rebaptized by the local Baptist minister. For seventeen years the Christian Association operated as a branch of the Baptists, until the younger Campbell's anti-creedalism aroused a storm of protest. The Baptists issued an eight-point manifesto, condemning the "reformers" for maintaining "that there is no promise of salvation without Baptism . . . that Baptism procures the remission of sins and the gift of the Holy Spirit . . . that no creed is necessary for the church but the Scriptures as they stand, and that all baptized persons have the right to administer the ordinance of Baptism."[2]

Three years after the Baptist ouster, the Campbellites were joined by Barton Stone, former Presbyterian minister who had formed a non-creedal group called the Christians. Excommunicated from the Presbyterians, Stone and his followers declared their "objections . . . to the Presbyterian Confession of Faith, and against all authoritative confessions and creeds formed by fallible men." They professed a "total abandonment of all authoritative creeds but the Bible alone as the only rule of faith and practice."[3] In 1832 a partial fusion of the Campbellites and Christians was effected at Lexington, Kentucky. When the question arose of a name for the merger, Stone insisted on "Christian," as the name given the followers of Christ "in the beginning by divine authority." Alexander Campbell and his friends preferred "Disciples" as less offensive to good people and quite as scriptural. The result was that no definite action was taken and to this day both names are used, the local organization being generally known as a "Christian Church" or a "Church of Christ," and rarely as a "Church of Disciples" or a "Disciples' Church."

The first national convention of the Disciples was held at Cincinnati in 1849, when 156 delegates from eleven states resolved on the formation of a Missionary Society "as a means to concentrate and dispense the wealth and benevolence of the brethren of this Reformation in an effort to convert the world."[4] Cincinnati was made the headquarters and Alexander Campbell was elected first president. A year later the first foreign missionary was sent "to engage in teaching, preaching and the practice of medicine among the Jews at Jerusalem."[5]

At the end of the nineteenth century, the Disciples counted more than a million members and were looking forward to the centennial celebration of the *Declaration and Address* when their ranks were split by a schism that was seventy years in the making. Alexander Campbell had been a Baptist from 1812 to 1829, during which time he advocated certain conservative policies, later abandoned by him but taken up and developed by a strong reactionary party among the Disciples. They were against open Communion outside the denomination and the use of "Reverend" as a title for the clergy. But their chief objection was against the organization of missionary and other societies, which they construed as a form of denominationalism and a concession to authoritarianism. On the ritual their main grievance was the installation of organs in churches.

After years of controversy in the pulpit and religious press, the conservatives felt they had enough solidarity to separate from the main body and, as far as possible, form a new denomination. In the government census for 1906 they were listed for the first time as a distinct religious body, the Churches of Christ, numbering at the time about two hundred thousand adherents.

The schism of the Churches of Christ was not the only disruption among the Disciples. At least six "mutually hostile and exclusive groups" have been identified within the denomination: "the pro-music, pro-organized-missions group . . . the pro-music, anti-organized-missions group . . . the anti-music, anti-organized-missions group . . . the anti-music, anti-organized-missions, anti-church-school group . . . the anti-music, anti-organized-missions, anti-alien-immersion group . . . the anti-music, anti-organized-missions, anti-Sunday-school group," each with separate and rival publishing headquarters.[6]

Although, in effect, at least two opposing bodies exist within the framework of the Disciples, the liberals and the fundamentalists, there is no prospect of a new schism for lack of sufficient unity among the different factions. One evidence of the increasing strength of the fundamentalists is the rising number of their missionaries, independently educated and supported, and the establishment of separate Bible colleges, generally small and non-accredited, but indicative of a growing dissatisfaction with the modernism that is rampant in the liberal half of the denomination.

Modernist Disciples have been outstanding in promoting the ecumenical movement. Though under fire from their co-religionists, who call the National Council of Churches an "ecclesiastical monstrosity" by which "the Reformation has been set back several hundred years," the liberals have contributed more than a proportional share to the church unity efforts in America. Unique among the constituents of the Council, the Disciples organized an administrative staff on a national scale, working through state and regional board members and supported by generous financial aid, with the result that Protestant ecumenism in the country is taking on more and more the non-creedal aspect of the Disciples of Christ.

In contrast with the relative homogeneity among the Disciples, the Churches of Christ can scarcely be said to have a denominational history since the break of 1906. Protesting they are not a denomination, their principal source of unity has been a steady resistance to the "human innovations" of other religious bodies, in the form of set creeds, church officials above the local congregation, and ritual requirements for membership. As distinct from the Disciples, they have been fairly consistent in opposing musical instruments in the churches, to such a degree that the Disciples commonly distinguish the Christians by describing them as the "non instrumental music" segment of the parent body. Their religious publications are carefully labeled "unofficial," their colleges and professional schools are "non-sectarian." While missionary societies are forbidden as having "no scriptural head, foundation, field or mission," foreign missionaries are privately sponsored by individuals or local Churches of Christ. In rare instances, if a church is too weak to completely support a preacher in other fields, then two or three congregations may co-operate in the effort, since this is co-operation without creating an organization.

DOCTRINE

Since both Disciples and Christians profess to be non-confessional, having no creed but Christ and no doctrines except those which are found in the New Testament, it would seem impossible to formulate their principal beliefs. In practice, however, they emphasize certain areas of faith which may be taken as representative of the two denominations.

The Scriptures. Disciples and Christians accept the Bible as the word of God, written by different persons at different times, somehow under the inspiration of the Holy Spirit. But even fundamentalists among them explain that "this revelation comes to us in many forms: in individual lives, in great epochs of history, in providence, in such organizations as the Church, in religious assemblies, but especially in men like the prophets, the apostles, the psalmists and the evangelists."[7] Allowance is therefore made for a difference of degree but not of essence between the "inspiration" of poetry or great genius and the supernatural inspiration of Sacred Scripture.

The Church. The Disciples and Christians are agreed in regarding the Church Universal as an essentially invisible "society of believers . . . instituted by Jesus Christ," and, by divine providence, indestructible.[8] "Single denominations and sects . . . after having served their purpose, may disappear and go the way of all flesh; but the Church Universal of Christ, in her divine life and substance, is too strong for the gates of hell."[9] Beyond this agreement on the existence of a world-wide spiritual society, the difference in concept of the visible Church of Christ is so radical between the Disciples and Christians that it practically constitutes the two religious groups. The Disciples frankly admit the existence and necessity of visible Christian bodies like the Methodists, Baptists, and their own denomination. "To become a member of the Church (invisible) it is necessary to have (only) an inner experience," but to enter the visible church of, say, the Presbyterians, it is further required to have "an outward expression (and) a new social attachment." As distinct functions, "the inner experience is to hear and believe the gospel and to repent of sin . . . The new social alignment is to become a member of the visible organization."[10]

Against this concession that denominations are according to the will of God, the Christians range all their apologetic writings. First they defend their own claim to being nondenominational. "It is possible," they admit, "to sectarianize the name church of Christ or Christian, but that is what we endeavor studiously to avoid. We spell the word church with a small letter . . . We are not a part of any religious denomination for we refuse to divide up into parties."[11] Moreover, denominations in general are opposed to gospel teaching. Starting with the assumption that Catholicism is a corruption of apostolic Christianity, the origin of denominationalism is explained as an apostasy, when "the commandments and inventions of men led to the gradual development of the Roman Catholic Church." Luther, Calvin, and others "tried to reform the Catholic Church, but their efforts only resulted in the establishment of more man-made churches. Their efforts gave birth to denominationalism with its hundreds of contradictory doctrines."[12] With minor differences, the Christians regard themselves as heirs of a new movement which began in the nineteenth century, "to restore the true church which had become lost to the multitudes because of the doctrines of Catholicism and denominationalism."[13] After the lapse of centuries, Thomas and Alexander Campbell rediscovered the fact that "faith in Jesus Christ as the Son of God (is) a sufficient profession to entitle a man or woman to become a member of the Church of Christ."[14]

A permanent tension among the Christians is how to operate their churches efficiently without some degree of unity beyond the local congregational level, and at the same time proclaim they are non-denominational in spite of their organization. They solve the problem by making concessions to co-operative effort among the churches, but always short of being on a national scale, assisted by books and periodicals from common publishing houses which serve to unite ostensibly independent congregations.

Sacraments. Two sacraments or ordinances are recognized by the Disciples and Christians: baptism and the Lord's Supper. Regarding baptism, Disciples are warned that, "We should neither overemphasize nor undervalue it."[15] Overemphasis would be to conceive it as efficacious independently of the active co-operation of the one baptized, e.g., a child, since "Baptism is (only) for all who understandingly, intentionally and sacrificially accept the Lordship of Jesus Christ, and want to declare that fact to the world."[16] Underestimation means a failure to realize that "Baptism is the experience that translates one from being a non-Christian to being a Christian," yet not "in any magical, commercial, formal or miraculous sense," as though sin is remitted or grace infused in virtue of the baptismal rite. At most, "it is the effort of the true Christian knight to honor Christ by the white flower of a stainless life. It is in this (promissory) sense that Baptism is for the remission of sins."[17]

Though variously described, the Lord's Supper for the Disciples and Christians is only "a sweet and simple memorial." Just "as we look at a flower from mother's grave in memory of man's truest earthly friend," or "we go to Washington's monument and stand with heads uncovered in memory of the father of our country, (so) also we gather around the Lord's table and take the Lord's supper in memory of Him who said, 'This do in remembrance of me.'"[18] Emphatically the Lord's Supper does not mean that "a real miracle, which changes the material elements into the actual body and blood of Christ, takes place in the elements."[19] That kind of miracle is unnecessary "to vitalize its power and enforce its influence over the soul."[20] Whatever the Eucharistic presence means to Campbell's disciples, it is not determined by the words of the minister pronouncing the words of institution, but by the living faith of the communicants, since "to partake of it without thinking of Christ, to partake of it simply as a 'church ordinance,' to partake of it because it is a custom or is expected of us, is to miss its depth and to eat of nothing but bread, to drink of nothing but the blood of the grape."[21]

WORSHIP AND RITUAL

Separate minister's manuals are available for the Disciples and the Churches of Christ, but the differences are slight. Both are relative innovations, and presented to the clergy with an apology. "The Disciples of Christ," are told they "have always been a free people, including a freedom from ritualism," but "with an increasing culture there is a growing desire that all things be done decently and in good order."[22] Hence the need of a uniform ritual. Ministers of the Churches of Christ are also cautioned that the manual of worship "should not be slavishly used, either to the exclusion of heartfelt personal expression, or of loyalty to what is believed to be the teaching of God's Word.[23]

Baptism. Alexander Campbell's conviction that only baptism by immersion is valid was based, he said, on extensive study of the meaning of the word *baptizo* in the Greek New Testament. He found that "the ancient lexicons with one consent give *immersion* as the natural, common, and primary sense of this word."[24] Disciples and Christians have remained faithful to this tradition, directing that "every congregation should have a baptistry inside the church edifice," which should be of adequate dimensions, since "humiliating experiences can be related of shallow baptistries." Also "there should be an abundant supply of leaded robes for both sexes," and "the water in the baptistry should be heated in cold weather." It is suggested that "the baptistry should be made as attractive as possible by simple lighting, or the careful arrangement of blooming flowers or potted plants. Garish or spectacular effects should be avoided."[25]

Before baptism a person is expected to go through a period of instruction. Ministers are encouraged to instruct candidates about cultivating their devotional life by regular habits of reading the Scriptures, meditating upon them, and engaging in private prayer.

The service of baptism may be a part of the regular morning or evening worship. Though customs differ, a growing number of Christian ministers follow a definite program as follows: prelude or processional hymn, announcement of the baptismal service, scriptural introduction, baptismal hymn, the Divine authorization of baptism (Matthew 28:18-20), and, just before the immersion, a baptismal prayer.

On reaching the position for baptism, the minister holds the clasped hands of the person and says quietly to him as he does so: "God is witness to what you are doing. Center your thoughts on Him, as I pronounce the baptismal formula." The baptismal pronouncement declares: "By the authority of our Lord Jesus Christ in whom you have confessed your faith, I baptize you . . . in the name of the Father, and of the Son, and of the Holy Spirit. Amen." Thereupon the minister says, "Now I am about to lower you gently into the water." The minister lowers the candidate backward into the water to the depth of a few inches, pausing long enough to count to himself, "One, two, three," to represent the burial. Then just as gradually he raises the person up.

The immersion is followed by a short baptismal blessing, a hymn of praise, and the benediction. Normally baptisms are administered early enough in the service to allow the newly baptized to participate in the worship service that follows. The congregation joins in the celebration of the baptism and of the special Lord's Supper ritual afterward.[26]

Lord's Supper. There are two principal types of service among the Disciples and Christians, Morning Worship with the Lord's Supper, and Evening Worship without Communion. Ministers are told to "avoid elaborate worship programs . . . Emphasis should always be placed on simplicity."[27] A standard "Order for Morning Worship" in the Churches of Christ, substantially the same for the Disciples, begins with a hymn by the choir, during which the minister comes to the platform and takes charge of the function. Following the first hymn is the doxology, an invocation, another hymn, scripture reading, and the Communion hymn which introduces the ceremony of the Lord's Supper.

Ministers have a choice of at least four "Orders of Observance" for the Communion Service, in which elders and deacons participate. During the singing of the Communion hymn, the elders take their places at each end of a table on which are placed wide-rim metal plates covered with pieces of bread, and wooden or metal trays filled with small glasses of wine. The deacons take their places in front of the table, while the congregation stands. Without announcement, "the elder at the right returns thanks for the bread," always quoting the words of institution from the Last Supper. Immediately "the elder at the left returns thanks for the cup," again using the words of institution. After the congregation has been seated the elders "distribute the bread to the alternate deacons," who in turn give Communion to the people. The remaining deacons close ranks and receive from the elders the trays of wineglasses to be served to the congregation. When the people have been served, the deacons give Communion to the elders, after which "the elders then serve the deacons and close the service with a song of thanksgiving."[28] An essential difference in the ritual of the Christians is the recommendation that "unleavened bread and the unfermented juice of the grape should be used."[29] The Disciples do not specify unleavened bread and allow the use of wine; they also provide "Simultaneous Communion which is being observed in an increasing number of their churches." Bread is distributed to the people and held in the hands; then, as the minister recites the words: "And he gave to the disciples, and said, 'Take, eat; this is my body,'" all eat together, each his own portion. The wine is distributed and taken in the same way.

Following Communion is the offertory, during which prayers of self-oblation are offered and contributions are made to the church as "a sacred and impressive part of divine worship." Then follows a sermon, which "should edify, inspire and secure decisive action on the part of the hearer."[30] After the sermon a benediction is invoked upon the congregation, with a choral response; and finally organ chimes are played to conclude the service.

A new feature of the Disciples' liturgy is the variety of introits and collects which they recommend for use by the ministers. By actual count, over seven hundred are offered for use. They cover a wide range of human needs for which the minister and faithful are invited to pray: Citizenship, Compassion, Grace to Follow the Crucified, Ecumenical Church, Family of Nations, Labor Day, Missions, Inner Peace, Surrender and Submission, and Women Workers in the Church.

Music in Public Worship. Historically the Churches of Christ differ from the Disciples by their opposition to the use of musical instruments in public worship. They agree that music has a place in New Testament worship, and freely use hymns in their church services. They also permit musical instruments to accompany religious songs for private devotion, but not for public acts of worship. The argument is that since the New Testament is silent concerning instrumental music in worship, it is evident that those who have it in the worship do so without scriptural authority. They should not presume to add to the divine pattern. The argument is supported by an appeal to the Protestant Reformers. Among others, Calvin is quoted as saying that musical instruments in celebrating the praises of God would be no more suitable than the burning of incense, the lighting up of lamps, or the restoration of the other shadows of the law. Catholics are said to have borrowed this from the Jews.

Parallel with this critical attitude of liturgical music is a remarkable tolerance in the other direction in many churches of the Campbellite tradition. Musical interludes are a commonplace in the standard Christian Service Book. There is even a special ceremony for the installation of a church organ. It begins with an organ recital and, after suitable readings from Scripture, the people say, "We dedicate this organ." To which the minister responds, "To summon His people to the hour of worship and holy communion . . . to lift man's soul to communions with Christ . . . and to bring to his life comfort, peace and hope which abide in Him."[31]

ORGANIZATION AND GOVERNMENT

While ministerial associations have been organized for mutual help and supervision, they have no authority among the Disciples and Christians, which are strictly congregational in their form of government. Local churches elect their own elders and deacons, "by voice, by show of hands, by ballot or by rising," followed by the ceremony of ordination if the officers are elected for a permanent term, to be ended by death or resignation. However, many congregations choose their ministers for a limited term only, usually three years, and the list is so arranged that one third of the officers is elected each year.

In the early days, ordinations to the ministry were rare. Even now the Disciples hold "there is no official distinction between the clergy and the laity . . . The real power of a minister is personal, not official, power of a strong compelling goodness of life and character."[32] This opinion is shared by the Churches of Christ. Yet ordinations are now a commonplace, and invested with considerable solemnity, as "the formal setting apart of a man to the work of the ministry." Essentially the ceremony consists in the laying on of hands by one or more elders, accompanied by the ordination prayer, for which there is no set formula except that it be "fervent, personal and short, asking the Lord to use the life now laid on His altar; to keep, guide and bless by making him a blessing to the church and for the saving of multitudes; and asking for him health of body, mind and heart and that he may be fully consecrated to the work whereunto he has been called."[33]

There is no juridical authority in the Churches of Christ beyond the local congregation. Only denominations are ruled by "ecclesiastical forms of government." But in so doing, say the Christians, they have ignored Christ, the head of the church, and have assumed the right of self-government. This is said to be clearly against the Scriptures, which tell us that, shortly before Christ ascended to the right hand of God, He declared, "All authority has been given me in heaven and on earth." Christ has all authority; therefore man has none. No doubt Christians hear much of "synods," "prebyteries," "councils," "general assemblies," and "conferences." In these delegations, "men legislate rules" independently of the law of God.

Also congregational in polity but fully organized as a denomination, the Disciples are grouped on three levels above the local church, into district and state conventions, and an International Convention which meets annually as a representative body of all the churches. There is no national body comparable to the Southern Baptist Convention or the Methodist General Conference. In fact, the Disciples' conventions have only advisory power and no final authority over the member churches. More direct supervision is exercised through a variety of boards, e.g., the Board of Church Extension, whose purpose is to assist Christian churches in the planning and financing of buildings; the Board of Higher Education, with numerous institutions like Texas Christian, Butler, and Drake Universities, "concerned with the education of youth in an atmosphere of Christian influence" and the training of the clergy; and the Christian Board of Publications, which operates a "Brotherhood-owned" publishing house "to propagate and support an effective program of Christian education," by providing a home journal, *The Christian Evangelist,* books, audio-visual materials, "and all other supplies" necessary for "Christian teaching, Christian evangelism and Christian stewardship in the local church."

While accurate figures are not available, there is good reason for believing that the Christian schism of 1906 was only the high point in a permanent trend within the Disciples of Christ toward an undistinguishable form of non-sectarianism. This is strikingly illustrated in the history of the *Christian Century,* founded in 1884 as a rival periodical to the denomination-minded *Christian Evangelist.* Remaining under the aegis of the Disciples, in 1908 the *Christian Century* was bought by Charles Clayton Morrison, and dedicated to "a new era of frank commitment to liberalism." Morrison was "far ahead of Disciple sentiment (in) advocating open membership" to all comers, regardless of their creedal prepossessions. By 1918, the paper carried the subtitle, "An Undenominational Journal of Religion." What many considered a "suicidal boldness in cutting loose from the position of the vast majority in the denomination of its origin," resulted in making the *Christian Century* acceptable to a wide circle of "liberals in all churches," until today it is the most popular interdenominational magazine in the country.

There is no counting the number of religious periodicals directly published by the Churches of Christ and the Disciples of Christ. Some have a venerable history that goes back before the *Christian Century*. Among these is the *Christian Standard*, founded in 1866 by Isaac Errett. To this day, the *Standard* is designed both to appeal to intelligent readers and to cultivate a broader culture than is common in many religious publications. A typical editorial illustrates the unique type of Christianity among the Disciples.

When is a church not a church? The question may appear somewhat ridiculous, but its implications are serious. A church is no longer a church when it becomes something other than a church. The church is the group of people, exclusively the Lord's, whose sum total of purpose is to extend and expand the Lord's influence on life, both of self and of others.

A church is no longer a church when it becomes a club. A club is a group of people meeting together for a common purpose, usually of social benefit.

A church is no longer a church when it becomes a bank. A bank is an institution that receives and keeps money for other people.

A church is no longer a church when it becomes a building. A building is a lifeless, bloodless, wood or stone structure, designed to facilitate a purpose.

A church is no longer a church when it becomes a self-centered group. A self-centered group is one that concentrates its effort on money, concern, time, love and thought on itself.

A church is no longer a church when it becomes an institution. An institution is an organization or society for a public or social purpose. An institution can be seen, defined, changed, directed, mistaken, aborted, confused, or dissolved. The church is an influence, not an institution.[34]

The above description of the Church of Christ as conceived by the Disciples perfectly synthesizes their ecclesiology. Whatever else the church is in their theory, it is not an institution. For "the church lives to serve, and serves to love." Its function is not to organize the People of God.

Episcopalians

In many ways Episcopalianism has more profoundly affected the history and fortunes of the Catholic Church, and is more closely akin to its doctrine and spirit, than any other Protestant denomination. The departure under Henry VIII and Queen Elizabeth was not only numerically considerable but, otherwise than in Germany or France, it involved the loss to the Church of a whole nation, and not only of one nation, but of many peoples who were later on to belong to the British Commonwealth. The only canonized English saints in modern times, John Fisher and Thomas More, and scores of beatified, were the victims of a persecution sanctioned by the Church of England. The same persecution contributed to solidifying the faith of the Irish people and to give the United States and other countries a large Catholic immigration and Catholic leadership.

From the ranks of the Anglican communion has come a stream of Roman Catholic converts, including some of the Church's outstanding priests and lay apostles. From the Episcopalian point of view, even though firmly attached to the doctrine, sacraments, and canonical position of their own church, many of them "hope ardently for ultimate reunion with Rome." In their opinion, "the Roman problem is the key problem of Christian unity, not only because the Roman is the most numerous Christian communion but because the papacy has within itself the potentiality of becoming many of the things which Roman Catholics now claim that it is."[1]

HISTORY

The historical origins of Episcopalianism cover a period of thirty-six years, from 1527 when Henry VIII first proposed to nullify the marriage with his wife, Catherine of Aragon, to 1563, when his daughter, Queen Elizabeth, by an act of Parliament promulgated the Thirty-nine Articles of the Anglican Church. Between these two dates, in rapid succession, the religious character of the English nation was radically changed. After seven years of vain effort to obtain papal approval for the nullification, Henry made himself supreme head of the Church of England, Parliament declaring that "the Roman Pontiff has no greater jurisdiction bestowed on him by God in the Holy Scriptures in this realm of England than any other foreign bishop."[2] During the minority of his son, Edward VI, the Book of Common Prayer was published in two editions (1549 and 1552), first along Lutheran and then Calvinist lines; a new Ordinal was issued (1550–52), following a Lutheran pattern, in which every mention of a priesthood offering sacrifice was carefully omitted from the ordination ritual; and the first draft of forty-two Articles of Faith was authorized in 1553. However, the complete rupture with Catholicism on a national scale did not come until 1563, when the Elizabethan Parliament made the Thirty-nine Articles of Religion obligatory on all citizens under heavy penalties.

Episcopalianism was brought to the American colonies by a group of English settlers who landed at Chesapeake Bay on May 6, 1607, and a week later founded what is now Jamestown, Virginia. For more than a hundred years, "The story of the Church of England in the thirteen colonies . . . is the story of what happens to an episcopal Church when it tries to live and thrive without a bishop."[3] England feared that allowing an indigenous colonial episcopate would produce an independent denomination in America. But in spite of these precautions, secession came as a result of the American Revolution. First a distinctive name was adopted. In 1783 the American Anglicans became known officially as the Protestant Episcopal Church: Protestant to distinguish them from Catholics, and Episcopal to mark them off from the Presbyterians and Congregationalists. In the same year ten representatives of the Church of Connecticut elected and sent Samuel Seabury to Scotland to be consecrated bishop by the Non-Jurors; in 1786 William White of Pennsylvania and Samuel Provost were sent to England for episcopal consecration. Finally in 1789 the church was united as a national body at the first General Convention in Philadelphia.

Among the resolutions adopted and still in force, it was decided that the Protestant Episcopal Church should be independent of all foreign authority, civil and ecclesiastical, and have full power to regulate its own affairs; its liturgy should conform to that of the Church of England; its ministry should consist of three orders, bishops, presbyter, and deacon; the canons of church doctrine and policy should be made by representatives of both clergy and laity; no powers should be delegated, as in England, to a general ecclesiastical government, except such as could not be conveniently exercised by individual state conventions; there should be bishops in each state, and they should have seats in the General Convention.

This first Convention also revised the English Book of Common Prayer. Though some writers call the revision slight, the nature of the changes was significant. Sixty-nine feast days were dropped from the church calendar, mostly of "persons subsequent to New Testament times or events not based on New Testament evidence"; the "Ornaments Rubric" requiring vestments was omitted; the Athanasian Creed was removed; in the Catechism, the sentence "the Body and Blood of Christ . . . are verily and indeed taken and received by the faithful in the Lord's Supper" was changed to read ". . . spiritually taken and received."[4]

For the first generation of the nineteenth century, the Protestant Episcopal Church was notoriously lax in its home missionary efforts, and as a consequence lost most of its communicants who migrated west of the Alleghenies. State dioceses felt this was the responsibility of the National Convention; the latter insisted it was the duty of the states. In 1829 the bishops decided that their mission society was the Church itself and not just a few zealous individuals. A missionary episcopate was therefore established, and, by tacit agreement, the Evangelical segment of the Church concentrated on foreign missions, while the High Church party emphasized the domestic field. The earliest surviving mission outside the country was in Liberia.

American Episcopalianism was deeply affected by the English Oxford Movement, led by Keble, Newman, and Froude. Although the full effect was slower to come in the States, the impact was felt already in the mid-nineteen hundreds, especially among the younger clergy, who began to wince at the appellation "Protestant." They were "inclined to be apologetic about the deplorable conditions of a Church which had so nearly forgotten its Catholic heritage. For them the Reformation was a de-formation, and the ancient Church of Rome, instead of being a target for their abuse, began to exert upon them an uneasy fascination."[5] Between 1825 and 1855, thirty American Episcopalian clergymen went over to Rome; and in the decade 1830–40, out of fourteen bishops elected, eleven were High Church advocates. This provoked a reaction, and in 1847 the Society for the Promotion of Evangelical Knowledge (S.P.E.K.) was established to combat Tractarianism.

Though unhampered by schisms as other denominations, even during the Civil War, the growth of the Protestant Episcopal Church in the nineteenth century was comparatively slow, as indicated in the following table:

Year	Members	Clergy	Ratio to National Population
1800	12,000	250	1 to 441
1830	31,000	760	1 to 417
1866	160,000	2,450	1 to 209
1901	751,000	5,067	1 to 102

During the same century, the Roman Catholic population in the country grew from 50,000 to 12,041,000 in membership; from 50 to 11,987 in the number of priests; and in population ratio from 1:1061 to 1:6.3.

Among the major changes which the Protestant Episcopal Church has undergone in the past fifty years, the most significant is in the reshaping of its liturgy. The American Book of Common Prayer was first revised in 1892 under the aegis of William Huntington, who began at Harvard as a Liberal and "as time went on became more Orthodox, more Catholic" —in fact, too Catholic for the General Convention, which adopted only a fraction of his suggested modifications. Meantime an "unofficial revision" of the liturgy went on apace. In 1891 the standard directory of ceremonial recommended interpolations from the Latin Mass, e.g., Offertory prayers and the Last Gospel. Later on *The People's Missal* boldly advocated the admission of the entire Latin Canon, and introduced a whole sequence of Introits, Secrets, Offertory prayers and Communion verses. Still later came the *English Missal,* which was "nothing but a bald translation of the Roman Missal, with side glances toward the Book of Common Prayer."[6] Ceremonial books simply reflected the changed liturgical practices. Colored stoles, vested choirs, processional crosses, fixed altars, choral services—all of which had at one time been the stigmata of a very "advanced" parish—were by 1900 commonplaces; indeed, an Episcopalian church which lacked them was scarcely orthodox. Eucharistic vestments, which had caused such a furor in the eighteen-sixties, were now nothing out of the way. In the experience of one clergyman, in 1892 the altar of his church was a plain wooden structure without any ornaments, in 1903 this was replaced by a marble altar furnished with a cross, in 1908 a vested choir and processional cross were introduced, in 1913 candles and an early communion celebration every Sunday, in 1933 Eucharistic vestments, and in 1938 the reservation of the Sacrament.

The Book of Common Prayer was revised again in 1928, this time from cover to cover, so that only the title page remained the same, and even here Bishop Guerry of South Carolina moved to strike out the word "Protestant," but his motion was killed in committee. An effort to drop the Thirty-nine Articles failed by a narrow margin, "but they were relegated to a harmless position as a sort of appendix." Most of the changes took the form of a revision of the ultra-Protestant Prayer Book of 1552, and a return to that of 1549. In the offertory, "the revision by-passed Cranmer, with his pathological fear of giving any countenance to the doctrine of sacrifice in the Eucharist."[7] New Collects, Epistles, and Gospels were added to the Eucharistic ceremony. In response to the demand for adding post-scriptural saints to the liturgy, a new proper was included, corresponding to the *Proprium Sanctorum* of the Roman Missal. The requiem mass for the dead, which High Churchmen had denounced in the 1870s, was now made legal. Reacting against the Protestant tradition, prayers for the dead were formally sanctioned. "After 1928, the Church at every Eucharist was remembering all the faithful departed, and beseeching God to grant them continual growth in His love and service . . . This was change of doctrine with a vengeance."[8] In the same way, the sacrament of extreme unction was restored, at least partially, "as a sacrament of healing."

The only significant schism in American Episcopalianism occurred in 1873 when a group of eight clergymen left the Protestant Episcopal Church in protest against what they considered Anglo-Catholicism. Their grievance was that Episcopalians had reverted to pre-Reformation concepts on the Eucharist and baptism. They rejected the idea that the Lord's table is an altar on which the body and blood of Christ are offered to the Father, that the presence of Christ in the Eucharist is anything more than a spiritual commemoration, and that regeneration is inseparably connected with the sacrament of baptism.

To emphasize their difference from the parent body, Reformed Episcopalians also deny that Christian ministers are priests in any other way than are all other believers "the royal priesthood." Consistent with the same principles, the Reformed Episcopal Church admits men to the ministry on letters of dismissal from other Protestant denominations and without reordination.

In the same spirit, they have modified their liturgy by removing what they consider "objectionable sacerdotal elements." Moreover, while some forms of worship are prescribed, ministers are encouraged to use extempore prayers and follow optional orders of service.

DOCTRINE AND WORSHIP

While the Thirty-nine Articles are still included in the American Book of Common Prayer, they are not considered representative of the doctrinal and ritual position of the Protestant Episcopal Church. For years it was felt that American Episcopalians needed a quasi-official exposition of their beliefs and practices, at once faithful to their Anglican tradition and yet embodying the distinctive characteristics of the Church in this country. A series of books was therefore "written to provide adults with the basic content teaching of the Episcopal Church." The present analysis is based largely on these volumes, produced under the auspices of the Department of Christian Education of the National Council, with parallel sources used when necessary.

The Church. By definition, "Episcopalians belong to a Church that is a member of the family known as the Anglican Churches." However, the term Anglican "does not imply adherence to the teachings of a religious leader as does 'Lutheran' or 'Calvinist.'" It means "that Christian tradition which became the ethos of the Church of England and spread thence to become the distinguishing mark of a vast worldwide Communion of Churches."[9] If we ask what is the most striking characteristic of the Anglican tradition, we are told it is the "combination in a single church life of Christian elements sometimes sharply divided by the words 'Catholic' and 'Protestant.'" Or, as affirmed by the Anglican Congress of 1954, the Anglican communion is "a fellowship of Churches at one and the same time Catholic in seeking to do justice to the wholeness of Christian truth, in emphasizing continuity through the Episcopate and in retaining the historic Creeds and Sacraments of undivided Christendom; and Evangelical in its commission to proclaim the Gospel and in its emphasis on personal faith in Jesus Christ as Saviour."[10]

The tension between these contraries has produced three types of Episcopalian parishes, sometimes mistaken as separate denominations—the high, low, and broad. In general, a high parish "emphasizes sacramental worship, the supreme value of the 'Catholic tradition' and a rather elaborate service of worship." At the other extreme, the low parish minimizes the liturgy; its "services are simple and a stronger emphasis is placed on the gospel and on personal religion." Between the two is the broad parish, "which may be either High or Low, (where) the importance of a rational understanding of the Christian tradition is stressed, with a concern for 'liberal' values."[11] Summarily, therefore, the High Church stresses what may be called the Catholic viewpoint, the Low Church is Protestant and Evangelical, and the Broad Church is more Liberal, Modernist, and Latitudinarian. Much of the conflict in present-day Episcopalianism, notably among the clergy, arises from the attempted assimilation of these disparate elements in a single body.

In spite of these tensions, there is a common core of beliefs and attitudes which Episcopalians regard as their special heritage. Their faith and worship are epitomized in the Lambeth Quadrilateral, which the Americans accepted in 1892: sufficiency of Scripture, the Apostles' and Nicene Creed, baptism and the Lord's Supper, and the historic episcopate. More realistically, however, and admitted by their writers, what has kept the Anglicans together is a triple visible bond of unity: "They all use the Book of Common Prayer; they are all in communion with the Archbishop of Canterbury; they all recognize bishops as their chief pastors."[12]

Sacraments. Technically only two sacraments are accepted as "ordained of Christ Our Lord," baptism and the Lord's Supper. While baptism is universally regarded as the sacrament of initiation into the Church, the degree of membership through baptism is still a matter of dispute. In his opening address to the General Convention in 1955, the presiding bishop urged the necessity of "a different . . . approach to the whole problem of Church membership."[13] As presently worded, the canons require after baptism one year of church attendance—hence rational maturity—for full membership in the Episcopalian communion. One of the main issues, still unsolved, is "whether a newly baptized baby would have to wait till he had attended church for a year before he could be counted as a member in good standing," i.e., a full-fledged member of the Protestant Episcopal Church.[14]

The Episcopalian concept of the Lord's Supper ranges from very "Catholic" to the opposite extreme, depending on two factors: the notion of the presence in the Eucharist, and the attitude toward the Eucharistic service. As regards the real presence, "The manner in which Christ is present and communicates Himself to His people in the Holy Communion has never been precisely defined by the Anglican Churches, although the certainty and reality of His presence have been strongly affirmed."[15] So too the Communion Service. Since the Prayer Book revision of 1928, countenance has been given to a sacrificial idea of the Lord's Supper, comparable to the Mass in the Roman rite. However, this must be sharply qualified by the still officially uncertain meaning of the Eucharist itself. In High Church circles, of course, there is no doubt about the Eucharist as a sacrifice, or about the sacrament as containing the Body and Blood of Christ.

The method of assisting at Mass consists in making oneself a part of The Action at each step. Surely this is the best method of "following the service." Thereby each worshipper is able to experience the true inner meaning of the Eucharist. For therein we and ours, with praise and thanksgiving are offered to God through the eternal sacrifice on Calvary, which same is made present and available to us every time Mass is celebrated, and is the divinely ordained means of the renewal and of the maintenance of our union with Christ who is our Saviour because he is our Sacrifice.

The phrase *Real Presence* does not mean that there can be an unreal presence. Rather, the words *Real Presence* reject the contrary idea of the real absence of Christ in favour of what every devout Communicant knows from experience, namely, that in this Sacrament Christ makes himself available to us in his humanity (which is the fundamental meaning of the phrase *Body* and *Blood*) as well as in his divinity. The real and whole Christ is here, after a fashion which enables us to receive him. He is present everywhere as God, but not in such a way as to enable us to receive him as our spiritual Food. In his humanity he is present only (a) in heaven where he continually makes intercession for us in the presentation of his eternal sacrifice; and (b) in the Sacrament which he has ordained to be the means whereby his heavenly presence and sacrifice is made available for us on earth.[16]

Among other benefits in America, the Oxford Movement has made the Episcopal Church willing to admit, in effect, the sacramental character of the five rites which the Thirty-nine Articles proscribe as "not to be counted for Sacraments."[17] Thus Confirmation is elevated to sacramental dignity, as a divinely ordained complement to baptism. Performed by the bishop, "with the outward and visible sign of the Laying on of Hands," it "calls down upon the candidates the Holy Spirit of God to strengthen them in their Christian profession."[18]

The same with penance. "Many Christians . . . have found it helpful to make a private and specific acknowledgement of their sins to God through sacramental confession in the presence of a priest of the Church. When they do this, they can receive from him both absolution from sin and assurance that they are restored by God to living membership in Christ's Body."[19] Church publications regularly list the times of confession in various churches. In many places confessions are heard at stated hours, e.g., Saturday from 12 to 1, 4 to 5, "and by appointment."

In matrimony, the ministers are said to be "the couple who are undertaking the marriage; by their promises they marry themselves . . . For Christians who are members of the Church of Christ, marriage is not merely a means of legalizing sexual relations; it is sacramental in nature, permanent in character, and must reflect the spiritual marriage and unity that exists between the Lord and His Church."[20] Consistent with the concept of marriage as a permanent contract, the canons of the Protestant Episcopal Church do not authorize the Church itself to grant divorce, in the technical sense. But they do provide ample grounds for annulment. Moreover, bishops may permit divorced persons to remarry, on certain conditions, and readmit them to Holy Communion, if they show themselves to be in good faith and trying to live a good Christian life. In view of its importance, the appropriate canon deserves to be quoted in full.

> Any person, being a member of this Church in good standing, whose marriage has been annulled or dissolved by a civil court of competent jurisdiction may apply to the Bishop or Ecclesiastical Authority of the Diocese or Missionary District in which such person is canonically resident for a judgment as to his or her marital status in the eyes of the Church. And any person, being a member of this Church in good standing, who desires to marry a non-member of this Church whose previous marriage has been dissolved or annulled by a civil court of competent jurisdiction may apply to the Bishop or Ecclesiastical Au-

thority of the Diocese or Missionary District in which he or she is canonically resident, for permission to be married by a Minister of this Church, provided in both cases that the judgment of the civil court has become final and that at least one year shall have elapsed from the date that the decree became final. Such application should be made at least thirty days before a contemplated marriage.

If the Bishop or Ecclesiastical Authority is satisfied that the parties intend a true Christian marriage he may refer the application to his Council of Advisors, or to the Court if such has been established by diocesan action. The Bishop or Ecclesiastical Authority shall take care that his or its judgment is based upon and conforms to the doctrine of this Church, that marriage is a physical, spiritual, and mystical union of a man and woman created by their mutual consent of heart, mind and will thereto, and is a Holy Estate instituted of God and is in intention lifelong.[21]

Without clarifying the fundamental ambiguity on the Eucharist as a sacrifice, and therefore of the ministry as a priesthood, the Episcopal Church nevertheless declares that "the act of ordination (of the clergy) has a sacramental character." By the imposition of hands, "God the Holy Ghost sets apart and authenticates these persons as ministers of Christ in His Church."[22] In the rite of ordination to the priesthood, the bishop and clergy present lay their hands "severally upon the head of every one that receiveth the Order of Priesthood." Then the bishop says: "Receive the Holy Ghost for the Office and Work of a Priest in the Church of God, now committed unto thee by the Imposition of our hands. Whose sins thou dost forgive, they are forgiven; and whose sins thou dost retain, they are retained. And be thou a faithful Dispenser of the Word of God, and of his holy Sacraments; in the name of the Father, and of the Son, and of the Holy Ghost. Amen."[23] The word "priest" was inserted into the prayer of ordination in 1661, attempting to correct the century-long defect in form which was one reason why Leo XIII, in 1896, declared Anglican Orders invalid. When the change was made in the seventeenth century, "a number of ministers, amounting it is said to two thousand, resigned their benefices," in protest against this and similar "Catholic" restorations.[24]

Extreme unction is proved to be scriptural by an appeal to the familiar text in St. James. Moreover, "the sacramental nature of this action is shown in the direction that the minister may use a prayer in which he says: 'I anoint thee with oil (or I lay my hand upon thee) . . . beseeching the mercy of Our Lord Jesus Christ, that . . . the blessing of health may be restored unto thee.' Coupled with this prayer is another, in which God is asked . . . 'to release thy servant from sin.' Here an outward and visible means is being employed so that an inward and spiritual gift may be received."[25]

De Novissimis. The Episcopalian position on hell is obscure. To the question of whether death in sin is punished by an irrevocable separation from God, the answer, in theory, or "in principle (is) yes . . . To deny hell in principle would be to deny man's freedom; to confine it to anything short of eternity would be to limit that freedom." But in practice, "when we come to think of how things will in fact work out, we must take into account our experience with God in this life . . . In that experience God never gives up His dealing with an individual soul." Of course, "whether His persistence and His loving ingenuity . . . will be enough to move all men eventually to turn to God, we do not know. We can hope and pray that the time will come, perhaps deep into eternity, when there will be no rebel areas, no pockets of resistance."[26] Thus the matter is left, admitting eternal punishment theoretically from the nature of man's freedom, while postulating universal salvation, not from reason or revelation but from our "experience" of God's mercy.

More clear-cut and a departure from the Protestantism in the Thirty-nine Articles is the teaching on purgatory. "The Romish Doctrine concerning Purgatory," says Article 22, "is a fond thing, vainly invented, and grounded upon no warranty of Scripture, but rather repugnant to the Word of God."[27] Yet now the Church allows belief in "purgatory (for) those whose enjoyment of God is not lessened by any defect in themselves, but it is not the full consummation in which the whole creation participates."[28] This attitude is fully sanctioned by the Prayers for the Dead in the revised (1928)

American Book of Common Prayer, e.g., "O God, whose mercies cannot be numbered; Accept our prayers on behalf of the soul of thy servant, and grant him (her) an entrance into the land of light and joy, in the fellowship of thy saints."[29]

Doctrinal Liberalism. American Episcopalianism seems not to have been plagued with such eminent liberals in its ranks as the late Anglican Bishop of Birmingham, Ernest Barnes, who taught that "miracles do not happen,"[30] and that St. John the Evangelist "thinks of the son of God in terms of a solar deity such as Mithra."[31] However, the liberal party in the Protestant Episcopal Church is neither small nor uninfluential. A popular manual on *The Episcopal Church* describes the Bible as "the literature of a great race, the literature of a great movement toward realizing the relation of God to man . . . But the Church does not ask you to make a formal statement of belief in the Bible." The writer admits that "every minister of the Church makes solemn affirmation at his ordination that he believes 'the Holy Scriptures of the Old and New Testaments contain all things necessary to Salvation.' But the Church imposes no such obligation upon its members."[32] In 1934, a group of "American priests" of the Episcopalian Church published a volume of essays called *Liberal Catholicism and the Modern World,* in which they defended the title "Liberal" as a good term. "It connotes freedom, adventure, independence, and that dignified quality of the human spirit by which it affirms its hostility to all enslavements."[33] A contributing factor in this de-Catholicization has been the practice of future Episcopalian scholars making their graduate studies at Union Theological Seminary. "There they came under the influence of Reinhold Niebuhr, Paul Tillich, and Richard Kroner, who were bringing to bear on the general American theological scene the latest ideas of Protestant theology from the continent of Europe."[34]

More recently, American Episcopalians have had such prominent moral theologians as Joseph Fletcher propounding a theory of situation ethics that leaves nothing to the imagination in its fusion of New Testament teaching and antinomian secularity. His program of situation ethics is a manifesto of individual freedom and autonomous responsibility, in which he claims to extricate modern man from the archaic rules and codes held sacred in Christianity.

We must flatly oppose the classical means-ends rule in Christian ethics and moral theology. We have to refuse to omit doing a preponderantly good deed just because the necessary means happens to be evil "generally" or because it entails some evil. For us, whether it is good or evil, right or wrong, is not *in* the deed but *by* its circumstances. William James liked to say that truth does not exist *ante rem,* before or apart from the facts as lived, but *in rebus*— in the lived event itself. And so with the good! Several years ago Congress passed a special bill giving citizenship to a Roumanian Jewish doctor, a woman, who had aborted three thousand Jewish women brought to the concentration camp. If pregnant, they were to be incinerated. Even accepting the view that the embryos were "human lives" (which many of us do not), by "killing" three thousand the doctor saved three thousand and prevented the murder of *six thousand!*

If, for example, the emotional and spiritual welfare of the parents and children in a *particular* family could best be served by a divorce, then wrong and cheap-jack as divorce often is, love justifies a divorce. Love's method is to judge by particularity, not to lay down laws and universals. It does not preach pretty propositions; it asks concrete questions, situation questions . . . We are quite clear about it: to will the end is to will the means.[35]

GOVERNMENT, LAWS, AND ORGANIZATION

The organizational structure of the Protestant Episcopal Church is strictly hierarchical, but unlike the government of the Catholic Church the Episcopalian hierarchy does not begin on an international level; it starts more locally with a separate denomination in each country. Also unlike the Catholic Church it includes a large measure of lay participation and aims to maintain a balance of power between the executive and legislative branches.

Anglican Communion. At the highest theoretical level, Anglican Churches in various countries regard themselves as members of a world association which they describe as the Anglican communion. There is no juridical bond, however, uniting these national churches, i.e., "there is no joint central executive or legislative body in the Anglican Communion. No archbishop or bishop is supreme, and no national Church has authority or jurisdiction over any other. A special position of honor is accorded to the Archbishop of Canterbury as head of the primatial See of the mother Church of England, and the test of membership in the Anglican Communion has traditionally been whether or not a diocese is in communion with the See of Canterbury. It is this background that gives this Church on the world scene the name Anglican, though the actual titles of the different Churches vary a great deal."[36] At the World Anglican Congress, which met in Milwaukee, the Archbishop of Canterbury, Primate of All England and Metropolitan, headed the list of attending dignitaries, and his speech was the concluding address of the Assembly. The same deference is shown the Primate at every gathering of Anglicans at which he presides.

Protestant Episcopal Church. The largest juridical unit, therefore, is always the national church, e.g., in England, the Church of England, in Scotland, the Scottish Episcopal Church, and in the States, the Protestant Episcopal Church. The latter comprises not only the churches in the continental United States, but also three other divisions, missionary in character, operating in eleven other areas, including Hawaii, Alaska, Liberia, Mexico, and Brazil.

As a national church, the denomination is governed by two executive-legislative bodies, one permanent, called the National Council, and another which meets every three years, called the General Convention. The National Council has thirty-one members, representing the denomination both nationally and as a composite of dioceses; among the members are bishops, priests, laymen, and laywomen. Heading the National Council is the Presiding Bishop. According to canon law, this central executive body "shall have charge of the unification, development and prosecution of the missionary, educational, and social work of the Church."[37] The changing status of the Presiding Bishop during the past century and a half is typical of the Church's adaptability to variable circumstances. Until 1919, he was always the senior member of the hierarchy, but this proved highly inefficient because of the man's age and often his ineptitude for the office; then a diocesan bishop was elected, who retained all the duties of his own see while managing the National Council—but this too was unworkable; finally in 1934 the Constitution was changed, providing for the election of a Presiding Bishop, to hold office until his sixty-eighth year, who is automatically relieved of diocesan responsibilities when he assumes the presidency.

Triennially the General Convention meets, usually in September, as the legislative arm of the Protestant Episcopal Church. Like the American Congress, the General Convention is bicameral, made up of a House of Bishops, composed of all the bishops of the Church, both active and retired, and a House of Deputies, consisting of eight delegates—equally clerical and lay—from each diocese. Meetings of the two Houses are held separately; and all acts of the Convention must pass both Houses. Perhaps the greatest difficulty in running the Convention arises from the large number of delegates, over one hundred bishops and upward of seven hundred deputies. Plans are being made for reducing the required number of delegates, while still preserving adequate representation.

Provinces. Immediately below the national Church are the Provinces, composed of a number of dioceses, presently eight in number for the entire Protestant Episcopal Church. Territorially the largest are the western Provinces; the smallest are in the East, where the Church's concentration is greatest. Organized after the pattern of the national body, the Provinces have their own representative governing organ, called the Provincial Synod, divided into a House of Bishops and a House of Clerical and Lay Deputies. However, the legislative power of the Synods is very restricted. They are "little more than official conferences by which the work of the Church in any given area may be increased in effectiveness and co-ordination."[38]

Dioceses. The fundamental ecclesiastical unit is the diocese, governed by the bishop in conjunction with the Diocesan Convention. Depending on its size, a diocese is named either after the principal city or the state. On the East Coast, the State of New York has six dioceses; in the Midwest, Iowa and Minnesota are separate diocesan territories. Although supreme in his diocese in many ways, the bishop is helped— and controlled—in the administration by a Diocesan Convention, sometimes called the Council, Synod, or Convocation, which consists of all the clergy and a number of lay representatives from each parish and mission. On certain major issues, the Convention must divide and vote as two Houses, clerical and lay, as on the national and provincial level. One of its chief functions is to adopt an annual budget, besides promoting the mission work of the diocese and its co-operation with the national Church. It also has the right to elect a bishop in case of vacancy, choose delegates to the General Convention and Provincial Synods, give financial aid to churches and missions, amend the diocesan Constitution, pass or repeal local canons, and receive the annual report of the bishop and intradiocesan organizations.

A large part of the national Church, especially in the West, is still too sparsely populated to be divided into dioceses. Missionary districts are temporarily set up, along state territorial lines, e.g., Nevada, Utah, and Arizona, which function analogously to a fully erected diocese, but with missionary bishops, and less rigidly, according to the amount and complexity of the work in the district.

Local Parish. At the lowest grade in the Church are the local parishes, which are not geographically distinct but draw their membership from all those who regularly attend the parish church (or mission) and contribute to its support. As a legal corporation, often called, "The Rector, Wardens and Vestrymen of —— Church," the parish is canonically united to the diocese and headed by the rector, who must be an ordained priest. Temporal administration is in the hands of vestrymen, men or women, from whose number are chosen wardens, who are vice-presidents of the vestry and *ex officio* delegates to the Diocesan Convention. Where a parish is still missionary, the bishop appoints the minister; but independent parishes have the right to call their own rector. According to canon law, a vestry may not elect a new rector until the bishop has been notified of the proposed candidate in sufficient time to discuss the matter with the vestry. Normally the bishop recommends certain candidates, on whom the vestry then votes and resubmits the name chosen for episcopal approval. Once appointed, a rector cannot resign without the consent of the vestry, "nor may he be removed except the bishop give his godly judgment thereto after a long canonical process."[39] A regular feature in the classified section of Episcopalian church magazines is the request for a priest to take charge of some parish or mission, giving the advantages of the position offered, or a priest advertising his services for parochial work and describing his special qualifications.

RELIGIOUS ORDERS

After three centuries of suppression in the Established Church, religious life was finally restored, "against tremendous obstacles, active opposition, not infrequently breaking out in persecution (and) general apathy."[40] In 1930, the Lambeth Conference expressed its appreciation of the work of those "who have given their lives in complete sacrifice as a supreme act of worship of God and for His immediate service."[41] Episcopalian canon law governing the ministry now recognizes the vocation of men and women who dedicate themselves by vow to the religious life, and provides for the regulation of their communities. Since 1842, when the Nashotah Community was first organized in Wisconsin, fifty-three different religious congregations have been established in the United States, twenty of men and thirty-three of women. Twenty-three of these (seventeen of women and six of men) have since become extinct, and four (three of men and one of women) have been received into the Catholic Church, among them the well-known Society of the Atonement (men and women) at Garrison, New York, which became Catholic in 1899. At present, there are twenty-six religious orders or congregations (eleven of men and fifteen of women) in the United States belonging to the Protestant Episcopal Church.[42]

Perhaps the best known among the communities for men is the Society of St. John the Evangelist, or, more popularly, the Cowley Fathers, founded in 1865 at Cowley-St. John, a suburb of Oxford, England. Associated with the founder, the Rev. Richard Benson, were an Englishman, Simeon O'Neill, and an American, Charles Grafton, later Bishop of Fond du Lac, Wisconsin. After living together for a year to test their vocation, these three men, in one another's presence, pronounced the vows of poverty, chastity, and obedience, on the Feast of St. John the Evangelist, 1866. This was the first successful effort in the Church of England to re-establish religious life for men. The rule of the society is described as modern, but based on a careful study of the rules of ancient and modern orders, with special affinity to those of the Society of Jesus and the Congregation of the Mission (Lazarists). There is a novitiate of at least two years, and no life profession under the age of thirty. Personal sanctification is fostered by sacramental confession, daily recitation of the Divine Office in choir, and daily meditation, an hour for priests and a half hour for lay brothers. Work in the apostolate includes parish ministry, retreats, missions, directing hostels, hearing confessions, spiritual direction of religious women, and the foreign missions. Cowley Fathers have been in the States since 1870; in 1914 they organized a separate American Province, and since 1921 have been an autonomous congregation.

The Order of St. Augustine is a purely contemplative society of ordained clerics and lay brothers, who follow the "Holy Rule written in A.D. 423." Their daily order is divided between prayer, study, and manual labor. Community Mass and the eight breviary Officers are the center of devotional life. Referred to as "monks," all the members assist with the manual labor, in the monastery and on the farm, besides taking care of a guest house for retreatants. After six months of postulancy and two years of novitiate, perpetual vows may be taken. Their one foundation in this country is at Orange City, Florida.

Among women religious communities, the Community of St. Mary was the first Anglican sisterhood established in

America. Founded in 1865 by Harriet Starr Cannon with only five sisters, the Society now has two American Provinces and a mission school in the Philippines. The Constitutions are based on the Rule of St. Benedict, with the twofold object of "advancing the glory of God and performing the spiritual and corporal works of mercy." Mass is offered each morning, and the Divine Office, "to which nothing is preferred," is recited daily from the *Monastic Diurnal,* an English translation of the Benedictine Office. Six months of postulancy and two years of novitiate are followed by perpetual vows. Heading the Community is the Mother Superior General, residing in New York City, who has the power of visitation and presides at meetings of the General Chapter, which is the basic source of authority in the organization. In 1935 the Community bought Racine College, Wisconsin, and renamed it the De Koven Foundation for Church Work. As a center for retreats and conferences, it has become a "stronghold of the Catholic movement in the Episcopal Church."[43]

Comparable to the Augustinian monks, the Poor Clares of Reparation and Adoration are a contemplative order, dedicated to prayer and penance, under the spiritual direction of the Order of St. Francis. Founded in 1922, they represent the Second Order of the American Congregation of the Franciscans, and follow "the primitive Rule of St. Clare," adapted to modern conditions. In the spirit of Franciscan poverty, they have no fixed source of revenue but are supported entirely by alms. Several hours a day are spent in the chapel, assisting at daily Mass, reciting the Divine Office, making meditation, "offering the community intercessions," and watching before the sacrament reserved and exposed on the altar. Regarded as austere, the Rule of St. Clare is not considered "beyond the strength of normal human beings." Among the requirements for admission are: age limit between eighteen and forty, freedom from obligation of debt or marriage, good health of mind and body, emotional stability, and a love of prayer sufficient to enable the candidate to live a cloistered life. A six months' postulancy is followed by at least a year's novitiate, three years under annual vows, and then perpetual profession. One of their forms of apostolate is the Fellowship of Prayer, by which they pledge themselves to pray daily, by name, for all who are duly enrolled. The Motherhouse is at Mt. Sinai, Long Island.

The *Constitution and Canons* for the government of the Protestant Episcopal Church in the United States has elaborate provisions for the direction of religious communities. These regulations reflect the growing interest in a life of perfection among American Episcopalians. While authentically Anglican, the canonical directives are also broadly Catholic, at least in their spirit and sometimes in verbal expression. There are nine sections to the canon dealing with religious communities. Every significant feature of community life is provided for.

1. A religious community of men or women desiring the official recognition of the Church shall submit for his approval its Rule and Constitution to the Bishop of the Diocese wherein the Motherhouse of the community is situated; and no change in the Rule or Constitution shall be made without his approval.

2. In such Constitution there shall be a distinct recognition of the Doctrine, Discipline, and Worship of this Church as of supreme authority.

3. No religious community shall establish itself in another Diocese without permission of the Bishop of that Diocese.

4. The community may elect a Chaplain, but if he be a Priest who is not canonically resident in the Diocese, he must be licensed by the Bishop. Any Priest ministering in a Chapel of a religious community shall be responsible to the Bishop of the Diocese for his ministrations, in the same manner as a parochial Clergyman.

5. In the Administration of the Sacraments the Book of Common Prayer shall be used without alteration, save as it may be lawfully permitted by lawful authority.

6. It shall be provided in the Constitution of a religious community that real estate and endowments belonging to the community shall be held in trust for the community as a body in communion with this Church.

7. Members of a religious community who are in Holy

Orders shall be subject to all canonical regulations concerning the Clergy.

8. Provision shall be made in the Constitution for the appointment of a Visitor, with the approval of the Bishop of the Diocese in which the Motherhouse is situated, if the Bishop is himself unwilling to serve in such capacity. It shall be the duty of the Visitor to see that the Constitution and Rule, as approved, are duly observed, and to receive and hear appeals either from the community or from individual members thereof as to transgressions of the Rule. No full member of a community shall be dismissed therefrom without appeal to the Visitor, nor shall any be released from his or her obligations thereto without the Visitor's sanction.

9. It shall not be within the power of a succeeding Bishop to withdraw the official recognition that has been given to a Religious Community; *Provided,* that the conditions laid down in this Canon are observed.[44]

APPROACHES TO CHURCH UNITY

Church unity efforts in the Protestant Episcopal Church on a major scale began in 1867, when nineteen American bishops joined in the first Lambeth (London) Conference to strengthen the solidarity of Anglican bodies throughout the world. Twenty years later in 1888, the American delegation successfully promoted the adoption of what has since become the doctrinal cohesive of world Anglicanism. Originally conceived by William Huntington, of Worcester, Massachusetts, the Lambeth Quadrilateral reduced to four statements the basic principles to which the Anglican Church subscribes, namely:

I. The Holy Scriptures of the Old and New Testaments, as "containing all things necessary to salvation," and as being the rule and ultimate standard of faith.

II. The Apostles' Creed, as the Baptismal Symbol; and the Nicene Creed, as the sufficient statement of the Christian faith.

III. The two sacraments, Baptism and the Supper of the Lord, ministered with unfailing use of Christ's words of institution, and of the elements ordained by Him.

IV. The Historic Episcopate, locally adapted in the methods of its administration to the varying needs of the nations and peoples called of God into the unity of His Church.[45]

Since 1888, the Lambeth Quadrilateral has been reinterpreted, but never revised. It still expresses the official position of the Church in relation to projects for union with Protestant bodies.

Before the end of the century, invitations for union on the basis of the Quadrilateral were sent to eighteen Protestant denominations. But only one, with the Presbyterians, reached anything like a negotiable stage, though even this was finally called off by the Episcopalians. Union efforts broke down over the crucial question of orders. Advocates of the Episcopalian-Presbyterian merger suggested holding formal services of "extension of authority to minister in the united Church," at which time clergy of each denomination were to be told: "The Ministry of the Word and Sacraments which thou hast already received is hereby recognized; and the grace and authority of Holy Orders as conferred by this Church is now added."[46] In 1946 the "Catholic" minority in the Protestant Episcopal Church successfully vetoed the Proposed Basis of Union, mainly on the grounds that the recommended formula for extension of orders was in no sense a supplementary ordination, and that, consequently, if adopted, "the united Church would have no priesthood in the Catholic and Prayer Book sense of the term."[47]

Equally unsuccessful were attempts at union with the Eastern Orthodox churches. "The chief obstacle on the other side was that the Orthodox Church was not prepared to affirm the validity of Anglican orders. The chief obstacle on this side was the watchful suspicion of the Evangelicals, who regarded these Eastern Churches as little better than the Church of Rome."[48]

However, a close degree of union was established with the Polish National Church, founded in 1900 and directed for fifty years by Francis Hodur, schismatic Catholic priest who was consecrated bishop at Utrecht by the Old Catholic Church. In October 1946, the House of Bishops of the Episcopal Church accepted the overtures of the Polish Nationals and received them into full intercommunion on the basis of the so-called Bonn agreement, which stated:

I. Each Communion agrees to admit members of the other Communion to participation in the Sacraments.

II. Each Communion recognizes the catholicity and independence of the other, and maintains its own.

III. Intercommunion does not require from either Communion the acceptance of all doctrinal opinion, sacramental devotion, or liturgical practice characteristic of the other, but implies that each believes the other to hold the essentials of the Christian Faith.[49]

On a global scale, the World Council of Churches directly owes its existence to the reunion efforts of the American Episcopalians. In 1910 Bishop Brent, Philippine missionary and later Bishop of New York, asked the House of Bishops of the Protestant Episcopal Church to appoint a committee inviting "all Churches which accept Jesus Christ as God and Saviour to join in conferences following the general method of the World's Missionary Conference, for the consideration of all questions pertaining to the Faith and Order of the Church of Christ."[50] Out of this grew the World Conference on Faith and Order, which in 1948 developed into the World Council of Churches.

The most significant development in ecumenism among Episcopalians of the United States is the Consultation on Church Union (C.O.C.U.), into which they entered in 1966. Jointly originated by Bishop James Pike of the Episcopal Diocese of California and Carlson Blake, former Stated Clerk of the Presbyterian Church U.S.A., the *Principles of Church Union* adopted by the Consultation have deeply affected the Protestant Episcopal Church. Those who favor the merger with other Protestant bodies like the Methodists and Presbyterians welcome the merger as a godsend. They are generally in the Low Church tradition and are little concerned over the implicit removal of the historic episcopate which for centuries has been one of the four pillars of Anglicanism. Anglican theologians like John Macquarrie, Reginald Fuller, and John Knox, on the other hand, look with misgiving at what they consider the dissolution of their religious heritage. It remains to be seen how the Protestant Episcopal Church in the United States will finally decide between the two directions that are open to it; either toward Rome where its Catholic ancestry seems to be leading, or toward Protestantism where its Reformation theology is often inclined.

Lutherans

Where other Protestant churches are satisfied to describe their religious similarities and differences without analysis, Lutheran writers are concerned with telling their people and others what they consider the essence of Lutheranism. A recent symposium allowed Lutheran theologians of varying degrees of orthodoxy to express their opinion on "What is Lutheranism's *raison d'être* as a distinct communion in the twentieth century?" While there was no agreement on the answer, there was revealed a basic divergency of attitude. On one side are conservatives, who distinguish Lutheranism as essentially an adherence to the principles enunciated in a half dozen "symbolic documents," beginning with the Confession of Augsburg (1530) and ending with the Formula of Concord (1577). Without this adherence, it would be quite impossible correctly to acknowledge God or call upon Him to preserve harmony in the Church and "to bridle the audacity of such as invent new doctrines."

At the other extreme are unionists, who are looking for a fusion of Lutheran and other denominations, and liberals, who do not hesitate to dismiss the Lutheran Confessions as dated, outmoded, and no more binding than any other statement of religious sentiment. Arguing against rigid conservatists, they insist that "symbolism" is no part of the original Lutheran faith. They point out that the full symbolic system was not adopted until 1580, after the Lutheran Church had existed more than half a century. Moreover, it is contended, the Formula of Concord itself states that the Scriptures alone are the norm by which "all doctrines are to be examined." Since the official declaration of historic Lutheranism plainly declares that with new light and more adequate interpretation of the biblical writings, changes in doctrine are not only anticipated but necessary, there is scarcely need, say the modernists, to explain that the Lutheran Confessions contain many views no longer tenable. They would, for instance, hesitate to call the Pope the Antichrist. They might well question the Christological doctrine on the ubiquity of Christ's body. Even the position which Luther took on the interpretation of the Eucharist may fairly be challenged.

Between these extremes is a variety of opinions that are hard to classify, while retaining enough historical continuity to permit a descriptive analysis of present-day American Lutheranism.

HISTORY

Lutheranism dates from October 31, 1517, when Martin Luther affixed his ninety-five theses to the church door of the castle of Wittenberg. Three years later, June 15, 1520, he was formally excommunicated by Pope Leo X, who also condemned forty-one propositions from Luther's writings, notably the denial of free will and the Roman primacy; and the claim that no matter how ostensibly good, every human act is a sin.

The religious crisis which Luther and his followers provoked in Germany occasioned a series of conferences or diets which became landmarks in the history of the Reformation. Summoned by Charles V to the Diet of Worms (1521), Luther refused to retract and was condemned as an outlaw, but the Elector of Saxony took him into protective custody. Eight years later, at the Diet of Speyer (1529), five Lutheran princes rejected the compromise of King Frederick that would allow their estates to practice the new religion while demanding the same rights for Catholics. Their statement of protestation has become historic since it gave the name Protestant to the whole opposition movement to the Catholic Church. When the Diet of Speyer proved inoperative, the Emperor summoned the Diet of Augsburg (1530) to effect a reconciliation between the Catholics and Reformers. A profession of the Protestant faith was drafted with Luther's assistance and approval and submitted to the Diet. After the Confession of Augsburg was challenged by the Catholic delegation, Melanchthon was commissioned to write an "Apology for the Confession of Augsburg." Both documents are now doctrinal standards in the Lutheran Church.

A year after Augsburg, the Lutherans organized an offensive and defensive alliance, the Schmalkaldic League, for which Luther wrote a set of Articles in 1537, thus marking the final establishment of the Lutheran *Landeskirche* as a distinct outward body completely separated from the Roman Church. Before his death in 1546, besides voluminous other writings now mostly of historical interest, Luther published (1529) two catechisms, a larger and a smaller, originally intended "for the improperly indoctrinated Roman clergy who had joined the evangelicals and to the teachers of the parochial schools," which have since become recognized as "probably the most useful and the most unique of his original publications."[1]

Already during Luther's lifetime, conflicts over doctrine arose among the leaders of the Reformation. With characteristic passion, Luther stigmatized his rival, Zwingli, as a pagan, Oecolampadius as having a corrupt heart and lying mouth, and Calvin and his followers as possessed of "in-devilled, over-devilled and through-devilled hearts."[2] After the reformer's death, the area of conflict was widened where different groups favored Calvinism or Zwinglianism in opposition to the orthodox Lutheranism of their founder. Questions of sin and grace, justification by faith, the use of good works, the person and work of Christ, and especially the Lord's Supper were the ground of violent dissension. A partial solution was effected, at least among Lutheran churches, by the Formula of Concord, the last of the Lutheran symbols, which was drawn up in 1577.

By the middle of the seventeenth century Lutheranism had been propagated not only in Germany and Central Europe but in Denmark, where the Lutheran Church was organized (1536) with the king as supreme bishop; in Sweden, where the Reformation was formally established in 1529; in East Prussia in 1525; in Iceland by 1550; and temporarily or among scattered regions in Poland (1573), Transylvania (1545), Hungary (1606), and Silesia (1524).

Although a Lutheran Christmas service was held at Hudson Bay as early as 1619, the first European Lutherans to make a permanent settlement in America came from Holland to the Dutch New Netherlands (Manhattan Island) in 1623. Under

Governor Stuyvesant they had to conform to the Reformed (Calvinist) ritual, but freedom of worship came when New Amsterdam (New York) was captured by the English in 1664. A second distinct body of Lutherans came from Sweden in 1637. Two years later they had a minister and organized the first independent Lutheran congregation in the New World at Fort Christina (Wilmington, Delaware). After 1771, the Swedes of Delaware and Pennsylvania dissolved their union with the Mother Church in Sweden and, not having English-speaking pastors of their own, chose ministers from the Episcopalian Church. Since 1846 these congregations have entered into full communion with the Episcopalians. The first colony of German Lutherans came from the Palatinate, arriving in 1693 and settling in Germantown, now a part of Philadelphia. Before the mid-1800s about thirty thousand German Lutherans found a permanent residence in eastern Pennsylvania, besides scattered groups along the Atlantic Coast, in New Jersey, Virginia, Georgia, and South Carolina.

The first systematic organization of Lutheran churches in the colonies was undertaken in 1742 by Henry Mühlenberg (1711–87), a Hanoverian, who is regarded as the patriarch of American Lutheranism. The basis of unity was the synod, territorial in extension and compassing all the churches in a given area. Thus in 1748 Mühlenberg founded the Synod of Pennsylvania, and in 1773 his son, Frederick, organized the Ministerium of New York, the second synod in America. The elder Mühlenberg was a pietist, his successors were tainted rationalists—with the result that indifferentism and schism crept into the churches. In 1792 the Pennsylvania Synod eliminated all confessional tests in its constitution, and the New York Ministerium substituted more liberal books for the older Lutheran catechisms and hymnals. Transition from German to English and sympathy in the German party for the German-speaking Reformed Churches caused divisions in many congregations. Added to these disrupting elements were the growing immigration from Europe and the westward movement, so that in 1820 a General Synod for all the Lutherans in America was formed at Hagerstown, Pennsylvania, to prevent a complete disintegration. Yet even at the beginning, some district ministeria remained aloof, and as time went on rival synods developed. In spite of opposition from confessional Lutherans, the General Synod rapidly absorbed new state organizations as they arose, until by 1860 it had 26 member synods, 864 ministers, and a reported 164,000 communicants. As a federation comprising more than half the Lutherans in America, the General Synod was directed by men who were "avowed enemies of the Lutheran Confessions. They denounced the Lutheran doctrines of baptism, the Lord's Supper, absolution, and the personal union of the two natures of Christ. They loved the doctrines of the Reformed Church, championed the revival, and advocated a union with the sects."[3]

At the time of the Civil War, when hopes ran high that the General Synod would form a solid national body, a schism occurred that was not healed for half a century. The slavery question and doctrinal differences occasioned the break. In 1863 five Southern synods withdrew to form the General Synod of the Confederate States, reorganized in 1886 as the United Synod of the South. Three years later, the Pennsylvania Synod, "contending for theological conservatism," sent out invitations to all American and Canadian synods to join in forming a new body. In answer to the invitation, thirteen synods consolidated into the General Council. Separated for fifty years, these three units were reunited in 1918 to form the United Lutheran Church in America, which, before it merged (1963) to become the Lutheran Church in America, was the largest Lutheran body in the United States.

Meantime the conservatives were busy organizing their own synods, on the triple basis of doctrinal fidelity to the Lutheran symbols, territorial limitation, and usually a common European background. In 1847 a group of Saxon immigrants, led by Carl Walther, organized the Missouri Synod. They had come to America because of their religious convictions, to escape the Prussian government's imposition of union of the Lutheran and Reformed churches. A like group of German immigrants founded the Wisconsin Synod in 1850; from a mild and conciliatory attitude, the Lutheranism of this synod developed into one of uncompromising fidelity to the Lutheran Confessions.

In 1869 the Missouri and Wisconsin Synods, while remaining autonomous, "joined fellowship" in a co-operative society, which has since aggregated three other groups (Norwegian, Slovak, and Negro) to form the Lutheran Synodical Conference of North America.

In June 1955, the Evangelical Lutheran Church (Norwegian) suspended fellowship with the Missouri Synod on the basis of Romans 16:17–18, as stated in a resolution of the ELC. Six years later (August 1961), the Wisconsin Evangelical Lutheran Synod adopted a similar resolution. The differences centered around the question of church fellowship and joint worship. In 1962 the two synods recommended the dissolution of the Lutheran Synodical Conference, and the following year both formally withdrew. At present the Synodical Conference includes only the Missouri Synod and the Synod of Evangelical Lutheran Churches, which consists mainly of first- and second-generation emigrants from Slovakia.

However, in 1964 the National Evangelical Lutheran Church was officially and organically merged with the Missouri Synod. Originally called the Finnish Evangelical Lutheran National Church of America, the NELC shared the Missouri Synod's acceptance of all the Lutheran Confessions as correct interpretations of the Bible.

Missouri Lutherans operate parochial schools throughout the country and direct the largest religious publishing house in the world, located at their national center in St. Louis.

According to its constitution, the Missouri Synod is primarily concerned with preserving and continuing the Christian faith, as interpreted in the historic Lutheran Confessions. It also resists every form of schism and secularism. To ensure orthodoxy, the clergy are carefully educated in seminaries—notably Concordia in St. Louis, Missouri—and a regular supervision over their ministry is maintained by directors appointed by the Synod. A system of parochial schools was established that is "confessedly Christian and Lutheran," and a religious press prepares and distributes a wide range of literature, from Sunday school manuals to a critical edition of the works of Martin Luther.

In their official statement of doctrine, members of the Synod insist upon the literal meaning of Scripture and will admit no compromise. They reject as "horrible and blasphemous" the theory that parts of the Bible are purely human and, therefore, may contain error. They hold that all churchmen who deny the Trinity are "outside the pale of the Christian Church," and therefore they warn against Unitarianism, which in America has "to a great extent" penetrated the denominations.

Missouri Synod Lutherans believe that men, because of the Fall, are dead in their sins, inclined to all evil and "unable through any efforts of their own" to rise above their sinful nature. Reacting against the Catholic position on grace and free will, they call "apostate from the Christian religion all doctrines whereby man's works and merits are mingled into the article on justification before God." To counteract "the notion that the Christian Church in the proper sense is an external institution," they insist that men become members of the church "by faith in the Gospel alone." The church, they hold, is "the invisible communion of all believers." It is not, as Catholics hold, a visible organism with external marks of unity, holiness, universality, and apostolic origin founded on the primacy of St. Peter.

The Synod also repudiates any claim, whether Catholic or Protestant, that power is vested "in the pope, or the bishops, or the order of the ministers, or the secular lords, or councils, or synods." According to this teaching, the people, and only they, have authority in religious matters; church officials, presbyteries, and conventions are delegates of the people and act on the people's behalf.

In view of its uncompromising attitude, it is not surprising that until recently the Missouri Synod has collaborated only slightly with other Lutheran bodies in the United States. Pressure from within the ranks by "unionist" churchmen, however, has led to some attempts toward union with other groups.

In 1967, the Missouri Synod entered into ecumenical relationship with the two other major Lutheran bodies in the United States, the American Lutheran Church and the Lutheran Church in America. A new organization, the Lutheran Council in the United States, was created. It replaced the National Lutheran Council, which was restructured in order to accommodate the Missouri Synod. Membership in the Lutheran Council in the United States does not deprive the participating bodies of their denominational autonomy.

A recent addition to the family of Lutheran denominations, the American Lutheran Church was born in 1960 as a result of the merger of three separate churches: the American Lutheran, whose name was perpetuated in the new church, Evangelical Lutheran, and United Evangelical Lutheran, each with a history of previous mergers.

As the largest member of the new body, the Evangelical Lutheran Church was a haven for 90 per cent of the Norwegian-descended Lutherans in America. It had been organized in 1917 under the name Norwegian Lutheran Church as an organic union of three independent groups: the United Norwegian Church, the Norwegian and the Hauge Synods. In 1946 the adjective "Norwegian" was changed to "Evangelical." Outside of the Synodical Conference (comprising the Missouri and Wisconsin Synods), it was one of the most conservative Lutheran bodies in the States.

Remarkably close-knit, the Evangelical Lutheran Church maintained a chain of small colleges stretching from Minnesota to Texas, foreign missionaries in Asia, Africa, and Latin America, and—because most of its membership was rural—promoted the largest home-mission program of any comparable denomination in the country. A multi-million-dollar project fund would finance every new congregational unit.

Almost equal in membership was the American Lutheran Church, which came into existence in 1930 through the merger of the German synods of Ohio, Iowa, and Buffalo. Though very conservative in doctrine, to the extent of working out a creedal agreement with the strict standards of the Lutheran Missouri Synod, the original American Lutherans have been more ecumenical-minded than other Lutheran bodies. Their merger efforts, however, have been based on the principle that unity in doctrine and worship is the only condition for church fellowship following the rule of "Lutheran pulpits for Lutheran pastors only, and Lutheran altars for Lutheran communicants only."

The smallest partner in the new denomination, the United Evangelical Lutheran Church, also resulted from a previous merger (1896), this between two Danish synods with strong devotional and revivalist traditions. In 1946 the word "Danish" was dropped from the official title, but doctrine and worship are still patterned, often word for word, on the parent church in Denmark. The largest membership is in Nebraska.

The formation of the new American Lutheran Church set a landmark in a little-known phase of the ecumenical movement. It united three nationally distinct bodies: German, Norwegian, and Danish; two of the partners were among the largest churches in the country, each with more than a million adherents; the basis of union was not merely social or dictated by external interests, but doctrinal and motivated by a common concern in theological issues.

All three parties to the merger, especially the Evangelical Lutheran Church, have been uncompromising in their confessional orthodoxy and unsympathetic with the ecumenical movement as it is commonly understood. Evangelical Lutherans would even refuse to pray with Lutherans belonging to other church bodies when meeting in conferences held for the purpose of developing better understanding among them. They believed "it is a Christian duty to separate oneself from those who teach contrary to the clear word of God." Unity among the churches, they maintained, becomes apostasy if based on anything less than the Bible. Symbolic of the same dogmatic firmness was the election of the former head of the Evangelical Lutherans as first president of the new denomination.

Smaller conservative bodies are being attracted by the church's professed fidelity to Reformation principles. Not more than a year after the American Lutheran Church was organized, the Lutheran Free Church (of Danish-Norwegian stock) asked to be affiliated and was received in 1963.

Although a latecomer to the merger, the Lutheran Free Church made a substantial contribution to its polity. Organized in 1897 as the result of differences in the United Norwegian Church over Augsburg Seminary, the Lutheran Free Church stressed the autonomy of the local congregations. Moreover, it favored ecumenical relations among Lutherans and with other Protestant bodies, preferring (according to its leaders) unity in diversity to unity in conformity. In the same spirit, the Free Church did not encourage elaborate liturgical services. Traditionally it emphasized more simple forms of public worship and permitted informal meetings of prayer, praise, and testimonies.

Headquarters of the American Lutheran Church are located in Minneapolis, Minnesota.

Organized in 1962, the Lutheran Church in America is a consolidation of four Lutheran denominations whose origins go back to the middle of the nineteenth century. It began to function as a new juridical institution on January 1, 1963, and represents one of the principal Protestant mergers in the present generation.

The four merging churches were the American Evangelical Lutheran Church, the Augustana Evangelical Lutheran Church, the Finnish Evangelical Lutheran Church, and the United Lutheran Church in America. Each group has an interesting history and each has had a profound influence on American Protestantism.

The American Evangelical Lutheran Church was founded in 1871 by missionaries from Denmark under the name of *Kirkelig Missionsforening* ("Church Mission Association"). Augustana Evangelical Lutherans became an organic body in 1860. Their constituency was mainly of Swedish extraction, along with sympathetic Danes and Norwegians who protested against the new liberalism among the immigrants from Europe. Finnish Lutherans became a separate denomination in 1890 and, until recently, were called the Suomi Synod. United Lutherans date back to the Ministerium of Pennsylvania, organized in 1748, and beyond that to early colonial days. They represent the union, in 1918, of the General Synod, the General Council, and the United Synod of the South. At the time of their latest merger, their membership was about two million, compared to a total of less than one million for the other three bodies.

It was relatively easy for the Lutheran Church in America to formulate a common confession of faith, since the merging churches were in the conservative evangelical tradition. A typical statement of doctrine reflects the tenor of its strong dogmatic foundation: "This church accepts the Apostles', the Nicene, and the Athanasian creeds as true declarations of faith of the church. This church accepts the unaltered Augsburg Confession and Luther's Small Catechism as true witnesses to the Gospel, and acknowledges as one with it in faith and doctrine all churches that likewise accept the teachings of these symbols." Significantly, the statement professes belief in the Scriptures as the norm of faith and life in the church, but without excluding tradition as a possible complement.

The Lutheran Church in America carefully avoids two extremes: the centralization of authority in the Roman Catholic Church and the congregationalism of Protestant denominations in the Free Church tradition. It has a central organization, but its authority comes from the congregations and is shared with them. The only unchangeable rule pertains to matters of doctrine.

Membership of the church consists of congregations and pastors. Congregations which enjoy the benefits of membership are expected to shoulder their fair share of the responsibilities, both in carrying out the adopted programs and in contributing to the work which is done in their name. Pastors qualify for membership by ordination. They remain members as long as they are doing the work of the ministry under call by a congregation or church agency or are retired after honorable service.

True to the Lutheran emphasis on education, the new merged church has already undertaken an educational program that will affect every level of religious instruction. More than thirty colleges and universities are affiliated with the Lutheran Church in America, besides numerous day schools for children in the primary and secondary grades. Unlike other conservative American Lutherans, church leaders in the Lutheran Church in America are sympathetic to the National Council of Churches and are active in the world ecumenical movement.

Although the Lutherans in the United States have succeeded in reducing their denominational separability from more than eighty different bodies in the mid-nineteenth century to less than ten, there are still a number of small groups that have not been merged.

The Evangelical Lutheran Church in America (Eielsen Synod) is a minuscule society brought to America from Norway in 1846. It takes its name from Elling Eielsen, who founded the group among the Norwegian immigrants. A schism in 1875 caused most of the members to organize under the name of Hauge's Norwegian Evangelical Lutheran Synod. The remnant kept the old name and elected Eielsen president. Eielsen Lutherans require proof of conversion as a condition for church membership.

The Apostolic Lutheran Church of America is a Finnish body founded in 1872 as the Solomon Korteniemi Lutheran Society. But in 1929 it was incorporated as the Finnish Apostolic Lutheran Church of America. In 1962 the word "Finnish" was dropped from the name. An unusual feature of the Apostolic Lutherans is their stress on the confessions of sins and absolution. Public sin must be expiated publicly by a confession before the community, and followed by absolution. A scriptural Christian experience is required for voting membership.

The Church of the Lutheran Brethren of America was started in 1900. In line with the Baptist tradition, the Lutheran Brethren require something more than orthodoxy. They demand the evidence of a personal experience of salvation of all their faithful. Consistent with the same Free Church tradition, they discourage liturgical worship.

The Evangelical Lutheran Synod was founded in 1918 by a minority group which declined to join the union of other merging bodies in 1917. There were doctrinal reasons to form the separation, mainly a dispute over the teaching regarding election and grace. In 1963 the ELS withdrew from the Synodical Conference, over doctrinal differences with the Missouri Synod. In 1958 the present name was adopted.

In 1928 a group of Wisconsin Lutherans separated from their synod to form the Protestant Conference (Lutheran). They were dissatisfied with the doctrinal teaching of the Joint Synod of Wisconsin and critical of its alleged spirit of self-righteousness. They sought to re-emphasize the "Gospel of forgiveness of sins through our Blessed Savior."

DOCTRINE

While Lutherans as a class have the reputation for being the most orthodox among Protestant denominations, this needs to be severely qualified. If by orthodoxy is meant fidelity to the principles of the Reformation, then, it is true, a sizable portion of American Lutherans is still orthodox, and on this basis we may find a substantial agreement among the various divisions. But there are wide deviations, not unlike the situation among Baptists in their adherence to Calvinism, or among the Methodists in their fidelity to John Wesley.

Our analysis will cover two aspects: the common doctrinal elements, and the differences in matters of faith. The creedal bases for whatever agreement there is among American Lutherans are the Ecumenical Creeds: Apostles', Nicene, and Athanasian; and the Lutheran Confessions composed during the first fifty years of the Reformation and comprehended in the Book of Concord, namely, the Augsburg Confession and its Apology, the two catechisms of Luther, his Smalcald Articles and the Formula of Concord. The evidence of disagreement is found in the various doctrinal statements made by the Lutheran churches, either officially or as found in their representative theologians.

The Church. Claiming to base its position on the teaching of the Fathers, the Augsburg Confession defines the Church as "the Congregation of saints, in which the Gospel is rightly taught [purely preached] and the Sacraments rightly administered [according to the Gospel]."[4] In the revised edition of 1540, the ambiguous "congregation of saints" was specified, in parentheses, as "the assembly of all believers."[5] This concept of the Church is equivocal, apparently defining it as invisible, since it is composed of all believers, and yet visible, because it exists wherever the gospel is rightly preached and the sacraments are rightly administered. As a result, two antithetical theories have arisen among the Lutherans. Liberals admit the Church's invisible character, but emphasize that "There could never be a Church which is merely invisible . . . Wherever the Word of God is preached and the

sacraments are administered, there is the true Church of
Jesus Christ."[6] Evangelicals teach the opposite, holding that
"The Church is *invisible* because the constitutive factor of
the Church, faith in the heart, is invisible for men and known
only to God." Consequently, "all who declare the Church to
be wholly visible—Romanists—or at least semi-visible—recent
Lutherans—are perverting the nature of the Christian
Church."[7] This interpretation of the "Romanists" and "recent
Lutherans" is countered by both, who hold that the Church
is not only visible but also, and especially, a spiritual entity
—the Mystical Body of Christ—animated by the invisible Spirit
of God.

Justification. Again appealing to the Fathers, the Augsburg
Confession teaches that "Men can not be justified [obtain
forgiveness of sins and righteousness] before God by their
own powers, merits or works; but are justified freely [of
grace] for Christ's sake through faith, when they believe that
they are received into favor . . . God imputes this faith for
righteousness before Him [Christ]."[8] Moreover, "ours teach
that . . . by faith alone is apprehended remission of sins and
grace."[9] As explained by confessional Lutherans, salvific faith
is a blind trust in God's mercy, to the exclusion of any good
work on the part of man, so that "faith is said to be the beginning, middle and end of justification . . . Man cannot
prepare himself for God's activity by a deep sorrow, an earnest longing . . . Man is justified solely by faith."[10]

It is a matter of history that Luther altered a famous passage in the Epistle to the Romans when translating the Bible
into German, to make it square with his theory of justification.
He inserted the adverb *allein* in St. Paul's statement that "A
man is justified by faith *alone* (Rom. 3:28)." When a cor-
respondent brought his attention to the interpolation, he told
him, "Your papist is tormented by this word *alone* which I
have added. Tell him Dr. Martin Luther wants it so . . . I
am not the papists' pupil, but their judge."[11] Modern Lutheran commentators defend it on the grounds that it "is demanded by the whole context of the Epistles to the Galatians
and to the Romans"—interpreted in Luther's sense.[12]

Free Will and Total Depravity. More significant in the light
of future developments was the denial of free will to do any

spiritual good, expressed by the Augsburg Confession. Consequent on Adam's sin, "Man's will has no power to work the righteousness of God, or a spiritual righteousness, without the Spirit of God."[13] Man is utterly corrupt, according to Luther; and this opinion is echoed by his literalist disciples, who teach that "Original sin . . . has so totally corrupted human nature that man is incapable of any spiritual good and inclined to all evil." Whatever good he may do is attributable solely to God. The truth of this teaching, it is said, "has been, is now, and will ever be confirmed by every Christian who has made a practical experience of the Law and the Gospel."[14] Liberal-minded Lutherans soften this doctrine. They feel that "Luther's insistence . . . upon man's total depravity is hardly tenable either on Christian, moral, or reasonably considered grounds . . . To propound the *utter* worthlessness of man implies the curious paradox in which salvation is conceived to be effected upon a worthless object . . . We must, therefore, on Christian, moral and reasonable grounds regard such extreme doctrine as *nonessential* in character."[15]

The Sacraments in General. Lutheran symbolical books are not specific on the number of sacraments, which are defined as "rites which have the command of God and to which the promise of grace has been added";[16] or as "signs of the New Testament, i.e., signs of the remission of sins."[17] First, in general, it is said the number of sacraments is unimportant. According to the Apology for the Augsburg Confession, "We do not believe it to be of any consequence if, in teaching, different persons count [the number of sacraments] differently."[18] However, in Luther's large catechism baptism and the Lord's Supper are considered essential, since they were "instituted by Christ," and therefore "without them there cannot be a Christian."[19] Melanchthon's Apology inclines to fix the number at three, popularly so-called, saying that "Baptism, the Lord's Supper, and Absolution, which is the Sacrament of Repentance, are truly Sacraments."[20] In the same way, the term "Sacrament" is conceded to "Holy Ordination," by the Apology and the Smalcald Articles. While denying that priests in the New Law are "called to offer any sacrifice," the Apology admits that "if Order is understood thus, neither will we refuse to call the imposition of hands a Sacrament."[21] With reservation, even matrimony is described as sacramental in the Apology. Older than the New Testament, marriage and its promises "pertain to the life of the body. Wherefore, if anyone wants to call it a Sacrament, he ought still to differentiate it from the preceding ones."[22] The objection to this use, that "calling Holy Matrimony a Sacrament opens the way to calling other vocations which have God's command, e.g., the magistracy, Sacraments,"[23] indicates how vague the term "Sacrament" is in the Lutheran Confessions. Finally confirmation and extreme unction are denied any sacramental quality, being only "rites received from the Fathers which even the Church does not require as necessary to salvation because they do not have God's command."[24] Most Lutherans, however, would allow them to be called sacraments, but "only in an improper sense."[25]

Baptism. There is some disparity between the wording of the symbolic books and the teaching of the Lutheran Churches, even the most orthodox, on the necessity of baptism. The Augsburg Confession, for example, without qualification states that baptism "is necessary to salvation," and condemns "the Anabaptists who allow not the Baptism of children, and affirm that children are saved without Baptism."[26] But the churches found this doctrine too difficult and, in fact, went to Luther himself to mitigate the absolute necessity of the first sacrament. "It may happen," wrote Luther, "that one has faith without having been baptized . . . If a person dies a believer but lacks Baptism, he would not be condemned."[27] To speak of faith without baptism in children would be unintelligible except that Luther held the theory of "infant faith" before the age of reason. Consequently, while modern writers admit that "Baptism is not a matter of choice, but a divine ordinance," they explain that "still one may not assert an absolute necessity of Baptism."[28] The "Papist" doctrine on Limbo for unbaptized children is dismissed as an effort "to soften somewhat the cruel nature of their error," which teaches that "infants dying without Baptism are deprived of the beatific vision of God, but subject to no torment."[29]

In the administration of the sacrament, although "the Matthew 28:19 [Trinitarian] formula of Baptism is" said to be "the most fitting, the simplest and the safest," still even otherwise strict Lutherans "acknowledge as valid a Baptism performed 'in the name of Jesus Christ,' if the baptizers are known as Trinitarians and confess their faith in the Holy Trinity."[30]

The Lord's Supper. In his small catechism, Luther asks: "You believe, then, that the true body and blood of Christ are in the Sacrament?" and answers, "Yes, I believe it."[31] Also, according to the Augsburg Confession, "The true body and blood of Christ are truly present in the Supper under the form of the bread and wine and are there distributed and received";[32] and still more clearly in the Apology, which says that "The body and blood of Christ are truly and substantially present in the Supper."[33]

What is the nature of the "Real Presence" in the Lord's Supper? The symbolic books define it mostly in negative terms. First against the Catholic doctrine, they reject "papistic transubstantiation, when it is taught that in the Holy Supper the bread and wine lose their substance and natural essence . . . that they are changed into the body of Christ and the outward form alone remains."[34] Then against the Calvinist position, "We unanimously reject and condemn . . . the doctrine that the bread and wine are only figures, similitudes and representations of the far absent body and blood of Christ."[35] More positively, however, "the expressions 'under the bread,' 'with the bread,' 'in the bread,' are used . . . to indicate the sacramental union of the intransubstantiated essence of the bread and of the body of Christ."[36] Again, "we do not hold that the body and blood of Christ are confined in the bread *localiter, i.e.,* locally, or are otherwise permanently united therewith apart from the use of the Sacrament." Therefore, "apart from use," when the Supper ritual is actually taking place, "we do not hold that the body of Christ is present."[37]

American Lutherans understand the "Real Presence" in different ways, depending on their adherence to the basic Confessions. At the orthodox level is the Missouri Synod, which teaches that "as far as the 'what' of the Real Presence is concerned, we occupy the same ground as the Roman—

that is, the Western—the Greek—that is, the Eastern Churches."[38] More liberal positions identify the body of Christ with His person, explaining that "The Greek term 'soma' means person." Consequently, in the Lord's Supper, "we get fellowship with the entire person of Christ," much as in the right preaching of the word, Christians experience fellowship with God.

Sacrament of Penance. Without calling it a sacrament, Lutheran symbolic books speak favorably of "Absolution, or the Power of the Keys," calling it "an aid and consolation against sin and a bad conscience." Furthermore, the "Keys truly remit sins before God, because God quickens through the word."[39] Beyond this, however, the rest is a departure from Catholic doctrine. Luther's catechism denies that penance is a distinct sacrament. "Repentance," he says, "is simply a return and approach to Baptism," although normally requested for Communion, since "it is not usual to give the body of the Lord except to them that have previously been examined and absolved."[40] Lutheran sources also distinguish between absolution and confession: the former is admittedly scriptural, the latter only human. Accordingly, "since private absolution originates in the Office of the Keys, it should not be despised, but greatly and highly esteemed."[41] As regards the confession of one's sins to a minister, though only "instituted by the Church," yet "on account of the great benefit of absolution, which is the chief and pre-eminent part [of confession], for the consolation of straitened consciences, and for a number of other reasons, we retain confession."[42]

Lutheran Churches in America practice confession, depending on how closely they follow the symbolic formulae. While maintaining there is no essential difference between what is known as *Privatbeichte* (private confession) and *Allgemeine Beichte* (general confession), pastors are told that private confession offers a certain advantage.

Lutheran pastoral theology is developing toward a gradual reinstatement of auricular confession.

The congregation should be informed that individual pastoral care in the form of private confession is available to all, and that there is in their midst a fellow-Christian who by virtue of his office is sworn to silence concerning all confidences he receives in the course of confession. Similarly, that he is enabled, by virtue of the office he holds, to pronounce the word of absolution on behalf of his Lord and to help relieve the penitent of his burden. It is necessary, if the church is to fulfill this important task through its ministers, that it should once more stand forth as the tangible presence of Christ ["the body of Christ"]; further, that the ministry should recover its original character as the number of those who represent Christ, and that one of its most significant tasks is to communicate on Christ's behalf [2 Cor. 5:20] the absolution and remission of sins, in accordance with the words of Christ: "If you forgive the sins of any, they are forgiven" [John 20:23].[43]

One formula of absolution reads: "Be it unto thee according to thy faith. And I, by the command of Our Lord Jesus Christ, upon this thy confession, forgive thee all thy sins, in the name of the Father, and of the Son and of the Holy Ghost. Amen."[44]

Marriage and Divorce. While Luther did not go as far as Calvin in secularizing marriage, and spoke of it as "Holy Matrimony," like Calvin he permitted divorce with remarriage. Although the basic Confession of Augsburg is silent on the subject, Lutheran tradition holds there are two legitimate grounds for divorce: infidelity and willful desertion. Manuals of pastoral theology explain that, in the event of infidelity, the pastor should first try to persuade the offended party to condone the injustice. But he must leave the final decision to the option of the innocent party, and if the latter has applied for, and obtained a legal divorce, the pastor, sufficient proof having been submitted, cannot, after the expiration of a proper period, refuse the solemnization of another marriage. The same is true in cases of "malicious desertion." However, a distinction between the two does exist. Desertion is regarded "in itself divorce," whereas infidelity "is not itself divorce, but cause of divorce." Referring the Pauline privilege to all cases of desertion, ministers are instructed that, "after having secured a legal divorce," the deserted party is "no longer bound to the former spouse, and must not be denied remarriage at the proper time." Significantly, pastors have to be cautioned against too great severity, lest they fail in charity by refusing to marry divorced persons.

Universal Priesthood. One of the basic premises of Reformation theology was Luther's denial of a distinct sacerdotal office or power, and the corresponding claim that all believers are equally priests before God. Where the context refers to offering "spiritual sacrifices," he rested his case on the words of St. Peter, saying, "You are a chosen race, a royal priesthood" (I Pet. 2:9). "By this text," he said, "I have proved that all Christians are priests, for Peter addresses all Christians, as the words themselves clearly prove."[45] This notion was later incorporated into the Smalcald Articles, and thus made confessional doctrine, after Luther had taken up the Catholic challenge and repudiated the very idea of a visible priesthood to be consistent with his theory of a purely invisible Church.

A great part of modern Lutheranism finds its basis and justification in the hypothesis of a universal priesthood. As a logical consequence, it rejects as unscriptural the doctrine "that only such are true ministers of the Church as have been ordained by bishops . . . that the different offices and ranks of the clergy are not of human but of divine origin . . . that only priests can forgive sins . . . that the power of excommunication does not belong to the whole congregation, but to the spiritual rulers of the Church."[46] But along with the exclusion of a distinct sacerdotal office, Lutherans inherited a problem which they have not yet resolved, namely, the exact status of the ministry, whether it is a divine or merely human institution. If there is no sacerdotal office instituted by Christ and all believers are equally priests, where does the Lutheran ministry derive its authority to teach, celebrate the Eucharist, absolve from sin, demand obedience, and punish the unworthy? In trying to answer this question, two schools of thought have arisen. The evangelical party "grants that the ministry is divinely ordained, but only in the sense as everything wise, appropriate, morally necessary can be said to have divine sanction, not in the sense that an express divine command for the establishment of the public ministry can be shown."[47] Against this position is the "strongly Roman doctrine of the ministry, namely, that the office of the public ministry is not conferred by the call of the congregation as the original possessor of all spiritual power, but is a divine institution in the sense that it was transmitted immediately from the Apostles to their pupils, considered as a separate 'ministerial order' or caste, and that this order perpetuates itself by means of the ordination."[48]

To date no solution has been found for the dilemma, and no compromise seems possible between these two conceptions of the ministry, which if not divinely ordained has no title to authority, and if divinely ordained seems to be the negation of a cardinal principle of Lutheran theology.

RITUAL AND WORSHIP

As much as they differ in ritual emphases, Lutheran Churches have in common the evangelical principle bequeathed by their founder, who made preaching of the gospel instead of the Mass the center of the Christian liturgy. Around this nucleus, however, even the most confessional bodies have developed a liturgical system that is in striking contrast with the colder formality of churches in the Calvinist tradition. A representative example is the liturgy of the Synodical Conference of North America.

Hymns. Luther's love of music is proverbial. Faithful to this memory, the number and variety of hymns in regular use can only be described as bewildering. The current *Lutheran Hymnal* lists 668 full-length hymns, giving the words and music, author, composer, and date of composition, and frequently extending to eight and ten stanzas. There is an alphabetical index of all the songs, an index of first lines, a metrical index of tunes, a classification of general doxologies, arrangement according to season and doctrinal content, and separate lists of authors, composers, and translators, giving their dates of birth and death. Among the authors are Sts. Ambrose, Bede, and Bernard of Clairvaux, the Dominican Savonarola, non-Lutheran reformers like Hus and John Wesley, and more recent writers like John Keble and William Cullen Bryant. Although most of the composers (161) are

Protestant, they include several names familiar to Catholics, like Palestrina, Prätorius, Gounod, and Tallis. Out of 700 hymns, not one is directed to the Blessed Virgin; one, the *Magnificat*, quotes her song of praise, and another makes reference to her virginity. This silence is consistent with Lutheran opposition to having "Mary, the Mother of Mercy . . . called upon for help."[49]

Holy Communion Service. The most elaborate liturgical service in the Lutheran Church is the "Order of Holy Communion," which is celebrated with varying frequency and closely approximates the sequence and even the words of the Roman missal.

1. The ritual opens with a public sign of the cross, followed by the Confession of Sins, in the form of a prayer recited by the congregation. The minister then pronounces the Absolution, saying: "Upon this your confession, I, by virtue of my office, as a called and ordained servant of the Word, announce the grace of God unto all of you, and in the stead and by the command of my Lord Jesus Christ, I forgive you all your sins, in the name of the Father and of the Son and of the Holy Ghost."[50]

2. An Introit is either chanted by the choir or recited by the minister. Different introits are provided for the changing seasons of the year. In form and content they are translations or paraphrases from the Catholic Mass.

3. Kyrie Eleison, in the vernacular, is said or chanted by the minister and the congregation; followed by the Gloria in Excelsis Deo, similarly recited or sung—somewhat abbreviated from the Latin Mass.

4. Salutation, "The Lord be with you," with the response, "And with thy spirit"; Collect for the day, taken verbatim or adapted from the Missal; the Epistle, announced and read to the people; one of a number of Graduals, chanted or recited, and concluded with a Hallelujah, which also differs for different seasons; the reading of the Gospel, facing the people, after which the congregation answers, "Praise be to Thee, O Christ."

5. The Nicene Creed is then recited by the people, followed by a hymn and the Sermon.

6. The Offertory Prayer, which may be sung or recited, is

always the same: "Create in me a clean heart, O God, and renew a right spirit within me. Cast me not away from Thy presence; and take not Thy Holy Spirit from me. Restore unto me the joy of Thy salvation; and uphold me with Thy free spirit. Amen."[51] Then follows a series of General Prayers: for the Church, civil rulers, enemies, those in "trouble, want, sickness, anguish of labor, peril of death, or any other adversity."

7. The Preface is preceded by three versicles and responses: "The Lord be with you . . . Lift up your hearts . . . Let us give thanks to the Lord our God." Nine proper Prefaces are provided, for Advent, Christmas, Epiphany, Lent, Easter, Ascension, Pentecost, Trinity, and "Days of Apostles and Evangelists." The wording is practically the same as in the Catholic Mass, e.g., the Trinity Preface:

> It is truly meet, right and salutary, that we should at all times and in all places give thanks unto Thee, O Lord, holy Father, almighty everlasting God, through Jesus Christ Our Lord, Who with Thine only-begotten Son and the Holy Ghost art one God, one Lord. And in the confession of the only true God we worship the Trinity in Person and the Unity in Substance, of Majesty co-equal. Therefore with angels and archangels and with all the company of heaven we laud and magnify Thy glorious name, evermore praising Thee and saying: Holy, Holy, Holy, Lord God of Sabaoth.[52]

After the Sanctus, the Lord's Prayer is recited, with the people adding, in song, "For Thine is the kingdom and the power and the glory for ever and ever. Amen."[53]

8. The Words of Institution of the Eucharist are recited or chanted by the minister. They are a literal translation of the Words of Consecration from the Mass.

9. Immediately after are the Pax Domini: "The peace of the Lord be with you always . . . Amen," and the Agnus Dei, saying three times the invocation: "O Christ, Thou Lamb of God, that takest away the sin of the world, have mercy on us."[54]

10. Communion is distributed while the congregation sings one or more hymns. In the act of distribution, "when the

Minister giveth the bread," he says, "Take, eat; this is the true body of Our Lord and Savior Jesus Christ, given into death for your sins." And "when he giveth the cup," he says, "Take, drink; this is the true blood of Our Lord and Savior Jesus Christ, shed for the remission of your sins."[55] After each distribution, he adds: "May this strengthen and preserve you in the true faith unto life everlasting."[56]

11. After distributing the elements, the minister recites a Prayer of Thanksgiving, following the chant of Nunc Dimittis by the congregation and preceding an optional Post Communion Hymn. The service is closed with the Benedicamus Domino and the Benediction said by the minister over the congregation, and answered by the people with a chanted "Amen."

Rite of Confirmation. The Confirmation ceremony is the solemn conclusion to a long period of instruction in the Lutheran religion. Since the ritual itself is denied to be sacramental, the emphasis is on the human element, technically called "indoctrination," which is "the necessary prerequisite of confirmation." Children must be at least twelve years old when confirmed; the usual age is fourteen, and "a year or two older is always better."

In the "Order of Confirmation," the two essentials are profession of faith and promises, and the imposition of hands by the presiding minister. Among the promises asked of the candidate is: "Do you . . . as a member of the Evangelical Lutheran Church, intend to continue steadfast in the confession of this Church, and suffer all, even death, rather than fall away from it?" The person then answers, "I do so intend, with the help of God."[57] During the imposition of hands, a choice of five formulas may be used by the minister, e.g., "N., May God, who hath begun the good work in thee, perform it until the day of our Lord Jesus Christ."[58] Adults who are baptized do not have to receive Confirmation.

ORGANIZATION AND GOVERNMENT

In the United States, the congregation is the basic unit of Lutheran church government. Normally the parish is administered by a church council, headed by the pastor, and composed of laymen elected to the office and variously called elders, deacons, or trustees. Pastors are elected and called by the congregation, but not deposed from the ministry.

Beyond the local level, the organization assumes two different forms. It may be a synod, like the Missouri or Norwegian Synods, composed of pastors and elected lay delegates from the congregations; or, more commonly, though organized on synodical lines, it is simply called a Church, like the American Lutheran Church or the Church of the Lutheran Brethren of America. In either case, this constitutive body is the denomination in a full juridical sense. Meetings are held at least triennially; between sessions the corporate work of the body is directed by a president, his officers, and a number of boards, commissions, and auxiliaries.

Some Lutheran bodies are not organized beyond the level of a synod. Generally, however, a group of synods bands together to form a conference (also called a "Church"), in which the member bodies relinquish a certain amount of autonomy for the privilege of mutual benefits in the larger organization. For example, the late American Lutheran Conference, which collaborated with the National and World Councils of Churches, included the American Lutheran, Augustana, Evangelical Lutheran, Lutheran Free, and United Evangelical Lutheran Churches. Organized in 1930, it was dissolved in 1954. A new concept of Lutheran co-operation is the council, which, as the Lutheran Council in the U.S.A., is the largest Federation of Lutheran Churches in the history of the country.

On the international level, in 1923 the Lutheran World Convention first met at Eisenach, Germany, and was attended by 147 delegates, representing 22 nations. After two other meetings in Copenhagen (1929) and Paris (1935), the Convention was reorganized in 1947, at Lund, as the Lutheran World Federation. Its doctrinal basis is "the Holy Scriptures of the Old and New Testaments as the only source and the infallible norm of all church doctrine and practice," and its main purpose is "to cultivate unity of faith and confession among the Lutheran Churches of the world," yet in such a way as "to foster Lutheran participation in ecumenical movements."[59]

Its Constitution states, "in the three Ecumenical Creeds and in the Confessions of the Lutheran Church, especially in the unaltered Augsburg Confession and Luther's Small Catechism [is] a pure exposition of the Word of God."[60]

Characteristically, the Lutheran World Federation has a Department of Theology, founded in 1952, the purpose of which is to develop and strengthen theological ties among the member churches. Although the department itself does not have the function of teaching, it actually serves its purpose by the exchange of theological professors and the publication of important doctrinal literature. Moreover, the department sponsors a program of guest professors for seminary and university faculties. Its broadest field of work, however, is the continuing study in depth which the department carries on with parallel commissions in the Federation.

Among the major contributions to the ecumenical movement produced by the Lutheran World Federation is the document on Confirmation issued by its Commission on Education. The Commission spent several years examining every phase of the subject and concluded that "Confirmation presupposes the practice of infant Baptism. It is closely tied up with it . . . But where the theology of baptism follows the Word and Reformation doctrine, Confirmation would never become an act which supplements and completes the work begun in Baptism." Along with this apparently uncompromising position—"the Roman Catholic and the Pietistic misconceptions that Confirmation is a supplement to Baptism must be rejected"—the Lutheran World Federation left the door open for a more irenic approach to the sacraments.[61] It stated that "We have become full members in Baptism. We should also become active and responsible members of the Church of Christ who are alive and conscious of their membership . . . this living membership is not the product of organizational activity and of education, but primarily a result of the work of the Spirit of God who gives life born of faith which makes us 'confirmed' members."[62]

Needless to say, this kind of theological analysis offers great promise for the future of the ecumenical movement.

Mormons

Mormons disclaim they are Protestants because their founder belonged to no other religious body and admitted no succession from another church society. Yet historically Mormonism is derived from the Reformation principle of religious freedom carried to the point of not only appealing to the inner voice of God for private interpretation of the Bible, but developing a new revelation parallel with the Scriptures of traditional Christianity.

As popularly conceived, Mormonism is identified with a peculiar group which at one time practiced polygamy, and still exists as a small sectarian body, but otherwise has no particular significance among the major churches in America. This conception needs to be revised. The Church of the Latter-Day Saints, for which "Mormons" is only a nickname, is one of the largest and certainly the most closely knit of ecclesiastical bodies in the United States. Its origin and history offer a modern study in religious psychology for which there is no counterpart in the Western world; its long insistence on plural marriage as divinely ordained and the conflicts this provoked played an important role in the constitutional development of the country; its phenomenal growth from one hundred thousand in 1890 to over a million members and above all its missionary zeal in every part of the world suggest the importance of the Mormon Church, even when its doctrinal system is so singular among religious bodies in the country.

HISTORY

The founder of Mormonism was Joseph Smith, a farmer's son, born at Sharon, Vermont, December 23, 1805. His family moved to Lebanon, New Hampshire, in 1811, to Palmyra, New York, in 1815, and four years later to the small town of Manchester, Ontario County, New York. Since it has a direct bearing on the origins of Mormonism, the following judgment on the Smith family should be quoted from a public statement by sixty-two contemporary residents of Palmyra. "We, the undersigned," they stated, "have been acquainted with the Smith family for a number of years . . . They were particularly famous for visionary projects; spent much of their time digging for money which they pretended was hid in the earth."[1] Sympathetic biographers describe Joseph Smith, Jr., as an agreeable young man, whose occupation of digging for treasure was brought by the Yankees from New England to New York. They further attest that he used a "peepstone" —a sort of native crystal in the rough—in which he saw where treasure was hid. He was then paid for revealing his discovery to others.

The first of a series of divine communications to Joseph Smith is supposed to have occurred at Manchester (near Palmyra) in 1820. He was praying for light to recognize the true church: Baptist, Methodist, or Presbyterian. "I saw two personages," he later wrote, "whose brightness and glory defy all description, standing above me in the air. One of them spake unto me, calling me by name, and said, pointing to the other—This is my beloved Son, hear Him." Then "I asked the personages who stood above me in the light, which of all the sects was right—and which I should join. I was answered that I must join none of them, for they were all wrong."[2]

Three years later occurred another revelation, regarded as the "celestial beginnings" of the Mormon faith. While in prayer on the night of September 21, 1823, a person clothed in white appeared to Smith, said he was sent from God and identified himself as Moroni. The messenger told Smith that his name "should be for good and evil among all nations," and explained how he must go about establishing a new religion. In Smith's words:

> He said there was a book deposited, written upon gold plates, giving an account of the former inhabitants of this continent, and the source from whence they sprang. He also said that the fulness of the everlasting Gospel was contained in it, as delivered by the Savior to the ancient inhabitants; also that there were two stones in silver bows

—and these stones, fastened to a breastplate, constituted what is called the Urim and Thummim—deposited with the plates: and the possession and use of these stones were what constituted seers in ancient or former times; and that God had prepared them for the purpose of translating the book.[3]

After three more revelations, Smith finally went to the place designated by Moroni (Hill Cumorah), found the plates, the Urim and Thummim, and the breastplate. The plates were engraved in an unknown language, but with the help of the "spectacles," i.e., the Urim and Thummim, he was able to translate the inscriptions into English. Smith later claimed that a linguistic scholar, Anthon, had certified that the characters of the unknown language were Egyptian, Chaldaic, Assyriac, and Arabic. On hearing this, Anthon issued a statement denying any such certification and branded the supposed hieroglyphs as "a hoax (and) a singular scrawl."[4]

There are those who claim that Smith himself was incapable of producing what is now the Mormon Bible, which grew out of the Moroni revelations. In this he is said to have been assisted by a Baptist revivalist, Sidney Rigdon, who was well educated, intelligent, and bent on starting a new religion in opposition to Alexander Campbell, whose success he envied in founding the Disciples of Christ. It is further suggested that the idea was not even original with Rigdon, but was borrowed in its historical portion from a manuscript by Solomon Spaulding, minister-archaeologist of Conneaut, Ohio.[5] While disclaiming assistance from Rigdon or Spaulding, Smith admitted that at least "people besides himself had seen the golden plates" containing the heavenly message. Eventually three of the main witnesses defected from Mormonism and withdrew their former testimony. In a sworn affidavit, the metal plates were identified as "gotten up" by a blacksmith and some friends, being "cut out of some pieces of copper," properly etched with nitric acid, and covered with a rusting mixture to give the appearance of antiquity.[6]

The subsequent history of the Saints is a sequence of new revelations vouchsafed to Smith. He was directed to relate these revelations to the people and his disciples, who followed him in a strange odyssey that ended in tragedy for the prophet. On April 6, 1830, at Fayette, New York, the group was formally organized as the Church of Jesus Christ of the Latter-Day Saints. Hostility to Mormon doctrines occasioned a revelation (1831) which told Smith that Kirtland, Ohio, was to be Zion, or the New Jerusalem, where Christ would reign after His return to the world. When trouble arose over some notes that Smith issued in a bank he had established, he had another revelation bidding him and Rigdon flee from Kirtland (1837) and found the new Zion in Jackson County, Missouri. Within two years, the Missourians declared war on the Latter-Day Saints, which induced a revelation telling Smith to lead his people into Illinois, where, on the banks of the Mississippi, they founded the city of Nauvoo, said to be the Hebrew for "beautiful place." The charges of polygamy, however, led to a schism in the ranks.

The military atmosphere of Nauvoo, its tremendous growth, its virtual political independence, and its block voting provoked an armed uprising by non-Mormons, whom Smith had come to designate as "gentiles." The opposition was determined to seize the prophet and his adherents and, if they did not surrender, a war of extermination was to be waged. The result was that Smith and his brother, Hyrum, were arrested and kept in jail at Carthage, awaiting trial. But the mob wanted no trial. They broke into prison, and on June 27, 1844, shot and killed the two brothers.

After the death of Smith, the Mormons split into several factions which have not yet been reunited. The largest segment, known as the Church of Jesus Christ of Latter-Day Saints, was led by Brigham Young to Utah, where they founded Salt Lake City in 1847. Through thirty years of uncompromising rule Young developed the Mormons of Utah and Idaho into a well-organized, self-sustaining religious body. At their centennial celebration in 1947, it was reported that over fifty thousand missionaries had been sent into the field, at their personal expense, most of them serving a full two years. Some ten thousand missionaries are regularly maintained in the States and at mission stations in thirty countries. The Church conducts four senior and three junior colleges in Utah, which has the highest percentage of college students of any State. A very low death rate is attributed to the practice of "Mormon abstinence" combined with an elaborate system of public welfare. Numerous storehouses for community food and clothing are maintained by the Church.

A smaller group of Mormons protested Brigham Young's assumption of authority, claiming that Joseph Smith's son had sole title to leadership. Young was also charged with having been the first to sanction polygamy. Led by Joseph Smith III, the Reorganized Church of Jesus Christ of Latter-Day Saints settled at Independence, Missouri, where the "gathering of Zion" is expected to take place before the second coming of Christ.

The Reorganized Church rejects the claim of the Mormons led by Brigham Young mainly on the grounds that Young and his followers abandoned the rule of succession as found in the *Book of Doctrine and Covenants*. The crucial revelation to which the Reorganized Saints appeal states that God removed any possibility of anyone legally succeeding Joseph Smith unless specifically appointed by the prophet: "None else shall be appointed unto this gift except it be through him." Moreover, "this shall be a law unto you, that ye receive not the teachings of any that shall come before you as revelations, or commandments; and this I give unto you, that you may not be deceived, that you may know they are not of me."[7] From these and similar passages the Reorganized Church concludes that the Utah branch of the Mormons is not the legitimate offspring of Joseph Smith.

The Missouri group argues that Brigham Young took the presidency of the church by election, and therefore contrary to the Mormon scriptures. On the testimony of Young's own followers, notably Lorenzo Snow (fourth president of the Church of Utah), Brigham "was appointed by the people." This is said to be a clear violation of God's law of succession.

Consistent with this theology, the Reorganized Church of Latter-Day Saints recognizes only the direct descendants of Joseph Smith as presidents of the Church. The first successor was Joseph Smith III, the second Frederick M. Smith, the third Israel A. Smith, and so on.

Four other splinter groups, with only a very small membership, were organized in protest against either Brigham Young or Joseph Smith's son. Their significance in Mormon history is negligible.

DOCTRINE AND RITUAL

There are three principal sources from which Mormons derive their teachings and practices: *The Book of Mormon,* discovered by Joseph Smith; *The Pearl of Great Price,* which contains Smith's translations from the Bible, the Book of Moses and the Book of Abraham; and *The Doctrine and Covenants,* which covers the private revelations of Joseph Smith.

According to Article 8 of the Mormon Creed, "We believe the Bible to be the word of God, as far as it has been translated correctly; we also believe the Book of Mormon to be the word of God."[8] Like the Scriptures, the Mormon Bible is divided into books, chapters, and verses. There are four books of Nephi, two of Mormon, and one each of Jacob, Enos, Jarom, Omni, Mosiah, Alma, Helaman, Ether, and Moroni. In a modern edition, the total runs to 522 pages in duodecimo, covering perhaps 200 chapters, divided into verses, and cited like the Bible, e.g., II Nephi 31:17. The Book of Mormon purports to be a record of events that took place from 600 B.C. to A.D. 421, telling the history of two nations: the Jaredites, who came to America after the confusion of tongues at Babel, and the Nephites, who migrated to America from Jerusalem about 600 B.C. The Nephites, in turn, died out at the beginning of the fifth century of the Christian era, but not before their best historian, Moroni [son of Mormon], wrote the annals of his people and hid them, along with a record of the Jaredites, "to be brought forth in the latter days, as predicted by the voice of God through his ancient prophets." It was this double record which Joseph Smith discovered in 1827 and translated from the golden plates, delivered to him by the "same Moroni, then a resurrected personage."[9]

Perhaps the most important doctrinal content of the Book of Mormon is the claim that after His Ascension Christ personally established a nascent Church among the Nephites in America; that after the passing of the Nephites a race of believers would arise as the Latter-Day Saints, blessed with the gift of revelation and prophecy and inaugurating an age of unparalleled prosperity among all nations. Underlying this mission of the Saints is the conviction that God did not intend fully to establish the true Church in Palestine at the time of Christ, but in America at the present day. All preceding events, e.g., the revival of learning, the Protestant Reformation, the discovery of a new world, the landing of the Pilgrims, American independence, were a prologue to the destiny set in store for the American nation, of which the Mormons are divinely chosen prophets.

In *The Pearl of Great Price,* the Book of Moses is an interpolation between Genesis 5:21 and 23, and contains some alleged visions of Moses. Among these are revelations that the devil organized the Freemasons to mislead the human race. Later on the Mormons changed in their opposition to Masonry, so that now some writers consider their cultus and ritual to be modeled after that of the Masonic Order. The Book of Abraham openly supports the practice of plural marriage.

The private revelations of Joseph Smith, called *The Doctrine and Covenants,* are the principal source of faith and practice in present-day Mormonism. They also provide a theoretical basis for the Church's absolute authority by means of continued divine communications to its spiritual leaders. Believers are told that "In view of the demonstrated facts that revelation between God and man has ever been and is a characteristic of the Church of Jesus Christ, it is reasonable to await with confident expectation the coming of other messages from heaven, even until the end of man's probation on earth."[10]

Although faith is professed in the Trinity, the Mormon concept of God is anthropomorphic. "We affirm," they say, "that to deny the materiality of God's person is to deny God; for a thing without parts has no whole, and an immaterial body cannot exist. The Church of Jesus Christ of Latter-Day Saints proclaims against the incomprehensible God, devoid of 'body, parts, or passions.' "[11]

Mormons believe in universal salvation, allowing for three kinds of resurrection from the dead: celestial glory, resplendent like the sun, for those who lived perfect lives; terrestrial, like the moon, for those who were somewhat unfaithful; and telestial glory, comparable to the stars, for all who did not receive Christ but were faithful to the Holy Ghost. The wicked will be punished, but not forever. Hell is said to be eternal only in the sense that it will last as long as there is sin to punish.

Man is defined as a union of pre-existent spirit and an earthly body. "This union of spirit and body makes progress from the unembodied to the embodied condition, and is an inestimable advancement in the soul's onward course."[12] In line with this pre-eminence of body over spirit, "marriage is a requirement to all who are not prevented by physical or other disability from assuming the sacred responsibilities of the wedded state."[13] Through marriage, pre-existent souls are given a chance to enter the advanced state of "embodiment" that might otherwise be denied them. Mormons further distinguish between temporal and celestial marriages; the former open to everyone, the latter "permitted to those members of the Church only who are adjudged worthy."[14] Celestial marriages are performed with special, secret functions, and the offspring "are natural heirs to the Priesthood."[15]

While claiming that baptism is necessary for salvation, Mormons oppose infant baptism on the grounds of a special revelation from Moroni.

> Little children need no repentance, neither baptism. Behold, baptism is unto repentance to the fulfilling of the commandments unto the remission of sins.
>
> But little children are alive in Christ, even from the foundation of the world; if not so, God is a partial God, and also a changeable God, and a respecter of persons; for how many little children have died without baptism!
>
> Wherefore, if little children cannot be saved without

baptism, these must have gone to an endless hell. Behold I say unto you, that he that supposeth that little children need baptism is in the gall of bitterness and in the bonds of iniquity, for he hath neither faith, hope, nor charity; wherefore, should he be cut off while in the thought, he must go down to hell.[16]

In a reported vision of 1830, the mode of baptism was revealed as including immersion in water and the Trinitarian formula, in which the minister says, "Having been commissioned of Jesus Christ, I baptize you in the name of the Father, and of the Son, and of the Holy Ghost, Amen."[17] As a correlative to the necessity of baptism for salvation, Mormons teach that if a person died without this rite, he may and should be baptized by proxy after death, since "Nowhere in scripture is a distinction made in this regard between the living and the dead."[18] A living relative or friend goes through the immersion ritual in place of the deceased, with no difference in baptismal effect.

The most important ritual function of the Mormons is the administration of the Lord's Supper, whose purpose is "to commemorate the atonement of the Lord Jesus." Participation in the Communion worship is "a means of renewing our avowals before the Lord, of acknowledgment of mutual fellowship among the members, and of solemnly witnessing our claim and profession of membership in the Church of Jesus Christ."[19] A revelation to Joseph Smith commanded him, "You shall not purchase wine nor strong drink." In obedience to this authority, "the Latter-Day Saints administer water in their sacramental service, in preference to wine."[20]

For administration of the Lord's Supper, the Aaronic priesthood is required, and as a matter of policy anyone "in a higher degree" has the right to officiate at the service. The ritual words are practically the same for "consecrating the emblems" of bread and water separately. While kneeling, the elder or priest calls upon God the Father and says:

O God, the Eternal Father, we ask thee in the name of thy Son, Jesus Christ, to bless and sanctify this bread [water] to the souls of all those who partake [drink] of it, that they may eat [do it] in remembrance of the body [blood] of thy Son, and witness unto thee, O God, the Eternal Father, that they are willing to take upon them the name of thy Son, and always remember him and keep his commandments which he has given them; that they may always have his Spirit to be with them. Amen.[21]

The real presence is denied explicitly, being called "the Great Apostasy," or the teaching that "the sacramental emblems by the ceremony of consecration lost their natural character of simply bread and wine, and became in reality flesh and blood—actually parts of the crucified body of Christ." No evidence to support the Mormon position is offered, since "argument against such dogmas is unnecessary."[22]

POLYGAMY

Plural marriage was advocated by Joseph Smith on the strength of a special revelation, in which the Lord is made to say:

> . . . If any man espouse a virgin, and desire to espouse another, and the first give her consent; and if he espouse the second, and they are virgins, and have vowed to no other man, then is he justified; he cannot commit adultery, for they are given unto him; for he cannot commit adultery with that which belongeth unto him and to no one else.
>
> And if he have ten virgins given unto him by this law, he cannot commit adultery, for they belong to him, and they are given unto him, therefore is he justified.
>
> But if one or either of the ten virgins, after she is espoused, shall be with another man; she has committed adultery, and shall be destroyed; for they are given unto him to multiply and replenish the earth, according to my commandment . . .[23]

Accepted as an article of faith by the Mormons in Utah, polygamy became the main source of their trouble until the turn of the century. As early as 1860, a bill was introduced in the House of Representatives in Washington "to punish and prevent the practice of polygamy in the Territories of the United States."[24] Though finally passed by the House and Senate and signed by President Lincoln in 1862, the legislation was inoperative. A stronger bill failed to pass the Senate in 1869 because it was assumed impossible to convict polygamists with any juries drawn up in Utah.

In 1878 a mass meeting of women of Salt Lake City sent a petition to Congress to suppress polygamous marriages which the Mormons were contracting in so-called Endowment Houses, where people were "sealed [married] and bound by oaths so strong that even apostates will not reveal them."[25] The next year, in his inaugural address, President Garfield declared that "The Mormon Church not only offends the moral sense of mankind by sanctioning polygamy, but prevents the administration of justice through ordinary instrumentalities of law."[26] President Arthur, in his message in 1881, spoke of "this odious crime, so revolting to the moral and religious sense of Christendom," and recommended legislation to secure convictions in the Utah territory.[27] Inspired by these recommendations, the Edmunds Law was passed in 1882—"the first real serious blow struck by Congress against polygamy."[28] Essentially it disfranchised any person who practiced plural marriage. In 1890, when the U. S. Supreme Court upheld the constitutionality of the anti-polygamy legislation, the Mormons finally yielded to circumstances and amended the doctrine of their Church.

This important step was not taken in the form of a new revelation, but simply as a proclamation. There was first a statement from the Mormon President, Wilford Woodruff:

> Inasmuch as laws have been enacted by Congress, which laws have been pronounced constitutional by the court of last resort, I hereby declare my intention to submit to these laws, and to use my influence with the members of the church over which I preside to have them do likewise.
> And now I publicly declare that my advice to the Latter-Day Saints is to refrain from contracting any marriage forbidden by the law of the land.[29]

Shortly after, the General Council of the Latter-Day Saints unanimously voted to accept President Woodruff's recommendation, declaring, "as a church in general conference assembled we accept his declaration concerning plural marriages as authoritative and binding."[30] The date of acceptance was October 6, 1890. Six years later the State of Utah was admitted to the Union, but not before Congress had passed an act allowing Utah's admittance, "provided that polygamous or plural marriages are forever prohibited" within its territory.[31]

As regards Mormon polygamy at the present time, several distinctions should be made. The Church, in its largest segment, juridically disavowed the practice only under pressure from political forces. So far from denying, it reaffirms the claim that polygamy is divinely revealed, but its practice must be held in abeyance. Under "submission to secular authority," an official Mormon publication gives as "an illustration of . . . suspension of divine law . . . the action of the Church regarding the matter of plural marriage. This practice was established as a result of direct revelation." But when "Federal statutes were framed declaring the practice unlawful . . . the Church, through its president thereupon discontinued the practice . . . solemnly placing the responsibility for the change upon the nation by whose laws the renunciation had been forced."[32]

Fundamentalists among the Mormons still practice polygamy and defend their right to plural marriage against civil authority. Periodically state officials "raid" a polygamous Mormon colony, separating the men and their wives and instituting court proceedings against the offenders.

At the other extreme the Reorganized Church of Jesus Christ of Latter-Day Saints absolutely disavows polygamy. It is not only that the civil law forbids the practice, presumably revealed, but the Missouri contingent denies there was ever a revelation on the subject. Joseph Smith, they say, was not a polygamist; he never taught plural marriages; and the clearest evidence that the Utah Church is not the true Church is the preaching and practice of polygamy by Brigham Young and his successors until the federal government forbade the innovation.

PRIESTHOOD AND GOVERNMENT

Priesthood and jurisdiction are intimately connected in Mormonism. Two types of priesthood are recognized, the lesser, called Aaronic, bestowed on Smith by John the Baptist, and the greater, known as the Melchizedek Order, given to Smith at the bidding of Peter, James, and John.

The special functions of the priesthood of Melchizedek "lie in the administration of spiritual things, comprising the keys of all spiritual blessings of the Church, the right 'to have the heavens opened unto them . . . to commune with the general assembly and Church of the Firstborn, and to enjoy the communion and presence of God the Father, and Jesus the mediator of the new covenant.'"[33] Its officers include twelve apostles, a number of patriarchs or evangelists, high priests "ordained with power to officiate" but primarily administrative, seventies—who are traveling preachers "ordained to promulgate the Gospel among the nations of the earth"— and elders ordained to perform the lower callings of the priesthood, including the power to ordain other elders, to baptize, to confirm, and to conduct meetings, "as they are led by the Holy Ghost."

To the Aaronic priesthood are committed the temporal duties of the Church, operating through ministers who are "appointed to preach, to teach, expound the scriptures, to administer the sacrament, to visit the homes of the members."[34] They may ordain deacons, teachers, and other priests. Next in dignity are teachers, or local officers, "whose function it is to mingle with the saints . . . They are to see that there is no iniquity in the Church," and are allowed to preach when directed to do so, but may not officiate at baptism, the Lord's Supper, or the laying on of hands. Finally, to the deacons, as the lowest office in the Aaronic priesthood, pertains the duty of caring for "the houses of worship, the comfort of the worshipers, and ministration to the members of the Church as the bishop may direct."[35]

Mormon ecclesiastical structure is rigidly hierarchical. At the head stands the First Presidency, made up of three high priests, a president, and two counselors. Its authority is absolute and universal, binding in matters spiritual as well as temporal. Below the Presidency is the Council of Twelve Apostles, which supervises the lesser patriarchs. Parallel with the Apostles is the Presiding Quorum of Seventy, whose unanimous decisions have the same authority as the Council of the Apostles. On the territorial level, working within the framework of the Church, are all the other officials. Their jurisdiction is based on geographical divisions, called stakes and wards. Heading each ward is a bishop, along with two high priests as his counselors. Being of the lower priesthood, the ward bishop has no direct authority over members of the Order of Melchizedek who are working within his territory. But subject to him are the priests, teachers, deacons, and auxiliary church organizations like relief societies and mutual improvement associations.

Mormons make a great deal of what they call "practical religion," which involves the church's dictation in the lives of its members down to the smallest details. In compliance with the law of tithing, "a man should make out and lay before the Bishop a schedule of all his property and pay him one-tenth of it . . . The next year he must pay one-tenth of the increase, and one-tenth of his time, of his cattle, money, goods and trade."[36] In matters of food, the believer is forbidden to drink "wine or strong drink"; also "tobacco is not good for men," and "hot drinks [tea and coffee] are not good for the body." While permitted to eat "the flesh of beasts and of the fouls of the air," they are to be used sparingly, and "only in time of winter, or of cold, or famine."[37] Yet with all these restrictions, the faithful Mormon professes to cherish nothing more than freedom, believing that "the right of choice is essential to salvation, and that anyone who seeks to enslave men in any sense is essentially in league with Satan himself."[38]

Current figures for the total number of ordained persons are not publicly available. But all the evidence indicates that the Church of the Latter-Day Saints is flourishing. What is less certain is the future of Mormonism. Friendly historians of the movement believe it is on the eve of its diaspora. For over a century the Mormons have concentrated on secular activities, social welfare, and bodily well-being, which in recent years have come under the aegis of the state. The basic need of Mormonism, therefore, may well become the search for a more contemplative understanding of the relationship of men to God. Given the strong emphasis on education, which is typical of the Latter-Day Saints, the religious future of their Church is even more promising than in the past.

Pentecostals

The beginnings of the Pentecostal movement in modern Protestantism may be traced to the ministry of Edward Irving, pastor of a Presbyterian church in London. Irving had witnessed an outburst of speaking in tongues and some cases of healing in Glasgow, Scotland. He reported back to his congregation that what he had seen could be repeated in London if only his people prayed earnestly enough that they, too, might be filled with the gifts of the Spirit. In a short time some of his parishioners began to speak in strange tongues and prophesy. When he was advised by his vestry to curb these manifestations, he refused to do so. By 1832, he had started a new congregation which professed to receive unusual blessings in answer to prayer.

Although the Irvingites are not the only ancestors of American Pentecostalism, their principles entered the mainstream of the movement in the United States.

According to the Irvingites, the glossolalia (gift of tongues) which they experienced was of the same nature as that which occurred on the day of Pentecost. Speaking in tongues was proof of Spirit baptism. They also regarded such an experience as necessary before receiving any other divine gifts. Other charismata were believed to be part of the permanent possession of the church. The Christians had lost these for centuries because of their disbelief. Moreover, the only hope of recovering these gifts was to organize new churches even if this meant departing from established denominations.

AMERICAN BEGINNINGS

American Pentecostalism goes back to the early nineteenth century, when the Quakers, Shakers, Irvingites, Mormons, and others were preaching that external manifestations are an essential part of Christian belief. However, the main influence was a protest movement among the followers of John

Wesley. After the Civil War, Methodists in different parts of the country began to charge their leaders with neglecting an important phase of Wesleyan belief, namely, that the justification of a sinner is only the beginning of his sanctification.

Called the Holiness Movement, it produced a new attitude toward the Christian religion. It also paved the way for the establishment of Pentecostal churches. Ideologically the Holiness people claimed that justification is followed by a special blessing which is distinct from conversion; that this blessing is to be sought and can be obtained through such collective outbursts of a fervor as revivals might produce; and that sanctified Christians should forsake the world and its sinful allurements.

At the same time two divergent interpretations began to appear among the Holiness devotees. One group felt that the experience of sanctification was basically an interior change, though it could be exhibited by such external signs as loud shouting or boisterous praying. Others were convinced that the internal grace had to be manifested by supernatural signs. The latter became the left wing of the Holiness Movement and helped to form the core of today's Pentecostalism.

Two names stand out in Pentecostal history: Charles Fox Parham and William J. Seymour. Parham was white and Seymour a Negro, which partly explains the interracial character of most Pentecostal churches.

Parham began as a lay preacher (1888) with a Congregational church in southwestern Kansas. While at college he temporarily lost his faith and soon after came down with rheumatic fever. Convinced that his sickness was due to rebellion against God, he made a vow to re-enter the ministry if he was cured. Unexpectedly cured, he became a Methodist minister and soon after began teaching what was substantially a Pentecostal understanding of John Wesley. Parham insisted that joining a church was useful but not necessary. Essential to salvation was a crisis experience, characterized by a violent struggle with sin and conscious self-renunciation. He further held that sanctification comes only after sin has been completely destroyed, that faith healing is part of the Christian message, and that the interior movements of the Spirit are externally revealed when a person is truly sanctified.

In 1898 Parham opened the Bethel Healing Home in Topeka, Kansas, which later became Bethel Bible College. Two years later on New Year's Eve, 1900, occurred the most dramatic event in Pentecostal history. Before he left on a mission trip, Parham instructed his students to investigate the subject of baptism in the Holy Spirit. When he returned they told him that the gift of tongues was conclusively this Spirit baptism. They asked him to impose hands on one of their number, a Miss Ozman. The moment he did so she was filled with the Holy Spirit and began to speak in several languages, besides talking in a strange tongue that not even accomplished linguists could understand. This experience of Miss Ozman is commonly held to be the first occasion that a direct request for baptism in the Holy Spirit produced the expected effects. Before long most of the students at Bethel became similarly gifted, and went out to preach the new gospel to all who would hear them.

Parham's disciple, William Seymour, carried the Pentecostal message to California. The Azusa Street revival, in Los Angeles, attracted large crowds. An eyewitness described what he saw. Seymour had one eye and was meek, plainspoken, and certainly no orator. He spoke the language of the uneducated. He might preach for three quarters of an hour with no more emotion than a post. Generally he sat behind two empty shoe boxes, one on top of the other, and kept his head inside the top one during the meeting, lost in prayer. When he finished the sermon, he would fall on his knees and begin to invoke the Holy Spirit. Everybody would follow his example. Then suddenly the manifestations began. Sounds would be uttered that no one had ever heard before. Some would weep, others prophesy. Most remarkable of all, the heavenly chorus would burst into song. Every man and woman in the crowd would break into spontaneous melody, in a language that no one understood, to a tune that no one had ever heard, and with a unison that thrilled every participant with celestial ecstasy.

In the next three years Azusa attracted the curious and fervent from all parts of America and even from overseas. In time the Spirit which Seymour engendered passed on to church leaders everywhere. His own work was short-lived. The name of his revival was changed to Apostolic Faith Gospel Mission; a new pastor succeeded Seymour; and, to the founder's regret, the Pentecostal groups he inspired began to separate along racial lines.

Pentecostal polity goes back to Charles Parham himself. Even while resisting any kind of "ecclesiasticalism," he advocated a simple congregational form in which individual churches were administered by local elders who were not responsible to any authority. He acted on his own principles when he wrote from Los Angeles where Seymour asked him to stamp out "the hypnotic forces and fleshly contortions" which had erupted in the Azusa Street Mission. "I have no desire," he said, "to assert my authority. For I have none to assert over the people of God, but to help and strengthen and forever make plain to all people that extremes . . . fanaticism and everything that is beyond the bounds of common sense and reason do not now and never had any part or lot in Apostolic Faith work and teaching."

The church that Parham founded still exists as the Apostolic Faith Movement. Its source of unity was the magazine, the *Apostolic Faith*, which his wife Sarah edited with her two sons.

Another organization with the same title as Parham's began independently of the parent organization. It was founded in 1907 at Portland, Oregon, by Florence Louise Crawford, who had experienced sanctification during an Azusa Street revival. Like Parham's group, the Apostolic Faith believes in sanctification, the ritual of foot washing, and a strict policy of not soliciting church funds. Women are told to attire themselves "in modest apparel, no extreme fads, no facial make-up, or bobbed hair."

PRINCIPAL DENOMINATIONS

It is estimated that over two hundred religious bodies in America would qualify as Pentecostal. The principal denominations are well organized and easily identified.

Church (Churches) of God. At least ten denominations in America are called Church of God and, though juridically distinct, they reflect a common reaction against denominationalism in all its forms. The very name implies a profession of faith in God as the only founder of the Church and a protest against other "man-made" institutions.

There are two main forms of Church of God in the United States, deriving either from the Holiness or the Pentecostal movements, and both tracing their ancestry to John Wesley, the founder of Methodism. In his original teaching, Wesley stressed the importance of rising above the level of justification by faith to a true conversion of spirit or sanctification by grace. The Churches of God have sought to give these Wesleyan principles organized expression; but unlike other Holiness or Pentecostal groups who are in the same tradition, they want to avoid anything savoring of a structured, authoritarian society and prefer to speak of themselves as a "reformation movement" among the various Christian bodies.

The three largest Churches of God account for almost 80 per cent of the American membership and are generally representative of the movement as a whole. One group calls itself simply the Church of God and has its headquarters in New York. It was founded in 1903 by A. J. Tomlinson, an American Bible Society salesman from North Carolina, and was headed by him until his death in 1943. As first conceived by Tomlinson, "There are no creeds connected with the Church of God, but only the Bible, rightly divided, with the New Testament as the only rule of faith and practice." Tomlinson's death was the signal for a chain of schisms that is still going on. He had designated his son Homer to succeed him, but the choice was opposed by a group of state overseers. Homer placed his younger brother Milton in charge. Shortly after, Homer was expelled from the church, whereupon he formed the New York group, which claims direct lineage from the elder Tomlinson.

Two other groups, Church of God, Anderson, Indiana, and Church of God, Cleveland, Tennessee, had independent beginnings and no relation to Tomlinson's organization. The Anderson body was started in 1880 by Daniel S. Warner and several minister companions who "severed their connection with humanly-organized churches" and maintained that "Scriptural, all-sufficient standard for Christians is membership in the body of Christ alone." In January 1881 Warner published the first issue of the *Gospel Trumpet*, which later (1963) became *Vital Christianity*, to give the church a weekly journal that, more than anything else, has kept the denomination organized and flourishing, beyond that of other Churches of God.

Like the Anderson group, the Church of God of Cleveland believes in the soul's personal encounter with God, but its emphasis is more extreme. It began in 1886 under the title of Christian Union, was reorganized in 1902 as the Holiness Church, and in 1907 adopted its present name. The *Church of God Evangel*, an inspirational weekly, serves to encourage the faithful to share their own conversion experience with others. Where the Indiana segment is more conservative, the Tennessee organization believes that the Holy Spirit manifests His presence in the soul through such extraordinary signs as the gift of tongues. Revivalism is prominent and mission work in countries such as Brazil caters to those who want a strong emotional appeal in Christianity.

Even when they are well organized, as in Anderson, the Churches of God are strictly congregational in polity. The highest directing body is the General Assembly, which meets annually or biennially. Ritually they recognize baptism by immersion, the Lord's Supper as a memorial of Christ's Passion, and (among some) foot washing as a divine ordinance. Ideally they are pacifist in their sentiments, oppose all secret societies, and abstain from alcoholic beverages.

The Churches of God may be described as anti-sectarian in their concept of Christianity, Wesleyan in their belief that divine grace offers the prospect of personal holiness, fundamentalist in theology, legalistic in the stress on external practices of morality (notably temperance), and charismatic in their expectation that the Holy Spirit will manifest His presence by extraordinary signs.

Besides the Churches of God, commonly so called, there is a body of Negro Pentecostals, the largest in the world, which has the same name with an addition, Church of God in Christ. It was started by Charles H. Mason, Baptist minister, who was baptized by the Holy Spirit during one of the Azusa Street revivals. The usual date of foundation is given as 1895, in Arkansas. More properly, it should be 1907, when Mason's partner in the ministry, C. P. Jones, withdrew after Mason changed his congregation into a Pentecostal group. Soon after Mason called for an assembly in Memphis, Tennessee, at which time he declared that the Church of God in Christ was now Pentecostal.

Serving the Negro people almost exclusively, Mason's church has experienced remarkable growth. Its missionary work in Jamaica, Haiti, Liberia, South and West Coast Africa has developed a strong sense of evangelism and deepened the ethnic solidarity between American Negroes in the Southern states and their confreres in other countries. Central authority is vested in a group of bishops residing in different states with headquarters in Memphis.

Pentecostal Holiness Church. This denomination came into being when three different Holiness bodies joined forces after they had embraced Pentecostalism. Partners to the merger were The Fire-Baptized Holiness Church, the Holiness Church, and the Tabernacle Presbyterian Church.

The Fire-Baptized Holiness Church was formed in the 1890s by Benjamin H. Irvin, a lawyer who became a Holiness preacher. Accused of the "third blessing heresy," Irvin created foundations as far west as Kansas and into Texas and Florida. When he defected from his own church, it almost went out of existence until Agnes Ozman, a Parham pupil, joined the association as pastor and evangelist.

The Holiness Church, second partner to the merger, was started by A. P. Crumpler; originally a Methodist, Crumpler was forced to withdraw from the Wesleyan group after his strong espousal of sanctification. Ironically Crumpler was later ousted from his own organization after most of the people became Pentecostals.

Crumpler's successor, A. H. Butler, led the newly created society in changing an essential article in the *Discipline*. The amended version was now to read: "We . . . need to receive the filling of the Spirit, the Baptism with the Holy Ghost, the abiding Comforter, that which was promised by John the Baptist (Matt. 3:11) and corroborated by Jesus Christ (John

14:15–17) that on receiving the baptism with the Holy Ghost we have the same evidence that followed Acts 2nd, 10th, and 19th Chapter to wit: The speaking in other tongues as the Spirit gave utterance."[1]

The last segment to join the Pentecostal Holiness Church was the Tabernacle Presbyterian Church, founded by Nickels John Holmes, who left the Presbyterians because he disagreed with their attitude toward holiness and the divine healing. His church entered the merger in 1915.

While having much in common with similar groups throughout the country, the Pentecostal Holiness Church differs from them in being more tolerant in matters of doctrine and more liberal in church policy. Where other Pentecostals are known to be sharply critical of the medical profession, this church merely says that divine healing is a more excellent way, but resorting to doctors is permissible. Equally tolerant is its position regarding baptism. Where others demand immersion, members of this group have the option of any mode of baptism. In fact, parents have the choice of either dedicating their child without baptism or having the child baptized according to their own preferred formula and method.

Unlike many other Pentecostal groups, the Pentecostal Holiness Church operates its own theological seminaries in Greenville, South Carolina, and Oklahoma City. Missionary work is spread throughout the world, in India and Africa, Mexico and South America. The national headquarters are in Franklin Springs, Georgia.

Assemblies of God. Until this organization came into existence, American Pentecostals had only two forms of government. They were either headed by a dynamic religious leader like Parham or Florence Crawford, or they were organized on a regional basis like the Churches of God. They had no national structure to care for the thousands of Pentecostals who did not live in the South or who were not in the Holiness tradition.

Pentecostal leaders who recognized this structural weakness had tried to do something about it as far back as 1909, when Parham and others thought of organizing special schools for their own clergy to serve prospective ministers from the whole country. It was not until 1913, however, that a serious move was made to federate all the existing Pentecostal churches in America. The announcement of the proposed organization occurred in December and in less than a four-month period it gathered so much momentum that a new denomination became inevitable. In April 1914, about one hundred twenty pastors and evangelists from twenty states and several foreign countries arrived in Hot Springs, Arkansas, for the first constitutional conference of the Assemblies of God. Their declaration is a concise statement of the basic principle by which this church still operates.

> We recognize ourselves as a GENERAL COUNCIL of Pentecostal (Spirit Baptized) saints from local Churches of God in Christ, Assemblies of God and various Apostolic Faith Missions and Churches, and Full Gospel Pentecostal Missions, and Assemblies of the like faith in the United States of America, Canada, and Foreign lands, whose purpose is neither to legislate laws of government, nor usurp authority over said various Assemblies of God, nor deprive them of their Scriptural and local rights and privileges, but to recognize Scriptural methods and order for worship, unity, fellowship, work, and business for God, and to disapprove of all unscriptural methods, doctrine and conduct, and approve all Scriptural truth and conduct, endeavoring to keep the unity of the Spirit in the bonds of peace, until we all come into the unity of the faith, and of the knowledge of the Son of God, unto a perfect man, unto the measure of the stature of the fulness of Christ, and to walk accordingly, as recorded in Eph. 4:17–32.[2]

The same constitutional conference took up the question of organization and a common statement of doctrine.

On the organizational side, the Assemblies of God adopted a varied kind of polity. Local churches are related to the national body on a basis of equality, unity, and co-operation. Each local church remains absolutely independent except in such matters of policy as would seriously affect the essence of Pentecostalism. A good description of the structure would be to call it Congregationalism joined to a sense of charismatic blessing.

It took two years to formulate the *Statement of Fundamen-*

tal Truths, which reflect a strong Trinitarian faith—to meet the challenge of the Unitarian drive among Pentecostals, and a pronounced Arminianism—to make sure that man's co-operation with grace would be recognized, against those who still held to the Reformed notion of man contributing nothing to his own sanctification.

Faith in the Trinity is explained in the Constitution in precise theological terms.

The terms "Trinity" and "persons" as related to the Godhead, while not found in the Scripture, are words in harmony with Scripture, whereby we may convey to others our immediate understanding of the doctrine of Christ respecting the Being of God, as distinguished from "gods many and lords many." We therefore may speak with propriety of the Lord our God, who is One Lord, as a Trinity or as one Being of three persons, and still be absolutely scriptural.

Accordingly, therefore, there is *that* in the Son which constitutes Him *the Son* and not the Father; and there is *that* in the Holy Ghost which constitutes Him *the Holy Ghost* and not either the Father or the Son. Wherefore the Father is the Begetter, the Son is the Begotten, and the Holy Ghost is the one proceeding from the Father and the Son. Therefore, because these three persons in the Godhead are in a state of unity, there is but one Lord God Almighty and His name one.

Wherefore, it is a transgression of the Doctrine of Christ to say that Jesus Christ derived the title, Son of God, solely from the fact of the incarnation, or because of His relation to the economy of redemption. Therefore, to deny that the Father is a real and eternal Father, and that the Son is a real and eternal Son, is a denial of the distinction and relationship in the Being of God; a denial of the Father and the Son; and a displacement of the truth that Jesus Christ is come in the flesh.[3]

Consistent with the general outlook of other Pentecostal churches, the Assemblies of God describe the baptism of the Holy Spirit in terms that leave no doubt about its necessity for the Christian faith.

All believers are entitled to and should ardently expect and earnestly seek the promise of the Father, the baptism in the Holy Ghost and fire, according to the command of our Lord Jesus Christ. This was the normal experience of all in the early Christian Church. With it comes the endowment of power for life and service, the bestowment of the gifts and their uses in the work of the ministry. This experience is distinct from and subsequent to the experience of the new birth. With the baptism in the Holy Ghost come such experiences as an overflowing fullness of the Spirit, a deepened reverence for God, an intensified consecration to God and dedication to His work, and a more active love for Christ, for His Word and for the lost.

The baptism of believers in the Holy Ghost is witnessed by the initial physical sign of speaking with other tongues as the Spirit of God gives them utterance. The speaking in tongues in this instance is the same in essence as the gift of tongues, but different in purpose and use.[4]

From the beginning, the Assemblies of God have been fervently mission-minded. They run Bible schools in more than seventy countries, with special concern for South America. The result has been that over one million members are claimed outside the United States, mainly first- and second-generation converts.

Pentecostal Church of God of America. As so often happens in the development of a new religious movement, adherents to the Pentecostal way of life have both united to form new churches and separated to form new divisions.

When the Assemblies of God were being organized in 1914, they aroused antagonism among those who claimed that spiritual liberty and the local autonomy of churches had been bartered away. By 1919, however, the anti-organization party organized itself as the Pentecostal Assemblies of the United States of America. Three years later the name was changed to the Pentecostal Church of God, and in 1933 the name was changed once more by adding the phrase "of America." This was done to avoid confusion with the local church which had the same title.

Although the Pentecostal Church of God ostensibly came

into being only as an afterthought to the foundation of the Assemblies of God, it is really a church with a distinctive doctrinal and governmental policy. It now has its own statement of faith, in sixteen articles, which verbally seems not to differ much from that of other Pentecostal bodies, but in practice has strictly followed the principle set down by its founder, John C. Sinclair, who taught that the Bible alone is sufficient for Christian belief and practice. Parallel with its doctrinal liberalism, the church also permits ordination with minimum creedal requirements and allows remarriage after divorce with more freedom than obtains in more conservative Pentecostal bodies. The church is centered in Joplin, Missouri, and has little administrative organization, except for a general superintendent and secretary.

Pentecostal Assemblies of the World. This group is not very large numerically but historically it represents a milestone in the development of American Pentecostalism.

At the time of the First World War, as Pentecostal organizations were being founded, they were faced with the critical problem of deciding whether true baptism must be in the name of Jesus only, or in the name of the entire Trinity. This issue split the movement into two factions, and the Pentecostal movement in the United States cannot be understood without taking stock of this basic cleavage.

The first significant group to go Unitarian was the Pentecostal Assemblies of the World. The date of its actual beginning is obscure. It certainly came into being after the fourth general council of the Assemblies of God in St. Louis in 1916, at which the *Statement of Fundamental Truths* was drafted. The opposition argues that the charter conference two years before had declared that the Scriptures alone are "all sufficient rule for faith and practice." Now a man-made creed was being proposed. Out of the conflict, the Assemblies of God immerged staunchly Trinitarian, but the "oneness" faction left the council to form its own Pentecostal Assembly of the World. Central offices are still in Indianapolis, where G. T. Hayward, a leading Negro evangelist, had already started a powerful "Jesus only" congregation.

United Pentecostal Church. The newly formed Pentecostal Assemblies of the World held together for about ten years.

In 1924 the white constituents withdrew on the grounds that interracial membership hindered their efforts in evangelism. They called the succeeding body simply the Pentecostal Church, Inc. Most of its affiliation was clustered on both sides of the Mississippi.

In 1931 a large number of independent Unitarian Pentecostals from the Mid-Atlantic and North Central states decided to form their own national society, the Pentecostal Assemblies of Jesus Christ.

It soon became apparent that since both federations had so much in common they could profitably coalesce. At its annual conference in 1934, the Pentecostal Assemblies of Jesus Christ approached their counterpart about a merger. It came into effect the following year at St. Louis as the United Pentecostal Church.

Unexpectedly for a religious group that was strongly congregational, this Unitarian segment of American Pentecostals has a well-developed central organization. This gives the church leaders access to all the resources on the local level and the freedom to use them in the interests of the common good. In the same spirit all the major activities of the church —missions, religious education, and publication—are placed under the jurisdiction of the general board, which directs denominational activities from St. Louis, Missouri.

In keeping with its general Unitarian policy, the United Pentecostal Church forbids baptism in the name of the Trinity. Instead, "water baptism . . . must be administered in the name of the Lord Jesus Christ, as consistently taught in the Bible."[5] Jesus Christ is declared to be the only person in the Godhead.[6]

The International Church of the Foursquare Gospel. This church was the creation of Mrs. (Sister) Aimee Semple McPherson, who at the age of seventeen was converted by her Baptist evangelist husband and became a preacher by divine revelation. A woman of striking appearance, dramatic ability, and adept in crowd psychology, Aimee McPherson managed to turn even alleged scandals to her own advantage. Thrice married, she used the names of her first and second husbands, omitting the third (David Hutton). After extensive travels in the Orient with Robert Semple, she settled in Los

Angeles in 1918; there years later she founded the Echo
Park Evangelistic Association and built the large Angelus
Temple. In 1927 she organized her thousands of followers
in the International Church of the Foursquare Gospel. At
her death the office of president passed on to her son, Rolf.
Though the church is less dramatic now than it was during
the lifetime of the foundress, it still attracts a large following.
Rallies and assemblies have replaced the pageants and lighting effects of Mrs. McPherson. Young people are banded into
Crusaders, and all are required to accept the Declaration of
Faith written by the first president. Foreign missions and
Bible colleges are established in ten countries, with a concentration in Latin America. Fundamentalist in doctrine, the
Declaration of Faith professes Spirit baptism following conversion, the gift of tongues and their interpretation, eternal
punishment for the wicked, and the power to heal in answer
to confident prayer. A radio station, KFSG, broadcasts from
Los Angeles.

Minor Pentecostal Groups. It is impossible to give a complete coverage of all the smaller Pentecostal bodies in the
United States. Their number is large and their variety so
complex as to defy classification. Moreover, they are often
short-lived organizations, or single congregations that rise and
disappear with bewildering frequency. Most of them are not
listed in any standard catalogue of American religious bodies.

A convenient way of reviewing these groups is to divide
them into regional, ethnic, and cultic societies, with obvious
overlapping.

One of the earliest charismatic churches came out of a
Baptist background in Kentucky. In 1903 the Church of God
of Ryan's Creek was formed in eastern Kentucky after ouster
by the United Baptists for preaching that a person can be
lost after he had been regenerated. Eight years later the
name was changed to The Church of God of the Mountain Assembly, with permanent central offices in Jellico,
Tennessee.

A similar organization came into being at Nicholson, Georgia, in 1918, when a group from the Pentecostal Holiness
Church quarreled with the parent body over the wearing of
ornaments and elaborate dress. The Pentecostal Fire-Baptized

Holiness Church prescribes simplicity of dress, and forbids association between the sexes, foolish talking, attendance at fairs, use of swimming pools, and the wearing of anything worldly, including jewelry and neckties. At the same time, spontaneity in worship is encouraged, so that loud shouting, crying, and hand clapping frequently punctuate the church services. An unusual doctrinal accent is the belief that sanctification follows baptism by the Holy Spirit, and speaking in other tongues comes only after sanctification.

In 1920 a large section of the Georgia Pentecostal Holiness Church separated, over the question of divine healing, to form the Congregational Holiness Church. Until the schism, the Georgia conference believed it was unnecessary to use human means of therapy besides the divine powers of the Spirit. The majority disagreed, claiming that God wants people to use ordinary means for restoring health and only then to look for miracles. This majority formed the Congregational Holiness Church not only to protect its doctrinal belief but also to ensure strict fidelity to a demanding code of morals. In addition to other restrictions, this faction also forbids membership in secret societies, playing games of chance, drinking alcoholic beverages, and attending any public place of entertainment. Membership is scattered through the Carolinas, Alabama, Georgia, and Virginia, with missions in Cuba and Nigeria.

John Stroup founded the Pentecostal Church of Christ in 1917 when a group of ministers in Kentucky joined him in preaching Holy Spirit baptism and Pentecostal experience. It is typical of so many other charismatic bodies in seeking to join fellowship with the larger Pentecostal churches.

The Elim Missionary Assemblies were established in 1947 and they illustrate a phenomenon that is common among the smaller denominations. Their foundation grew out of a desire of the graduates of an independent Pentecostal school —Elim Bible Institute—to start a new church. Confined mainly to New York and Pennsylvania, they are unique in the number of missionaries they have overseas, one to every ten church members at home.

It is not surprising that Pentecostalism became stratified along national and ethnic lines from the beginning of its

American development. The main division was between Negroes and white, but other segments divided on a language
basis, as among Spaniards and Italians in the large urban
centers of the country.

As early as 1908 the Fire-Baptized Holiness Church of God
of the Americas departed from the predominantly white Fire-
Baptized Holiness Association of America. The Negro minority said they were leaving to form a new church because of
"the growing prejudice that began to arise." By 1922 the
colored faction was joined by another Holiness church from
Knoxville, Kentucky, at which time the present title of the
church was adopted. There is nothing doctrinally distinctive
about the Fire-Baptized Pentecostals except their strong opposition to "the teaching of the so-called Christian Scientists,
Spiritualists, Unitarians, Universalists, and Mormons."

Another Pentecostal Association began as a Negro offshoot
of the Apostolic Faith Mission. It was started by W. P. Phillips
in Alabama in 1916 as the Ethiopian Overcoming Holy Church
of God. When Phillips quarreled with other church leaders,
he left to form a group of his own. In 1927 he changed the
word Ethiopian to Apostolic in the official title. Religious
services in the Apostolic Overcoming Holy Church of God
are free emotional affairs that unfriendly critics have called
bizarre, with participants speaking in a babel of tongues and
engaging in ecstatic dances. Their songs are spirituals; rhythm
is essential, with drums, tambourines, stomping of feet, and
the clapping of hands to accompany the ritual of the presiding
minister.

The latest feature of American Pentecostalism has been its
ecumenical outreach, not only among traditional Protestants
but also in some quarters of Catholicism.

Pentecostal ministers are available to congregations or interested groups who desire their services. Unexpectedly those
who are attracted by this form of Protestantism are not only
the socially disadvantaged. University students and faculty
members are drawn to experiment with Spirit baptism and
in many cases are deeply affected by what they find.

Commentators on the religious movements in the country
point out that Pentecostals offer what other more sedate
churches have failed to give their people: a sense of the

sacred and a realization of God's saving grace in those who believe. Not unlike the situation that gave rise to modern Pentecostalism, as Christianity becomes overly intellectual and lacking in concern for basic human needs, it creates new forms that promise personal experience to the faithful and the benefit of divine assistance in visible signs.

Presbyterians

Unlike the Baptists, whose name is derived from the stress on a single ritual practice, or the Lutherans, who are named after their founder, the Presbyterians are called after the principal characteristic of their form of Church government. Their name is a doctrinal synthesis in one word, born of the historical issues out of which the church arose as a distinct denomination.

In contrast to other churches, Presbyterianism is an ecclesiastical system in which ultimate authority on earth is not vested in one person, the Pope, as in Roman Catholicism; or in the bishops, as in Episcopalianism; or in the local congregation, as in Congregationalism—but in a group of persons representing a number of churches, and called the presbytery. This approach looks upon the visible church as an institutional society; Church government is entrusted to a highly structured, quasi-democratic organization, in which delegates from the various congregations represent the highest authority in spiritual matters.

HISTORY

John Calvin is commonly regarded as the founder of Presbyterianism. However, it would be more correct to say that he originated a theological system out of which developed the Huguenots in France, the Dutch Reformed Church in Holland, and the Presbyterians in Scotland and America. Calvin was born at Noyon in Picardy, France, July 10, 1509, and died at Geneva, May 27, 1564. Contrary to popular opinion, he never met Luther, although Lutheran books and teachers undoubtedly influenced his departure from the Catholic faith in 1533, after he had given up the study of law to prepare for the ministry. In 1536, Calvin published the *Institutes of the Christian Religion,* which to this day remains the most authoritative exposition of Protestant theology. The same year he went to Geneva where he stayed two years until banished for attempting to exclude public sinners from the Communion table. After three years' exile, he returned to establish a stronghold of moral rigorism in Geneva. Here in 1553 Michael Servetus was executed for denying the Trinity, and within sixty years, 150 people were burnt for witchcraft. Calvin's attitude toward his former coreligionists is summarized in a letter he wrote to Somerset, the English Regent, during the minority of Edward VI. In his viewpoint, Separatists and Romanists were equally to be resisted by the civil law.

The link between Calvin and American Presbyterianism is John Knox (c. 1515–72), an ex-priest who because of his implication in the death of Cardinal Beaton was a prisoner on the galleys for nineteen months. After release, during his travels on the continent, he met Calvin and lived at Geneva under his direction for three years. When he returned to Scotland, Knox was instrumental in having Queen Mary Stuart dethroned and Presbyterianism established as the state religion by an act of the Scottish Parliament in 1560. Meanwhile the Puritans in England had adopted Calvinist principles, while favoring a congregational form of government. In 1643, the Westminster Assembly of divines, called by a Puritan English Parliament, met to resolve the struggle over the compulsory use of the Anglican Book of Common Prayer. After five years' session, the Assembly produced a Larger and Shorter Catechism, a Directory of Worship, a Form of Government, and, most important, the Westminster Confession of Faith, which became the doctrinal standard of Scottish, British, and American Presbyterianism.

Presbyterianism in the United States had three origins, all due to migrations from Europe. In 1623 the Dutch settled in New York as members of the Calvinist Reformed Church; in 1629 the Puritan refugees from England landed in Massachusetts at Salem, and although they first merged with the Pilgrims to form the Congregational Church, eventually many of them changed their allegiance and became Presbyterians; and in 1685 Ulster men, or Scotch-Irish, arrived in New Jersey and Pennsylvania under the leadership of Francis Makemie, "the father of American Presbyterianism." Before

Makemie's time, Presbyterians were to be found scattered throughout the colonies, but without having over them any presbytery, which is essential to the Calvinist ecclesiastical system. To Makemie goes the credit of organizing in 1706, at Freehold, New Jersey, the first presbytery, and thus establishing the Church as a corporate entity in America. Between 1705 and 1775, about 500,000 Scotch-Irish arrived in America to swell the ranks of American Presbyterianism in New Jersey, Pennsylvania, Maryland, Virginia, and the Carolinas.

The first milestone in American Presbyterianism was the Adopting Act of 1729, which decided that every minister and candidate for the ministry had to declare the Calvinist Westminster Confession and the Larger and Shorter Catechisms "in all essentials and necessary articles, good forms of sound words and systems of Christian doctrine."[1] This was approved over the protests of those who questioned the Trinity and the divinity of Christ. To satisfy the latter, the concession was made that if any minister had scruples about any parts of these standards, he should propose them to the synod, which would then decide whether his difficulties involved anything "essential" that would warrant his exclusion.

There was a temporary break in Presbyterian unity from 1741 to 1758 over conflicting interpretations of "essential and necessary articles" of faith in the Westminster Confession. The matter was settled by expunging the controversial phrase "essential and necessary articles." Instead, candidates for the ministry were to be examined as to their "experimental acquaintance with religion."[2] This amity lasted until 1810, when the Cumberland Presbytery seceded to form a separate denomination, known as the Cumberland Presbyterian Church. Its grievance was the Calvinist doctrine on predestination, which was rejected as "fantastic." Although a partial reunion took place in 1906, the Cumberland Presbyterian Church continues its autonomous existence in two segments: the Cumberland Presbyterian Church for the whites, and the Colored Cumberland Presbyterian Church.

Another temporary schism, lasting thirty years (1837–69), divided the Presbyterian Church into the Old School and the New School, the former rejecting the Plan of Union with the

Congregationalists. The issue at stake was acceptance or rejection of "the novelties of New England [Congregational] theology."

In 1857, a more serious and lasting split took place over the slavery question. In that year several Southern synods withdrew to form the United Synod of the Presbyterian Church. They were joined eight years later by forty-seven Southern presbyteries, called the General Assembly of the Presbyterian Church in the Confederate States of America. The new merger (1865) became known as the Presbyterian Church in the United States, and has remained separated from the parent body to this day. Frequently called the Southern Presbyterian Church, its doctrinal position is notably conservative and the membership is mostly urban. Efforts have been made to reunite this body with the Northern segment, one as late as 1955, but adoption of the merger failed. Following the general pattern in the South, the Presbyterian Church in the United States has segregated Negro churches; these are organized into separate presbyteries, and are made up exclusively of Negro clergy and laity.

The Northern denomination retained the name of the Presbyterian Church in the U.S.A., adopted in 1821, and has the reputation of being more tolerant of theological liberalism. Its latest Confession of Faith was a landmark in the development of Calvinist theology in modern times.

Merger plans were completed for an absorption of the United Presbyterian Church of North America by the Presbyterian Church, U.S.A., before the end of 1958. No change of doctrinal position or ecclesiastical structure was involved. Except for a fusion of personnel and a prefix to the title, United Presbyterian Church in the U.S.A., the new denomination carries on the liberal tradition of Northern Presbyterianism.

Parallel with the rise of the two main segments of American Presbyterianism, a variety of smaller groups came into being, some reaching back to colonial times.

A secessionist body within the Church of Scotland, organized in 1733, is the ancestor of the Associate Presbyterian Church of North America. Scottish missionaries founded the Associate Presbytery in 1754, which in 1782 merged with the Reformed Presbytery. Reacting against the merger, the

Associate Presbytery in Pennsylvania became a separate church. The Associate Synod of North America came into existence after other presbyteries joined the Pennsylvania section. In 1858 another merger was made, this time with the Associate Reformed Presbyterian Church of North America. The majority joined the Associate Reformed Presbyterians to form the United Presbyterian Church of North America. A minority refused to enter the merger and continued instead as the Associate Presbyterian Church of North America.

While the polity of the Associate Presbyterians does not differ substantially from other churches in that same tradition, its policy is more demanding. Restricted Communion, expulsion of members who join secret orders, and the exclusive use of psalms are typically distinctive features.

The Cumberland Presbyterian Church was born in 1810 in Dickson County, Tennessee. Those who organized the new church were dissatisfied with the doctrine of predestination in the Westminster Confession of Faith and unwilling to accept the demands for extensive education of the clergy in the frontier regions of America. A century later (1906), the Cumberland Presbyterians were only partially successful in reuniting with the Presbyterian Church, U.S.A. National headquarters are in Memphis. After the Civil War (1871), the Negro segment of the Cumberland body formed a separate denomination. It accepted the Westminster Confession with a number of strong reservations, notably the denial of eternal punishment and universal redemption.

Another Scottish derivative, the Reformed Presbyterian Church of North America, traces its lineage to the Covenanters in Europe. Its first minister came to this country in 1752, but the synod was not constituted until 1809. By 1833 it split into two segments, the Old Light and the New Light, in a quarrel over citizenship. The Old Light faction forbade its members to vote or participate generally in public affairs. This is the present Reformed Presbyterian Church of North America (Old School). The New Light group allowed its members to vote and hold public office. As the Reformed Presbyterian Church in North America (General Synod), they followed the Westminster standards and strict Presbyterian polity.

In 1965 the Reformed Presbyterian Church in North America (General Synod) joined with the Evangelical Presbyterian Church to produce the Reformed Presbyterian Church, Evangelical Synod. The Evangelical Presbyterians acquired this name four years earlier after changing it from the Bible Presbyterian Church in protest against Carl McIntire, who in 1956 had organized a rival Bible Presbyterian Church. He had broken away (1937) from the Orthodox Presbyterian Church, which he considered modernistic. Later on he became head of the American Council of Christian Churches, in protest against the National Council of the Churches of Christ.

DOCTRINE

It is comparatively easy to analyze Presbyterian doctrine because the Church professes to have a creed. "Some denominations have none; but Presbyterian elders, ruling or teaching, accept at ordination the Westminster 'Confession of Faith' as 'the system of doctrine taught in the Holy Scriptures.' "[3] An appraisal of the Westminster Confession, therefore, will give us a substantially accurate picture of the doctrinal mentality of American Presbyterians, with one important reservation since the Presbyterian Church in the U.S.A. has considerably modified the Westminster formulary. These modifications will be noted, while omitting such doctrines as the Trinity and the Incarnation, which are substantially the same as in Reformation Christianity.

Of special significance are the developments reflected in the 1967 Confession of the United Presbyterian Church in the United States of America. It would be a mistake to suppose that the new Confession essentially changed any of the doctrines in the great Reformed creedal documents. In fact, the new Confession explicitly states that the United Presbyterians are guided by: the Scots Confession, the Heidelberg Catechism, and the Second Helvetic Confession from the era of the Reformation; the Westminster Confession and the Shorter Catechism from the seventeenth century; and the Theological Declaration of Barmen from the twentieth century. All these statements of faith remain normative for the Church. Among these, however, the Westminster Confession is still the most distinctive.

Where the Confession of 1967 reflects any modification of the Westminster formulary, this will be indicated.

The Church is conceived in two ways. As "the catholic or universal Church, which is invisible, [it] consists of the whole number of the elect," whereas "the visible Church, which is also catholic or universal under the gospel—not confined to one nation, as before under the law—consists of all those throughout the world that profess the true religion, together with their children, and is the Kingdom of the Lord Jesus Christ."[4] Then to make a clear distinction between itself and the Roman Catholic Church, it is stated that "There is no other head of the Church but the Lord Jesus Christ. Nor can the pope of Rome in any sense be head thereof; but is that anti-christ, that man of sin, and son of perdition, that exalteth himself, in the Church, against Christ, and all that is called God."[5] This passage was revised by the Northern Presbyterians in 1903 during the pontificate of St. Pius X; the direct reference to the Pope was deleted and the new version reads: ". . . the claim of any man to be the vicar of Christ and the head of the Church, is unscriptural, without warrant in fact, and is a usurpation dishonoring to the Lord Jesus Christ."[6] The latest revision of the Presbyterian creed has not changed this wording.

Predestination, regarded as the keystone of Calvin's theology, has been the focus of practically every doctrinal schism since the origin of Presbyterianism. We should therefore expect radical changes in the expression of this doctrine. Actually, a compromise has been reached, as in the Presbyterian Church in the U.S.A., which retained Calvin's teaching verbally intact in the body of the Confession, and then added an appendix to soften its implication. As found in the Confession, we read that "By the decree of God, for the manifestation of his glory, some men and angels are predestined unto everlasting life, and others foreordained to everlasting death."[7] Lest there be any doubt about the latter, it is further declared that no others are "redeemed by Christ, effectually called, justified, adopted, sanctified, and saved but the elect only. The rest of mankind, God was pleased, according to the unsearchable counsel of his own will . . . to ordain them to dishonor and wrath for their sin, to the praise of his glorious justice."[8] But in 1903 the Presbyterian Church in the U.S.A. added an interpretation which modified the foregoing rigid predestinarianism. "Concerning those who perish," it said, "the doctrine of God's eternal decree is held in harmony with the doctrine that God desires not the death of any sinner, but has provided in Christ a salvation sufficient for all . . . men are fully responsible for their treatment of God's gracious offer . . . his decree hinders no man from accepting that offer . . . no man is condemned except on the ground of his sin."[9]

The United Presbyterian Church further qualified the Calvinism inherent in the Westminster Confession in the new Confession of Faith published three hundred and twenty years later. In several passages, the Church affirms its belief in God's universal salvific will and in man's duty to respond freely to the voice of God.

> The risen Christ is the savior for all men. Those joined to him by faith are set right with God and commissioned to serve as his reconciling community.
>
> The same Jesus Christ is the judge of all men . . . All who put their trust in Christ face divine judgment without fear, for the judge is their redeemer.
>
> Man is free to seek his life within the purpose of God: to develop and protect the resources of nature for the common welfare, to work for justice and peace in society, and in other ways to use its creative powers for the fulfillment of human life.
>
> The gift of God in Christ is for all men. The Church, therefore, is commissioned to carry the gospel to all men whatever their religion may be and even when they profess none.[10]

Sacraments are defined as "holy signs and seals of the covenant of grace," but not in the Catholic sense of conferring grace by their intrinsic efficacy.[11] Only two sacraments are recognized: baptism and the Lord's Supper. The first is administered by immersion, pouring, or sprinkling, together with the invocation of the Trinity. Unlike Baptists, Presbyterians hold that "infants of one or both believing parents are to be baptized."[12] And though it is regarded a sin to contemn this sacrament, "yet grace and salvation are not so inseparably annexed unto it as that no person can be regenerated or saved without it."[13] To clarify the lot of those who die without baptism before reaching the age of reason, the Presbyterian Church in the U.S.A. added the following: "We believe that all dying in infancy are included in the election of grace, and are regenerated and saved by Christ, through the Spirit, who works when and where and how he pleases."[14] It is assumed that death in infancy is an infallible sign of salvation, whether the child is baptized or not.

The concept of the Lord's Supper is the same as Calvin's, with no modification in any of the modern Confessions. Christ is said to be only represented in the sacrament, so that even after the "prayer of consecration" the elements, "in substance and nature . . . still remain truly and only, bread and wine, as they were before."[15] In keeping with the Calvinist tradition, the Sacrifice of the Mass, as offered by the Catholic Church, is called "most abominably injurious to Christ's one only sacrifice."[16]

As a commentary on the Westminster Confession of Faith, the latest creedal document of the Northern Presbyterians does not substantially change the traditional doctrine.

> The Lord's Supper is a celebration of the reconciliation of men with God and with one another, in which they joyfully eat and drink together at the table of their Savior. Jesus Christ gave his church this remembrance of his dying for sinful men so that by participation in it they have communion with him and with all who shall be gathered to him. Partaking in him as they eat the bread and drink the wine in accordance with Christ's appointment, they receive from the risen and living Lord the benefits of his death and resurrection. They rejoice in the foretaste of the kingdom which he will bring to consummation at his promised coming, and go out from the Lord's Table with courage and hope for the service to which he has called them.[17]

Marriage is not considered to be a sacrament. Nevertheless Christians are reminded that they have a duty "to marry in the Lord." Consequently, "such as profess the true reformed religion should not marry with infidels, Papists, or other idolaters."[18] In 1953, the Presbyterian Church in the U.S.A. completely modified the Westminster Confession on marriage, removing all reference to "infidels, Papists, or other idolaters."

In the basic Westminster creed, divorce with remarriage is allowed for "adultery, or such willful desertion as can in no way be remedied by Church or civil magistrates," which are considered "sufficient of dissolving the bond of marriage."[19] The Presbyterian Church in the U.S.A. professed this doctrine as late as 1939. But in 1953 a revision was made, laying down no restrictive conditions beyond declaring that ". . . remarriage after a divorce granted on grounds explicitly stated in Scripture or implicit in the gospel of Christ may be sanctioned in keeping with his redemptive gospel, when sufficient penitence for sin and failure is evident, and a firm purpose of an endeavor after Christian marriage is manifest."[20]

FORM OF GOVERNMENT

The organizational system of the Presbyterian Church most clearly distinguishes it from other Protestant denominations. And just as the doctrines of faith are substantially embodied in the Westminster Confession, so the essentials of the Church's juridical structure are specified in the Form of Government, which was drawn up along with the Confession by the Westminster Assembly in 1647. Since all Presbyterian bodies follow the same general pattern, our analysis will be confined to the Form of Government presently in use by the Presbyterian Church in the U.S.A.

Officers in the Church. Three grades of church officials are recognized: bishops or pastors, ruling elders, and deacons. First in dignity is the pastor, who is given no less than eight titles, depending on the aspect from which his office is considered. "As he has the oversight of the flock of Christ, he is termed bishop. As he feeds them with spiritual food, he is termed pastor. As he serves Christ in his Church, he is termed minister. As it is his duty to be grave and prudent, and an example of the flock, and to govern well in the house and Kingdom of Christ, he is termed presbyter or elder. As he is the messenger of God, he is termed the angel of the Church. As he is sent to declare the will of God to sinners, and to beseech them to be reconciled to God through Christ, he is termed ambassador. And, as he dispenses the manifold grace of God, and the ordinances instituted by Christ, he is termed steward of the mysteries of God."[21] Under all these names, however, the pastor has only one essential function, that of *teaching* the word of God.

Next in dignity are the ruling elders, who are "properly the representatives of the people, chosen by them for the purpose of exercising government and discipline."[22] Thus the Presbyterian Church has two kinds of elders, the teaching and the ruling, so that every congregation duly constituted has a pastor, or teaching elder, and a group of ruling elders. Both types are specially ordained to their office. However, the essential element is their previous election to this office by the laity of the congregation, and "a Presbyterian church" may be defined as "a church with a representative form of government by elders elected by the people."[23]

Last in rank are the deacons, "whose business it is to take care of the poor and to distribute among them the collections which may be raised for their use. To them also may be properly committed the management of the temporal affairs of the Church."[24] Deacons must also be elected before ordination.

In order to provide workers in the ministry who are not forthcoming from the ordained, Presbyterian polity allows the laity to become preachers in the local churches, normally for a period of three years which may be renewed, and without the duty of ordination. Both men and women are eligible for lay preachership, the sole condition being their acceptance by the presbytery after declaring, among other things, that they "believe the Scriptures of the Old and New Testaments to be the Word of God, the only infallible rule of faith and practice."[25]

Governing Bodies. There are four hierarchical levels in the church organization: session, presbytery, synod, and general assembly, each with clearly defined functions and specific directors.

The local church, in Presbyterian parlance, is called a session, and "consists of the pastor or co-pastor and ruling elders of a particular congregation."[26] Ordinarily the pastor is moderator of the local session, which has the right to admit and dismiss members, "to admonish, to rebuke, to suspend or exclude from the sacraments," and, in general, "to concert the best measures for promoting the spiritual interests of the congregation."[27]

Next in authority and so distinctive that it denominates the whole church is the presbytery, "which consists of all the ministers, in number not less than five, and one ruling elder from each congregation, within a certain district."[28] Presbyteries are usually organized on a geographical basis, but some exist to take care of separate language groups or racial minorities within a larger area. Although there are still two grades of jurisdiction technically higher than the presbytery, the latter is, for practical purposes, the principal governmental body in Presbyterianism, having "power to receive and issue all appeals, complaints and references that are regularly brought before it from church sessions . . . to examine and license candidates for the holy ministry; to ordain, install, remove, and judge ministers; to examine and approve or censure the records of church sessions; to resolve questions of doctrine or discipline seriously and reasonably proposed; to condemn erroneous opinions which injure the purity or peace of the Church; to visit particular churches, for the purpose of inquiring into their state and redressing the evils that may have arisen in them; to unite or divide congregations, at the request of the people, or to form or receive new congregations, and, in general, to order whatever pertains to the spiritual welfare of the churches under their care."[29]

As presbyteries grow in number, they are united into synods, with at least three presbyteries to each synod. Membership in the synod is by election among the presbyteries, with equal representation of pastors and ruling elders. In general, the function of the synod bears the same relation to the presbytery as the latter does to the session. It meets at least once a year to decide on such varied issues as erection of new presbyteries, passing judgment on appeals and complaints, and settling all questions submitted to it "that do not affect the doctrine or constitution of the Church."[30]

At the highest juridical level stands the General Assembly, which consists of an equal delegation of pastors and elders from each presbytery. Like the synod, it meets once a year to make decisions "in all controversies respecting doctrine and discipline," in any church, presbytery, or synod. It may erect new synods, divide old ones, and especially has the right of "corresponding with foreign Churches [and] of suppressing schismatical contentions and disputations."[31]

A striking example of the Assembly's suppression of schismatical contentions was the action which the Presbyterian Church in the U.S.A. took in 1936 against two of its ministers, Carl McIntire, who was later to become the president of the International Council of Churches, and J. Gresham Machen, founder of the Presbyterian Church in America, a group which called themselves Orthodox Presbyterians after an injunction was brought against their use of the former name. According to his account, McIntire was ousted by the General Assembly for opposing his church's theological liberalism and compromise with Christian fundamentals. The Assembly declared it found him guilty of "advocating rebellion against the constituted authorities of the Church."[32] After a series of legal battles, McIntire lost his parish property, but the parishioners sided with their pastor and renounced the jurisdiction of the denomination. The late Machen established his church with a strong emphasis on the infallibility of the Bible, original sin, the Virgin Birth, divinity, sacrificial atonement, and the resurrection of Christ. Doctrinal disputes with Machen led McIntire to split with his former professor and found a church of his own, the Bible Presbyterian Synod.

One of the striking features of Northern Presbyterian polity is their growing interest in the church's social involvement in the world. The 1967 Confession of the United Presbyterians, for the first time in American Presbyterian history, incorporated into its creedal position a strong commitment to the Christian apostolate.

Thus God is said to have created the peoples of the earth

to be one universal family. In His reconciling love He is said to overcome the barriers between brothers and to break down every form of discrimination based on racial or ethnic differences, real or imaginary.

The church is called to bring all men to receive and uphold one another as persons in all relationships of life: in employment, housing, education, leisure, marriage, family, church, and the exercise of political rights. Therefore the church labors for the abolition of all racial discrimination and ministers to those injured by it. Congregations, individuals, or groups of Christians who exclude, dominate, or patronize their fellowmen, however subtly, resist the Spirit of God and bring contempt on the faith which they profess.[33]

RITUAL AND WORSHIP

The ritual of the Presbyterian Church in all denominations is fundamentally the same, and is founded on the Directory for the Worship of God composed by the Westminster Assembly in the seventeenth century. In keeping with the spirit of Calvin and Knox, and their theological presuppositions, the Presbyterian order of worship is markedly grave and restrained. Thus, says the Directory, "in time of public worship, let all the people attend with gravity and reverence."[34] When beginning public worship, it is declared fitting to adore "the infinite majesty of the living God, expressing a sense of our distance from him as creatures, and unworthiness as sinners, and humbly imploring his gracious presence."[35]

However, a liturgical revival is taking place, with a growing sense of the need for reform, if not to restore the ritual splendor of the Church of antiquity, at least to introduce many elements that go beyond the Calvinistic tradition. Accordingly a new Book of Common Worship was drawn up for American Presbyterians, after years of sifting and compilation from many sources. Looking to the improvement of Presbyterian worship, the liturgical movement "seeks . . . not only to provide the minister with the treasures in thought and expression that are the inheritance of the Church, but to encourage Christian congregations to more active participation in Christian worship, which was the custom in the Early Church."[36] The whole ritual setup has been recast. Following the Anglican tradition, a lectionary was added, giving two sets of readings from Scripture, for the morning and evening of each Sunday and feast day of the year: from the Psalms, the Old Testament, the gospels, and the epistles. Four new forms of public worship for morning and evening were added. Three orders (rites) for Holy Communion are now provided. An order for giving Communion to the sick has been included. Important changes were made in the ritual for baptism of infants and adults, though retaining the Trinitarian formula in each case. An alternate ritual for administering the Lord's Supper was provided, removing the repetition of the words of institution and only once, as in the Roman Missal, pronouncing over the bread and wine the prayer of consecration: "This is My Body . . . This cup is the New Covenant in My blood."[37] However, both services still enjoin that "after the celebration, reverent disposition of the Elements which remain shall be made by the Minister and Elders."[38]

A typical development was the order for the celebration of Holy Communion for the sick. The minister enters the sickroom and pronounces the Invitation: "Beloved in the Lord, hear what gracious words our Savior Christ saith unto all who truly turn to Him, 'Come unto Me, all ye that labor and are heavy laden, and I will give you rest . . . I am the Bread of Life, he that cometh to Me shall never hunger.'" Then the minister uncovers the elements and proceeds to repeat the words of institution from St. Paul's letter to the Corinthians. He quotes Christ's command, "Take, eat: this is My Body, which is broken for you . . . This cup is the new covenant in My Blood: do ye, as oft as ye drink it, in remembrance of Me."

Before the minister gives the elements to the sick person, he prays at some length and concludes by repeating the words of institution separately over the bread and cup, first communicates himself, and then administers Communion to the sick person. He concludes with two prayers that are familiar from pre-Reformation liturgy.

We thank Thee, O God, for Thy great mercy given to us in this Sacrament, whereby we are made partakers of Christ. So enrich us by the Holy Spirit that the life of Jesus may be made manifest in us, and the remainder of our days may be spent in Thy love and service.

O Lord, holy Father, by whose loving-kindness our souls and bodies are renewed: Mercifully look upon this Thy servant, that, every cause of sickness being removed, *he* may be restored to soundness of health; through Jesus Christ our Lord. *Amen.*[39]

Along with a comprehensive change in the ritual there has been a revision in congregational singing, always an essential part of Protestant worship. A co-operative Hymnbook was published by the Northern and Southern Presbyterians, the United Presbyterian and the Reformed Churches, representing 95 per cent of American Presbyterianism. Although "there is some question whether the melange has the integrity of any one of the participants' own tradition," the hymnal is looked upon as a "portent" of greater unity among Presbyterian denominations.

Quakers

For three centuries the Society of Friends, or Quakers, has exerted an influence on American thought out of all proportion to its numbers—less than a quarter million. It is not sufficient to explain this influence superficially by pointing to outstanding Quakers like William Penn, John Greenleaf Whittier, Herbert Hoover, or Whittaker Chambers. A more likely explanation was suggested by the philosopher William James, who considered the Quaker religion "something which it is impossible to overpraise" because it is rooted in "spiritual inwardness." So that, "as our Christian sects are evolving, they are simply reverting in essence to the position which . . . the early Quakers so long ago assumed."[1]

More than any other offspring of the Reformation, the Quakers have consistently applied the principle of private interpretation and independence of ecclesiastical authority. There is even a question of whether they should properly be called Protestants. They prefer to call themselves "a 'third way' of Christians" emphasizing fundamentals differently from Roman Catholics and Protestants. Roman Catholics emphasize Church authority, the hierarchy, and an absolute creed. Protestant denominations emphasize one or another interpretation of religion as found in the Holy Bible. But the Society of Friends puts its mark on religion as a fellowship of the Spirit."[2] It is this emphasis on responsibility to God alone which is so appealing to non-Catholic Christians, who see in Quaker theology "the most protestant form of Protestantism" and the ultimate of religious autonomy.

HISTORY

The Religious Society of Friends was founded in England by George Fox (1624–91), a "restless seeking spirit" who reacted against the prevalent Anglican emphasis on ceremonial. Fox was an earnest young man whose trials and temptations disturbed his peace of mind. He sought counsel from the official guides in the Church, but without success. Finally, he records in his *Journal,* "when all my hopes in men were gone, so that I had nothing outwardly to help me, nor could I tell what to do, then, O then, I heard a voice which said, 'There is One, even Christ Jesus, that can speak to thy condition.' And when I heard it, my heart did leap for joy."[3]

Enthusiastic over the discovery of this Inner Light, in 1647 Fox began to preach to others and gradually organized a group of followers who called themselves "Children of the Light," "Friends of the Truth," or simply "Friends." Hailed into court for his opposition to the Established Church, Fox warned the judge to "tremble at the Word of God." The judge called him "Quaker" in derision at his agitation over religious matters; but the name caught the popular fancy and eventually was accepted, though never formally adopted, by the Friends.

Persecution, imprisonment, and in some cases death only served to increase the prestige of the Society and swell its numbers. Quakers came to America as early as 1655, and by 1661 were sufficiently organized to hold their first Yearly Meeting in Rhode Island. Fox's visit to the Colonies (1671–73) helped encourage the Friends to remain steadfast in spite of pressure from the churches and the civil power. Four were hanged at Boston. In the 1680s and '90s, West Jersey and Pennsylvania were established as Quaker settlements. Here Friends, under the leadership of William Penn, undertook to carry out "a holy experiment" in conducting a government on New Testament principles.

The charter of Pennsylvania, granted to William Penn in 1681, gave him the opportunity to try out the "holy experiment" of a haven for his fellow Quakers and other persecuted persons on a large scale, and to undertake at the same time a promising business venture.

Penn's preface to the Frame of Government of 1682 summarized some of his basic concepts about civil government. He was unembarrassed about interweaving religious ideas and political theory.

Government seems to me a part of religion itself, a thing sacred in its institution and end . . . They weakly err, that think there is no other use of government than correction, which is the coarsest part of it; daily experience tells us, that the care and regulation of many other affairs, more soft, and daily necessary, make up much of the greatest part of government; and which must have followed the peopling of the world, had Adam never fell, and will continue among men, on earth, under the highest attainments they may arrive at, by the coming of the Second Adam, the Lord from heaven.

I know what is said by the several admirers of monarchy, aristocracy and democracy, which are the rule of one, the few, and many, and are the three common ideas of government when men discourse on the subject. But I choose to solve the controversy with this small distinction, and it belongs to all three: Any government is free to the people under it [whatever be the frame] where the laws rule and the people are a party to those laws, and more than this is tyranny, oligarchy, or confusion.[4]

Faithful to these convictions, the Quakers remained in political control in Pennsylvania until 1756, at which time they preferred to give up their seats in the Assembly rather than vote in favor of war against the Shawnee and Delaware Indians.

The same pacifist spirit kept most Quakers from active participation in the American Revolution. As early as 1800, their hatred of "traffic in the bodies of men" forbade membership in the Society to sellers or purchasers of slaves. Since the Civil War, they have taken a leading part in protecting and promoting the education of Negroes. During the First and Second World Wars, and since, the American Friends Service Committee has been doing welfare and reconstruction work on a wide scale, including the staffing of hospitals, plowing fields and driving ambulances in wartime, famine relief and child-feeding programs in Serbia, Poland, and Russia, allocation and housing of refugees. In 1947 the American Friends Service Committee and the Friends Service Council (London) were jointly awarded the Nobel Peace Prize.

The long history of pacifism among the Quakers also explains their actions during the Vietnam conflict. One of the more publicized events (1967) was the voyage of the *Phoenix*, on which medical supplies were carried to North Vietnam. A Quaker Action Group from Philadelphia, knowingly acting in contravention to the federal Trading with the Enemy Act, sponsored the venture. On questioning, the group rested their case on a biblical imperative: "We recognize no boundaries," they said, "in our moral obligation and desire to heal the sick and bind the wounds of war." Later in that same year, Quaker Americans crossed the Peace Bridge from Buffalo to Fort Erie, Ontario, "on an errand of mercy to civilian victims of the Vietnamese war." Representatives of the Canadian Friends Service Committee there received a substantial contribution to their medical aid program for civilians in Vietnam—North as well as South. This, too, was in violation of federal laws. But in neither case did the American government see fit to prosecute.

Along with these external labors of charity, "outreaching" in Quaker terminology, there has been an internal disunity that is not surprising in view of the creedal freedom professed by the Society of Friends. Though all Quakers look upon George Fox as their founder, they have about the largest variety of denominations of any comparable religious group in America. To avoid ecclesiastical terminology, two generic synonyms are used for church: the term "Meeting" designates a particular Quaker body, which is qualified as "Yearly" or "Five Years," depending on the frequency of its General Conference; or a group is called "Religious Society of Friends," with an added name to distinguish it from other Friends in a different denomination.

The largest Quaker body in the United States is the "Five Years Meeting of Friends," which was formed in 1902 by the loose federation of fourteen Yearly Meetings. Headquarters are located in Richmond, Indiana. Current membership includes affiliated groups in Africa and the West Indies. In 1965 the name was changed to Friends United Meeting.

Next in size is the Religious Society of Friends, General Conference, nicknamed the Hicksites, with a central office in Philadelphia. It came into existence in 1827 as a modernist party within the Quakers under the leadership of Elias Hicks, a liberal, whose disciples were accused of denying the Trinity. They are concentrated in the Eastern and Midwestern states. In 1900 they developed into the present General Conference. Among American Quakers they symbolize the conflict between rationalism and orthodoxy, the latter based on Methodist ideas of evangelism. Their major contribution has been in the field of religious education and social welfare. In 1955 the Philadelphia Yearly Meeting joined the General Conference.

There are six Yearly Meeting denominations, identified by the state or region in which they are localized: Central in the central states, Kansas, Ohio, Oregon, Pacific, and Philadelphia. Until recently there were two Philadelphia Yearly Meetings, distinguished by the street on which their headquarters were located: Arch Street and Race Street. In 1955 they joined forces "in a single Yearly Meeting [as] an outward and visible embodiment of inner unity."[5]

DOCTRINAL POSITION

Quaker teaching is fluid and unpredictable. While broad doctrinal differences are generally determined by the spirit of a particular group, individual Quakers enjoy a maximum of freedom in matters of faith as the logical consequence of the Inner Light theory of George Fox. To know what they mean by this Light is to understand something of the essence of Quakerism, which, in spite of appearances, is only peripherally interested in social welfare and primarily concerned with man's personal relations with God.

In the writings of Quaker leaders, the Inner Light is variously called the Light Within, the Seed, the Christ Within, the Eternal Christ, the Divine Principle, and the Presence of God in Man. Used indiscriminately, these titles are drawn from the New Testament, mostly from Sts. John and Paul, and radically based on the reference in John's Prologue to "the true Light, which enlightens every man that comes into this world."[6]

No Quaker has improved on the description of this Light

given by George Fox, and all Quakers subscribe to his definition:

> The Lord God hath opened to me by His invisible power
> how that every man was enlightened by the divine Light
> of Christ; and I saw it shine through all; and they that
> believed in it came out of condemnation and came to the
> Light of Life, and became the children of it; but they that
> hated it, and did not believe in it, were condemned by it,
> though they made a profession of Christ. This I saw in the
> pure openings of the Light, without the help of any man,
> neither did I then know where to find it in the Scriptures,
> though afterwards, searching the Scriptures, I found it. For
> I saw in that Light and Spirit which was before Scripture
> was given forth, and which led the holy men of God to give
> them forth, that all must come to that Spirit—if they would
> know God or Christ or the Scriptures aright—which they
> that gave them forth were led and taught by.[7]

According to Fox, therefore, all men are naturally endowed
with a divine Light which they have only to recognize and
follow to be saved. Profession of faith in Christ is meaning-
less, says Fox, unless a man believes in this Light; and given
such faith, it matters little what else he professes to believe.
The first function of the Light is to emancipate a person from
adherence to any creed, or obedience to ecclesiastical authority, or submission to any prescribed form of worship.

Quakers are divided on the exact nature of the divine Light.
They are agreed, however, that "the Light Within is not to
be identified with conscience, which is the human faculty,
imperfect because human, through which the Light shines."[8]
It is something divine. An English contemporary of Fox described it as "a free grace of God . . . that comes from
Christ."[9] More recently, a Quaker Commission reported to the
World Conference on Faith and Order that "The main differences between ourselves and most other bodies of Christians
arise from the emphasis we place on the Light of God's Holy
Spirit in the human soul . . . This direct contact between the
Spirit of Christ and the human spirit we are prepared to trust
to, as the basis of our individual and corporate life."[10]

Over the years, Quaker belief in the Inner Light has come into conflict with practically every doctrine of traditional Christianity. As a result, many Christian concepts had to be revised, others were adapted, and not a few were simply discarded as incompatible with divine illumination.

Sacred Scriptures are highly respected. Yet they are secondary to the Inner Light. The latter is personal and constant; it also is unfailing, whereas the Bible calls for interpretation.

From these revelations of the Spirit of God to the saints have proceeded the Scriptures of truth, which contain: 1. A faithful historical account of the actings of God's people in divers ages, with many singular and remarkable providences attending them. 2. A prophetical account of several things, whereof some are already past, and some yet to come. 3. A full and ample account of all the chief principles of the doctrine of Christ, held forth in divers precious declarations, exhortations, and sentences, which, by the moving of God's Spirit, were at several times, and upon sundry occasions, spoken and written unto some churches and their pastors.

Nevertheless, because they are only a declaration of the fountain, and not the fountain itself, therefore they are not to be esteemed the principal ground of all truth and knowledge, nor yet the adequate primary rule of faith and manners.

Nevertheless, as that which giveth a true and faithful testimony of the first foundation, they are and may be esteemed a secondary rule, subordinate to the Spirit, from which they have all their excellency and certainty; for as by the inward testimony of the Spirit we do alone truly know them, so they testify that the Spirit is that guide by which the saints are led into all truth: therefore, according to the Scriptures, the Spirit is the first and principal leader. And seeing we do therefore receive and believe the Scriptures, because they proceeded from the Spirit; therefore also the Spirit is more originally and principally the rule, according to that received maxim in the schools, "That for which a thing is such, that thing itself is more such."[11]

The Church is wholly invisible, conditioned only on acceptance of the Light, and transcending the barriers of sectarian belief. It is a "great error," consequently, to "set up an outward order and uniformity and to make men's consciences bend thereto," when "the true Church government is to leave the conscience to its full liberty . . . and to seek unity in the Light and in the Spirit, walking sweetly and harmoniously together in the midst of different practices."[12]

Christ's Divinity and the Trinity are understood in various ways. An early English Quaker, Barclay, spoke of Christ as "the Mediator betwixt God and man, being Himself God, and partaking in time of the human nature."[13] The poet John Whittier regarded Christ as "the highest possible manifestation of God in man."[14] More vaguely, Rufus Jones, the prophet of American Quakerism, held that "Christ was divine" in the sense that we see "the divine possibilities of man revealed in Christ."[15] At the other extreme, there is a Quaker tradition of anti-Trinitarianism, at least in the States, which goes back to William Penn, who attacked the doctrine of the Trinity in his *Sandy Foundation Shaken* and was imprisoned as a consequence. Modern followers of Elias Hicks, in the General Conference Quakers, are openly Unitarian.

WORSHIP AND PRACTICE

Acceptance of the Light of Christ as the unique source of religious experience would seem to eliminate the need of a ministry. In practice, however, there is a ministerial office among Quakers, with two limitations: it is not a "monopoly of priestly caste through whom alone [divine grace] can be ministered to others"; and "anyone may experience 'the anointing' and, if that is known, may be called to minister to others of what God has given."[16] Hence there is no real distinction between the clergy and laity, and no ordination of ministers.

Quakers admit they are compelled "to stand apart from other communions in such matters as . . . forms of public worship, and the use of outward sacraments."[17] They do not "make use of the outward rites of Baptism and the Lord's Supper, but . . . believe in the inward experiences they symbolize." The underlying claim is "to actuality of this experience even without the external rite."[18] The usual practice is to dispense with any formal program for the Worship Meeting. Nothing is prearranged. Worshipers gather at the appointed time and just wait silently until the Spirit moves someone to speech or action. Out of this inspiration come divine communications, individual or community prayer, reading the Scriptures, testimonies of faith in the form of sermons, and even bodily healing—from anyone in the congregation. After about an hour of such worship, the assembly is closed by a general shaking of hands with one's neighbor, following the lead of the overseers, who sit on a bench facing the people during the meeting. In some Quaker societies there is a fixed program for worship, which is called a Pastoral Meeting. But this is an exception to the traditional custom.

Behind this insistence on the inwardness of Christianity is a principle of Quakerism, introduced by George Fox and developed by Robert Barclay; it has ever since been professed as a cardinal position by the Society of Friends. Barclay's Thirteenth Proposition in his *Theses Theologicae* remains as true of the Friends today as when first written in the late seventeenth century.

> The communion of the body and blood of Christ is inward and spiritual, which is the participation of his flesh and blood, by which the inward man is daily nourished in the hearts of those in whom Christ dwells; of which things the breaking of bread by Christ with his disciples was a figure, which they even used in the church for a time, who had received the substance, for the cause of the weak; even as "abstaining from things strangled, and from blood; the washing one another's feet, and the anointing of the sick with oil;" all which are commanded with no less authority and solemnity than the former; yet seeing they are but the shadows of better things, they cease in such as have obtained the substance.[19]

Marriage among Quakers is a concern of the whole Society. In the ideal situation, where bride and groom are members of the same congregation, they write a letter to the church officials stating their intention of getting married. This letter is presented to a session of the Monthly Meeting, at which a Committee on Clearness or Family Relationships takes up the matter. Since the committee's report is normally approved at the next session, a minimum of two months is required before wedding invitations may be sent out. The actual ceremony is "a meeting of worship within which a marriage takes place. In an atmosphere of quiet and reverence, the promises of the bride and groom are made without the help of a third person. Thus they enter into a binding relationship before God and in the presence of their friends."[20]

Quaker simplicity is said to begin "inside, with the quality of the soul. It is first and foremost the quality of sincerity, which is the opposite of duplicity or sham."[21] In effect it extends to all the details of daily life. A conscientious Quaker avoids luxury in dress and living quarters; he does not gamble or trade in the stock market, abstains from tobacco and intoxicating drinks, and is restrained in his speech and recreation. The use of "plain language" is confined nowadays to conversation among Quakers and in family life. It means avoiding the pronoun "you," in plural, when referring to one person, and using "thee" and "thou" instead. Also, instead of saying Sunday, Monday, etc., they use "First-day, Second-day," and for January, February, and the other months, they substitute "First-month, Second-month . . . ," on the principle that the names of days and months are pagan in origin and hence not to be employed by those who profess Christianity. Opposition to judicial oaths is "not merely a negation but is a positive affirmation of an ideal of sincerity for the regulation of life. A man's word should be as good as his sworn statement."[22] Quaker agitation from colonial times has contributed to the change in federal law in most states, which permits a simple statement instead of sworn testimony in legal processes.

GOVERNMENT AND ORGANIZATION

Quaker organization is necessarily very simple. Since all members are considered priests or ministers, there is no hierarchy of jurisdiction and no recognized superiority of clergy over lay people. Nevertheless, there are church officers, called elders or ministers. They are not ordained but chosen "by acclamation" for their ability in leadership.

The governmental structure is an adapted form of congregationalism, in which four strata of authority are distinguished. At the bottom level is the Preparatory or Congregational Meeting, whose only function is to prepare and digest business for the Monthly Meeting. Except in large "parishes," the Preparatory Meeting is absorbed by the Monthly Meeting, which is the fundamental unit of Quaker polity, receiving and recording members, extending spiritual care and, if necessary, material aid to its adherents. "It provides for the oversight of marriages and funerals; for dealing in a spirit of restoring love with those who fail to live in accordance with Friends' principles and testimonies; for the collection of funds required to carry on the work of the Meetings; for holding titles to property and for the suitable administration of trust funds."[23] Three officers, a clerk, treasurer, and recorder, are appointed for definite terms.

Above the Monthly Meeting is the Quarterly Meeting, which is "designed to bring together a larger group for inspiration and counsel and to consider more varied interests than a Monthly or Preparative Meeting can undertake. It is composed of constituent Monthly Meetings, each of which shall appoint representatives to attend it."[24]

Finally, in most Quaker groups, "the Yearly Meeting is composed of the entire membership of its constituent Monthly and Quarterly Meetings, members of which have both the privilege and the responsibility to attend all sessions and to participate in the deliberations. Members of other Yearly Meetings and any interested persons are welcome."[25] Those few Societies that operate on a five-year plan add one juridical unit to the previous three, in which case the Yearly Meetings are self-sustaining, but they meet every five years in a given locality for advisory purposes and without the authority enjoyed by the lesser bodies.

Among the important submeetings used by Quakers, the best known is the Meeting for Sufferings, established in 1756 as a standing committee of the respective Yearly Meetings.

Its name was derived from a similar organization founded in England, "to care for and relieve members and their families suffering persecution for their testimonies." Because the name was misunderstood, it was changed in 1955 to the Representative Meeting. Its purpose is manifold, notably to popularize the Quaker way of life, defend it against opposition, and assist "any individuals suffering because of maintaining Friends' testimonies." A recent outlet for this phase of Quaker piety was to provide moral and financial help for conscientious objectors during World War II. Quaker camps were organized for pacifists of all denominations. When a national board for religious objectors was set up by the Friends, it was generally accepted as the co-ordinating agency for this kind of work.

It is not commonly known that behind much of the Quaker opposition to war and insistence on freedom from military service is a theological position that is part of the whole fabric of their spiritualized Christianity. In the words of their greatest spokesman, Barclay, "All true and acceptable worship to God is offered in the inward and immediate moving and drawing of his own Spirit." Consequently "all other worship . . . which man sets about in his own will . . . whether they be a prescribed form, as a liturgy, or prayers conceived extemporarily . . . they are all but superstitions, will-worship, and abominable idolatry in the sight of God; which are to be denied, rejected, and separated from, in this day of His spiritual arising."

Quakerism is consistent in applying the same principle to civil authority. Just as no institutional church is authorized to prescribe liturgical forms, no political institution has a right to dictate a man's moral conduct or presume to enlighten his conscience.

> Since God hath assumed to himself the power and dominion of the conscience, who alone can rightly instruct and govern it, therefore it is not lawful for any whatsoever, by virtue of any authority or principality they bear in the government of this world, to force the consciences of others; and therefore all killing, banishing, fining, imprisoning, and other such things, which men are afflicted

with, for the alone exercise of their conscience, or difference in worship or opinion, proceedeth from the spirit of Cain, the murderer, and is contrary to the truth; provided always that no man, under the pretense of conscience, prejudice his neighbor in his life or estate, or do any thing destructive to, or inconsistent with human society; in which case ministered upon all, without respect of persons.[26]

While there is no organic unity among the Quaker groups, they collaborate in social activities on a fairly large scale. For example, all Societies of Friends contribute to the American Friends Service Committee. They all support Pendle Hill, an educational community (outside Philadelphia) for religious and social study, open to persons who are sufficiently mature to use their time profitably without the incentive of grades, examinations, and degrees.

Not surprisingly, the Friends are prominent members of the National and World Councils of Churches, where they testify to the same experience through corporate silent worship and the lay ministry.

Salvationists

A common misunderstanding is to regard the Salvation Army as only a social welfare organization which is sponsored by dedicated citizens for the purpose of relieving poverty and other temporal necessities. In reality the Army is a Protestant denomination in the fullest sense of the term, with a mandatory body of doctrine, following a prescribed ritual and worship, and governed by a well-defined ecclesiastical authority.

It is not detracting from the creditable work of the Salvation Army in feeding the hungry and comforting the sick to say that this phase of its ministry is purely secondary. "Its primary aim," according to an official declaration, "is to preach the gospel of Jesus Christ to men and women untouched by ordinary religious efforts."[1]

HISTORY

First known as the East London Revival Society and later as the Christian Mission, the Salvation Army was organized in 1865 by William Booth (1829–1912), an ordained minister of the Methodist Church in England. "Filled with compassion for the wretched multitudes outside the influence of the religious agencies of the time," Booth left the pulpit of the Methodist New Connection Body to preach to the people on the street corners in the slum district of East End, London. His original plan was to supplement the work of the churches, but when the latter refused to accept his converts into active membership, Booth decided to establish a religious society of his own. He was moved to this decision by the appalling indifference of the existing religious bodies to care for the dregs of humanity, numbered in the thousands, living in the heart of a supposedly Christian capital. "Drunkenness and all manner of uncleanness," he wrote, "moral and physical, abound . . . A population sodden with drink, stupid in vice, eaten up by every social and physical malady, these are the denizens of Darkest England [analogous to Darkest Africa] amidst whom my life has been spent, and to whose rescue I would now summon all that is best in the manhood and womanhood of our land."[2] What a cruel satire, he complained, that the existence of these colonies of heathens and savages should attract so little concern. To his mind, "it is no better than a ghastly mockery to call by the name of One who came to seek and save that which was lost those Churches which in the midst of lost multitudes either sleep in apathy or display a fitful interest in the chasuble. Why all this apparatus of temples and meeting-houses to save men from perdition in a world which is to come, while never a helping hand stretched out to save them from the inferno of their present life?"[3]

Consistent with this attitude toward the churches, Booth changed the original Methodist structure of his movement into a quasi-military organization. Instead of being a church, the society should be called an army; from superintendent, Booth became general; the traditional articles of faith became "Articles of War"; converts from sin became recruits and then cadets; after a period of training they rose to the rank of lieutenants, captains, and finally majors. Mission houses were changed into "citadels," and prayer meetings were transformed into "knee drills."

Within a decade, the Army spread to other countries, Ireland, Scotland, and Wales, coming to the United States in 1880. Booth personally nurtured the American foundation in four visits that he made to the States, and in 1904 appointed his daughter, Evangeline, the first American commander.

The variety and scope of the Army's work of social rehabilitation in the United States is unique among the Protestant churches. Certainly no other denomination with comparable numbers has a greater reputation for being the friend of the poor and homeless or of more effectively dealing with the problems of moral degradation, especially those of alcoholism. Salvation Army hotels for homeless and transient men and women, maternity homes, general hospitals, children's homes and nurseries add up to several hundred institutions, besides summer camps, missing persons' bureaus and prison-gate homes; sympathetic observers have been prompted to call the Salvationists "the most powerful minority in the world."[4] Their work is not only extensive, it is highly efficient. In 1954, both Houses of Congress passed a complimentary resolution which proclaimed the week of November 28 through December 4, 1954, as National Salvation Army Week. President Eisenhower added an official proclamation to the nation, urging citizens to honor the Salvation Army because of its work and principles.

In the history of the Salvation Army, there were two schismatic departures that affected the United States and Canada. The first defection started shortly after the Army came to the United States in 1880. Major Thomas E. Moore, Army chief in America, would not obey General Booth's order to leave the States and take command of the work in South Africa. He preferred to organize a Salvation Army of his own and, in fact, assumed the title of general. For some time his group was commonly known as The Salvation Army of America to distinguish it from the "World-wide" or the Salvation Army of England. Prudent handling of the situation from England gradually reconciled most of the American Salvationists to the parent body.

A number of posts in America turned down the English offer of reconciliation and became incorporated in 1896. They reorganized in 1913 as the American Rescue Workers. Unlike the Army, the Workers observe baptism and the Lord's Supper. Otherwise their theology is the same as that of the Salvationists. Most of their rescue mission work (lodgings, clothing, food) is confined to the East with headquarters in Philadelphia.[5]

The second break from the Salvation Army occurred in 1896, when the Volunteers of America were founded by Ballington and Maud Booth. Ballington was the son of William Booth, founder of the Salvationists, and Maud was Ballington's wife. They reacted against what they considered the autocratic and foreign control of the Army and wanted the American contingent to be more democratically organized. Like the American Rescue Workers, the Volunteers also restored the sacraments of baptism and the Eucharist that William Booth had dropped. Their theology is expressed in a series of ten statements, issued by the National Society of the Volunteers of America. They are a concise summary of that phase of American Protestantism, started by John Wesley, which has applied Christianity to human needs while remaining faithful to the basic principles of the traditional faith.

1. We believe in one supreme God, who is "from everlasting to everlasting," who is infinitely perfect, benevolent and wise, who is omnipotent and omnipresent, and who is creator and ruler of heaven and earth.

2. We believe in a Triune God,—The Father, Son and the Holy Ghost. We believe these three Persons are one, and while separate in office, are undivided in essence, coequal in power and glory, and that all men everywhere ought to worship and serve this Triune God.

3. We believe the contents of the Bible to have been given by inspiration of God, and the Scriptures form the Divine rule of all true, Godly faith and Christian practice.

4. We believe that Jesus Christ, when upon earth, was truly man and yet was as truly God—The Divine and human being blended in the one Being, hence His ability to feel and suffer as a man and yet supremely love and triumph as the Godhead.

5. We believe that our first parents were created without sin, but by listening to the tempter and obeying his voice fell from grace and lost their purity and peace; and that in consequence of their disobedience and fall all men have become sinful by propensity and are consequently exposed to the wrath of God.

6. We believe that Jesus Christ, the only begotten Son of God, by the sacrifice of His life, made an atonement for all men, and that whosoever will call upon Him and accept His overtures of grace shall be saved.

7. We believe that in order to be saved it is necessary (a) to repent toward God; (b) to believe with the heart in Jesus Christ; and (c) to become regenerated through the operation of the Holy Spirit.

8. We believe that the Spirit beareth witness with our spirit, that we are the children of God, thus giving the inward witness of acceptance by God.

9. We believe that the Scriptures teach and urge all Christians to be cleansed in heart from inborn sin, so that they may walk uprightly and serve Him without fear in holiness and righteousness all the days of their lives.

10. We believe the soul shall never die; that we shall be raised again; that the world shall be judged by God; and that the punishment of the wicked shall be eternal, and the joy and reward of the righteous will be everlasting before the throne of God.[6]

As will be seen in the analysis of its doctrine, the Salvation Army professes many of the same beliefs. But where the Volunteers refuse to change the creedal premises, the Salvationists adjust them to a new religion. It is correct, then, to say that the Volunteers of America are Protestants in the Methodist tradition engaged in the social apostolate; whereas the followers of the elder Booth are a post-Reformation development with only a historical tie to their Protestant origins.

DOCTRINE ON FAITH AND MORALS

The basic tenets of the Salvationist creed are set forth in a series of eleven propositions, first elaborated by William Booth in 1878, and since then accepted as "the principal doctrines held and taught by the Salvation Army . . . extending to all enactments and settlements throughout the world under which its property is held."[7] However, a bare examination of this creed would not reveal much of its inner meaning, which is supplied by the *Orders and Regulations for Officers of The Salvation Army* and the *Handbook of Doctrine,* containing "an exposition of the principal Doctrines" obligatory on the "officers of all ranks." Unlike other denominations, the Army allows a minimum of freedom in the interpretation of its articles of faith.

Jesus Christ. The divinity of Christ is professed unambiguously, for "Jesus Christ has been God from all eternity: He is God and will be God for evermore."[8] Among the proofs offered for the deity of Christ, Salvationists learn that "the Bible repeatedly calls Him God . . . ascribes to Him those

wonderful powers and perfections which belong only to God
. . . shows that Jesus made claims so tremendous that they
could rightly have been made only by God."[9] While developing this theme, the *Handbook* is strangely silent on
Christ's appeal to miracles to prove His claim to divinity.
Also a characteristically revivalist attitude is betrayed in saying that "the experience of those who are truly saved shows
that Jesus must be God," when they realize that forgiveness
comes only through the merits of Christ and no one less than
God could atone for their sins.[10]

Redemption and Salvation. The Salvationist concepts of
original sin and redemption are considerably removed from
those of Luther and Calvin. Through Adam's sin, "all men
are born with a sinful nature, which early leads to actual
wrongdoing."[11] Nevertheless, ". . . although prone to evil,
man is a free agent. His spiritual powers were marred but
not destroyed by the Fall."[12] Also contrary to the Protestant
idea of redemption as a mere "covering over of sin," the
Salvationists believe that forgiveness of sin is the first and
greatest blessing of Christ's death on the cross. "God," they
say, "forgives or justifies a sinner completely," with consequent "regeneration [which] is of the nature of a new birth,"
whereby man is "brought into a new spiritual world and has
a new spiritual force within him." He thus becomes an
adopted son of God, who "receives into His family the par-
doned and regenerated sinner and makes him His own
child."[13] Unlike many Protestants, the Army teaches that
"persons who are truly saved may backslide entirely and be
eternally lost."[14] The opposite opinion is branded as "contrary to the general teaching of the Bible. It is based upon
[a misinterpretation of those] passages which speak of the
security of God's faithful people, especially: 'My sheep . . .
shall never perish' [John 10:27–28]." Basically, the possibility of a relapse even after conversion arises from the fact that
"otherwise we should not be free agents."[15]

Entire Sanctification. Quite different from most religious
bodies who are preoccupied with sin, the Salvationist religion offers prospects of spiritual perfection or "entire sanctification," which is described as a "complete deliverance from
sin, and dedication [or consecration] of the whole being,

with all its gifts and capacities, to the love and will of God."[16] From God's point of view this is to be regarded as being "overpowered by divine grace."[17] From man's side it means having "a clean heart . . . freedom from sin . . . perfect love . . . rest from inward conflict and from anxious care."[18] It is not to be expected, however, that perfect sanctity will take place at the moment of conversion. "It is only later, when [people] discover the true nature and power of inborn sin, that they realize further need; then they earnestly seek deliverance and God sanctifies them."[19] This ideal of Christian perfection is held up to the officers of the Army as a goal to be attained already in this life and well before eternity. Hence "the idea that sanctification cannot take place at or near the time of death is contrary to the teaching of the Bible."[20] The secret lies in understanding that perfection, like every gift of God, is conditional. Four conditions are laid down: conviction of the malice of sin and that holiness is possible; consecration to God of oneself and of all that one has "to live only to please Him"; faith, which is "the act of simple heart-trust by which a soul commits itself to God and believes that He does now sanctify according to His promise"; and most practically, renunciation, which is "giving up everything opposed to the will of God," forever and entirely.[21]

Renunciation will affect many common habits to which other people are accustomed, but which a consecrated soul will sacrifice to the glory of God. A faithful Salvationist must give up "the use of strong drink, even in moderation . . . because the practice is wasteful, injurious, and productive of misery, wickedness and ruin; because the influence of a moderate drinker may lead weaker people to drunkenness." He should also abandon "the use of tobacco . . . because the practice is wasteful, injurious, dirty, often selfish and annoying to others." He must discontinue "the wearing of fashionable dress and worldly adornment . . . because it tends to gratify and encourage pride; it absorbs time, thought and money which could be better employed." He should avoid "worldly amusement and selfish indulgence . . . it being realized that attendance at gatherings with associations of an unworthy kind, also frivolous conduct and the reading of trashy literature are detrimental to spiritual life."[22]

The Sacraments. A negative feature of Salvation Army teaching is its repudiation of the sacramental system, inherited from William Booth. "Various opinions are held," it is said, "as to how many Sacraments there are. Roman Catholics observe seven, many Protestants only two, namely, Baptism and the Lord's Supper." However, ". . . as it is the Salvation Army's firm conviction that these ceremonies are not necessary to salvation nor essential to spiritual progress, we do not observe them."[23]

Various arguments are given to support this negativism: isolated scriptural texts which describe Christianity as interior are quoted and "the religion of Jesus Christ" is said to be wholly "a spiritual religion."[24] The ritual practices of Christ and the early Church, e.g., the Eucharist, are dismissed as "carried over from the Jewish dispensation."[25] And most critically it is argued that some people "who observe the Sacraments give no evidence of a spiritual change, while others who do not observe Sacraments give definite evidence of such a spiritual change." Moreover, since the "Sacraments are sometimes a hindrance to spiritual life, in that many people rely upon them rather than upon Christ," they have no essential function in the spiritual life of a Christian.[26]

This doctrinal position was determined by Booth, who in the early days of the Army baptized infants and administered the Lord's Supper at all Salvationist stations. Gradually he gave up both practices, and eventually legislated against them. He was moved to this decision by the Society of Friends (Quakers), "which came into being and exercised so mighty an influence when England was full of the practise of external religion, but almost dead in respect of vital Christian experience. George Fox and his followers, being convinced that the Church Sacraments were merely symbols of spiritual truth, had laid them aside and sought after the experience which these symbols represented."[27]

Booth was willing to retain the Lord's Supper except for certain practical considerations. Many of his converts "had been slaves of strong drink, to whom the taste, even the odour, was a danger."[28] Should he expose them to temptation by placing in their hands "the cup of remembrance" of Christ's Passion? He was also determined to have women enjoy perfect equality with men in his Army. But the prevalent attitude was against the administration of the sacraments by women. He therefore chose to eliminate the Eucharist rather than deprive his wife and other women of the privileges of the ministry. A final explanation lay in the conciliatory nature of the founder of the Salvation Army, who "wished to avoid anything that might cause disorder."[29] Since the Lord's Supper had been the cause of so much controversy over the centuries, Booth decided to drop it rather than stir up dissension.

Divorce and Remarriage. As marriage is not recognized as a sacrament, divorce with remarriage is permitted to Salvationists, though with some qualifications. Officers contemplating divorce or legal separation must notify the Commander and relinquish their office before the commencement of divorce proceedings. Reinstatement is not encouraged, although the innocent party is given every consideration for readmission to his rank in the Army. "In the event of the reacceptance of a divorced person, or one whose marriage has been annulled, the Chief of Staff will, at the same time, give a ruling in regard to the time which must elapse before remarriage can be considered."[30] But not even these mild regulations apply to the Army privates, who have no official rank in the society.

RITUAL AND WORSHIP

Although he excluded the sacraments, Booth did not leave his followers without a complicated ceremonial. Salvationists are now told that "too much importance cannot be attached to ceremonies . . . in which vows are registered and covenants entered into between the soul and God."[31] Five principal kinds of ceremonies, in addition to Salvation Meetings, are prescribed by the Army manuals.

The Swearing in of Soldiers is the solemn installation of Salvationists when they sign the "Articles of War," professing their faith in "the truth of the Army's teaching," promise to abstain from intoxicating liquors, anything low or unclean, and pledge to support the Salvation War in obedience to their officers.[32]

The Presentation of Colors, or the Army Flag, is "emblematical of the aggressiveness of Salvation warfare." The principal feature of the ceremony is a homily on the meaning of the flag: red standing for the Blood of Christ, yellow for the fire of the Holy Spirit, and blue for the purity of God.[33]

Covenant Services are of two kinds, referring to holiness or to the Salvation War, in which the candidate makes a solemn promise to God, vowing to maintain holiness of life and promote the work of the Army until death, asking that "the promises I make on earth be ratified in heaven."[34]

The Dedication of Children is a substitute for baptism and consists in the officer accepting a child while pronouncing the formula: "In the name of the Lord and of the — Corps of the Salvation Army, I have taken this child, who has been fully given up by his (her) parents for the Salvation of the world. God save, bless, and keep this child. Amen."[35]

Marriages are governed by detailed regulations, which increase in number and severity with the rank of the Salvationist. Officers, e.g., may not have courtships during training, the men must have served at least two years and be twenty-three years of age, they may marry only another Salvationist, and the woman partner must be younger than the man. The marriage ceremony is prescriptive and includes a profession of the "Articles on Marriage," among them a solemn promise that "we will not allow our marriage in any way to lessen our devotion to God, our affection for our comrades, or our faithfulness in the Army."[36]

While upward of thirty types of meetings are provided by the *Orders and Regulations,* the most familiar is the Ordinary Meeting, "at which a determined and usually a prolonged effort is made for the Salvation of sinners."[37] A typical program begins with "a united Salvation song, to enlighten and cheer everyone," followed by prayer, a chorus, Bible reading, and a brigade or united song. Then "testimonies, or short address, with singing interspersed, collection and Band music, announcements," and a solo or chorus to introduce the main function, which is an appeal for sinners. One method of procedure is to preach a sermon, after which "a call may be given to silent prayer, during which the leader should gently urge the unsaved to tell God there and then whether or not they will accept His salvation."[38] The appeal for sinners to repent is made over and over again, "as long as any unsaved remain in the Meeting." Every possible motive is presented: "the claims of God, the uncertainty of life, the terrible condition of the lost . . . the blessedness of the saved both here and hereafter, the thraldom and disappointment of sin even in this life . . . should all in turn be brought forward as reasons for immediate decisions." In addition to these verbal appeals, "the singing is highly important. The Officer should consider what songs are best calculated to help sinners to the Mercy Seat, and when there, to lead them to commit themselves to the Saviour." A further suggestion is, "bombarding a sinner or backslider, [which] if wisely, earnestly, and believingly done, frequently helps the person concerned to yield. For instance . . . it may be very helpful for a few praying Salvationists to surround him, and while one pleads with him directly the others pray for his Salvation. Some of the best Salvationists have been literally 'compelled' into the Kingdom after this fashion."[39]

ORGANIZATION AND GOVERNMENT

The organizational structure of the Salvation Army is rigidly military. "Without any intention, in the first instance, on the part of its leaders to adopt military organization, the Salvation Army government has come to resemble the military form. Experience has proved this system of administration to be best adapted for preserving order and conducting aggressive warfare, and is, as all who have practical acquaintance with the management of men know, more prompt, forcible, and energetic than any other."[40]

Accordingly the governing personnel is strictly hierarchical. At the head of the Army stands the General, who is elected by the High Council and may be removed from office by the same authority. "The control of the General extends to every part of the Salvation Army, and to every phase of its operations throughout the world."[41] Under the General are the officers, who are divided into two classes: the field and staff officers. The first group, in turn, are variously ranked, from Probationary Lieutenant to Brigadier; the second from Lieutenant Colonel to Commissioner. All positions of authority are held by the officers, under whom serve the rank and file of the Army, called the Soldiers.

The basic juridical unit of the Army is the corps, of which there are some twenty thousand in the world. Each corps is commanded by an officer, from Lieutenant to Brigadier, who is responsible to divisional headquarters which direct larger areas, corresponding to the whole or part of a state, e.g., Indiana, Iowa, and eastern Michigan. Divisions are further organized into territories, the Eastern, Western, Southern, and Central, with headquarters in New York, San Francisco, Atlanta, and Chicago, each governed by a territorial commander and all united under a secretary at the national headquarters in New York.

Ultimate control of the organization, however, is vested in the General, who directs the Army's activities from the International Headquarters in London. Immediately under the General are the Chief of Staff and the heads of all the departments—finance, audit, literary and translation, overseas, public relations, youth and education. "The work of all officers at International Headquarters is inspired by our Lord's command: 'Go ye into all the world, and preach the gospel.'" This ideal is implemented through a number of corporations, like the Salvation Army Trustee Company and the Reliance Bank, which offers "varied types of banking services." Not more than a thousand pounds may be deposited in any one year and no fees are paid to directors; the profits after providing for reserves are paid over to the Salvation Army. The Salvation Army Assurance Society operates on the same nonpersonal profit basis. Currently handling over two million policies and having a comparable premium income, it is an insurance company with a "fundamental difference," where "the policyholder is not only a client, but a friend of the Salvation Army, and the Salvation Army assurance agent or officer is the 'padre of the people.'"[42]

Indicative of the complete dependence on the International Headquarters are the rules governing property and finance. "All Army property in any Territory is dealt with by the Headquarters of that Territory, under the direction of the General." Again, "The Headquarters concerned is responsible to the General for the oversight and care of all property, receiving the rents [where rent is payable], and paying the charges due in respect of it."[43] Correlative to this dependence are the "chief means by which the General controls the world-wide operations of the Army," namely, "by Orders and Regulations, which all Officers and Soldiers are under obligation to obey . . . by appointing Officers to represent him . . . by the administrative control of the property of the Army . . . by having reports of the Salvation War regularly presented to him [and] by personal inspections and visitations."[44]

Such responsiveness to superiors implies a training in discipline during childhood. "As a soldier under authority, which with all its human limitations he broadly accepts as from God, the Salvationist is a disciplined citizen of heaven [whose] conscience is instructed from childhood upward."[45] Behind this "outward man" of obedience, the Army professes to follow an "inner law," which it calls its faith in the redeemability of human nature and in the power of divine help. Opposed to the main stream of Protestant thought, it believes that "there is salvation for all who will come to Christ in sincere repentance." It will ". . . not countenance any restrictiveness in the grace of God [and] doctrines which deny the universality of redemption."[46] The result has been "the most widespread social program" in Protestant Christendom, based on the "Catholic" principle of William Booth's Methodism, which he borrowed from John Wesley and which denies man's utter depravity while affirming his power of free co-operation with the grace of God.

Unitarians and Universalists

Judged by traditional standards, the Unitarians are not really Christians because they deny the divinity of Christ. And even among Protestants they are ostracized by professedly Christian societies, like the National Council of the Churches of Christ. But Unitarians have their own definition of Christianity. They argue that "If to be a 'Christian' is to profess and sincerely seek to practice the religion of Jesus, so simply and beautifully given in the Sermon on the Mount, then Unitarians are Christians."[1] In fact, they are more Christian than their critics, since "the orthodox Christian world has forgotten and forsaken the real, human Jesus of the Gospels, and has substituted a 'Christ' of dogmatism, metaphysics, and pagan philosophy."[2]

Behind this critical attitude toward dogma is the real spirit of Unitarianism as an ecclesiastical institution built on the foundations of anti-supernaturalism. Essentially naturalistic, its corporate existence is a symbol of the limits to which Protestant liberalism can go and still call itself an heir of the Reformation.

HISTORY

Although Unitarians as individuals or groups denying the Trinity may be found in the first century of the Christian era, the actual beginnings of the denomination go back less than two hundred years. Theologically the genesis of Unitarianism can be traced to the liberal reaction against Calvinism as understood by the Congregational churches in colonial New England. Under the influence of deistic ideas imported from England, liberal-minded Congregationalists began publicly to preach doctrines that contradicted the Calvinist elements in their Church's confession. "The doctrine that Jesus is God, the principle of predestination, the belief in the depravity of human nature, the dogma of the atonement, the conception of Deity as a God of wrath, damnation and hell-fire—all these teachings were challenged."[3]

American Unitarianism was consequently born as a secessionist movement in the Congregational Church, though the first church to profess Unitarian teaching was the Episcopalian King's Chapel, Boston, which in 1785 modified its liturgy by eliminating the Athanasian and Nicene Creeds and all references to the Trinity. In 1802 the oldest Pilgrim church, founded at Plymouth in 1620, became Unitarian. Within a short time, twenty out of the twenty-five original churches in Massachusetts became Unitarian, until approximately 125 churches broke with the conservative Congregational body or were forced to resign as unorthodox and essentially unchristian. Drawing from the intelligentsia among the liberals and lacking creedal cohesion, the secessionists felt that an official Unitarian publication would help to unify them. Thus in 1821 the *Christian Register* was founded, which is reputedly the oldest religious journal of continuous publication in America.

Two landmarks in Unitarian history which laid down the principles for future development were the Baltimore sermon in 1819 of William Ellery Channing, outstanding Congregationalist preacher, and the address delivered by Ralph Waldo Emerson at the graduation exercises of Harvard Divinity School in 1838. Channing proclaimed that the liberal position is more soundly based on Scripture than traditional Calvinism. Emerson's speech was more radical. He proposed to change the foundation of religion from historical documents and external events, i.e., from the Scriptures and miraculous phenomena, to the subjective life within man. "Jesus Christ," for him, "belonged to the true race of prophets . . . Alone in all history he estimated the greatness of man. One man was true to what is in you and me. He saw that God incarnates himself in man, and evermore goes forth anew to take possession of his world. He said in the jubilee of this sublime emotion, 'I am divine.'"[4] Like his contemporary, David Strauss, Emerson thought this picture of the man-Christ suffered distortion in the early Church. "The understanding caught this high chant from the poet's lips, and said, in the next age, 'This was Jehovah come down from heaven' . . . Christianity became a Mythus, as the poetic teaching of Greece and Egypt before."[5]

Emerson, who is regarded as one of the founders of American Unitarianism, later left the ministry and organized a group of Transcendentalists. Eventually he replaced the Unitarian deity by a vaguely pantheistic Over-soul and rejected the idea of personal immortality.

The American Unitarian Association was established in 1825 as a society of individuals interested in promoting the influence of Unitarianism, to be reorganized sixty years later as an association of churches. The Beacon Press was started in Boston in 1902 as the official publishing house of the American Unitarian Association. Two years later the Starr King School for the Unitarian Ministry was founded in Berkeley, California.

In the early 1930s, the "Unitarians suddenly awoke to the realization that a long period of neglect of organizational matters had brought the denomination to the verge of collapse." They were also under pressure from "outside forces illiberal and totalitarian in character," and "slowly made up their minds to accept the undeniable fact that they could no longer depend upon the generosity of a few men and women of great wealth to support their denominational program."[6] The result was a complete overhauling of organizational structure to make previously disparate agencies more co-operative; a new emphasis was placed on social and youth services; the United Unitarian Appeal was made into a permanent institution, drawing funds from local churches for national and corporate ventures, and, perhaps most important, the Beacon Press entered on a more "bold policy in the publication field." Among the best sellers were Paul Blanshard's trilogy: *American Freedom and Catholic Power* (1949), *Communism, Democracy and Catholic Power* (1951), and *The Irish and Catholic Power* (1953). The Beacon Paperback series is a library of several hundred titles in unorthodoxy, including such eminent writers as Coulton, Dewey, Freud, and Harnack.

DOCTRINAL POSITION

The doctrinal position of the Unitarians can be defined as a
radical deism which denies any validity to the supernatural,
whether as revelation, divine grace, or an order of reality beyond the natural, i.e., beyond what is due to man as a human
being. Thus, as regards revelation, the Scriptures are equated
with the Moslem Koran and the Hindu Vedas, and summarily
described as mythical:

> In all cultures men's keenest thoughts, deepest longings,
> most haunting fears, and boldest affirmations about life's
> meanings have been expressed in legend, folk tale, and
> myth. The lives of their heroes have been told and retold.
> Accepted ways of getting along with one another have been
> preserved in precept and in codes of law. In many instances
> much of this material has been written down, collected,
> edited, and re-edited. These are the sacred literatures or
> Bibles of the world, often considered by the peoples that
> have produced them as the very word of God. The Judeo-
> Christian Bible is a remarkable collection of this sort.[7]

Consequent on this anti-supernaturalism, the Unitarians as
a body reject all the basic dogmas of Christianity. "We neither believe," writes one of their ministers, "in the unique
divinity of Jesus as the supernatural son of God nor in the
human depravity which was supposed to make a supernatural
savior necessary. We believe that, as he was, so are we all—
as Paul said—offspring of the Eternal, 'in whom we live and
move and have our being.'" Consequently, "It is not the details of Jesus' teaching, nor the doctrines about his birth and
death, but the quality of the spirit in which he met his problems and lived his faith that we find inspiring. It is as an inspiration to living, not as the price paid to free us from sin
and mortality, that we look to him."[8]

Unitarianism is often misunderstood and its critics accuse
it of being hostile to Christian tradition. The standard Unitarian reply is that in all human institutions, notably in the
church, tradition tends to become fixed and unchangeable.

Unitarians boast that theirs is a fellowship which consciously resists this tendency.

The issue comes to focus for them as to whether they are Christians or not. Of course, they say, the only sensible answer is the exasperating one: It depends on who is talking and what he thinks Christianity is. They are not concerned with whether they are Christian; they claim to be concerned only with whether they are right.

> We are not concerned whether we hold to the teaching of the elders; we are concerned whether the tradition to which we hold is good. Our attitude toward tradition is neither to embrace it completely nor to reject it completely. We wish to keep whatever in the past is valid, while letting go whatever is not.
>
> Our genius lies, not in a particular break with a particular tradition, but in a constant willingness to break with whatever elements of tradition threaten to bind us. Whenever our practice ceases to reflect the highest aims we can imagine and seek to serve, whenever our worship is of something less than what we conceive to be the Most High, we are compelled to make a break with the past through gradual reform, if possible, but if not, by revolt— even by the formation of a new church.[9]

One of the distinctive features of the Unitarian movement is its acceptance of open questions. Unitarians do not claim to be the only church to hold this view, but they find their identity in the degree to which they insist that the Spirit must be unfettered in all its expressions. Put negatively, their principle declares: Truth cannot be reduced to a creed. Stated positively, they claim: Ours is a church in which creedal matters are purposely kept open.

The followers of Channing and Emerson admit that individual members of other denominations who wrestle with theological problems may also look upon them as open rather than closed. But there is a difference which is fundamental. In other religious bodies, theological doubt is personal. It is not institutional. It is the individual who struggles with problems of faith, but the church as church professes an unquestionable faith. Among Unitarians, doctrinal skepticism and religious agnosticism is a community experience. They have set at the heart of their Church not a creed or a confession of faith but the principle that no religious truth can receive unwavering loyalty. Students of Unitarian history suggest that it is more in the nature of a psychological attitude than a theological position. Unitarians as a rule are above average intellectually, often reacting against an oppressive creedalism in their early training and always impatient with those who prefer to believe with security than to question with anxiety. They can be eloquent in describing this type of creedless religion.

By no stretch of the imagination can this be called *security*. At least, it is not the kind of security which makes us feel snug and safe and protected against the barbs and thrusts of life. "Nothing is secure," says Emerson, "but life, transition, the energizing spirit." With this perspective we achieve a larger conception of religion. If we would find solid ground beneath our feet, we must have courage enough to give up our illusions of a protected life and accept our role as the servants of life, the agents of transition, the children of the energizing spirit: subject to all the shocks and stresses of life, but confident and buoyant through them all. This is religion at its greatest, not as a petty search for protection, or as a pinched hope of buying God off, but as the wonderful adventure of life itself.[10]

While Unitarianism as an institution is conveniently identified with a kind of deism, individual Unitarians, including leaders in the Church, go beyond the mere denial of the supernatural. Their concept of God and the real distinction between Creator and creature can be very vague. "All Unitarians would agree," for instance, "that there is something within the range of human experience—whether in the reality of God or in what Wordsworth called 'the still sad music of humanity'—that properly calls forth the responses of reverence, wonder, appreciation and humility. It is known by many names and expressed in many ways."[11] Less vague and more nearly monistic is the declaration that "The Cosmos [Nature, Universe] is the highest unity that we know. Many and varied are the things and beings of the world; yet all are parts of one vast and enduring Whole or Cosmos . . . The Cosmos . . . is creative. This does not mean making something from nothing, but rather making the new out of the old . . . Since the Cosmos is the highest known unity and is creative, we call it God. God and the Cosmos are one."[12]

After years of negotiation, the American Unitarian Association agreed to consolidate with the Universalist Church of America, whose philosophy originated with the doctrine of universal salvation. In May 1961, the two bodies merged to form the Unitarian Universalist Association. Their combined church membership is only a fraction of those who are known to be sympathetic with the principles of Unitarianism.

Originally the Universalists or Universal Salvationists, as they are also called, professed classical predestinarianism, namely that God elected some people to salvation and damned others to hell by an eternal decree. In time they completely reversed this Calvinism by teaching that God actually predestined everyone to salvation in such a way that no one will be lost.

Universalism as an organized religious body began in London in 1750 and the first American society was founded by John Murray, whom the Methodists excommunicated in 1779 because of his unorthodox Wesleyan preaching. One of the first charter members of the Universalists was a Negro, and as early as 1790 the organization became officially opposed to human slavery.

In the meantime the Universalists adopted the Unitarian idea of Ballou and others, to the point that by the turn of the last century there was no basic difference between the two movements. Among the prominent early Americans whom the Universalists claim as their forebearers were Benjamin Rush, signer of the Declaration of Independence, and Clara Barton, who founded the American Red Cross.

WORSHIP AND LITURGY

Unexpectedly, the Unitarian churches have an elaborate system of corporate worship, sufficiently uniform to be compiled in an official *Services of Religion*. Liturgical functions, orders of service, with hundreds of prayers and hymns which have been edited by the Unitarian and Universalist Commission on Hymns and Services, are to be used by the member churches as "a sound norm which can be followed to advantage." Sources from which the formularies are drawn are mostly Roman Catholic and Protestant, with additions and alterations from "the religious ideals of our own day."[13] The editors' apology for using sectarian material is that "Although the theological content of those traditional forms, whether of the Roman Catholic Church or of the older branches of Protestantism, frequently expresses a way of thinking about religion which is far removed from that of the modern man, the pattern upon which the older services have been built up is often beautifully and nobly devised, and offers a norm which may well be followed."[14] Thus we find among the 576 hymns in the Service Book such familiar pieces as *"Adoro Te Devote"* (words changed), *"Adeste Fideles"* (words retained), *"Tantum Ergo"* (words changed), *"O Salutaris Hostia"* (three melodies, words changed in each), *"Stabat Mater"* (no words), *"Magnificat"* (words retained), and "Lead Kindly Light" (words retained).

To provide for every taste, sixteen Orders of Services are offered by the manual, five for festive occasions, and eleven for the regular Sunday and occasional functions. The First Order of Service, in sequence, covers twenty different acts of worship, including:

Litanies, with the minister and people alternating in such petitions as: "From all ambition and greed, which bring want and distress to multitudes and debase the bodies and souls of men, shutting them from the fulness of life . . . O Lord deliver us."[15]

The *Offertory,* which consists of sentences from the Scriptures with corresponding prayers, such as: "We give thee, Lord, what is thine own, for all we have comes from thy bounty to enrich our lives. Grant us thy grace with these outward offerings to present ourselves willingly before thee, dedicated anew to thy service in the spirit of Jesus Christ."[16]

The *Benediction,* which means the reading of selections from the Scriptures, frequently described as "adapted." Thus

II Corinthians 13:14 reads: "The grace of the Lord Jesus Christ . . . and the love of God, and the fellowship of his Holy Spirit be with us all, this day and forevermore. Amen."[17]

Two kinds of invitation to the Communion Service are provided, one at which the elements are distributed, and another in which "The bread and wine will not be passed, the communion being wholly symbolic."[18] Corresponding provision is made in the ritual when the elements are not given to the people. After the words of institution, the minister says: "Let us partake in spirit with those who, remembering him, have shared the bread of life and the wine of sacrifice." Then, lifting up the plate with the bread and also the cup, tasting a little of each, he says to the people: "We take and eat this in remembrance of Christ . . . We drink this in remembrance of Christ."[19]

ORGANIZATIONAL STRUCTURE

Unitarian churches in the United States are always congregational, which means that the local church is juridically independent. Each church has its own set of bylaws and statement of purpose. It chooses its own minister, who is given a position of leadership, not in order that he may dogmatically instruct the congregations in beliefs and practices, but in order that he may stimulate the members in their own free development of religious belief and action. The minister holds no ecclesiastical authority given to him by external agencies.

When Unitarian and Universalist churches became more numerous, they took on the organizational form of the Congregational Church from which they seceded, so that, at present, the administrative setup is not unlike that of the parent denomination: Local churches are organized into Conferences, which form natural geographical associations and vary in size from seven or eight to twenty member churches. The projects initiated by the Conferences vary greatly, from the founding of new churches to the establishment of homes for aged people. But the major purpose of the Conference

usually is to help churches and church members to become
acquainted with one another and to promote more effectively
the cause of Unitarianism in their area.

As Conferences grow, they unite into regional bodies,
largely the outgrowth of a study by the Commission on Appraisal (1934–36), which recommended a decentralization of
administrative functions. The Southern Unit is called the
"Thomas Jefferson Conference Region" in tribute to that historical figure's avowed Unitarianism. Leading the Regions
are elected Council boards, charged with policy decisions,
with the employment of executive directors, and with the
budgeting of funds which are secured in the main from the
United Unitarian Appeal.

With the formation of the Unitarian Universalist Association, American Protestant liberalism entered on a new phase
of existence. According to its new constitution the Association has become promotional to a degree that was unknown
in the past history of either partner.

> The Unitarian Universalist Association is empowered to,
> and shall devote its resources to and exercise its corporate
> powers for, religious, educational and charitable purposes.
> It is further empowered: to solicit and receive funds sepa-
> rately or with others to support its work; to make appropri-
> ations to carry on its work, including appropriations to its
> associate members and to other organizations to enable
> them to assist the Unitarian Universalist Association in
> carrying on its work; and without limitation as to amount,
> to receive, hold, manage, invest and reinvest and dis-
> tribute any real and personal property for the foregoing
> purposes.[20]

Consistent with these corporate purposes, members of the
Association dedicate themselves to the advancement of a
"free faith" which they hope to communicate to others by
uniting in their common endeavor. In the words of the Constitution, they covenant in seeking:

> 1. To strengthen one another in a free and disciplined
> search for truth as the foundation of our religious fellow-
> ship;

2. To cherish and spread the universal truths taught by the great prophets and teachers of humanity in every age and tradition, immemorially summarized in the Judeo-Christian heritage as love to God and love to man;

3. To affirm, defend and promote the supreme worth of every human personality, the dignity of man, and the use of the democratic method in human relationships;

4. To implement our vision of one world by striving for a world community founded on ideals of brotherhood, justice and peace;

5. To serve the needs of member churches and fellowships, to organize new churches and fellowships, and to extend and strengthen liberal religion;

6. To encourage cooperation with men of good will in every land.[21]

When the two parties to the merger consolidated, they also pooled their subordinate activities. In practice it is more often these supporting organizations that exercise the greatest influence in the advancement of Unitarian Universalism. Such, among others, are the Unitarian Universalist Women's Federation, with several hundred branches doing educational, interfaith, and lay leadership work; the Layman's League, charged with recruiting for the ministry, besides other duties; the Liberal Religious Youth, which aims to instill the ideas of creedless Christianity into the minds of the young; the Student Religious Liberals, which caters to the university population; and the Unitarian Universalist Fellowship for Social Justice, founded in 1908, to sustain its members "in united action against social injustice and in the realization of religious ideals in present day society."[22]

During the thirties the Fellowship for Social Justice opposed Father Coughlin and it is now co-operating with other groups "to prevent any further encroachment on the state by the church."[23] In 1953 it presented its annual award to Mrs. Vashti McCollum, active Unitarian in Urbana, Illinois, "who so courageously took her case on released-time religious education to the United States Supreme Court—and won."[24]

A new development will be the joining of forces between the Unitarian Historical Society and the Universalist Histori-

al Society. Both have already proved their worth in the
field of scholarship to further the cause of American religion,
free from dogmatic presuppositions. There is still greater
promise, it is said, for the future.

United Church of Christ

Congregationalists

The United Church of Christ came into existence in 1957 as the result of a merger between the Congregational Christians and the Evangelical and Reformed bodies. The legal controversy which this merger occasioned received national publicity. After years of litigation in the civil courts, certain decisions have been handed down which are deeply significant for future church and state relations in this country.

Leaders of the merger plans have substantially kept intact the doctrinal and ritual characteristics of the respective bodies. Even the ecclesiastical structure of the uniting parties was not much altered. For this reason it seems best to treat the Congregational Christian and the Evangelical Reformed Churches separately, in order to do full justice to the distinctive elements of each.

Two years after the merger, representatives of the two churches adopted a Statement of Faith for the United Church of Christ. Known as the Oberlin Confession of Faith, it is a model for religious bodies in the Free Church tradition.

We believe in God, the Eternal Spirit, Father of our Lord Jesus Christ and our Father, and to his deeds we testify:

He calls the worlds into being, creates man in his own image and sets before him the ways of life and death.

He seeks in holy love to save all people from aimlessness and sin.

He judges men and nations by his righteous will declared through prophets and apostles.

In Jesus Christ, the man of Nazareth, our crucified and risen Lord, he has come to us and shared our common lot, conquering sin and death and reconciling the world to himself.

He bestows upon us his Holy Spirit, creating and renewing the Church of Jesus Christ, binding in covenant faithful people of all ages, tongues, and races.

He calls us into his Church to accept the cost and joy of discipleship, to be his servants in the service of men, to proclaim the gospel to all the world and resist the powers of evil, to share in Christ's baptism and eat at his table, to join him in his passion and victory.

He promises to all who trust him forgiveness of sins and fullness of grace, courage in the struggle for justice and peace, his presence in trial and rejoicing, and eternal life in his kingdom which has no end.

Blessing and honor, glory and power be unto him. Amen

Understandably this statement was called a testimony rather than a test of faith. It reflected the intention of the joining partners to avoid anything like substituting a new creed for an old one and, less still, drafting a substitute for either of the merging denominations.

On the eve of their merger, Congregationalists boasted of being the most ecumenically minded of the Protestant Churches: "No other ecclesiastical group has participated in a greater number of unions with other groups." Congregationalists "will cooperate with any Christian communion which will cooperate with them. In any community, they oppose religious isolationism and denominational exclusiveness."[1]

Tangible evidence of this ecclesiastical co-operativeness is the fact that twice in less than thirty years the Congregational Church fused with other denominations on a national scale, and altered its name to the point of absorption. Comparable to their desire for organic merger is the active promotion by Congregationalists of church union among other religious bodies. If they are sometimes called "the interdenominational denomination," this title is well deserved.

HISTORY

As the name suggests, the Congregational Christian Church is a union of two denominations, the Congregational and the Christian. Actually it is the amalgamation of at least six religious bodies, going back to the late sixteenth century. The origins of Congregationalism are commonly dated from the founding, in 1581, of a church in Norwich, England, by Robert Browne, a Separatist Anglican minister. Browne, a Cambridge graduate, was demoted from the ministry for teaching "seditious doctrines," notably that the basis of church membership was not submission to episcopal authority but acceptance of a covenant, to which a group of people gave their mutual consent. Pressure from the government forced Browne's followers to move to Holland, and then to America, where, as the Mayflower Pilgrims, they landed at Plymouth, Massachusetts, in 1620.

As Separatists without a ministry, "who had broken away from the arbitrary rule of the episcopacy and from what they regarded as the empty and unchristian forms prevailing in the Church of England," the Pilgrims would probably have disappeared as an ecclesiastical body had they not been joined in 1629 by the immigrant Puritans, whose Massachusetts Bay Colony was chartered in the same year.[2] Unlike the Pilgrims, the Puritans admitted the validity of a state church in England, but they sought to reform this body from within. Basically Calvinist in doctrine, they were willing to remain in the Established Church on condition that there was "more preaching and less liturgy, fewer vestments and more well-educated Clergy"; they wished to cleanse English worship "of any vestige of Roman Catholicism."[3] On August 6, 1629, the Salem Puritans united to form a church by covenant, elected and ordained a pastor and teacher, and sent their first "letter missive" to the Plymouth Separatists, asking for approbation and guidance. The Plymouth Church was happy to comply and sent delegates to Salem to extend the right hand of fellowship. "This was the real inception of American Congregationalism."[4]

In striking contrast with present-day liberalism among Congregationalists, the early days of the group (c. 1640) showed a fanatical intolerance of other religions, which their own historians admit "was a blot on the escutcheon of the Puritan colonists."[5] Quakers and Baptists especially were maltreated and persecuted, even to death. The Salem executions for witchcraft belong to this period.

While the Puritan element in Congregationalism gave it a doctrinal basis of unity, the Separatist "independency" of thought and policy slowly neutralized the Calvinist foundation until, by 1730, the Congregationalist churches had become quite thoroughly secularized. This induced a reaction, called "The Great Awakening," ushered in by Jonathan Edwards, pastor at Northampton, Massachusetts, who was "consumed by the sovereignty of God, the fateful brevity of life and its eternal issues."[6]

During the next century, Congregationalists were concerned with six principal developments: higher education, missions, the Presbyterian question, the Unitarian separation, the formation of a system of government, and the formulation of a uniform statement of doctrine. In education, the Congregational Church was a pioneer. Harvard, founded in 1636, and Yale, founded in 1701, were established to prepare students for the Congregational ministry. Dartmouth (1769), Williams (1793), Amherst (1821), Bowdoin (1794), and Middlebury (1800) were among the first senior colleges in New England. By 1952, fifty-one colleges and fourteen seminaries in the United States had professedly Congregational-Christian origins or affiliations.

The missionary zeal of the Congregationalists spread the denomination far into the West, but also brought on the Presbyterian crisis which threatened to dissolve Congregationalism in America. For economic reasons, the two Churches had joined forces according to the Plan of Union (1801), but "the more authoritative and tough-fibered Presbyterians' order was better suited to loose frontier conditions," with the result that in fifty years about two thousand churches became Presbyterian, many of them originally Congregationalist.[7] The Plan of Union was rejected in 1852, and Congregational-Presbyterian relations have been somewhat aloof ever since.

The Unitarian departure is an epic in American Protestantism as illustrative of the changing theological order among the denominations. Shortly after the American Unitarian Association was founded in 1825, about 125 Congregational churches seceded in favor of the liberals. Ironically, a century later Congregationalist historians regretfully observed that although the Unitarians left because they were opposed to dogmatism, especially Christ's divinity, "the position theologically of the first generation of Unitarian preachers would now hardly provoke a Congregational examining council to argument";[8] so far has Congregationalism broken through "traditional conventionalities and . . . creedal literalism."[9]

Until 1852 American Congregationalists were united largely by ties of common origin and informal co-operative efforts among the churches. In that year, however, the first general meeting of Congregational representatives was held at Albany, New York—drawn together by the need for material support of the churches and missionary enterprises in the West. The existing jurisdictional structure of the Congregational Christian Churches eventually grew out of this initial meeting.

In 1913, at Kansas City, the National Council adopted a statement of faith, polity, and fellowship that still remains the primary cohesive force in American Congregationalism. The article on faith begins: "We believe in God the Father . . ." and goes through a sizable portion of the Apostles' Creed, ending with the words ". . . we look with faith for the triumph of righteousness and the life everlasting."[10] Regarding polity, the full article declares, "We believe in the freedom and responsibility of the individual soul, and the right of private judgment. We hold to the autonomy of the local church and its independence of all ecclesiastical control. We cherish the fellowship of the churches, united in district, state and national bodies, for counsel and cooperation in matters of common concern."[11] The declaration on "Wider Fellowship" is a single sentence, stating that, "While affirming the liberty of our churches, and the validity of our ministry, we hold to the unity and catholicity of the Church of Christ, and will unite with all its branches in hearty cooperation, and will earnestly seek, as far as in us lies, that the prayer of

Our Lord may be answered, that they all may be one."[12] Among the tangible results of this doctrine on wider fellowship was the incorporation into the body of Congregationalism of two major bodies, the Protestant Evangelical in 1925, and the Christian Churches in 1931. A more significant effect is the impulse which Congregationalism has officially given in promoting the ecumenical movement in the United States and throughout the world. The constitutional basis of the World Council of Churches as "a fellowship of churches," whose function is to "offer counsel and provide opportunity of united action" among its constituents, is a paraphrase of Congregational principle expanded to global proportions.[13]

Four groups of Congregationalists did not participate in the 1957–61 merger negotiations. They have remained juridically distinct and have since begun denominations of their own.

The largest of the dissenting groups was the Congregational Christian Churches (National Association). The National Association differs from the other derivatives in having national scope. Its function is to bring local churches together for counsel, inspiration, and fellowship, while preserving the independence of the local unit. Six commissions carry on the religious and social programs of the Association.

An unusual feature of the Association is the right of 10 per cent of the churches and a two-thirds vote to change any action or proposal of any of the national bodies or that of the officials of the Association.

The Congregational Holiness Church had been founded in 1921 by a group of ministers who left the Pentecostals in order to maintain a more democratic church polity. Stressing divine healing, abstention from tobacco and other forms of worldliness, they also believe in the typical Pentecostal doctrine of "the second rain," which means the conferral of special gifts such as speaking in strange tongues. Women are licensed to preach, but, unlike the situation in the United Church of Christ, they are not ordained to the ministry.

The Conservative Congregational Christian Conference was founded in Chicago during 1948. Its beginnings go back to the efforts of H. B. Sandine, pastor in Hancock, Minnesota. Two reasons especially prompted the Conference not to join the United Church merger: As conservative Protestants, members of the Conference were uncomfortable with the known creedal liberalism of the rising merger; and, as Congregationalists, they were too sensitive to local church autonomy to be willing to sacrifice it in the interests of ecumenical co-operation.

The Evangelical Congregational Church was started in 1894 in protest against the "usurpation of powers in violation of the discipline" by church leaders in the Evangelical Association. The latter had been founded by Jacob Albright, the Lutheran revivalist and forerunner of the Evangelical United Brethren. Except for a Congregational policy on the ownership of local church property, the Evangelical Congregationalists profess an Arminian theology of grace, strong evangelism, and a Wesleyan form of government. Their administrative council is headed by a bishop and their various boards of operation are similar to those of the Methodist Church.

DOCTRINE

Before attempting to make a summary of Congregationalist doctrine, it is essential to see the two sets of principles which, according to the best commentators, are the focal points between which the whole concept of Congregationalism oscillates:

The Principle of Independency allows the greatest freedom in matters of faith and doctrine. According to the Congregationalists, doctrinal creeds are not expressions of stable verities which have prior importance in man's dealings with God. They are merely "intellectual statements of religious experiences [which] represent landmarks along the pathway of religious thought." Consequently, ". . . as experiences and intellectual capacities change . . . it is inevitable that creeds should change."[14] Assuming that religious doctrine is objectively fluid, Congregationalism logically requires no subscription to any set creed as a condition for membership. "No member," therefore, "is ever told that he must believe any specific religious tenet in order to be a good church member."[15]

The Principle of Fellowship is a corrective and limitation of doctrinal freedom. It means that certain people band together into a congregation, and local churches unite into associations and councils, out of a "sense of comity."[16] They feel they have a common purpose, not unlike that of "the group of disciples who were gathered about Jesus . . . to be with him and to be like him."[17]

If Congregationalist doctrine were examined only on the principle of independency or freedom, there would be practically nothing to describe, except the extremes of dogmatic liberalism permitted within the denomination; whereas fellowship suggests that the members and member churches have at least some convictions in common, which may be classified and compared with the corresponding doctrines of the traditional Christian faith.

Revelation and the Bible. The Congregationalist catechism answer to the question "What is divine revelation?" describes it as ". . . the process by which God has helped men to find out about Him."[18] But this is not to be understood as a supernatural communication from God, made in times past, now closed, and to be regarded as the inerrant and immutable word of God. The Scriptures are only a natural, although sublime, record of the religious sentiments of their authors, since "the Bible grew out of the religion of a people. Originally it was not so much a guide for their living as a statement of their experience." As such experiences were conditioned by the capacity of the writer and the times in which he lived, so it is "inevitable that there should be differences of value in different parts of the Bible." To illustrate: "Belief in demons was once a part of the framework of common thought. That belief would of course creep into the record. [But] why should any sensible reader allow an outgrown category of thought to rob him of a permanent truth or cast a shadow over an abiding experience?" The experience in this case is described as a sense of evil which was so intense as to give it personality.[19]

The Church and Churches. In Congregationalist terminology, the church has two basic meanings which are not mutually exclusive. There is first the "One Holy Catholic Church" of the Apostles' Creed. This is "the Church Universal [which] includes all who accept Jesus Christ as Master, determining to do His will whatsoever it may cost. This is greater than all Churches together, for there are people who accept Jesus as Saviour who may not belong to any organization." Accordingly "the Church Universal is the whole body of Christians."[20]

While everyone who accepts Christ as Savior belongs to the Church Invisible, many Christians have banded together into separate groups, since "it is much easier to be a real Christian as a member of some congregation with which one may regularly worship, pray, study and receive the inspiration of preaching and fellowship."[21] Among these auxiliaries is the Congregational Christian Church, which is "democratic in organization. As the name 'Congregational' indicates, the *Congregation* is the final authority. Each individual church, through the action of its members, calls its own ministers, plans its own programs, regulates its own finances, determines its own policies. The principle of cooperation is recognized in that individual churches group themselves together in local associations of churches, state conferences, and the General Council of the Congregational Christian Churches. The decisions of these larger groups, however, are never mandatory unless approved by the local church."[22]

In practice, a new Congregationalist church is formed on the basis of an agreement or covenant, by which "a group of people bind themselves together in Christian fellowship 'to walk in the ways of the Lord, made known or to be made known to them.'" Here "you have the true basis of a Congregational Church. To join a church is to make a Christian confession," i.e., to profess Christ as one's Savior, and "to accept the covenant."[23] In virtue of the Christian confession, a man becomes a member of the Church Universal; by reason of accepting the covenant, he becomes a Congregationalist. Verbally expressed, the covenant may be only a short formula, as, for example, "We covenant with God and one another, and do bind ourselves in the presence of God to walk together in all His ways according as He is pleased to reveal Himself unto us in His blessed word of truth."[24] But in private it means that the members of a parish agree to believe and worship substantially alike, allowing malcontents the option of going elsewhere or forming another congregation if they so desire.

Divinity and Personality of Christ. While permitting acceptance of the Nicene Creed, which declares, "I believe . . . in one Lord Jesus Christ, the only-begotten Son of God," the Congregational Christian Churches explain the divinity of Christ in terms which negate the hypostatic union. In answer to the question "What made Jesus divine?" we are told: "To be fair with the rest of humanity, we have to suggest that it was not special privileges . . . The divinity of Jesus was due to a complete surrender of his own will and an absolute opening up of his life until at the end, all that was human was shot through with divinity. His divinity was achieved, as well as endowed. Had he yielded to temptation, he would have weakened and ultimately destroyed his divine nature."[25] Comparable to Christ's achievement, we can become equally divine. "Our endowment of a divine nature cannot be claimed unless we deny the invitations of sin. Jesus is the source of our confidence that we can live as children of God. What God did in Jesus, He can and will do in any life which will persistently say 'No' to sin, and 'Yes' to righteousness."[26] Thus the Congregationalist idea of Christ's divinity is distinctly Arian. "Jesus had a profound and unique sense of God. To him, more than to any other man that has lived, God was real. He lived in constant fellowship with God . . . He said that he and the Father were one in purpose and spirit," not in substance and nature.[27]

The Sacraments. Congregational Christians define sacraments as "sacred ceremonies observed from earliest times by the Christian Church, to remember Christ and to receive his spirit."[28] Two sacraments are commonly observed, baptism and the Lord's Supper. Baptism is recognized as "the Sacrament of Christian Dedication in which we dedicate ourselves or our children to God. Water is used as a symbol of the cleansing of the soul by the Holy Spirit."[29] The Trinitarian formula is used in the administration of baptism, which may be by immersion, ablution, or aspersion, depending on the person's choice; although the customary way is "to sprinkle a few drops of water on the head of the person to be baptized."[30] Infant baptism is permitted and encouraged; sponsors are optional. However, baptism is not regarded as essential for salvation, or even for membership in the Church. As expressed by a writer for the Commission on Evangelism, "Some Christians, notably the Quakers, believe only in a baptism of the spirit and do not use water baptism at all. Like many other Congregational ministers, my experience has been that our churches gladly receive members of the Society of Friends without requiring water baptism. We leave it to their conscientious choice."[31] Although the phrase "sacrament of cleansing" occurs in the baptismal ritual, the doctrinal explanations sedulously avoid reference to the remission of sin, original or actual. Congregationalism, we are told, turns away from the external magical concept which "makes of Baptism a saving ordinance"; it regards as ". . . tragic . . . the idea that infants dying unbaptized were lost—though medieval theology modified their 'lostness' somewhat by providing for them a special compartment called 'Limbo' in the world to come, which would not be a place of torture, like hell, but not quite heaven, either!"[32]

The Lord's Supper is accorded a place of honor in the Congregationalist *Book of Worship* and is generally described as a sacrament. But the real presence is admitted only in the spiritual, symbolic sense of John Calvin and Ulrich Zwingli. Attributing the Catholic doctrine of transubstantiation to a late innovation, official only "since the year 1215,"[33] the Eucharistic change from bread and wine to the Lord's Body and Blood is said to consist "not in a physical change in the material properties of the elements on the altar, but in a moral and spiritual change in the ethical and religious nature of the worshipers assembled before it."[34] The "reality" in the real presence, therefore, is purely subjective. Since Christ tells us He is present where two or three are gathered in His name, then "surely he may be truly and especially present, in a spiritual sense, in the hearts of the worshipers and among them when we assemble before the table upon which are spread the symbols of his life and death, the bread and wine of the sacrament."[35] Congregationalists argue, as did Calvin, that it is not necessary "so literally" to understand Christ's words of institution. They arrive at this position as a corollary to their interpretation of the Bible and their denial of objective validity to Christian tradition, which, from apostolic times, has proclaimed a corporeal presence of Christ in the Eucharist.

Life after Death. In response to the catechism question "What is life everlasting?" the answer is that ". . . life everlasting is the never-ending life of the soul with God."[36] Not only is life everlasting admitted for the soul, but the resurrection of the body is also accepted, at least by the authors of the Commission on Evangelism and Devotional Life. "How shall we live in [the] future state?" one of the writers asks, and answers, hesitatingly, "I do not know. Jesus thought of it as a place of activity. Heaven would not mean all we want it to mean unless we could have fellowship with living personal spirits . . . Our bodies will be different. Paul said that 'flesh and blood cannot inherit the kingdom of heaven.' But we must have some body."[37] Unfortunately no distinction is made between bodily immortality and the immortality of the soul—the first accepted on faith and the second also known from reason. Moreover, faith in an afterlife is reduced to a native instinct, since Christians are simply urged to "cherish this immortal hope. You cannot and need not prove it. You are born with it . . . You are going somewhere; you are becoming something."[38]

There is no mention of hell in the standard doctrinal treatises. In fact, a place of eternal punishment seems to be ruled out by an implicit belief in universal salvation, since ". . . what man begins here he will be given the opportunity to finish hereafter."[39] Life everlasting is unequivocally equated with blessedness, the "never-ending life of the soul with God," which means "the triumph of righteousness [in] the final victory of good over evil, which must come because God wills it."[40]

RITUAL AND WORSHIP

Since 1948, the Congregational Christian Churches have had a *Book of Worship* that was ten years in the making and involved the co-operative labor of a group of ministers appointed for the task by the General Council of the denomination. This is admittedly a major departure from the Calvinist austerity of the colonial Puritans. "Standing as we do in the non-liturgical tradition, our Congregational Christian Churches have not commonly made much use of symbols in their worship."[41] But under pressure from the people, the need was felt for a reintroduction into religious service of many things which "at the time of the Reformation the reformed churches did away with."[42]

The result is that, while keeping the matter optional, the ritual now provides, in detail, for the use of an altar, covered with three white cloths; Eucharistic candles which "may be present [on the altar] at all times, but should be lighted only for the Lord's Supper";[43] flowers on the altar, which "are works of God's creative power and remind us of the marvelous beauty of his natural world";[44] a cross, although "a crucifix [with corpus] is almost never used in a Congregational Christian Church";[45] following the Catholic tradition, "the church is often built in the shape of a cross";[46] the vestments worn by the minister now include a cassock, surplice, and stole, which "is the sign of an ordained clergyman," and which may be of various colors.[47] While offering twenty-five pages on liturgical symbols, which "can become a language of great potency and beauty," the ritual is careful to point out "there is a grave and constant danger of losing our sense of values in the minutiae of forms." Consequently, "it is of the greatest importance that the congregation be ever aware of the facts or objects for which the symbols stand; that children and newcomers be instructed; and that simplicity be guarded."[48]

Among the ordinary services provided by the Congregational ritual, the most important is the worship with Communion. The sequence adheres closely to the Anglican formulary, modeled on the Roman Missal. Following the "Prayer of Consecration" are the "Words of Institution," verbatim from the Scriptures. But in giving Communion to the people, the minister expressly says: "Ministering to you in His Name, I give you this bread . . . I give you this cup."[49]

The ordination ceremony is the most elaborate in the ritual, "since this is, by common consent, a most solemn and sigificant occasion."[50] Presiding at the functions is an ordained minister who publicly examines the candidate on his fitness for the office. Then, while the ordinand is kneeling, the officiating minister, together with the other ministers present, lays his hands on the head of the neophyte and says: "O Lord our God . . . as now in thy name, and in obedience to thy most blessed will, we do, by laying on of hands, ordain this thy servant, and set him apart to the office of the holy ministry, committing unto him authority to proclaim thy word and administer the sacraments and to bear rule in thy flock."[51] Three ritual actions follow the laying on of hands: a pulpit gown is presented, with the words "Take thou this robe as a symbol of thine office. Wear it when thou shalt minister of the things of Christ."[52] A copy of the Scriptures is handed the newly ordained, as he is told, "Take thou the authority of the Church of Christ to preach the Word of God and to administer the holy sacraments."[53] Finally, "the right hand of fellowship" is extended from the ministers to the new member of the clergy. What is specially distinctive among Congregationalists is their admission of women to ecclesiastical office. Referring to the rites of ordination and liturgical functions, the office Manual declares that "although the masculine pronoun is used . . . women are eligible to all stages of the ministry in Congregational Churches."[54]

As in other denominations organized along similar lines, ordination to the Congregational ministry does not take place until after a person has "received a call to become the minister of a local church, or to serve a mission board or other church-related body. It is the general principle of our fellowship that ordination is given only for service in a local church or church-related organization requiring ordination."[55] This is in accordance with the Cambridge Platform, adopted by the Congregational Synod held at Cambridge, Massachusetts, in 1648, which reduced the ordained ministry to mere functionalism. "Ordination," it stated, "we account as nothing else but the solemn putting a man into his place and office in the church."[56] And though ordination and installation are now ritually distinct, in principle the ordination does not confer essentially higher powers than those possessed by the unordained lay preacher, who may, if necessary, perform the duties of ministers, including the rite of the Lord's Supper.

ORGANIZATIONAL STRUCTURE

The structure of the Congregational Christian Churches before their merger was remarkably well organized along quasi hierarchical lines, beginning with the local congregations and terminating in the General Council.

Local Churches were individually responsible for the doctrine, ministry, and ritual of their own congregation. They appointed delegates (one or more) to the Associations and Conferences. This has not substantially changed since the rise of the United Church.

The *Associations* had authority to recognize local churches, promote co-operation, exercise discipline, license, ordain, install, and dismiss ministers. This too holds since the new merger.

The *Conferences* were generally organized to correspond to state territories, including Hawaii. Heading each Conference was a superintendent, now called the Conference minister. Conferences recognized Associations, directed and in many cases financed missionary activities within their territory. Basically a board of recommendation and counsel, the Conference specialized in promoting educational work among young people and women. Together with the Associations, Conferences elected the members of the General Council. Since the United Church came into existence, the General Council has become the Executive Council, but the basic structure has remained the same.

The *General Council* recognized Conferences, elected the legal holding body of the Council, published the Congregational Yearbook which listed and rated the ministers, elected delegates to the National Council of the Churches of Christ and collaborated with a variety of national organizations like the Board of Home Missions, the Council for Social Action and the Annuity Fund for Congregational Ministers. Technically a voluntary society of Congregational Christian

Churches, which met every two years, the General Council's primary purpose was "to provide a gathering for useful discussion of questions of concern to the churches and to furnish inspiration for increased devotion and effectiveness."[57] It was therefore "not a legislative body with ecclesiastical authority over the churches, the associations or the conferences." As part of its function, it could pass recommendations to the lower organizations, or bear "testimony to its faith through approved statements or resolutions on various topics." But all these expressions carried "with them no authority beyond the weight of their own wisdom."[58] In recent years, the General Council had been severely criticized by certain lay leaders in the church for its heavy clerical membership. "In the General Council," they charge, "a minister has 250 times the voting power he has in the local church."[59] The movement for greater lay representation was occasioned by the General Council's approval of the Council for Social Action, a subsidiary of the Congregational Church, which, according to lay conservatives, "has openly advocated socialist doctrines . . . has at times presumed to speak for all Congregationalists . . . has expended nearly a million dollars that would otherwise have been used to further the missionary program of the churches."[60] Competent observers regarded this as a symptom of the growing "anti-clericalism" developing in Protestant churches where the clergy have controlling influence.

Delegates of the two churches which merged in 1957 were painfully conscious of these criticisms, and the United Church which they organized has since taken action to strengthen lay representation. At the same time they structured the new body along lines that are less Congregational than was true before, at least among the Congregational Christian bodies. It was, in fact, precisely this new direction which occasioned dissatisfaction with the merger on the part of those who held that local church autonomy is of the essence of Congregational polity. Departure from this policy, they charged, is a defection from the tradition of Congregationalism.

CHURCH MERGERS

The principle of fellowship is not a dead-letter ideal in American Congregationalism. For almost a century it has found expression in a constant series of mergers, achieved or attempted, with other denominations. In 1866 an effort was made to reunite the Free Baptists who had seceded from the Congregational churches a century before. But the proposed union never took place apparently because the Baptists rejected infant baptism. In 1892 the General Council admitted "into fellowship" a group of Methodist churches from Georgia and Alabama. Between 1895 and 1923, serious attempts were made to join the Congregational and Episcopalian denominations. These were unsuccessful because of the intransigent position of the Episcopalians on the subject of orders. They interpreted the term "historic episcopate" so as to "require all other denominations to accept the order of bishops as officially superior to that of the ministry," and therefore, "to receive ordination through bishops who claim uninterrupted apostolic succession." Equivalently the Episcopalians refused "to recognize the clergy of other denominations either fraternally or officially as possessing a valid ministry."[61] Since Congregational ministers believed that "their ordination is valid . . . they would not accept reordination if it brought into question their Congregational ordination."[62] So the merger did not materialize. A projected union with the Disciples of Christ failed because the Disciples insisted on baptism by immersion. After years of negotiation, a merger with the United Brethren also foundered when the Congregationalists refused to give up the idea of local church autonomy.

In 1925 the Evangelical Protestant Churches, "noted for their liberal views and theology, and for their consciousness of need for social amelioration," were joined to the Congregationalists with a minimum of difficulty.[63] More trying and protracted over forty years was the merger of the Congregational and Christian bodies, finally completed in 1931. When originally proposed in 1895, there were difficulties on both sides. Congregational churchmen observed that the Christians' "rejection of all man-made formulas and creeds has sometimes led to the idea that they are Unitarians, because they will not adopt the word 'Trinity' which they do not find in the Bible."[64] On the other side, certain Christian leaders felt that "any merger with a church bearing a denominational name was departing from their principles . . . They contended their churches could not become affiliated with a 'sect' which they considered the Congregationalists to be."[65] The matter was shelved until 1931, when the two joined to form a new body, the Congregational Christian Church, based upon "the acceptance of Christianity as primarily a way of life and not upon uniformity of theological opinion or any uniform practice of ordinances . . . The autonomy of the local congregation and the right of each individual member to follow Christ according to his own conscience" was left undisturbed.[66]

For several years efforts were made to unite the Congregational Christian with the Evangelical and Reformed Church, and in June of 1955, at a joint meeting of the two church councils, it was decided that a formal merger should take place on June 25, 1957. The proposed name for the new amalgam was the United Church of Christ, which meant the absorption of Congregationalism, at least nominally, after three centuries of relative autonomy in the United States. When the merger took place, it was only after the opposition of conservatives had been overcome. They appealed to the civil courts to block the merger, but lost by a 4–2 decision of the New York State Court of Appeals, which decided in 1953 that the government had no jurisdiction over the proposed union.

Undaunted, the minority sponsored a two-day conference of protest in Detroit (November 1955) under the titles of the Committee for the Continuation of Congregational Christian Churches, and the League to Uphold Congregational Principles. As reported by one of the delegates, "I am afraid I hadn't thought or known very much about Congregationalism before I went to Detroit. If I am critical of what went on there it is because I want desperately to believe that historic Congregationalism is a better, more Christian, more informed thing than I found there. There was in two days of discussion not one whisper of a suggestion that anyone there knew or cared about what the church of Christ is and/or ought to be."[67] Back of the agitation "that is stirring this denomination to its depths is the determination of some of its members, mainly laity with conservative social and political views, to destroy its claim to be a denomination and to establish that it can never be anything more than a loose congeries of autonomous local congregations."[68]

Since the establishment of the United Church of Christ, the attitude of individual church communities has remained fluid. In any given city, especially the large metropolitan areas, churches are variously identified as United Church of Christ, or —— Congregational Church, or —— Evangelical and Reformed Church, with no attempt to further identify them as members of the United Church except on the juridical level through the ministers and delegates to the coordinating agencies. As might be expected, churches differ in their degree of fidelity to the tradition of their origin—Congregational Christian or Evangelical and Reformed—depending on the pastor's attitude and his people's preference.

The United Church of Christ continues in the ecumenical spirit of the Congregational and Christian bodies. Its leaders are among the most active churchmen in the National Council of Churches.

Evangelical and Reformed Church

Historians of the ecumenical movement point out that one measure of success in restoring unity to a fragmented Protestantism is the degree to which groups of different religious backgrounds finally unite in a single denomination. By this standard, the Evangelical and Reformed Church is the best large-scale example of progress in American ecumenism during modern times. Whereas the majority of church mergers take place between societies that were once united and came together again, the Evangelical and Reformed body was born of two religious groups which had only the remotest historical affinity to each other.

However, while illustrating the strength of the ecumenical movement, the Evangelical and Reformed Church also reveals its fundamental problem, which is the preservation of doctrinal beliefs while serving the needs of greater organizational efficiency. The adjustments made by the Reformed Church when it joined the Evangelicals have been further extended in the new merger with the Congregational Christians, whose "genius [in] subordinating ecclesiastical structure and creedal definition [has] made it peculiarly hospitable to far-reaching Christian fellowship."[1]

HISTORY

The Evangelical and Reformed Church was formed in 1934 by the merger of two bodies of German and Swiss origin, the Evangelical Synod of North America and the Reformed Church in the United States. Hailed as unique in American history, it was the first merger where the uniting denominations did not belong to the same religious family and were of approximately equal size and strength.

The larger and older of the parent societies was the Reformed Church, which had its origin among the Dutch Calvinist immigrants of the early eighteenth century. On October 25, 1725, the traditional birthday of the denomination, the first Communion Service was celebrated at Falkner Swamp, about forty miles north of Philadelphia. Ministers were scarce and the congregations were scattered along the Atlantic seaboard. In September 1747, Michael Schlatter came to America as a delegate of the Synods of Holland, to organize the Coetus (Synod) of Philadelphia. Not until 1793 did the American branch declare its independence from Holland and become reorganized as the Synod of the German Reformed Church.

In its early history, the Reformed Church had no educational institutions, boards, or established missionary work. As the Church spread westward, pastors were sent to open mission stations. Membership grew until by 1819 the Synod divided into eight districts known as Classes. Five years later the Ohio Classis was made into a synod, with powers similar to those of the Mother Church in the East. A theological seminary was opened in 1825 at Carlisle, Pennsylvania, and later moved to Lancaster where it still stands. About the same time, the American Missionary Society was started in Frederick, Maryland, and a Board of Foreign Missions was established for work in the Orient. Competing with the Eastern Synod, the Ohio contingent built its own seminary at Canton, which was later transferred to Dayton, started an independent Mission Board, and published a separate denominational newspaper, the *Western Missionary*. Conscious of the inefficiency of this competition and stimulated by the tercentenary celebration of the Heidelberg Catechism (1563), the two synods combined in 1863 as the General Synod of the German Reformed Church. The word "German" was dropped in 1869. Comparable to the union of the Ohio and Eastern Synods was the split and reunion in 1837 of the pro-English and pro-German factions in the Reformed Church. Two Hungarian Classes were added in 1924 from the old Hungarian Reformed Church. On the eve of the 1934 merger there were about 350,000 members in the Reformed body, operating a dozen institutions of higher learning and concentrated in the states of Pennsylvania and Ohio.

The Evangelical Synod was an offshoot of the Evangelical United Church of Prussia, an amalgam of Lutheran and Reformed believers ordered into existence by the Prussian king, William III. Six ministers of the German society met at Gravois Settlement, near St. Louis, on October 15, 1840, to form the Evangelical Union of the West. Beginning as a ministerial association, the Union was permanently organized in 1849. Similar groups had sprung up in Ohio, the East, and the Northwest. By 1872 they had all joined the original St. Louis union, and in 1877 adopted the name of the German Evangelical Synod.

Other congregations of German-speaking people, of Lutheran or Reformed background, and four synodical groups identified themselves with the nuclear body, which in 1884 extended its work beyond the States through the Board of Foreign Missions. Gradually the word "German" was dropped from the title.

In the opinion of a Lutheran authority, the growing success of the Evangelicals in America and their eventual union with the Reformed is explained by the latitudinarianism and pietism which they inherited from their compromising Prussian forebears. Except for these factors the Evangelicals would not have received the help from Europe which assured their continued existence as a distinct religious body. "Though there was at no time an organic union with the Evangelical Church of Prussia, the Evangelical Synod received moral and financial support from the State Churches of Germany, and especially from the Basel, the Berlin, and the Barmen Mission Societies. These societies espoused the unionistic and pietistic principles of the Prussian Union, and its emissaries implanted these trends upon the Evangelicals in America."[2] There were somewhat less than 300,000 members in the Evangelical Synod at the time of the merger in 1934.

The fusion of the Evangelicals and Reformed was directly occasioned by the Stockholm Ecumenical Conference of 1925, at which "the relationship of the [Reformed] Synod to other church bodies, both at home and abroad, had been strongly emphasized."[3] Merger relations were initiated by the Reformed Church and promoted, among others, by H. Richard Niebuhr, brother of Reinhold Niebuhr and former President of Elmhurst College. When the new denomination was born, it was hailed as a model in the history of American ecumenism since the union "was entered upon in a spirit of complete mutual respect and confidence, the united body having been formed without even drafting a constitution or setting up a new doctrinal formula."[4]

DOCTRINE AND WORSHIP

The doctrinal position of the Evangelical and Reformed Church is summarized in the opening paragraphs of the Constitution adopted in 1936 and periodically amended by the General Synod:

The Holy Scriptures of the Old and New Testaments are recognized as the Word of God and the ultimate rule of Christian faith and practice.

The doctrinal standards of the Evangelical and Reformed Church are the Heidelberg Catechism, Luther's Catechism and the Augsburg Confession. They are accepted as an authoritative interpretation of the essential truth taught in the Holy Scriptures.

Wherever these doctrinal standards differ, ministers, members and congregations, in accordance with the liberty of conscience inherent in the gospel, are allowed to adhere to the interpretation of one of these confessions. However, in each case the final norm is the Word of God.[5]

While the three standards of doctrine are theoretically of equal value, in practice the Heidelberg Catechism is given special prominence and generally featured as the distinctive possession of the Evangelical and Reformed Church. It was jointly written by two young theologians at the University of Heidelberg, Zacharias Ursinus (1534–83), a pupil of Melanchthon, and Caspar Olevianus (1536–87), a follower of John Calvin. Frederick III, Elector of the Palatinate, had ordered the Catechism in order to reconcile the warring factions among the Protestants. Frederick defended the Augsburg Confession as modified by Melanchthon, but he inclined toward the "Reformed" point of view, as distinguished from the Lutheran, insisting on the self-sufficiency of Scripture and "repelled by the bigotry and intolerance of the 'ultra-Lutherans.'"[6] Published in 1563, the Heidelberg Catechism "combined in a remarkable manner the conciliatory spirit of Melanchthon, the friend and assistant of Luther, and the practical spirit of Zwingli and Calvin."[7] Though still holding a place of honor in the Church's "sources of doctrine," the Heidelberg Catechism has been interpreted, sometimes quite liberally, to suit the needs of a group which "constantly endeavors to promote the unity of the Spirit in bond of peace [with] other Christian communions."[8]

Divinity of Christ and the Trinity. According to the Heidelberg Catechism, Christ is the only-begotten Son of God, "because Christ alone is the eternal and natural Son of God; but we are children adopted by God, by grace, for His sake."[9] More recent teaching of the Evangelical and Reformed Church is less traditional. A manual of instruction for Confirmation explains the title "Son of God" by quoting the words of Christ, "He who has seen me has seen the Father," remarking, "How near he must have felt to God to be able to say that . . . All through the years Christians have called him 'Son of God.' To say it in another way, in Jesus God walked the earth as in no other person."[10]

Equally fluid is the Church's current teaching on the Trinity. When the early Christians used the word "person" relating to God, "a part at least of their meaning was that the one God had come to them in three different roles, just as an actor can play three different parts, or as one man can be a son, a husband, and a father at the same time." God meant so much to the followers of Christ that "they could not put all he did mean in one word or statement, but had to use three."[11]

Whatever fluidity of doctrine is found in the manuals of instruction, it is consistent with the neo-orthodoxy among the ministers of the gospel. An outstanding example was Reinhold Niebuhr, late professor of Christian Ethics at Union Theological Seminary and registered minister of the Evangelical and Reformed Church. Regarded by admirers as the most fearless theological critic of our age, Niebuhr was unalterably opposed to the dogma of the Incarnation. He characterized the Council of Chalcedon, which defined the union of two natures in Christ, as "wooden-headed literalism of orthodoxy."[12] For Niebuhr, the hypostatic union was not only non-existent, but impossible. He argued that "since the essence of the divine consists in its unconditional character, and since the essence of the human lies in its conditional and contingent nature, it is not logically possible to assert both qualities of the same person."[13]

The Church. In answer to the question "What do you believe concerning the Holy Catholic Church?" the Heidelberg Catechism says: "That the Son of God, from age to age, gathers and preserves unto Himself, by His Spirit and word, a chosen communion, out of every race, agreeing in true faith."[14] Within the denomination, two types of membership are recognized: communicant members who have been baptized and confirmed and have made a profession of faith; and unconfirmed members who are only baptized.

Sacraments and Rites. As stated in the Constitution, "The Sacraments of the Church, instituted by Christ, are Holy Baptism and the Lord's Supper . . . The Rites of the Church are confirmation, ordination, consecration, marriage and burial."[15]

In the sacrament of baptism, God is said to impart "the gift of the new life unto man, receives him into his fellowship as a child, and admits him as a member of the Christian Church."[16] The accepted custom is to sprinkle a few drops of water three times on the head of the person being baptized, while pronouncing the Trinitarian formula. Sponsors are permitted, but the parents of the child must be present to answer all the questions in the service. Unlike the Baptists, the Evangelical and Reformed Church "recognizes the Baptism of all Christian Churches."[17]

There is considerable ambiguity on the exact meaning of the Lord's Supper, partly the effect of a conflict between the Evangelical and Reformed segments of the denomination. On the Reformed side, as expressed by the Heidelberg Catechism, the communicant is told to pray, "May I receive, not only the bread and wine, but also become partaker of the Lord Himself by His Spirit."[18] The Evangelical version is less Zwinglian and states quite simply that "The Lord's Supper is the sacrament by which we receive the body and blood of our Lord Jesus Christ as the nourishment of our new life."[19] Further evidence of a compromise attitude is the liberty of using either wine or unfermented grape juice in the Communion Service. Moreover, "members of other denominations," not only may but "should be invited to participate in the Church's administration of the Lord's Supper," regardless of what they believe about the real presence in the Eucharist.[20]

As prescribed by the *Book of Worship*, "the Sacrament of the Lord's Supper should be administered in every Congregation four times a year, and preferably more often."[21] The ritual follows the Roman Missal rather closely, and in sequence uses the Confession of Sins, Kyrie Eleison, Gloria in

Excelsis Deo, Collect, Reading of Scripture, Creed (Apostles' or Nicene), Sermon, Offering, Preface, Sanctus, Intercession, Agnus Dei, and Communion. A notable exception is the time when the words of institution are pronounced: "This is my body . . . my blood," is not said until the moment when the minister is giving the bread and wine to the communicant.

Although children are baptized in infancy, it is understood that this does not make them full-fledged members of the Church. It is claimed that although in the early Church there were two parts to the rite of Confirmation, anointing with oil and laying on of hands, "as the years went by confirmation was usually separated from baptism, *and* the first part of the rite was used less and less."[22] The Evangelical and Reformed Church "uses only the second part." After due instruction, the children make a public profession of "their faith in their Savior, Jesus Christ, promise obedience to him until death, and are received by the Church into active membership," in the ceremony of Confirmation.[23]

In the rite of ordination of ministers, there is an imposition of hands and a declaration that "we ordain, consecrate and appoint you to the office of the Christian Ministry."[24] But in special cases a man who has finished the prescribed theological studies may be temporarily licensed "to preach the gospel and administer the sacraments and rites of the Church," even before ordination.[25]

The rites of marriage and burial are practically the same as in other Protestant churches. But the rite of consecration is distinctive. Essentially it means the dedication of a lay member of the church, man or woman, to some auxiliary service like pastor's assistant, director of religious education, lay worker in the home or foreign missions, deaconess, or full-time worker in any other recognized department of the Evangelical and Reformed Church. After due promise is made by the kneeling candidate that he will labor with diligence in his vocation, the "Minister shall proceed to consecrate him, saying . . . We consecrate you a Commissioned Worker of the Church and appoint you to the office to which you have been called."[26] Consecrated persons are entitled to special privileges not granted to ordinary members, which are not forfeited by reason of illness or old age. Deaconesses retain their family name but are called "Sisters," and are so designated in official statements of the denomination.

ORGANIZATION AND MERGER

Evangelical and Reformed Church polity was not basically changed by the merger with the Congregational Christians. Indeed, the structure of the United Church of Christ shows many features of the Evangelical and Reformed tradition. On the local level the new Constitution explicitly provides that "The autonomy of the local church is inherent and modifiable only by its own action. Nothing . . . shall destroy or limit the right of each local church to continue to operate in the way customary to it." Beyond this level, however, a Presbyterian form of organization now becomes evident. There is a general synod which represents the whole body of the church. Meeting biennially as a delegation chosen by the conferences, it effectively governs along Presbyterian lines.

Territorial synods are united into the General Synod, which is the highest governing body, consisting of equal representation of lay and clerical delegates. Elected by the General Synod and working under its supervision are denominational boards and commissions which take care of the Church's social and educational activities: 20 homes for the aged, 12 hospitals and homes for the feeble-minded, 10 orphanages and homes for children, 14 colleges and seminaries in the States and 396 educational institutions in foreign countries, including 34 primary schools in India and 2 colleges in Japan.

In 1942 the Congregational Christian and Evangelical and Reformed Churches entered into negotiation with a view to organic merger. The final edition of the basis of union was drafted in 1947, and the name chosen, the United Church of Christ, expressed "a hope that in time soon to come, by further union between this Church and other bodies, there shall arise a more inclusive United Church."[27] Nevertheless, the basis of union deliberately left many questions to be settled by the United Church itself. Following a declaration of faith which is Trinitarian, the plan of merger called for a reorganization of the Church along Congregational lines, where "the liberty and independence of the local Church as the basic unit of the organization of the United Church of Christ is affirmed and safeguarded."[28] A like concession was made in favor of the Evangelical and Reformed party by providing for a General Synod which "shall carry on the general work of the church and shall meet the responsibilities of the Church for foreign missions, home missions, education and other activities."[29]

When in 1949 the General Council of the Congregational Church decided that a 72 per cent favorable vote of its churches was "sufficient to warrant consummation of the Union," it provoked a storm of protest that continued for years. In 1950 the opposition Congregationalists won a decision from the Supreme Court of the State of New York, which declared that "the General Council of the Congregational Christian Churches was permanently restrained from entering into union with the General Synod of the Evangelical and Reformed Church."[30] This decision temporarily halted further negotiations. In the meantime the Evangelical and Reformed group was invited to unite with the Presbyterian Churches, but turned down the invitation, since "we have made a promise to the Congregational Christian Churches, and because they are temporarily in trouble, we do not intend to go back on our promise."[31]

Three years later the New York State Court of Appeals reversed the 1950 decision of the lower court (nominally the Supreme Court of the state), "on the law and the facts, with costs, and complaint dismissed with costs." The judgment stated that "in controversies such as this, ecclesiastical or doctrinal questions may be inquired into only in so far as it is necessary to do so to determine the civil or property rights of the parties."[32] A joint meeting of the two General Synods in 1955 decided that the merger would take place in June of 1957. The union was completed in July 1961, when the Constitution was adopted in Philadelphia. The Church's national headquarters are in New York City.

The United Methodist Church

METHODISTS

EVANGELICAL UNITED BRETHREN

Methodists

After years of negotiation, The Methodist Church and the Church of the Evangelical United Brethren joined to form a new denomination, The United Methodist Church. Prior to the vote on union in 1966, delegates from the two Churches offered a prayer that may go down in religious history as a symbol of the new spirit in American Protestantism.

O God, our Father, we do not ask in this moment to see the distant scene, one step is enough. We do not ask for all prophecies to be fulfilled in this one moment, but, O God, may our hearts be ready for the next thing that Thou would say to us.

We thank Thee for those who have loved and labored, who have served sacrificially, who have forgotten themselves because they have dedicated themselves to a great cause; and now in this moment of silence, with each of us before Thee, our Father, searching his own heart, standing before his own judgment bar of conscience and conviction, may we hear Thy voice, and may Thy voice be saying to each one of us, this is the way, walk ye in it.

In this spirit may we come to this moment of decision for which we have been seeking to prepare ourselves. Lord, grant that Thy Holy Spirit may indeed give us leadership, and that we may take counsel not of our fears but of our faith, that we may dare to dream and move ahead, knowing that before us even as behind, Thou art, and all shall be well.

Forgive what we have been. Amend what we are. Order what we shall be in this moment and in the long days ahead, as we must live with ourselves, and with the choice that we make.

In the Master's name and for his sake, we pray. Amen.[1]

In the Plan of Union drawn up by the merging parties, they stressed how much they share in common: "They hold the same fundamental doctrines of faith. Ecclesiastical organization is similar. They are Protestant churches, whose streams of spiritual life and thought come out of the Protestant Reformation of the sixteenth century."[2]

Since their beginning, they had lived and worked side by side in friendly communication. Were it not for the difference in language, the Methodists working among English-speaking people and the Evangelical and United Brethren among those of German ancestry, they might have been one Church since their first organization in America. They both found that the language barrier is no longer in existence and the uniting of forces for their common task seemed appropriate and timely. In the Constitution of the new Church the uniting bodies recognized that each has a distinctive history. This would naturally color what each had to bring to the prospective merger and would correspondingly affect the future denomination. For this reason it seems wiser to the author to treat each coalescing body as a separate entity, with its own past history, doctrinal stress, ritual practice, and organizational structure. For years, perhaps for generations to come, The United Methodist Church will reflect the characteristic features of its respective partners. There is no better way of understanding these features than by seeing the source from which they came, namely, the religious tradition of the Methodists and the Brethren.

A number of provisions in the Constitution of The United Methodist Church deserve to be singled out for special mention. They indicate something more than the sentiments of two Protestant denominations and reveal a development of Protestant ecclesiology that will deeply affect the ecumenical movement.

Preamble. The church is a community of all true believers under the Lordship of Christ. It is the redeemed and redeeming fellowship in which the Word of God is preached by men divinely called, and the Sacraments are duly administered according to Christ's own appointment. Under the discipline of the Holy Spirit the church seeks to provide for the maintenance of worship, the edification of believers and the redemption of the world.

The Church of Jesus Christ exists in and for the world and its very dividedness is a hindrance to its mission in that world.

The prayers and intentions of The Methodist Church and The Evangelical United Brethren Church have been and are for obedience to the will of our Lord that His people be one, in humility for the present brokenness of the church and in gratitude that opportunities for reunion have been given. In harmony with these prayers and intentions these churches do now propose to unite, in the confident assurance that this act is an expression of the oneness of Christ's people.

Name. The name of the church shall be The United Methodist Church. The name of the church may be translated freely into languages other than English as the General Conference may determine.

Inclusiveness of the Church. The United Methodist Church is a part of the Church Universal which is one Body in Christ. Therefore all persons, without regard to race, color, natural origin, or economic condition, shall be eligible to attend its worship services, to participate in its programs, and, when they take the appropriate vows, to be admitted into its membership in any local church in the connection. In The United Methodist Church no conference or other organizational unit of the church shall be structured so as to exclude any member or any constituent body of the church because of race, color, national origin, or economic condition.

Ecumenical Relations. As part of the Church Universal, The United Methodist Church believes that the Lord of the Church is calling Christians everywhere to strive toward unity and therefore it will seek, and work for, unity at all levels of church life: through world relationships with other Methodist churches and united churches related to The Methodist Church or The Evangelical United Brethren Church, through councils of churches, and through plans of union with churches of Methodist or other denominational traditions.[3]

On the important question of the episcopacy, the uniting churches agreed that the powers, privileges, and duties of bishops in The Methodist Church and The Evangelical United Brethren Church are essentially identical. Whatever differences may have existed, the constitutional document decided that they were thereby "reconciled and harmonized . . . so that a unified superintendency and episcopacy is hereby created and established of, in, and by those who now are and shall be bishops of The United Methodist Church."[4] By this action, John Wesley's concept of the episcopate was canonized. According to Wesley, the episcopate does not depend on apostolic succession, as is commonly understood in the Anglican and Roman Catholic traditions.

While treating each of the merging bodies as separate denominations, it should further be kept in mind that the Plan of Union intends to keep their respective traditions basically unchanged. "It is proposed," the document states, "that this vital heritage be cherished and its authentic development insured." Throughout the new Constitution and supporting legislation, this theme is constantly emphasized: that the merger does not mean the absorption of one church by the other and, less still, the exclusion of anything significant in one tradition at the expense of the other.

If ever a Protestant society was built around a dynamic personality and its continued existence was due to the infusion of his spirit, that society is Methodism. John Wesley not only founded the Methodist Church but left his followers with a reverence for himself which is unique among the Reformers.

This is not a study of Methodist theology. If it were, we should have to examine in detail Wesley's character and doctrine to see how his insistence on "salvation for all" diverted the course of Protestantism in the English-speaking world and brought it closer to the Catholic teaching on freedom and good works. Although our present concern is more practical and limited to a review of Methodism as an ecclesiastical institution, even here the organizing genius of John Wesley, his personal asceticism and inflexible pursuit of an ideal believed to be from God are still discernible. Where Methodists have compromised in matters of faith or allowed material interests to obscure the spiritual, they have, on their own admission, departed from the principles of their founder.

HISTORY

The founder of Methodism was born in Epworth, England, June 17, 1703. He died in London, March 2, 1791. Graduated from Oxford with an M.A., he was ordained a priest in the Church of England in 1728. Returning to Oxford as a lecturer, he joined a group of Bible-reading students, nicknamed Methodists by a cynical wit because of their methodical application to Scripture study and prayer. Wesley came to the American colony of Georgia late in 1735, but returned to England two years later, after an unfortunate court trial involving the "excommunication" of a woman in his parish. He had hoped to marry the lady, but could not reach a decision; in the meantime she married someone else, and then her being repelled from the Lord's Supper looked like revenge. Disillusioned, Wesley remarked on what he had learned from his American stay, "that I, who went to America to convert others, was never myself converted to God."[5]

The turning point in Wesley's life and the birthday of Methodism came on May 24, 1738, at a prayer meeting in London, during the reading of Luther's preface to the Epistle to the Romans. He felt his heart "strangely warmed" as Luther's teaching on justification by faith penetrated his soul. Immediately he set on a career of evangelization that for zeal and magnitude has no counterpart in the history of Protestantism. He preached three times a day for over fifty years, traveled over 200,000 miles on horseback throughout the British Isles, including forty-two visits to Ireland, published four hundred books and pamphlets, and with his brother, Charles, composed 6500 hymns. His labors and exertions, descibed by admirers as "wholly dedicated to God and the service of his fellowmen," have earned for him the title of "Methodism's saint."[6]

Moral laxity among the clergy and people of the Church of England was the background of Wesley's evangelism, although it was never intended by him to mean a complete severance with the Anglican communion. A year before his death, Wesley still proclaimed his loyalty to the Established Church, declaring that "I live and die a member of the Church of England, and none who regard my judgment will ever separate from it."[7] When his doctrine on the internal witness of the Spirit and free grace barred him from the pulpits, he answered, "The world is my parish," and began field-preaching. Societies of the "saved" were formed throughout England with Wesley as the final authority in all matters of doctrine and discipline. He drew up a list of rules for his followers as early as 1739, but the Methodists were not legally recognized in England until 1784.

American Methodism had three independent beginnings. In 1760, the Irish Robert Strawbridge from Ulster organized a group of Methodist preachers in Maryland; the following year another group of Irish immigrants from County Limerick founded the first Methodist meetinghouse in New York; and finally, between 1769 and 1772, Wesley personally appointed and sent chosen missionaries from England to the Colonies.

The Methodist Church in America grew in numbers during the Revolutionary War, but also weakened to the point of near disintegration for lack of Anglican-ordained clergy to care for its needs. When the Bishop of London refused to ordain ministers for Methodist societies in the colonies, Wesley on his own authority first ordained Thomas Coke, Richard Whatcoat, and Thomas Vasey, and then consecrated Coke to the episcopacy. "I can scarcely believe it," wrote his brother Charles, "that in his eighty-second year my brother, my old intimate friend and companion, should have assumed the episcopal character, ordained elders, consecrated a bishop, and sent him to ordain our elder preachers in America."[8] On his part, Wesley believed he had been divinely inspired to this action. "Know all men," he stated in a formal manifesto, "that I, John Wesley, think myself to be providentially called at this time, to set apart some persons for the work of the ministry in America."[9] Besides the inspiration, he argued that "he had been convinced of his scriptural authority as a presbyter to ordain, since it had been the practice of the ancient church in Alexandria for presbyters to ordain bishops, never suffering the interference of a foreign bishop."[10] This assumption of episcopal powers is still the main barrier of separation between the Episcopal and Methodist Churches.

During Christmas week of 1784, within two months of the landing of Coke, Whatcoat, and Vasey in New York, the Methodist Episcopal Church in America was juridically constituted and established as a religious body independent of the Church of England. The immediate fruit of this founding Conference, held in Baltimore, was the publication in 1785 of the first Methodist *Discipline*. As a carefully planned and detailed code of doctrine, ritual, and policy, drawn up according to directives received from John Wesley, the *Discipline* became an instrument of ecclesiastical unity for American Methodism, much as the Book of Common Prayer is in Anglicanism.

The greatest name in American Methodist history is Francis Asbury, who was ordained elder and consecrated bishop during the Christmas Conference of 1784. As an evangelist, he outrode Wesley in distance covered (275,000 miles) and revivals held (4000), during his thirty years of missionary travel. His genius in organizing lay preachers (one thousand by 1816) placed laymen into governing power in the Church, and thus completely severed Methodism in the United States, both legally and doctrinally, from the Church of England.

Three years after the Church's American establishment occurred the first secession from the parent body. In 1787 a group of Negro Methodists met in Philadelphia to organize the African Methodist Episcopal Church. Their grievance was the discrimination practiced against their brethren by the white members of the denomination. A few years later, in 1796, the African Methodist Episcopal Zion Church was similarly started because of racial discrimination in New York.

Within a dozen years of Asbury's death, lay representation in church policy contributed to the third major schism in

American Methodism. In 1828 the Methodist Protestant Church seceded over the juridical question of appeal for restoration of expelled ministers, and the more basic issue of equal participation of laymen and clergy in church government.

In 1845 another division occurred over the slavery question, bisecting the Methodist Episcopal Church into the Methodist Episcopal Church, North, and the Methodist Episcopal Church, South. The proximate occasion for the split was the mandate of the 1844 General Conference, ordering Bishop Andrew of Georgia to desist exercising his office so long as he remained a slaveholder. This enraged the Southern delegates, who went home to begin their own denomination the following year.

Shortly after the Emancipation Proclamation, the Methodist Episcopal Church, South, was faced with the problem of retaining in its body the thousands of liberated Negro slaves. On the Negroes' own initiative, the Colored Methodist Episcopal Church was founded in 1870.

The last two decades of the nineteenth century witnessed an "ominous change" in American Methodism. No longer were Methodists drawn from the lower and humbler economic and social groups, but rather represented the great middle class, and, as Mr. (Theodore) Roosevelt asserted, constituted "the most representative church in America." Moreover, to an increasing degree the business of the Church fell more and more into the hands of laymen. Illustrative of this new spirit was the celebrated Vanderbilt University case, tried in the courts, which resulted in the university's withdrawal (1914) from Methodist auspices in order to obtain the funds under control of the Peabody Foundation.

As a balance to this secularizing tendency, Methodist organizations like the Church Extension Society upheld traditional Wesleyan principles of evangelization. The Church Extension Society was founded in 1864 "to secure suitable houses of public worship and such other church property" as might assist the propagation of the faith. Within the first ten years, the Society collected three million dollars for its projects, and at present is promoting missionary enterprises in Hawaii, Alaska, Central America, and among the Negroes and Indians in the States.

Comparable to the evangelical balance to the inroads of secularism was the tendency toward reunion among Methodist bodies to offset the century and a half of schismatic fragmentation. After years of negotiation, on May 10, 1939, a Plan of Union was adopted at Kansas City, which united the Methodist Episcopal Church, the Methodist Episcopal Church, South, and the reformed Methodist Protestant Church into one organic body, The Methodist Church. The historical basis for the fusion, as stated in the Plan of Union, was that all three denominations "had their common origin in the organization of the Methodist Episcopal Church in America in 1784, A.D., and have ever held, adhered to and preserved a common belief, spirit and purpose, as expressed in their common Articles of Religion."[11]

In November 1966, the General Conferences of The Methodist Church and the Evangelical United Brethren approved a formal constitution for their long-discussed union. Ratification was presumed by the annual regional conferences of both churches. The new United Methodist Church came into being in the spring of 1968.

The United Methodist Church does not mean a complete reassessment of Wesleyan principles or restructuring of the whole denomination. Only minor changes were made in the two uniting bodies. In most cases, the Evangelical United Brethren adjusted to Methodist polity, e.g., to elect bishops for life and not for renewable four-year terms, and to have district superintendents appointed by bishops instead of elected by the annual conferences.

DOCTRINE OF FAITH AND MORALS

The Methodist Church accounts for 80 per cent of the membership of all Methodist bodies in the country and substantially expresses their common principles and policy. Its codification, therefore, of belief and worship in the *Doctrine and Discipline of The Methodist Church* may be taken as fairly representative of the nature and function of American

Methodism at the present day. Going back to the first days of the Church's establishment in colonial America, the *Discipline* has become an authoritative source book which the clergy urge the people to have "found in every Methodist home." It is revised every four years by the delegates to the General Conference, and has run to as much as eight hundred pages in duodecimo.

The heart of the Methodist profession of faith is the *Articles of Religion* which John Wesley sent to America in 1784, and which now hold the place of honor in the *Discipline*. Although based on the Thirty-nine Articles of the Anglican Church, they have been modified and supplemented to meet the needs of a growing democratic society.

Explicit faith is declared in "one living and true God, everlasting, without body or parts, of infinite power, wisdom and goodness." In the "unity of this Godhead are three persons, of one substance, power and eternity—the Father, the Son and the Holy Ghost."[12] Having stated that the Son of God "took man's nature in the womb of the blessed Virgin," the *Discipline* explains that He "truly suffered, was crucified, dead and buried, to reconcile His Father to us." After His passion and death, He is said to have risen from the dead, ascended into heaven, until He "return to judge all men at the last day."[13] Then follows a series of propositions, briefly worded in the *Articles of Religion* and expanded elsewhere in the *Discipline*, more than half of which the Methodists admit "are a protest against the errors of Roman Catholicism," since "our Methodist Articles are protestant articles."[14]

Scripture and Revelation. Without using the term, tradition is eliminated as a source of revelation, because "the Holy Scriptures contain all things necessary to salvation; so that whatsoever is not read therein nor may be proved thereby, is not to be required of any man that it should be believed as an article of faith, or be thought requisite or necessary to salvation."[15] In listing the canon of Scripture, those books are accepted "of whose authority [there] was never any doubt in the Church."[16] Accordingly seven books of the Old Testament are dropped, notably the Book of Wisdom and the two Books of Machabees.

Sin, Faith, and Justification. Original sin is first declared against the Pelagians not to consist in the mere "following of Adam," and then positively identified, with Luther and Calvin, as "a corruption of the nature of every man," which is so deep that "of his nature" man is "inclined to evil, and that continually."[17] As a result of this condition, "we have no power to do good works, pleasant and acceptable to God, without the grace of God preventing us."[18] Luther's doctrine of justification by faith alone is restated almost in the words of the Tridentine condemnation, that "We are accounted righteous before God only for the merit of our Lord and Saviour Jesus Christ, by faith, and not for our own works or deservings. Wherefore, that we are justified by faith only is a most wholesome doctrine, and very full of comfort."[19]

For an adequate concept of the Methodist idea of faith and conversion, the statements in the *Discipline* must be seen in the context of Wesley's own writings on the subject. As regards salvific faith, by which a sinner feels that he is converted to God, Wesley conceived it as something deeply personal, involving a direct quasi-sensible experience of the divine presence, a consciousness of "the immanent activity of the Holy Spirit."[20] In Wesley's own words, "Faith is the divine evidence whereby the spiritual man discerneth God, and the things of God. It is with regard to the spiritual world, what sense is with regard to the natural. It is the spiritual sensation of every soul that is born of God."[21] His attitude toward man's co-operation in the work of salvation is ambiguous. Faced with parallel passages from Wesley, in which he first seems to favor and then to oppose the Catholic teaching on good works, some Methodists confess that "if . . . Wesley is here falling back upon human causality in salvation, then we must be content with a final unresolved contradiction in Wesley's thought. Wesley has rendered man powerless and, in spite of that, requires him to respond freely to grace."[22] Whatever may be said in theory, Wesley's constant exhortation to the practice of Christian virtue meant an implicit repudiation of the denial of man's freedom and an admission that liberty must be rightly used as a condition for salvation.

Definition of the Church. The Methodist concept of the

Church includes three aspects, the universal, the visible, and the local, clearly defined by the *Discipline:*

> The Church Universal is composed of all who accept Jesus Christ as Lord and Saviour, and which in the Apostles' Creed we declare to be the holy catholic Church.[23]
>
> The visible Church of Christ is a congregation of faithful men in which the pure word of God is preached, and the Sacraments duly administered.[24]
>
> The local church is a connectional society of persons who have professed their faith in Christ, have been baptized, have assumed the vows of membership in The Methodist Church, and are associated in fellowship as a local Methodist Church.[25]

According to Methodism, therefore, the Church is not essentially an organized society founded by Christ. It was not He but His followers who may be said to have established an institutional church by their common acceptance of Him as their Savior. Not even a common faith in a definite body of doctrine, but only a trustful hope in the mercy of God is required to belong to the society called the Church Universal. However, if they wish, Christians may further express their solidarity by forming a structured church with not only a mutual trust in their Redeemer, but a common preaching discipline and sacramental ritual, like the Lutherans or Episcopalians. Finally, on the local level, the members are united by a voluntary submission to the Methodist form of Christianity, which makes no claim to exclusiveness as the true Church of Christ, but only has the title to individuality, to distinguish it from other equally orthodox bodies.

Rites and Ceremonies. Since the Church is not essentially organizational, it has no need of visible symbols to express and preserve its unity. Negatively, then, "It is not necessary that rites and ceremonies should in all places be the same, or exactly alike; for they have always been different, and may be changed according to the diversity of countries, times and men's manners." And positively, "every particular church may ordain, change or abolish ceremonies and rites, so that all things may be done to edification."[26] It is interesting to note that in drafting this last regulation, Wesley substantially altered Article 34 of the Thirty-nine Articles of the Anglican Church, which allowed the churches to modify rites and ceremonies that have been "ordained by man's authority."[27] Wesley deleted the restrictive clause.

The Sacraments. Only two sacraments, baptism and the Supper of the Lord, are said to be found in the gospel. The other five, commonly called sacraments, "are not to be counted for Sacraments of the Gospel; being such as have partly grown out of the corrupt following of the apostles, and partly are states of life allowed in the Scriptures."[28] In a statement directly aimed at the Catholic doctrine of the reserved presence in the Eucharist, the *Discipline* says that "the Sacraments were not ordained of Christ to be gazed upon, or to be carried about; but that we should duly use them."[29] This is substantially Article 25 of the Thirty-nine Articles. Although baptism is not explicitly said to effect the remission of sins, yet implicitly this function is suggested in the two synonyms given in its definition. It is "not only a sign of profession and mark of difference whereby Christians are distinguished from others that are not baptized; but it is also a sign of regeneration or the new birth."[30] Still there is strong evidence that Wesley, and the Methodists after him, would not regard baptism as remissive of moral guilt. Article 16 of the Anglican Articles begins: "Not every deadly sin willingly committed after Baptism is sin against the Holy Ghost."[31] The corresponding Article 12 of the Methodist Creed begins: "Not every sin willingly committed after justification is the sin against the Holy Ghost."[32] A reasonable conclusion is that Wesley substituted "justification" for "Baptism" to fit more logically into his system of justification by faith alone, since infants are presumably incapable of making an act of justifying faith; consequently whatever else happens to them at baptism, it is not the remission of sin.

The Supper of the Lord. The term "Eucharist" is nowhere used to describe the Sacrament of the Altar. Instead it is called the Lord's Supper or Holy Communion. Thus "transubstantiation, or the change of the substance of bread and wine in the Supper of the Lord" is said to be contrary to the plain words of Scripture, following the Protestant tradition in the Church of England. However, there is a sense in which

Christ may be considered present in the Lord's Supper, after a heavenly and spiritual manner. And the means whereby the body of Christ is received and eaten in the Supper is faith."[33] Unlike the Anglicans, from whom the wording of this doctrine is drawn, there is less evidence of a sacramental or "Catholic" interpretation of the real presence among the Methodists.

Marriage and Divorce. Although the marriage ceremony is taken almost verbally from the Roman Ritual, the contract itself is denied to be a sacrament instituted by Christ. Correspondingly it is not a permanent union, but may be dissolved.

A remarkable change, however, has taken place in Methodist thinking on this subject in the past decade. As late as 1952, the Methodist discipline was still quite specific in the reasons it gave for allowing a minister to solemnize a second marriage while both spouses were still alive. The full text then read:

> No minister shall solemnize the marriage of a divorced person whose wife or husband is living and unmarried; but this rule shall not apply (1) to the innocent person when it is clearly established by competent testimony that the true cause for divorce was adultery or other vicious conditions which through mental or physical cruelty or physical peril invalidated the marriage vow, nor (2) to the divorced persons seeking to be re-united in marriage. The violation of this rule concerning divorce shall be considered an act of maladministration.[34]

Hence the Methodist Church did not claim the right to grant a divorce on its own authority, but it conceded this right to the state and the married persons under several conditions:

1. The subsequent marital union of one party automatically gives his (or her) partner the right to a valid remarriage before a Methodist minister.

2. The innocent party in case of adultery, physical or mental cruelty may be validly remarried.

3. The victim of vicious conditions, or one exposed to physical danger may be validly remarried.

By 1964 the attitude had become quite different. Instead of spelling out the grounds for dissolving a previous marriage, the *Discipline* now merely warned the faithful of the evils of divorce and encouraged the remarrying couple to make adequate preparation for their new partnership:

> The minister shall make his counsel available to those under the threat of marriage breakdown in order to explore every possibility of reconstructing the marriage.
>
> In view of the seriousness with which the Scriptures and the Church regard divorce, a minister may solemnize the marriage of a divorced person only when he has satisfied himself by careful counseling that: (a) the divorced person is sufficiently aware of the factors leading to the failure of the previous marriage, (b) the divorced person is sincerely preparing to make the proposed marriage truly Christian and (c) sufficient time has elapsed for adequate preparation and counseling.[35]

This attitude is further reflected in the *Methodist Social Creed*, which is also part of the Church's *Discipline*, where the Church advocates "improved marriage and divorce laws."[36] In other words, legal divorce is taken for granted.

The same kind of liberalization is reflected in the changed attitude toward contraception. The 1952 *Discipline* is silent on the subject. Now the *Discipline* includes a detailed defense of contraception and its recommendation for society at large. As part of the *Methodist Social Creed*, its influence has been felt far beyond the Church's membership. Encouragement of contraception is given under the general heading of "Our Declaration of Social Concern"—with special reference to the family.

> We believe that planned parenthood, practiced with respect for human life, fulfills rather than violates the will of God. It is the duty of each married couple prayerfully and responsibly to seek parenthood, avert it, or defer it, in accordance with the best expression of their Christian love. Families in all parts of the world should have available to them necessary information and medical assistance for birth control through public and private programs. This issue

must be seen in reference to the pressing population problem now before the whole world.[37]

Individual Methodist churchmen, like the late Bishop G. Bromley Oxnam, have further advocated compulsory planned parenthood, pointing out that "Communities which fail to provide . . . child-space service are recreant in their trust."[38]

Religious Education. Until recently Methodist churchmen had been outspoken in their support of public schools, and in their opposition to any kind of subsidy for private education. Their position was concretized in the Methodist *Discipline* as late as the early fifties.

> The Methodist Church is committed to the public schools as the most effective means of providing common education for all our children. We hold that it is an institution essential to the preservation and development of our true democracy.
>
> We are unalterably opposed to the diversion of tax funds to the support of private and sectarian schools. In a short time this scattering process can destroy our American public school system and weaken the foundations of national unity.
>
> We believe that religion has a rightful place in the public school program, and that it is possible for public school teachers, without violating the traditional American principle of separation of church and state, to teach moral principles and spiritual values.[39]

The foregoing policy statement is omitted from the latest Methodist *Discipline*, which suggests a less critical attitude toward church-related schools. As a matter of fact, American Methodists have a long tradition of supporting and maintaining educational institutions. Their National Board of Education is officially committed to "the promotion of Christian education."[40] Moreover, its Division of Higher Education was founded for "establishing and maintaining individual institutions and . . . ministering to students without respect to race or national origin [whereby] the church continues its historic work of uniting knowledge and vital piety."[41]

Temperance. The traditional Methodist reform attitude toward alcoholic beverages goes back to John Wesley, who wrote in his sermon on "The Use of Money" that "Neither may we gain by hurting our neighbor in his body. Therefore, we may not sell anything which tends to impair health; such is evidently all that liquid fire, commonly called drams or spirituous liquors."[42]

In accordance with this principle, until lately the *Discipline* declared in forthright language what was the official Methodist stand on the sale and use of intoxicating drinks:

> Our Church reasserts its long-established conviction that intoxicating liquor cannot be legalized without sin. The Church of Jesus Christ from its very nature stands at variance with the liquor traffic. For it to be silent in its opposition would be to be disloyal in its function. Therefore, to be true to itself the Church must be militant in opposition to the liquor traffic . . . Adequate relief can come only through total abstinence for the individual, and effective prohibition for the state.[43]

These norms were given positive expression in the Board of Temperance, with headquarters in Washington, D.C., whose duty it was "to promote by an intensive educational program . . . voluntary total abstinence . . . to promote observance and enforcement of constitutional provisions and statutory enactments which suppress the traffic in alcoholic liquors and in narcotic drugs; and to aid and promote such legislation."[44] Since the General Conference of 1872, American Methodists had steadily promoted the necessity of "total legal prohibition." They were the most influential group in securing the passage of the 18th Amendment, and in 1932, just before the Amendment was repealed, the General Conference stated that "As a church we can follow no course except the one that will reduce the consumption of beverage alcohol to the minimum. We are convinced that national prohibition is that method."[45]

With this long-standing tradition, it may come as a surprise to know that The Methodist Church has since modified its position on alcohol. The Board of Temperance has been absorbed by a larger body, the Board of Christian Social Concerns; no longer are Methodists formally committed to advocating legal prohibition; and, in general, the whole stress is on education and developing personal responsibility rather than legislating against alcoholic beverages.

WORSHIP AND RITUAL

The contrast between Methodist doctrine and worship is striking. Where the Articles of Religion describe the Church as one whose only bond of unity is a common trust in the Redeemer, the Methodist ritual emphasizes the need for a corporate and visible worship that goes into minute details of posture, gesture, and order of procedure.

Methodist Orders of Worship. To avoid imposing complete uniformity on the ministers, the *Discipline* allows different types of religious service called "Orders of Worship," suitable for Sunday or weekday celebration. "But while liberty is given in the use of these orders of worship, it is urged that all ministers and congregations make use of some one of these orders."[46] The Order of Worship—Brief Form—will illustrate the general procedure:[47]

ORDER OF WORSHIP—BRIEF FORM

Let the people be in silent meditation and prayer upon entering the sanctuary. Let the service of worship begin at the time appointed.

At the end of all prayers the people shall say "Amen".

PRELUDE

SCRIPTURE SENTENCES, or CALL TO WORSHIP. To be said or sung.

HYMN. The people standing.

PRAYERS. Here the minister may use an invocation or collect and prayers of confession and the Lord's Prayer.

PSALTER OR OTHER ACT OF PRAISE. To be read responsively or in unison, the people standing; then shall be said or sung the *Gloria Patri*.

ANTHEM

THE SCRIPTURE LESSONS

AFFIRMATION OF FAITH. The people standing; then may be sung a doxology.

PASTORAL PRAYER

OFFERTORY. Here parish notices may be given.

The minister may read Scripture sentences before the offering is received. An anthem may be sung during the receiving of the offering. Following the presentation of the offering a prayer of dedication may be said or sung.

At the discretion of the minister the offertory and prayers may follow the sermon.

HYMN. The people standing.

THE SERMON

INVITATION TO CHRISTIAN DISCIPLESHIP

HYMN. The people standing.

BENEDICTION. The people may be seated for silent prayer.

POSTLUDE

The Lord's Supper. Two different services for the administration of the Lord's Supper are allowed by the Methodist *Discipline,* substantially alike, and both intended to replace the regular order of morning worship when the sacrament of the Lord's Supper is administered. A preliminary rubric directs that "The Lord's Table should have upon it a fair linen cloth. Let the pure, unfermented juice of the grape be used."[48] The Communion ritual is long and elaborate. Alternating prayers are said by the minister and congregation, texts from the Old and New Testaments, e.g., the Decalogue and the Sermon on the Mount, and finally the Prayer of Consecration, which is practically verbatim from various parts of the *Missale Romanum:*

O merciful Father, we most humbly beseech thee, and grant that we, receiving this bread and wine, according to thy Son our Saviour Jesus Christ's holy institution, in remembrance of his death and passion may also be partakers of the divine nature through him;

Who in the same night that he was betrayed took bread (*Here may the minister take the bread in his hands*); and when he had given thanks, he broke it, and gave it to his disciples, saying, Take, eat; this is my body, which is given for you; do this in remembrance of me. Likewise after supper he took the cup (*Here may the minister take the cup in his hands*); and when he had given thanks, he gave it to them, saying, Drink ye all of this; for this is my blood of the new covenant which is shed for you, and for many, for the remission of sins; do this, as oft as ye shall drink it, in remembrance of me. Amen.[49]

After another short prayer, the minister communicates himself and then distributes the elements to the people. The substitution of "bread and wine" for "body and blood" in the Prayer of Consecration and the reference to "faith" in the Communion Prayer reveal the Methodist idea of the Eucharist as mainly subjective; there is no physical reality independently of the mind of the communicant.

In giving the bread the minister says, "The body of our Lord Jesus Christ, which was given for thee, preserve thy soul and body unto everlasting life. Take and eat this in remembrance that Christ died for thee, and feed on him in thy heart by faith with thanksgiving." And in giving the grape juice, he continues, "The blood of our Lord Jesus Christ, which was shed for thee, preserve thy soul and body unto everlasting life. Drink this in remembrance that Christ's blood was shed for thee, and be thankful."[50] Unexpectedly the minister is given an option when distributing Communion to use either the statement referring to the body and blood of Christ or to the remembrance that Christ died and shed his blood. The choice is an accommodation to either High or Low Church Methodism.

The closing prayers are a paraphrase of the *Hanc Igitur* of the Latin Mass and a benediction which says: "The blessing of God Almighty the Father, the Son, and the Holy Spirit, be among you, and remain with you always. Amen."[51]

The Administration of Baptism. The only other sacrament admitted by the Methodists is baptism, in which every adult person, and the parents of every child to be baptized, have the choice of sprinkling, pouring, or immersion. Two rituals are provided for the administration of the sacrament, one for infants, another for youths and mature adults. The sequence in each is an explanation of the meaning of the rite, a prayer to God, an exhortation and questions addressed to the sponsors or candidates for baptism, a passage from the Gospels and the actual conferring of the sacrament. The words of administration are the same in both cases, namely: "N., I baptize thee in the name of the Father, and of the Son, and of the Holy Spirit. Amen."[52]

A common practice in many Methodist churches is to administer the sacrament by "application." The minister merely applies a moist object, e.g., a piece of cloth or cotton or even his hand, but there is no flow of water.

There is a significant difference in the questions asked of sponsors presenting an infant and those asked of a youth or adult presenting himself to be baptized. In the infant ritual, there is no reference to sin infecting the soul. The question is put to the sponsors, as to whether they solemnly promise to see that the child is brought up a Christian. Whereas in adult baptism, there is explicit reference to sin and sorrow, when the candidate is asked: "Do you truly and earnestly repent of your sins and accept Jesus Christ as your Savior?" They should answer, "I do."[53] Nevertheless even in the baptismal rite for youths and adults, the context shows that the sin factor pertains only to actually committed faults, since there is no suggestion of inherited sin being deleted in the sacrament.

Minister of the Sacraments. The Methodist *Discipline* distinguishes four grades in the ministry of the church, one lay and three clerical. To the lay ministry belong the preachers, who may be either local (stable) or traveling (itinerant). To the clerical belong deacons, elders, and bishops, who are specially ordained to their office.

All the above classes of persons, even lay preachers with a permanent pastorate who have never been ordained, are permitted to administer the sacraments of baptism and Holy Communion. Here is a paradox between ritual and practice. On the one hand, the ritual of the Lord's Supper uses the words of institution and prescribes the "Prayer of Consecration." What before the prayer was referred to as bread and unfermented grape juice, afterward is called "Holy Communion," which may be received by the people "while they are devoutly kneeling." Also in the rite of ordination of elders, when the bishop imposes hands on the ordinand, he says, "Be thou a faithful dispenser of the Word of God and of his holy Sacraments," whereas in ordaining deacons he explains that "It appertains to the office of a deacon . . . to assist the elder in the administration of the Holy Communion."[54] Thus a clear distinction is set up between the order of elder and deacon, the latter being ordained only to help in the ministration of Communion, while the former is ordained specifically to dispense the Sacred Mysteries. But in practice no distinction is made between deacon or elder, cleric or layman, in conducting the full ritual of the Lord's Supper, which requires a formal "consecration" of the elements.

ORGANIZATION AND GOVERNMENT

The government of The Methodist Church is highly organized. Centering around the Conference, the duties and functions of Methodist officials form an integrated unit which is an elaboration of the norms set down by John Wesley and which historians of Protestantism regard as "unsurpassed for the accomplishment of the spiritual mission of the Church." The same organizational structure is duplicated, on a minor scale, by the smaller Methodist bodies.

Conferences. There are six types of Methodist Conferences, hierarchically stratified from the General Conference on a global level to the Church Conference in the local congregation.

The General Conference, which meets every four years, is "the legislative body for the entire church . . . having full legislative powers over all connectional matters."[55] It has authority to enact laws which define the powers, duties, and privileges of the bishops; to decide on the content and form of the Hymnal and ritual; to initiate and direct Church publications, evangelization and the missions, social and charitable enterprises; to direct and decide the Church's judicial administration. Lesser Conferences are ultimately responsible to the General Conference for all matters of common interest to the whole denomination. Delegates to the General Conference are elected by the Annual Conferences. One half the delegates are ordained ministers and one half lay members. The Judicial Council, elected by the General Conference, is the final court of appeal in The Methodist Church.

The Jurisdictional Conference is "the representative body in the United States, established by the Plan of Union [1939], composed of ministerial and lay delegates [50-50] from the several Annual Conferences of a jurisdiction and meeting every four years."[56] There are six jurisdictions in the country; all are geographically distinct, with the exception of the Central, or Negro Conference, which is being phased out. Election of bishops is the Jurisdictional Conference's most important function.

The Annual Conference is "the basic administrative body in The Methodist Church, having supervision over the affairs of the Church in a specific territory."[57] Technically the territories so administered are called Annual Conferences, most of which correspond to the individual states. Three fundamental items referred to the Annual Conference are: constitutional amendments, election of delegates to the general and jurisdictional conferences, and matters relating to the character and function of the clergy. Reading of official appointments at the close of the Annual Conference is one of the most spectacular events in Methodist procedure.

The District Conference is "an assembly held annually in each district where authorized by the Annual Conference."[58] Its duties include inquiry into the spiritual state of the Church, promotion of mission work in the district, support of churches and colleges, hospitals and publications, and examination of candidates for the Methodist ministry.

The Quarterly Conference is "the governing body of the pastoral charge."[59] It unites the parish with the larger sphere of Methodist activity, and is composed of the preachers, lay leaders, and other representatives of the local churches. Although the Conference may convene four times a year, only two annual meetings are obligatory. Among the duties it may handle, the most important is to act as a "sounding board" for the people, to determine whether a given pastor is satisfactory to his congregation. If not, the Conference is authorized to inform the minister, call for adaptation to the people's wants, and, if necessary, urge the pastor's removal.

The Church Conference is "an assembly of the members of a charge or church for review and planning of the church's work [and], when so authorized by the Quarterly Conference, for election of church officers."[60] Its immediate purpose is to co-operate with the pastor in carrying out the duties of his office and to extend the influence of the local church into the whole community.

Church Ministers and Officials. Highest in rank is the bishop, who is a general superintendent within his territory. He is an elder, specially ordained, and generally holding office for life. Although nominally an executive, his duties are severely limited by the democratic structure of The Methodist Church, in which the Conferences play the major role. One large power he enjoys, however, is to appoint pastors and other ministers of the gospel, after consultation with the district superintendents. To him also belongs the consecration of bishops and the ordination of elders, deacons, and deaconesses. Since 1939, when the non-episcopal Methodist Protestant Church was absorbed into membership, the episcopacy in The Methodist Church has become more than ever functional and executive. Except for the right of appointment, which also may be challenged, the bishop's power and real influence is largely a matter of his personality and abilities. These lie in the direction of his presidencies over conferences, directing business, and maintaining accord among the members. He serves on many boards of the Church, sometimes as the presiding officer, but mostly as just a member.

Next in ministerial rank is the elder who has been "duly ordained by the laying on of the hands of a bishop and other elders." Below the elder is the deacon, who is also ordained by the bishop. A deaconess is "a woman who has been led by the Holy Spirit to devote herself to Christlike service under the direction of the Church, and who, having met the requirements, has been duly licensed, consecrated, and commissioned by a bishop."[61] As provided by the *Discipline*, deaconesses may engage in any of the social, educational, and missionary activities proper to The Methodist Church, in America or overseas. They receive a fixed salary, are given periodical leave of absence or sabbatical leave, and provision is made for their financial security after retirement from active service. Of the deaconesses in active service in the United States, the largest number belong to The Methodist Church.

Peculiar to The Methodist Church is the importance of the laity in the religious ministry. A person may be licensed to serve as pastor of a charge (church) even though he is not ordained as elder or deacon. If he is properly licensed, he is technically a minister or preacher, and entitled to the full exercise of the Methodist ministry. Lay trustees manage the property interests of the local congregation; while lay stewards handle the finances and generally guide the spiritual work of the parish under the pastor's direction. The 1956 General Conference legislated the admission of women to the full exercise of the ministry, not only locally, as before, but even to serve as "itinerant preachers" and to participate in the General Conference of The Methodist Church.

SMALLER METHODIST BODIES

Unlike the Baptists, whose denominationalism affects all the churches in that tradition, Methodists in the United States are less fragmented than statistics may indicate. The United Methodist Church accounts for 80 per cent of the professed followers of Wesley in the United States. Nevertheless, there are a large number of smaller Methodist bodies, which often differ considerably among themselves and especially from The United Methodist Church.

The two largest churches, apart from the United Methodists, are Negro denominations. Together they represent one seventh of the total Negro population in the country.

The African Methodist Episcopal Church was established in 1787, when a group of Negro Methodists withdrew from the Methodist Episcopal Church in Philadelphia. Their grievance was mainly against practices of discrimination. Until 1816, the church was only a co-operative of dissident Negro bodies who were dissatisfied with the dominantly white congregations. In that year, Richard Allen was consecrated first bishop of the church by the Methodist Bishop Asbury. Before the Civil War the church was confined to the Northern states, but its membership is now represented in almost every state of the union. While its doctrine and polity are similar to that of other Methodist bodies, the African Methodists are especially active in a widespread home missionary program.

Another group of Negroes separated from the parent organization in 1796, in protest against discrimination in New York City. Since their first church (1800) was called Zion, they later made the term a part of the denominational name. The African Methodist Episcopal Zion Church spread quickly over the Northern states, and by the beginning of the present century was also established in all the Southeastern states. Home-mission evangelism and church extension are emphasized, with foreign missionaries laboring in Liberia, Ghana, Nigeria, and South America.

The Christian Methodist Episcopal Church was known until 1954 as the Colored Methodist Episcopal Church. Otherwise than the foregoing, it was formed in 1870 in the South as a result of a friendly agreement between white and Negro members of the Methodist Episcopal Church, South. At the time of the Emancipation Proclamation, about a quarter million Negro slaves belonged to the Methodist Episcopal Church. By the end of the Civil War, most of them withdrew from the parent body and asked for a separate church of their own. The ethnic bond remains dominant to this day, but there is also a distinctive feature of organizational policy. Its national work is supervised by seven boards, each presided over by a bishop who acts as chairman under the direction of the College of Bishops.

In 1852 the Methodist Episcopal Church, South, lost a number of members in Georgia who withdrew in objection to certain features of the episcopate and the traveling ministry. Two denominations were created, the Congregational Methodist Church and the Congregational Methodist Church of the U.S.A. Both agree that the episcopacy and itinerant ministry lack biblical foundation and favor a congregational form of government.

More recently the Evangelical Methodist Church was

started at Memphis, Tennessee, in 1946 on the threefold premise of being "fundamental in doctrine, evangelistic in program, and congregational in government." On its own testimony, the church is Arminian in theology and Wesleyan in doctrine. Very conservative in their interpretation of the Bible, the church opposes "substituting of social, educational, or other varieties of cultural salvation" in place of the redemptive message of Christ. Its international headquarters are in Wichita, Kansas.

Probably the most direct challenge to large-scale Methodism in the United States comes from the Free Methodist Church of North America. Its beginnings go back to 1860 when a group of lay members and ministers met at Pekin, New York, to protest against what they called the abandonment of original Wesleyanism.

The Free Methodists insist that it is the duty and privilege of every believer to be sanctified wholly, and to be preserved blameless unto the coming of the Lord Jesus Christ. They are mainly characterized by great strictness in Christian conduct. Typical provisions of their teaching reveal what this means.

Temperance. A spirit of self-denial is indispensable to Christian character. A large proportion of the crime and pauperism of the country is caused by strong drink. The Spirit of Christ never leads one to countenance the use or sale of intoxicating liquor as a beverage.

Marriage and Divorce. We do not prohibit our people from marrying persons who are not members of our church, provided such persons give evidence of being converted to God; but we are determined to discourage their marrying those who do not come up to this standard.

We recognize no other ground for divorce than that permitted in the word of God (Matthew 5:32; Mark 10:11–12). Any person guilty of a violation of this law shall have no place among us.

Dress. We insist on the rules concerning dress. This is no time to give encouragement to superfluity of apparel. Therefore, receive none into the church till they have left off superfluous ornaments.

Secret Societies. Voluntary associations are not necessarily sinful because they are secret. But secrecy is always a ground of suspicion. Evil works instinctively incline to darkness. Good works draw good light.

Militarism and War. Militarism is contrary to the spirit of the New Testament and the teachings of Jesus Christ. Even from humanitarian principles alone it is utterly indefensible. It is our profound conviction that none of our people should be required to enter military training or to bear arms except in time of national peril and that the consciences of our individual members should be respected. Therefore we claim exemption from the bearing of arms for all members of our church who are conscientious objectors.[62]

Quite different from the Free Methodists is the Primitive Methodist Church of the U.S.A., whose ancestry goes back to 1812 when Lorenzo Dow, an American revivalist, went to England to organize societies that were more Congregational than Wesleyan. The leaders of these societies were dropped from Wesleyan connection. Their derivatives have since organized into a loosely structured denomination which has no bishops or district superintendents. Ministers have no time limit on their pastorates; they are invited by the local churches, who designate their first, second, and third choices. Foreign mission work is done in Guatemala, Kenya, and Brazil.

There are two Reformed Methodist bodies of considerable influence. In 1885 the Reformed Methodist Union Episcopal Church withdrew from the African Methodist Episcopal Church at Charleston, South Carolina. The schism arose over the election of ministerial delegates to the General Conference. Originally intended as a non-episcopal denomination, it has since adopted the complete structure of the Methodist Episcopal Church. Class meetings and love feasts are featured in the local congregations. The Reformed Zion Union Apostolic Church is another Negro body, formed in 1869 by James R. Howell, who withdrew from the African Methodist Episcopal Zion Church in protest against white discrimination by their fellow Methodists. Internal friction completely disrupted the church by 1874 and it was reorganized in 1881–82 under its present name. The standard Methodist doctrine and polity are followed except that the only ordination is that of elder.

When The Methodist Church was created in 1939, a dissident group broke off in protest to form the Southern Methodist Church. It favors a strong position on racial segregation, stating that "holy writ teaches the separation of peoples at least to the extent of three basic races, namely, Caucasian, Mongoloid, and Negroid."

One of the first Negro denominations to become an independent church was the Union American Methodist Episcopal, formed at Wilmington, Delaware, in 1805. It went through a series of changes in name and experienced a number of defections over administrative policy. It is still concentrated in the New York area and the Atlantic seaboard.

The Wesleyan Methodist Church of America started at Utica, New York, in 1843 during the agitation of the slavery question in the Methodist Conferences of New York State. After the Civil War and the passing of the slavery issue it began to stress the doctrine of higher sanctification. Candidates for membership must give up the use, sale, or manufacture of tobacco and alcoholic beverages and are forbidden membership in secret societies. It will almost certainly be merged in the near future with like-minded denominations like the Free Methodists or one of the Holiness bodies.

Evangelical United Brethren

In the Church of the Evangelical United Brethren we see a confluence of practically all the major streams of classic Protestantism. Among its founders were a Dutch Calvinist, a Mennonite perfectionist, a Methodist exhorter, and a converted Lutheran. Its organizational structure is fundamentally Methodist, and the body might have been incorporated into John Wesley's society except for the language obstacle. The Methodist bishop, Asbury, was reluctant to allow preaching in

German. Its doctrinal position is modeled on the Thirty-nine Articles of the Anglican Church.

While professedly non-liturgical, Evangelical United Brethren became unusually interested in the liturgy, which points to the influence of pre-Reformation Christianity at work in the denomination. They found that ritual worship can be "a vital factor in the faith and life of Christian people." One recommendation was that church buildings be "remodeled for the purpose of making the sanctuary more suggestive of worship." Recently the General Council of the Church ordered the publication of *Christian Worship in Symbol and Ritual,* which left nothing to be desired in careful direction to ministers on how to prevent the liturgy from becoming "an empty form or passing fad." They are instructed in the historical background and development of the liturgy from early Christian times, and in the meaning of liturgical symbols and practices. And though "public worship in non-liturgical Protestant churches has no fixed pattern," the clergy are even advised to follow uniform directives so that services "be performed in a manner fitting to their purpose."[1]

HISTORY

As a distinct denomination, the Evangelical United Brethren Church was born of a merger at Johnstown, Pennsylvania, in 1946, between the Church of the United Brethren in Christ and the Evangelical Church, each with a history that goes back to the early nineteenth century.

The Church of the United Brethren was founded at Frederick County, Maryland, in 1800, by two itinerant preachers, Philip Otterbein (1726–1813) and Martin Boehm (1725–1812). Otterbein was a missionary of the Reformed Church, having migrated to Pennsylvania in 1752 from the German duchy of Nassau. His religious training at home and in school was an "emphatic though moderate" Calvinism. Later he was influenced by the prevalent German pietism, in which "the core of religion was held to be life committed to God, not baptism nor assent to creed. Bible reading, confession, free prayer, hymn singing—these were the avenues to achieve an active, biblical faith."[2]

Martin Boehm was of Swiss ancestry, born in Lancaster County, Pennsylvania. At the age of thirty-one he was chosen by lot to be pastor of the local Mennonite church. But his use of English instead of German and his promotion of revivals aroused opposition. The Mennonites denounced him for "associating with men that allow themselves to walk on the broad way, preaching warfare and the swearing of oaths," and finally expelled him from the denomination.[3] Meantime Boehm had met Otterbein, and together they formed a fellowship of seven evangelist preachers. By 1800 this voluntary association was formalized into a group called The United Brotherhood in Christ Jesus. Otterbein and Boehm were elected superintendents or bishops. Depending on the locality, the organization was known by different names: The Freedom People, The New Reformed, The New Mennonites. At the foundation conference in 1800, they considered themselves "unsectarian." By 1821, however, the name was permanently changed to The United Brethren in Christ. As early as 1817, a *Discipline* of doctrines, ritual, and organizational rules was published, in order to raise the United Brethren above the "free and easy fellowship of unsectarian revivalism." An elaborate Constitution was formulated in 1841, with special emphasis on prohibition of membership in secret societies and opposition to slavery.

Parallel with the steady growth of the Brethren and before their merger with the Evangelicals, there arose a domestic conflict over lay participation and secret societies, with a proposed change of the Constitution. A minority group seceded in 1889 to form the Church of the United Brethren in Christ (Old Constitution), permitting the ordination of men and women and forbidding participation in war and membership in secret societies like the Freemasons.

Independently of the Brethren, the Evangelical Church was started as a revivalist movement by Jacob Albright (1759–1808), a Lutheran by baptism but a Methodist preacher by profession. Alternating between preaching and farming, Albright was finally "certified" in 1803, when "evangelical and Christian friends" from five mission centers drafted a statement declaring "Jacob Albright . . . a truly evangelical minister in every sense of the word and deed."[4] This was the only ordination Albright received. Before his premature death of overwork in the ministry, Albright had converted a Lutheran youth, George Miller (1774–1816), who in 1809 organized his master's followers into The So-Called Albright People. In 1816 they held their first General Conference as The Evangelical Association. A schism was averted in 1831 when John Hamilton was deposed for his anti-denominationalism. Finally in 1839 John Seybert was elected the first bishop of the Association, and through twenty-one years of tireless preaching and administration did more than anyone else "in molding the expansion and character of the Evangelical Church" in America.

As the denomination spread, the German language was replaced by English in preaching and the religious press. Missionary work was organized in a separate society in 1839, and gradually expanded to Germany, Switzerland and Russia, Africa, China and Japan. Like the United Brethren, the Evangelicals were divided by a schism, but on a larger scale. In 1894, delegates of the opposition met in Naperville, Illinois, to organize The United Evangelical Church, thus splitting the parent denomination in a 60-40 ratio. "A chain of untoward events, a number of incompatible leaders, coupled with varying opinions regarding the character of episcopal power," formed the background of the secession. After thirty years of separation and bitter recrimination on both sides, the two segments were reunited in 1922 to form The Evangelical Church.[5]

When the United Brethren and The Evangelical Church merged in 1946, the union came as a result of more than a century of ecumenical efforts by both parties. In the early 1800s the United Brethren were negotiating a union with the Methodists, planning the formation of a Wesleyan Methodist-United Brethren Church, which never materialized. In the mid-century, the Evangelical Conference actually approved by a majority of one to unite with the Methodists, but failed to carry out the resolution. At the turn of the present century, a fusion of Presbyterians, Christians, Methodists, Congregationalists, and United Brethren was discussed but unrealized after the Christians and Congregationalists dropped out. In 1933 the United Brethren and Evangelicals entered into active negotiations, "which resulted in the happy union of the two" on November 16, 1946. Historians of the new denomination trace its creation to almost fifty years of collaboration of Brethren and Evangelicals in the world ecumenical movement, working together as delegates to the Foreign Mission Conference at New York in 1900, at Edinburgh in 1910, at Madras in 1939. When the World Council of Churches was formed, Evangelicals and Brethren joined. Inevitably a union took place, on the assumption that "the creedal statements of these two Churches grew out of common and profound religious experience of the fathers, and were formulated in accord with their discerning interpretation of the Holy Scriptures and by careful study of other ecclesiastical confessions." Consequently, states the Plan of Union, "it is not strange that these creedal statements are found to be in agreement. In all basic and enduring verities of the Christian faith, their respective positions are in the most intimate and beautiful accord."[6] At the time of the merger, the United Brethren had a membership of approximately half a million; the Evangelical Church, half that number.

DOCTRINE AND WORSHIP

The "Confession of Faith" was prominently placed at the head of the *Discipline of the Evangelical United Brethren Church*, and summarized in thirty-two Articles, comparable to the twenty-five Articles of Faith of The Methodist Church, and largely derived from Methodist and Anglican sources. But whatever merger took place in 1946, it did not produce a common statement of belief. The thirty-two Articles of Faith were really two sets of doctrinal statements, thirteen for the Brethren and nineteen for the Evangelicals, not combined but juxtaposed, and in more than one instance hard to reconcile dogmatically.

The Church. In keeping with the Calvinist tradition, the "holy Christian Church" was said to be "composed of true believers in which the Word of God is preached by men divinely called, and ordinances are duly administered."[7] To avoid misunderstanding of the word "Catholic" in the Apostles' Creed, the term was explained to mean "the holy general church," divinely instituted for the threefold purpose of "maintenance of worship . . . the edification of believers, and the conversion of the world to Christ."[8]

Depravity and Justification. There was no compromise with Reformation theology on the state of man since the Fall. "Apart from the grace of our Lord Jesus Christ," man is considered "not only entirely destitute of holiness, but is inclined to evil, and only evil, and that continually."[9] Originally the United Brethren used the expression "depravity" with reference to man's condition, and only after years of controversy was the offensive word omitted from the examination of candidates for the ministry. But the concept remained unchanged. Reminiscent of John Wesley, the Evangelical United Brethren conceived justification of the sinner as a personal experience of the divine presence. Accordingly, "the witness of the Spirit is an inward impression on the soul, whereby the Spirit of God, the heavenly Comforter, immediately convinces the regenerate believer that he has passed from death unto life, that his sins are all forgiven, and that he is a child of God."[10]

Sacraments. In spite of protestations to the contrary, the doctrine on the sacraments is an instance of the incompatibility that existed between the Evangelical and United Brethren in spite of the merger. The Brethren part of the Confession of Faith admits two sacraments, baptism and the Lord's Supper, and then liberally adds that "the mode of baptism and the manner of observing the Lord's Supper are always to be left to the judgment and understanding of each individual."[11] A few pages later, the Evangelist statement leaves practically nothing to free choice. Baptism is described at length as "not merely a token of the Christian profession . . . but it is also a sign of internal ablution or the new birth."[12] Likewise the Lord's Supper is "not merely a token of love and union . . . but is rather a mystery or a representation of our redemption by the sufferings and death of Christ."[13] Without challenging transubstantiation as does the Methodist *Discipline,* the real bodily presence is simply denied, declaring that "the changing of the bread and wine into the body and blood of Christ cannot be supported by the Holy Writ."[14]

Baptism is administered by pouring, sprinkling, or immersion, according to the preference of a child's parents or the adult convert. The Trinitarian formula is used.

More than anywhere else, in the administration of the Lord's Supper there is evidence of a liturgical rebirth among the Evangelical United Brethren. The united denomination published its first *Discipline* in 1947. In the latest edition of the *Discipline* issued by order of the General Conference, the changes in the service of Holy Communion can only be described as radical. Self-consciously the new directive tells the people that this Eucharistic service "is thoroughly evangelical in theology"; but actually it is notoriously not evangelical and betrays the rising dominance of the "High Church" party. In 1947 the *Discipline* prescribed that "unfermented wine shall be used."[15] Now there is no prescription and "fermented wine" is freely allowed. Formerly the clergy were told that "this order is . . . in accordance with the usage of non-liturgical Churches."[16] Now the "form and order for celebration of the Holy Communion is an adaptation of the traditional order which can be traced back to early history of the Church."[17] In the previous directives, "The Prayer and Consecration" avoided all mention of Christ's body and blood and referred only to "this memorial of his death" and "this bread and wine in remembrance of his passion."[18] All this is changed. There is now an explicit "Consecration of the Elements," during which the minister prays, "that we . . . may be partakers of his most blessed body and blood." Following this, he separately takes up the bread, breaks it, and says, "This is my body," and the chalice, saying, "This cup is the new covenant in my blood."[19] Then, to remove any lingering doubt about the new attitude toward the Eucharist, after the words of Institution are pronounced, the bread and wine are said to be "Consecrated Elements," and after giving Communion to the people, the minister is charged to "return the sacred vessels to the Lord's Table and reverently cover them."[20] The "end result" of this reformed Eucharistic rite "is to give us the consciousness that we are part of the church catholic in all ages and in all places."[21]

Moral Standards. Correlative to the idea of Christian perfection, the Evangelical United Brethren Church makes considerable demands on its members for the practice of the moral virtues. Against the human tendency to idleness and sloth, "The Church believes in the proper use of time. The waste and misuse of idle hours . . . obligate every church to provide wholesome activities . . . through worship, music, reading, study, fellowship, recreation and service" facilities. Accordingly, "the Church views with alarm the widespread circulation and reading of salacious literature . . . Strict censorship of motion pictures in order to protect society from evident evils is advocated."[22] Alcoholic beverages, gambling, narcotics, and tobacco are forbidden, but in descending order of emphasis. "The manufacture, sale and use of intoxicating liquors as beverage . . . are strictly prohibited."[23] Less absolute but still forbidden is gambling, which is "a menace to society," so that "all members of the Church are expected to abstain from gambling in any form."[24] In like manner "the Church is unalterably opposed to the use of and the traffic in habit-forming drugs . . . and calls upon its members to abstain from the use of narcotics."[25] Lastly "the Church believes that the use of tobacco in any form is injurious and a needless waste of time . . . All members of the church are urged to abstain from its use."[26] Along with these restrictions is a leniency in the matter of divorce which loses none of its compromise by an appeal to the Scriptures. After stating that "the Church shall consistently regard as valid only such divorces as are granted on the ground of adultery," and ministers are told not to solemnize "marriages in cases where there is a divorced husband or wife living," a concession is granted which practically negates the prohibition, since "this does not apply to the innocent party to a divorce caused by adultery."[27]

Occasional Services. A notable feature of Evangelical United Brethren worship is the variety of services for special occasions. There is a service for the dedication of an organ, for the dedication of a parsonage, for the charge of the trustees of a parsonage, for commissioning of missionaries, and even for the burning of a mortgage. The ritual is quite impressive. For example, the solemn dedication of a home begins with the singing of an "instrumental prelude," and a declaration by the minister that "Before the state, the school, or the church were established, the home had come into being . . . We have come to invoke the divine blessing upon this home."[28] After prayer, said by the minister, and Scripture reading, the husband, wife, and family alternate in a "Responsive Service" which includes the lighting of a candle and reciting a series of invocations:

> *Husband*—To thee, O God, who dwellest with the humble . . . and maintainest their lot;
> *Family*—We dedicate this home and light the candle of devotion.
> *Wife*—As a house of friendship, where others may come for fellowship . . . and be enabled to go forth strengthened, in body, mind and spirit;
> *Family*—We dedicate this home and light the candle of friendship.
> *Husband*—To beauty in art and literature, where pictures and books shall be friends, and music and song the language of comfort and inspiration;
> *Family*—We dedicate this home and light the candle of beauty.
> *Wife*—To the Great Guest, Jesus Christ, our Lord . . . who brought the light of heaven and the peace of God to people like ourselves;
> *Family*—We dedicate this home and light the candle of service and hospitality.[29]

The dedication closes with a triple blessing by the minister, asking that "Jehovah lift up his countenance upon thee and give thee peace. Amen."[30]

GOVERNMENT AND ORGANIZATION

The organization of the Evangelical United Brethren follows the general plan of The Methodist Church, with thirty-three Annual Conferences or jurisdictional areas which roughly correspond to the territory of one or more states. In addition there are eleven Missionary and Overseas Conferences which cover such areas as Florida, Kentucky, and Puerto Rico. Subordinate to these are the Quarterly Conferences, supervised by district or conference superintendents. The major Conferences are grouped into Episcopal Areas, currently eight in number, presided over by a bishop.

Bishops are simply elders who have been chosen by the General Conference for a term of four years to supervise and administer the territory committed to their care. "They are agents of supervision, not a separate order. Their distinctiveness is administrative, not priestly, and they lack the special 'grace' which pertains to bishops in genuinely episcopal churches. Such prerogatives as they hold are entrusted to them for a specific term of office."[31] Behind this severe limitation of episcopal power lies a theory of ecclesiastical structure which the Evangelical United Brethren believe was inspired by John Calvin. They proudly regard it as "the golden mean" between Congregationalism and Episcopalianism, affirming that "the people through their chosen representatives should administer the Church, thus providing a church government that was democratic without being subject to chaos [as among Baptists and Congregationalists], and authoritative without the peril of tyranny [as among Episcopalians and Roman Catholics]."[32]

In contrast with the purely administrative function of bishops, Evangelical United Brethren ordain their elders in order to give them definite spiritual powers. As the bishop lays hands on the head of the candidate, he asks that "The Lord pour upon thee the Holy Spirit for the office and work of an Elder," and bids him receive "authority to preach the Word of God, and to administer the holy sacraments in the Church."[33] Inconsistently, however, even before ordination a man may be "licensed to preach in accordance with the Order and Discipline of The Evangelical United Brethren Church," and also administer the sacraments.[34] The latter privilege is granted to "probationers" who are looking forward to eventual ordination, "by special annual grant from [their] Annual Conferences."[35] Since 1946, the question arose whether this concession of administering the sacraments without ordination refers also to ministers from other churches who are serving as licensed, though unordained, preachers in the E.U.B. The General Conference answered that while "it is not the policy of the denomination to provide such rights for unordained Ministers of other denominations serving in our pulpits, however, where the emergency exists, the Annual Conference itself must determine" and may grant the privilege.[36]

Great care is taken to provide maximum lay participation in the church government. Laymen have equal representation with the clergy in the Annual and General Conferences. To forestall clerical intrusion beyond set limits, the meaning of what constitutes a lay person is clearly defined. Not only elders, but "no Minister [who may be a layman], Minister's wife, nor anyone recommended to the Annual Conference for licence to preach, should be eligible for election as a Lay Member or Alternate for an Annual Conference."[37] In governing the Church, therefore, "laymen and ministers sit side by side during the conference session, enjoying equal rights and privileges," with two exceptions: Only the clergy may vote on granting a license to preach and in advancing a lay candidate to eldership.[38]

The federated character of its organization enabled the Church to operate numerous boards and agencies on a national scale that would be impossible in a less closely knit society. The Board of Missions, for example, directed the Church's evangelism on all levels, from the local town and county to the foreign missions in West Africa. Besides other duties, the Board of Christian Education had general supervision of the two denominational seminaries with authority to "make such recommendations as will be of assistance in increasing the effectiveness of these institutions."[39] Typical of the ecumenical changes taking place before the 1968 merger with the Methodists was the constitution of the new United Theological Seminary, formed in 1947 by the union of Bonebrake and Evangelical Schools of Theology. The statutes of Bonebrake had required each professor on the day of his inauguration publicly to declare that he would not teach or insinuate anything contrary to the Constitution, the Confession of Faith, and the rules of the Evangelical United Brethren Church.[40] United Theological Seminary no longer requires such a declaration.

One feature of the denomination which is rather singular among American Protestants is its attention to the status of women and an organized effort to solicit their co-operation in the Church's activities. There is a Women's Society of World Service, operating on a national and local level, whose purpose is "to unite all the women of the church in Christian fellowship to make Christ known throughout the world, to deepen the spiritual life of each of its members and to develop a sense of personal responsibility for the whole task of the Church, through a program of education, service, prayer and giving for the maintenance and advancement of the missionary work of the Evangelical United Brethren Church."[41] A Girls' Missionary Guild has the same general purpose on a minor scale. Growing out of these women's societies is a denomination-wide program of Missionary Education for Children, whose aim is to develop in boys and girls "a spirit of friendship for all children, to create in them a desire to help all children to know and love Jesus Christ, to lead to a desire to share with others the good things of life which Christianity has brought to the world."[42] One result of this enlistment of women and interest in the children was an unusually high enrollment in Sunday school classes: almost a one-to-one relationship of children to church membership.

PART TWO

MINOR PROTESTANT DENOMINATIONS

Any attempt to classify Protestant denominations is bound to be inadequate. There is, first of all, a great deal of overlapping from one group to another. Holiness bodies, for example, show many qualities of the Pentecostals, Legalistic churches may belong to the Reformed family, certain Anti-Trinitarian groups indulge in Spiritualistic practices. Also, within a given body, as in the mental and moral improvement societies, there are several characteristics: They are esoteric, claim to be mystical, and they are frequently called New Thought.

In spite of these inadequacies, however, the classification which has been adopted is not arbitrary. It is based on specific elements of historical origin and doctrinal emphasis which otherwise disparate bodies have in common, and which Protestant writers generally recognize as constituting an ecclesiastical family, made up of denominations, which are further divided into subdenominations composed of the local churches.

Anti-Trinitarian Bodies

The Unitarians were founded on the basic denial that there are three Persons in one God and that Christ is possessed of two natures: human and divine. Other religious bodies in America also deny the Trinity, but not all in the same way. A number of respected groups, like the United Church of Christ, allow a great deal of latitude in the interpretation of orthodox doctrine. We are here concerned with still another class: those who may verbally profess the Trinity but officially teach that there is only one Person in God. They differ from the Unitarians in not having been organized originally on this negative principle.

The Swedenborgians, called the Churches of New Jerusalem, are founded on the teachings of Emanuel Swedenborg (1668–1772), a Swedish scientist turned theologian. Before he turned to theology, he distinguished himself in mathematics, geology, cosmology, and anatomy. According to his followers, "no other individual in the world's history ever encompassed in himself so great a variety of useful knowledge, or ever wrote so vast a range of practical subjects, serving at the same time in various public capacities." He is credited with having founded the science of crystallography, and of having discovered the function of the ductless glands. His first experiences with the other world initiated his prodigious writings in the field of religion. He claimed that he had almost daily visions of heaven and hell. He wrote also about his frequent conversations with angels and disembodied spirits, including those of Luther and Calvin. Through these he learned that a new Christian church was to be born and that his writings were to be its foundation.

Swedenborg died after leaving his followers a library of writings on theological works. A bare listing of their titles suggests the wide range of his interests. They include commentaries on the spiritual sense of Genesis and Exodus and an explanation of the Apocalypse, in addition to such volumes as *Heaven and Hell—From Things Heard and Seen, Conjugial Love,* and *The True Christian Religion.* His theological writings alone number sixteen thousand pages in a modern edition.

After Swedenborg's death a group of his disciples decided to organize what they felt was a new church implicit in the New Revelation. It was started in London during 1783 when Robert Hindmarsh, a printer, began discussing Swedenborg's writings. In 1815 a general conference of these discussion groups was established. In the meantime (1792) the first Swedenborgian society was founded in Baltimore, out of which two denominations have developed: the General Convention of the New Jerusalem, often referred to simply as the New Church, which is the parent body; and the General Church of the New Jerusalem that came into existence in 1897 under its present title. The latter started as an academy of the New Church in 1876 and from 1890 was called the General Church of the Advent of the Lord. The European contingent is called the General Conference of England. There is not much difference between the two American bodies except that the older branch controls the Swedenborg

Foundation, which publishes and distributes the founder's writings. The smaller General Church of the New Jerusalem claims to follow Swedenborg's theology with greater fidelity.

It is next to impossible to systematize the combination of theology, mysticism, and spiritism of Emanuel Swedenborg. The general convention, however, has summarized his teaching in five points and incorporated it into the Swedenborgian liturgy.

1. That there is one God, in whom there is a Divine Trinity; and that He is the Lord Jesus Christ.
2. That saving faith is to believe on Him.
3. That evils are to be shunned, because they are of the devil and from the devil.
4. That good actions are to be done, because they are of God and from God.
5. That these are to be done by a man as from himself; but that it ought to be believed that they are done from the Lord with Him and by Him.

Some famous Americans have been professed Swedenborgians. Helen Keller called the Swedish mystic "one of the noblest champions true Christianity has ever known." The father of Henry and William James was a Swedenborgian clergyman, and the popular poet Edgar Guest was a member of the Church of the New Jerusalem.

It seems legitimate to classify the Swedenborgians as anti-Trinitarians in view of the fact that Swedenborg held that the Trinity represented merely three aspects of Christ. Moreover, the present-day creedal position of his followers simply identifies the Divine Trinity as the Lord Jesus Christ.

Christadelphians or Brethren of Christ were started in 1844, by Doctor John Thomas, an immigrant from England who had left the Disciples of Christ. He was dissatisfied with the Disciples because he felt that they had apostatized from the church of the Scriptures and that many important biblical doctrines had been neglected. The American groups which he organized did not become a church, properly so-called, until the Civil War when his followers preached nonresistance and they took the name Brethren of Christ, or its Greek equivalent, Christadelphians.

They are a relatively small body, Unitarian and Adventist, pacifist and interested in primitive Christianity. They believe that the kingdom of God will be established in Palestine on the personal return of Christ to the earth.

Their theology rejects belief in the Trinity and a personal hell. They claim that the Bible does not teach that Christ was the Son of God; that the Scriptures show him to have been a mere man, in no sense pre-existent, yet born of Mary by the Holy Spirit. Man is said to be mortal in body and soul and his only prospect of immortality is through the merits of Christ.

Local churches follow a strictly congregational form of government, to the point that each congregation, known as ecclesia, elects serving Brethren, which includes managing Brethren, presiding Brethren, and lecturing Brethren. There are few church buildings and meetings are generally held in private homes or other temporary accommodations.

Self- and Society-improvement Religions

Among the improvement religions, Christian Science is the best organized and certainly the most influential, but it represents only a fraction of the total membership of similar groups in America. Though widely different in the cultural levels on which they operate, they have enough in common to classify them under a few generic names. As idealistic movements, they believe in the immanence of the Divine in every human being; the power of God becomes universally accessible; with Mrs. Eddy, man is said to be the idea of his loving Father-Mother God; but unlike Christian Science, the existence of matter is not denied, yet evil and error are considered only products of mortal mind. As religions of moral or psychological betterment, their radical principle is an absolute confidence in the power of the mind to cure any evil and solve any problem of human life. Their main concern is to acquire or maintain bodily health and peace of mind by means of correct mental attitudes. Many groups like Psychiana are too loosely organized to be considered denominations. Others like the Biosophical Institute and the Chapel of Truth are too small even to be listed in the *Yearbook of American Churches*. But their influence, especially on the millions of unchurched Americans, is considerable. Ethical Culture belongs in this category by reason of its preoccupation with the improvement of society, in terms of tangible human experience.

New Thought. As a religious movement, New Thought is any form of modern belief in the practice of mental healing other than those associated with traditional Christianity. The name came into vogue in 1895, and was used as the title of a magazine published for a time in Melrose, Massachusetts, to describe a "new thought" about life, based on the premise that knowledge of the real world of ideas has marvelous power to relieve people of various ills.

The movement began with the work of Phineas P. Quimby (1802–66) of Portland, Maine, who practiced mental and spiritual healing for over twenty years and greatly influenced Mrs. Mary Baker Patterson, better known as Mary Baker Eddy, foundress of Christian Science.

Quimby went through two stages of development in his science of healing. At first he practiced unqualified mesmerism. The client would sit opposite the doctor, who then held the person's hands and looked him intently in the eye. As the patient went into a mesmeric sleep, Quimby spoke to him and talked him out of his ailment, often manipulating the affected part with hands that were wetted for greater efficiency. Later on Quimby became convinced that disease was simply an error of the mind and not a real thing, so that mesmerism could be dispensed with and equal, or even better, results assured. In time he came to claim that his only power consisted in the knowledge he had that sickness is illusion and in the ability to communicate this assurance to others. In a circular addressed to the sick, Quimby thus described his own system: "My practice is unlike all medical practice. I give no medicine, and make no outward applications. I tell the patient his troubles, and what he thinks is his disease; and my explanation is the cure. If I succeed in correcting his errors, I change the fluids of the system and establish *the truth, or health. The truth is the cure.* This mode of practice applies to all cases."

Quimby organized no society, but persons whom he had helped adapted his method and passed it on to others, though not without additions or changes of their own. Two of his followers, Warren F. Evans and Julius A. Dresser, co-ordinated the master's ideas and reduced them to systematic form. They are regarded as the intellectual founders of New Thought and its allied movements.

Evans published six books on the subject, of which the most significant were *The Mental Cure* (1869), *Mental Medicine* (1872), and *Soul and Body* (1875). According to Evans, disease has its roots in wrong belief. Once that is changed, disease is cured. A devoted Swedenborgian, he had long been familiar with the writings of Berkeley and other idealists. His own character and personal experiences further led him to a point where he was ready to apply an extreme form of idealism to the healing of disease.

Julius Dresser was cured by Quimby in 1860, but Dresser's major work in mental healing was not started until 1882, in Boston, where he and his wife Annetta were competing with Mrs. Baker Eddy. Dresser's clients were curious to learn how they had been healed. He obliged with a series of twelve class lectures, which included a study of the divine immanence and a consideration that the spiritual life is continuous, that men already live in eternity. "To realize that our real life is spiritual was to overcome the illusions of sense-experience with its manifold bondages." Dresser's son and biographer popularized his father's teaching.

Evans and Dresser remained faithful to the memory of Quimby, whereas Mrs. Eddy disclaimed all dependence on her benefactor, whom she called "an ignorant mesmerist." Mrs Eddy's followers became organized in a tightly knit society, the Church of Christ, Scientist; the disciples of Quimby founded numerous small groups under different names like Divine Science, Unity, Practical Christianity, Home of Truth, and the Church of the Higher Life. Before the turn of the century, these came to be known as New Thought and in 1894 the first national convention was held. In 1908 the name National New Thought Alliance was adopted, and six years later the organization became international; its membership now extends to all the major countries of the world.

New Thought has not substantially changed since Quimby or Evans and Dresser. There has been an expansion of scope, however, to cover a broader perspective than healing sickness. The Declaration of Principles, adopted by the International Alliance in 1917, begins by affirming "the freedom of each soul as to its choice and as to belief." Accordingly, no creedal profession is necessary. "The essence of the New Thought is Truth, and each individual must be loyal to the Truth he sees. The windows of his soul must be kept open at each moment for the higher light, and his mind must be always hospitable to each new inspiration."[1]

Allowing for a monistic interpretation of the universe, the Declaration states, "We affirm the new thought of God as Universal Love, Life, Truth and Joy, in whom we live, move, and have our being, and by whom we are held together; that His mind is our mind now, that realizing our oneness with Him means love, truth, peace, health, and plenty."[2] In the same strain, taking monistically Christ's words about the kingdom within us, New Thought asserts that "we are one with the Father."[3]

In keeping with Quimby's theory of the mind's influence, it is held that "Man's body is his holy temple. Every function of it, every cell of it, is intelligent, and is shaped, ruled, repaired, and controlled by mind. He whose body is full of light is full of health. Spiritual healing has existed among all races in all times. It has now become a part of the higher science and art of living the life more abundant."[4]

Consistent with its stress on present well-being, New Thought believes that "Heaven is here and now, the life everlasting that becomes conscious immortality, the communion of mind with mind throughout the universe of thoughts, the nothingness of all error and negation, including death, the variety in unity that produces the individual expressions of the One-Life."[5] All of this is to be understood against the background of an idealism that some have traced to Hegel and others to Berkeley. "We affirm," the Declaration concludes, "that the universe is spiritual and we are spiritual beings."[6]

New Thought considers itself a form of Christianity, while denying the Trinity, original sin, and the divinity of Christ. It proposes instead a cosmic hypostatic union that reflects the Christology of David Strauss. Every man is an incarnation of God; the New Thought teaches that anyone who recognizes this and lives in conscious and harmonious union with Spirit automatically becomes Christ.

Unlike other mental health bodies, such as Christian Science, New Thought permits dual membership. Many of its adherents are active churchgoers in the more liberal Protestant denominations.

Unity School of Christianity. The founders of this society described it as a religious educational institution devoted to demonstrating that the teachings of Christ are a practical, seven-days-a-week way of life. Because of its professed nonsectarian emphasis on Christian teaching and healing, the Unity School of Christianity regards itself as a school rather than a church, "prepared through its activities to help anyone, regardless of church affiliation, to find health, peace, joy, and plenty through his day-by-day practice of Christian principles."

The organization was founded by Charles and Myrtle Fillmore, residents of Kansas City, Missouri, who had previously been connected with Christian Science. In 1892, husband and wife wrote a now famous *Dedication and Covenant,* in which they said:

> We, Charles Fillmore and Myrtle Fillmore, husband and wife, hereby dedicate ourselves, our time, our money, all we have and all we expect to have, to the Spirit of Truth, and through it, to the Society of Silent Unity.
>
> It being understood and also agreed that the Said Spirit of Trust shall render unto us an equivalent for this dedication, in peace of mind, health of body, wisdom, understanding, love, life and an abundant supply of all things necessary to meet every want without our making any of these things the object of our existence.
>
> In the presence of the Conscious Mind of Christ Jesus, this seventh day of December, 1892.[7]

What led the Fillmores to make this lifetime dedication was the wife's being suddenly cured of tuberculosis, after she had discovered in 1887 "a mental treatment that is guaranteed to cure every ill that flesh is heir to." Her husband had not been very religious until then. But his wife convinced him that prayer can do all things. As described by their son, Lowell, the father began to study the Bible and other religious writings, and attended lectures on metaphysics. He spent a great deal of time in prayer and meditation, and "many things were revealed to him." Much as happened to his wife, Charles was also healed of a withered leg and a chronic catarrh that had handicapped him since childhood. He became aware of God's presence as he worked during the day, and later decided to give up the real estate business to devote himself entirely to the promotion of health of mind and body through prayer.

Lowell Fillmore explained what his parents meant to do when they established the Unity School. They had no ambitions to found a new church.

> This work is known as Unity and is described as practical Christianity. My father and mother never claimed to teach anything new. They simply applied the truths taught in the Bible, especially the teachings of Jesus, in a very practical way. Father and mother believed that teachers are necessary only to help the student find the inner Christ so that the Spirit of truth can reveal all Truth to him. God is no respecter of persons, and each follower of Christ must ultimately find the Truth of God within himself.[8]

The Unity School of Christianity has since developed into a self-consciously coherent religious society which periodically explains its creedal position. One of the most recent explanations begins with the avowal that "Unity has some very specific teachings." Among these is the declaration that it is a mysticism, but a practical mysticism. It also claims to have elements of objective idealism: "We teach that reality is of the nature of mind." Unity also believes itself to be a return to the Christianity of Jesus and the apostles, "to the religion Jesus had."

On a broader plane, Unity teaches that life is an eternal unfoldment, that God does not put souls here—for seven minutes or seventy years—and this is all the time for unfoldment they have; that if they fail to fulfill themselves now, they are everlastingly damned. Souls have eternity in the sense that life is an evolution.

The further explanation of this evolving process allows for belief in reincarnation and encourages metempsychosis without insisting on it. As a matter of fact, Unity is almost exclusively concerned with the here and now rather than the hereafter. "What is important is what we are making of the present moment. God has brought us this far; we can trust Him for the rest."[9]

Although Unity writers use the familiar terms about God and speak of the Trinity, they emphasize the impersonal aspect of the Deity. "God is principle. God is not separate and far away and hard to reach. God is in you. In you! God is part of you, as you are part of Him. God is right where you are. You have constant, instant access to Him."[10]

Unity is centered at Lee's Summit, Missouri. It has no official membership and no fixed levies or charge for its students (as adherents are called). Magazines are well written and sell for a nominal price. But free literature is sent to some ten thousand hospitals, prisons, and other institutions throughout the world; individuals receive the same literature free of charge if they cannot afford to pay.

Silent Unity writes to more than half a million persons every year and maintains a constant vigil of prayer, yet its work has always been wholly supported by freewill offerings. Anyone who wishes may write; he receives the prayers he asks for and instructions on how he himself should pray. He is never asked for money, no matter how often he writes or how many letters of help he receives. Unity writers agree that this ministry of Silent Unity is the most important work the Unity School carries on.

The School prides itself on the fact that for over seventy years someone in Silent Unity has been engaged in prayer, on request, and has thus given without asking for remuneration.

Starting with literature only in English, Unity now publishes in twelve languages and sends its ideas to every corner of the globe. Without having missionaries, its evangelism has been considered most effective among people who are literate and suffering from the inner trials of spirit that are common in affluent societies.

The response from various peoples has been phenomenal. Forty thousand pieces of mail received in one week is not unusual. Radio and television programs broadcasted over more than seventy stations further suggest the impact (and benefit) of the Unity School of Christianity.

There are two sides to Unity, however, and both should be seen to make a proper evaluation of its place among the religions of America.

More commonly, Unity describes itself as only a school and methodology. Unity, it is said, is not doctrine so much as attitude; it is not a church but a call to prayer. In this sense, it has much in common with all established religious systems, and certainly is typical of a large segment of American Protestantism. The Fillmores remained believing Protestants all their lives. If there is one stress that distinguishes Unity, it is the insistence on the nearness of God's presence and the ease with which He may be invoked, with results that transcend ordinary laws of nature, even to the healing of disease or the sudden granting of some unexpected favor from on high.

However, Unity is not only a school. It is also a religion, depending always on who is interpreting its tenets and what the issue under discussion is. As one reads *Unity's Statement of Faith*, there is no doubt that its principles are more than functional; they are creedal in the full meaning of that term.

We believe in the twelve disciples, the twelve powers of man, going forth into mind and body, with power and authority to teach, preach, heal and wholly save man and the world from sin, sickness and death.

We believe that through indulgence in sense consciousness men fell into the belief in the reality of matter and material conditions. We believe that the "kingdom of God" can be attained here and now by overcoming the world, the flesh, and the Adversary through Jesus Christ.

We believe that the "second coming" of Jesus Christ is now being fulfilled, that His Spirit is quickening the whole world.[11]

Commentators on the Unity faith are clear in stating that the Fillmores had a vision of religious truth which gives them a right to be considered on the same line as all the great religious founders. Rarely has a religion been consciously and deliberately started. In each case, say the leaders of Unity, "there was one moving experience followed by the natural urge to convey the 'truth' to others—to help others make the same inner discovery and share the same experience. Thus did the Buddha begin his mission of teaching, as did Mohammed, and Jesus Christ."[12]

There is a difference, however, as regards Charles and Myrtle Fillmore. Where other systems all tend in time to become so caught up in a religion of form that the communicants no longer really communicate with God, Unity transcends these limitations. With Ralph Waldo Emerson, it asks, "Why should we not have a first-hand and immediate experience of God?" With thousands in America asking themselves this question, Unity offers an answer, outside all denominational strife and happily untouched by the formalism of established church institutions.

Religion should be a unifying force among people. It should foster peace and create harmony. "Yet the shocking fact is that the religions of the world have often separated mankind into groups between which have arisen prejudices, conflicts, and some of the most savage wars in history." Unlike these partisan rivalries, Unity offers its followers "the unifying, harmonizing, healing principle of love."[13] It gives believers, especially in a country of two hundred religious divisions, what they most need: a sense of spiritual oneness in spite of their numerous creeds.

Ethical Culture. The term Ethical Culture is commonly applied to a movement started by Felix Adler (1851–1933) in New York City during 1876. It has since come to be applied also to the societies which owe their origin to the principles of Ethical Culture, even when affiliated with other religious bodies or institutions.

Felix Adler, the founder of Ethical Culture, was a German immigrant from the Rhineland who came to the United States as a child. After his graduation from Columbia, he became a teacher of Oriental literature at Cornell University. His religious background was Jewish and, in fact, he was to have succeeded his father as rabbi of Temple Emanu-El in New York City. The struggle that Adler underwent in conflict with traditional Judaism resulted in his revolt against the synagogue. He became a Christian by internal conviction that Jesus Christ offered the best understanding of human nature and the best norm for human conduct. In this fundamental sense he was a Protestant, closer in spirit to George Fox and Emerson than to Martin Luther and Calvin—yet authentically a Protestant reformer and among the most influential in modern American history.

At first only a few friends joined Adler in his search for moral betterment through reinterpretation of the Judaeo-Christian religion. But soon a coterie of followers pledged themselves "to assert the supreme importance of the ethical factor in all relations of life, personal, social, national and international, apart from any theological or metaphysical considerations."

Among the formative factors to which Adler attributed his discovery of Ethical Culture, the moral teachings of Jesus were of paramount importance. Christian ethics, he said, has promoted the moral development of mankind in a thousand ways. It has emphasized the inner springs of conduct. However, like every product of the mind and aspirations of man, it exhibits the limitations of the time and of the social conditions under which it arose. The conditions have since changed. It was Adler's contention that with the help of Christianity a philosophy of life can be developed that will dispense with the theology of the Gospels and bring up to date the ethical ideals of Jesus of Nazareth. Adler believed that he could even improve on these ideals, and Ethical Culture still claims to be an improvement on the New Testament.

The single doctrine of the ethical aim as the supreme purpose of life is the basis of Ethical Culture. It emphasizes the fact that individual opinions on such questions as the existence of God or the immortality of the soul are secondary, and therefore membership in Ethical societies does not depend on credo belief or disbelief. Theists, deists, and atheists are equally welcome. Since Felix Adler had been a Jew and because not a few leaders in Ethical Culture came from Reform Judaism, the movement has sometimes been mistakenly identified with extreme liberal Jewry.

It is difficult to isolate the essential features of Ethical Culture on its theoretical side mainly because it denies on principle the priority of mind over will and asserts, with Immanuel Kant, that the only good thing in the world is a well-disciplined will. Nevertheless, certain aspects of its voluntarism may be analyzed in traditional Christian terms.

Ethical Culture vaguely identifies human nature with the divine and often speaks of the "potentially divine nature in men," which needs actuation to be brought into fullness of being.

The character of every person according to the Culturists contains contrary elements. The two kinds of qualities may be called the fair and foul, or more simply the plus and minus traits. Some people predominate in the good qualities, others in the minus traits, but potential plus qualities exist in the worst characters and potential negative traits can be found even in people who are most respected.

A working hypothesis of Ethical Culture postulates that certain definite minus traits always go along with certain plus qualities. In other words, the best of us have a *corresponding* evil nature, and the worst characters have *correlative* virtues that lie hidden. The problem of human existence is to know which of our virtues go with which of our vices, on the assumption that ostensibly good people hide their latent defects and seldom even discover their wickedness. In the same way, apparently evil persons have to learn that beneath the vicious crust lies a substance of deep goodness.

The method which Adler and his followers propose for the cultivation of virtue is twofold. First, a man is to study himself to discover his good and bad potential, otherwise he may become presumptuous over his good qualities or despondent over his bad ones. Secondly, merely having good tendencies does not make a man virtuous. Unless he also cultivates these tendencies and exercises them at the cost of self-sacrifice, he remains only a potentially good person but is not actually virtuous.

A classic example used by Ethical Culture to describe true virtue is the case of a person who works for others as a means of exalting the idea of self to the mind of the doer. Instead of using others as sacred personalities, worthwhile on their own account, he cleverly exploits them by benefiting them. He uses people as things by which to achieve a higher estimate of himself. He may even go to the greatest lengths of devotion for his friends, and perform for them the most repulsive tasks. He may freely assist them financially, while denying himself comforts and even necessities of life in order to free them from difficulty. If he is a doctor, he may watch through the night at their bedside and jeopardize his own health in order to help others recover their health. He may be willing to forego their gratitude because the lofty image of self which he is trying to create would be marred by such crude selfishness. Yet in all this he may be egocentric in the extreme. Unless self-sacrifice has no alloy of self-seeking, and excludes every self-complacency, it is vice masking as virtue and arrogance appearing as love.

Behind this high idealism in Ethical Culture stands an implicit reaction to the moral life of Christians who verbally follow the teachings of Christ but actually deny in their lives what they profess to believe in faith. In fact, Ethical Culture can best be understood as a negative reaction to practical Christianity, with its demanding creed and code, because Christians so often contradict their religion in the conduct of life. Why not dispense with the theological principles which seem to have so little effect in producing the goodness which should be there as their natural fruit? Culturists are ruthless in their insistence that all belief is irrelevant, unless and in so far as it results in ethical improvement.

One aspect of Ethical Culture that runs as a theme through its literature is the philosophy of suffering first stated by Adler and developed by his disciples. Suffering and evil, it is said, cannot be explained and the "explanation" given by many Christians is only their rationalization of a mystery. But if suffering cannot be explained, it can be utilized for a definite spiritual end. That end is to achieve through the ministry of frustration and the persistence of effort toward the unattainable the consciousness of the reality of the spiritual universe and of our membership in it. This statement summarizes the nearest thing to the essential teachings of Ethical Culture.

While membership in Ethical societies includes men and women from the established churches, most Culturists are from the great mass of the "unchurched." Reflective meditation and study are the mainstay of Ethical Culture services. Songs and inspirational readings are also encouraged, but always with a reluctance to imitate the ritual of traditional Christian bodies.

Holiness Churches

The Holiness spirit in Protestantism stems from the teaching of John Wesley, who believed there were two stages in the process of justification: freedom from sin and sanctification, or the "second blessing." In this Wesley departed from the doctrine of the earlier Reformers, who were too preoccupied with man's depravity to allow him any chance of holiness or growth in Christian perfection. With the decline of Wesleyan principles among American Methodists, there sprang up protest groups of various sizes, emphasizing sanctification as an essential part of the Methodist tradition. Popularly called the Holiness Movement, it gave birth to scores of religious bodies, juridically distinct, but united in professing the following tenets of Protestant perfectionism:

1. Besides justification, which is a sense of security that past sins are forgiven, there is a "second blessing," in which a person feels himself closely united with God.

2. There is an emotional experience produced in the heart by a direct action of the Holy Spirit. Although instantaneous, the "second blessing" may require years of preparation. It may be lost and regained, and may be increased in efficiency. But there is no mistaking the presence of the Spirit when He comes. More radical groups, called Pentecostals, were discussed earlier. The milder Holiness churches identify the

Spirit's coming and abiding presence by an exalted feeling, inner impression, bodily emotion, and a deep sense of awareness of God's loving kindness.

3. As a group, Holiness denominations depreciate the teachings and practices of the larger denominations for having abandoned the true faith and compromising with modernism. Their theology is fundamentalist and rigidly biblical.

4. The favorite method of preaching is the popular revival —always for winning new converts, and in some cases revivalism is the essence of the denomination.

5. Most of the Holiness societies profess, without always stressing, the imminent second coming of Christ, which is to inaugurate a millennium of earthly peace and happiness before the last day.

It is difficult to estimate the total membership of typical Holiness churches in America, scattered through about twenty established bodies and an unknown number of transient congregations. Some are microscopic in size, like the Hephzibah Faith Missionary Association, which derives its name from the prophecy of Isaias regarding the new Jerusalem, and Kodesh Church of Immanuel, organized in 1929 as an offshoot of the African Methodist Episcopal Zion Church.

Not the least difficulty describing churches in the Holiness tradition is how to identify them. The problem arises from the fact that, in practice, the line of distinction between Holiness churches properly so called and denominations that are technically Pentecostal is very thin and often not discernible. Thus most of the Churches of God qualify as Holiness bodies, but so many of them believe in miraculous healing and expect their members to receive the gift of speaking in tongues that they are more accurately classified as Pentecostal institutions.

Two sizable denominations belong by right to the Holiness movement, without Pentecostal implications: the Pilgrim Holiness Church and the Church of the Nazarene.

Pilgrim Holiness Church. This church was started by a Methodist minister in Cincinnati, Martin Wells Knapp, who in 1897 urged his people to return to the original spirit of John Wesley. In his own words, he wanted them to revive "apostolic practices, methods, power, and success." Divine healing was among the expectations. At first he was satisfied with a union of Holiness and Pentecostal groups, but later gave up the idea and formed a typical Holiness denomination by drawing together a variety of small communities, ranging from the Pilgrim Church of California to the Pentecostal Rescue Mission of New York. What was formerly the International Apostolic Holiness Union became the Pilgrim Holiness Church with headquarters in Indianapolis.

While close to the Church of the Nazarene in doctrine and organization, Knapp's foundation has consistently stressed Arminianism in theology and a combination of Episcopal and Congregational polity. Belief in the Trinity is required, but the mode of baptism is optional. Strongly conservative, membership is preceded by an examination before an advisory board and the church congregation. Men and women are ordained to the ministry, and foreign missions are among the most flourishing for a denomination of its size. Typical of the concern for creedal orthodoxy, the church supports five colleges and has a strong Sunday school program, with an enrollment almost three times that of the adult church membership.

The Church of the Nazarene was established in 1908 by a merger of the Association of Pentecostal Churches of America (New York and New England), the Church of the Nazarene (California), and the Holiness Church of Christ (Southern states). Official documentation favors October 8, 1908, and Pilot Point, Texas, as the date and place of the church's origin. It was first called the Pentecostal Church of the Nazarene, but in 1919 the term "Pentecostal" was dropped from its name. By that time the church leaders decided to dissociate themselves in the public mind from any connection with other Pentecostal groups which taught or practiced speaking in strange tongues. As might be expected, the church has ever since remained a haven for Wesleyan-minded persons who were concerned with sanctification but not comfortable with Pentecostalism.

In the same way, the church has slowly receded from its strong perfectionist emphasis. Nazarene schools have eliminated the sanctification label from their names. Texas Holiness University became Peniel College, and Illinois Holiness University is now Olivet College. None of the six denominational colleges retains the doctrinal "Holiness" name.

In its official *Constitution and Special Rules*, the Church of the Nazarene spells out in detail the conditions for active membership. First a preamble, and then specific regulations are given.

> To be identified with the visible Church is the blessed privilege and sacred duty of all who are saved from their sins, and are seeking completeness in Christ Jesus. It is required of all who desire to unite with the Church of the Nazarene, and thus to walk in fellowship with us, that they shall show evidence of salvation from their sins by a godly walk and vital piety; that they shall be, or earnestly desire to be, cleansed from all indwelling sins; and that they shall evidence this:
>
> *First.* By avoiding evil of every kind, including:
>
> 1. Taking the name of God in vain.
>
> 2. Profaning of the Lord's day, either by unnecessary labor, or business, or by patronizing or reading secular papers, or by holiday diversions.
>
> 3. Using of intoxicating liquors as a beverage, or trafficking therein; giving influence to, or voting for, the licensing of places for the sale of the same; using tobacco in any of its forms, or trafficking therein . . .
>
> *Second.* By doing that which is enjoined in the Word of God, which is both our rule of faith and practice, including:
>
> 1. Being courteous to all men.
>
> 2. Contributing to the support of the ministry and the church and its work, according to the ability which God giveth.
>
> 3. Being helpful to those who are of the household of the faith, in love forbearing one another . . .[14]

Among its most effective means of evangelism, made possible by the generosity of church members, is the radio program "Showers of Blessing," which broadcasts over more than three hundred stations throughout the world. As reported by its own missionary personnel, "At present all of South Africa is blanketed with 'the voice of the Church of the Nazarene' and the mail response indicates that a large radio audience listens every week."[15] The Nazarene Publishing House, with a current output of forty distinct periodicals, follows up the radio apostolate with appropriate literature.

Always an essential part of the Nazarene message is the idea of perfection promised to those who would follow Christ, as Wesley said, in "humility, meekness, gentleness, love lost to mankind, and every other holy and heavenly temper."[16]

Jehovah's Witnesses

An explanation is in order for including the Jehovah's Witnesses among the Protestant denominations. Though both sides would probably repudiate the identification, it is warranted for several reasons. Modern writers accept the term "Protestant" to mean everyone who calls himself a Christian and is not in communion with Rome, with the exception of members of the Eastern Churches. In common with traditionally Protestant communions, the Witnesses disclaim an infallible authority outside the Bible. And most importantly, they consider themselves the spiritual heirs of the Reformation. Martin Luther to them is "the successful challenger who courageously defied the all-powerful domination of the popes of Rome [and] made possible the current four hundred year era of freedom, progress, enlightenment, education and democracy of the western world."[17]

History. The Jehovah's Witnesses were founded in Pittsburgh in 1872 by Charles Taze Russell, former Congregationalist and Allegheny haberdasher. They have changed names three times: beginning as the Russellites, they then became the Millennial Dawnists, the International Bible Students, and, in 1931, the Jehovah's Witnesses. At his death in 1916, Russell was succeeded by Judge J. F. Rutherford, a Missouri lawyer who had defended Russell in his several conflicts with the civil authorities. During his twenty-six years of presidency, the Witnesses developed their present hierarchical system and highly authoritarian form of government. In 1942 Rutherford was succeeded by Nathan Homer Knorr, of Allentown, Pennsylvania, formerly a member of the Reformed Church, who had been associated full time with the Watchtower Society since his graduation from high school in 1923. His chief preoccupation was with foreign missions, and his most important contribution has been to shift the Society's emphasis from the head to the members, which is exemplified in the banishment of the portable phonograph (carrying Judge Rutherford's voice) as standard equipment of the Witnesses in making house-to-house calls. Knorr may be regarded as the last autocratic head of the Witnesses.

Doctrine. A relative consistency in doctrine is maintained by means of a rigid authoritarianism, in which the writings of Russell and Rutherford must be accepted without question. Russell's interpretation of Scripture is said to be "far more extensive than the combined writings of St. Paul, St. John, Arius, Waldo, Wyclif and Martin Luther—the six messengers of Christ who preceded him." In fact, "the place next to St. Paul in the gallery of fame as expounder of the Gospel of the Master will be occupied by Charles Taze Russell."[18] When Russell died, it was necessary to prove his divine mission. This was done by interpreting the prophecy of Ezechiel which foretells the coming of a seventh messenger of God to "mark Thau upon the foreheads of the men who sigh and mourn for all the abominations that are committed" (Ezechiel 9:4). Russell was this seventh man. He introduced the germinal concepts on which the present Watchtower Society is founded, but the development of these notions into a doctrinal system was the work of Rutherford.

Theocracy, or the rule of God, is the foundation of the Bible Tract Society. According to Rutherford, when Lucifer rebelled he became ruler of the world, and from then on the human race has followed his lead. Satan remained in heaven until he was driven out by Christ in 1914, reflected on earth in the calamities of the First World War. But Lucifer is still master on earth, where he organized the visible part of his empire by founding churches, the great capitalistic organizations, and civil societies. The great tragedy of history is that Satan has forced mankind to practice religion through this triple alliance of ecclesiastical, commercial, and political powers. Since 1914 Christ has been fighting Satan invisibly, and will finally defeat him at Armageddon, annihilating the army of the devil with the help of a host of angels. This will usher in the millennium, a thousand years of earthly happiness for all the righteous, who will be resurrected. The wicked will not rise from the dead. After the millennium, Satan will rise again for a short time, only to be utterly destroyed so that even his memory will disappear. At the same time the righteous begin to live forever in peace and blessedness.

The Trinity and divinity of Christ are explicitly denied as "the Devil's doctrine, fraudulently imposed upon men to destroy their faith in Jehovah."[19] To admit Christ's divinity, Rutherford argued, would be inconsistent with the concept of a theocracy which requires that men obey only God, and never a human being. The Holy Spirit is denied to be either God or even a personality.

Immortality for the human soul is said to be an invention of the devil propounded by earthly philosophers and which became the cornerstone of Roman Catholicism. Jehovah alone is immortal; Christ received this gift as a reward for his virtue, to be earned by others if they are faithful to Jehovah in resisting the devil. Hell is denied as a place of eternal punishment by an appeal to divine mercy, since a "loving God could not torment any of his creatures."[20] Instead of going to hell, the wicked will be annihilated. On the other hand, a complicated theory of heaven provides for two kinds of paradise, one earthly and the other celestial. Only the 144,000 who were faithful followers of Jesus "will stand victorious with him on the heavenly Mount Zion," minus their bodies and living in spirit alone. "All the rest of mankind who take advantage of salvation to everlasting life through Jesus' sacrifice will remain on earth."[21]

Organization and Practices. Jehovah's Witnesses consider themselves a "Society of ministers," and accuse Protestant sectarians of watering down Luther's teaching on the universal priesthood of the laity. The public ceremony of water immersion sets one apart as a minister of Jehovah, with four classes of clergy to which a Witness may belong. On the lowest level are "Publishers" or part-time workers, who are expected to devote sixty hours a month to spreading the Society's literature; at the top level are "Pioneers" or full-time laborers; in between are the "Special Pioneers" and "General Pioneers," who give 175 and 150 hours monthly to the Witness apostolate.

With all their opposition to ecclesiastical authority, the Witnesses have a closely knit hierarchy consisting of the four hundred members of the Watch Tower Bible and Tract Society (New York), one of three legal corporations through which the Witnesses do their work. The other two are the Watch Tower Bible and Tract Society, Inc. (New York), and the International Bible Students Association (England). However, the principal officers of all three corporations are virtually the same. They elect a director who becomes international head of the Jehovah's Witnesses. Ministers working in administration or in the field get no pay. Officers get fourteen dollars a month plus room and board. To support themselves, most Witnesses do secular work.

Characteristic practices of the Witnesses flow naturally from their doctrines. They refuse to bear arms, salute the flag, or participate in affairs of the secular government because they regard all civil authority as satanic. In the same way they exhaust the language of vituperation in attacking the Catholic Church as an emissary of the devil. They refuse blood transfusions as being against the Bible, which says, "Whatsoever man . . . eats any manner of blood, I will cut him off from among his people" (Leviticus 17:10), since it makes no difference whether a person is "fed" blood through the mouth or nose or intravenously.

Witnesses look upon the opposition they arouse as a sign of divine approval, quoting the words of St. Paul that "all who will live godly in Christ Jesus shall suffer persecution" (2 Timothy 3:12). Their insistence on freedom to preach and proselytize, along with their refusal to do military service and salute the flag, has involved them in more legal suits than any other denomination in America. During a recent period of less than twenty years, there were forty-six United States Supreme Court cases involving the Jehovah's Witnesses, with the majority decided in their favor. Most of the litigations center around exemptions from military service and door-to-door propaganda work. In 1940 the Supreme Court ruled that a Connecticut conviction for breach of peace by playing a phonograph record which attacked the Catholic Church violated the freedom of speech and religion guaranteed by the First Amendment. Within three years, the Supreme Court reversed itself in another case and decided that compulsory saluting of the flag was unconstitutional. In delivering the majority opinion, Justice Robert Jackson declared: "If there is any fixed star in our constitutional constellation, it is that no official, high or petty, can prescribe what shall be orthodox in politics, nationalism, religion, or other matters of opinion or force citizens to confess by word or act their faith therein."[22]

Many advocates of religious freedom are willing to call the Witnesses "intolerant," but they also feel that these "simple, sincere" people are rendering a service to the cause of liberty under our Constitution as a result of their persistence.

Legalistic Bodies

Unlike the Holiness churches or even the Pentecostals, which emphasize the operations of the Holy Spirit in man's relations with God, legalistic Protestant bodies stress the importance of certain human actions or practices in the work of sanctification. Correlative with this legalism is a belief in the immediacy of the Holy Spirit's action on the human soul. Like the Quakers, they repudiate all formal creeds and rely on the Inner Light which requires no other illumination. They trace their origin to the wave of Pietism, especially in Germany, which rebelled against the formalism in public worship and the "spiritual barrenness" of continental Protestantism, as they saw it in the seventeenth and eighteenth centuries.

The Churches of the Brethren, sometimes called German Baptists, is a common name for at least seven distinct religious groups in the United States, with more than a dozen subdivisions that are difficult to classify.

The most accurate classification is to divide the Brethren into the Dunkers (from the German *tunken*—to immerse), who originally came from Schwarzenau in Germany; the Plymouth Brethren, who are independent of the German branch and trace their origin to reaction against the Established Anglican Church in England and Ireland; and the River Brethren, a group of Pietists and Anabaptists from Europe who settled along the Susquehanna River in Lancaster County, Pennsylvania.

River Brethren are the smallest of the three segments, and owe their organizational structure in America mainly to the need for legal recognition as a church at the time of the Civil War. Since non-resistance has been one of the hallmarks of Brethren polity, the River Brethren came into corporate existence in 1863, when they first officially adopted the name Brethren in Christ Church. They were incorporated in 1904. Sectarian differences split the parent body to create two rival groups, besides the Brethren in Christ: Old Order (or Yonker) Brethren, who prefer to meet in private homes rather than in regular churches; and the United Zion Church, essentially the same as the Brethren in Christ, but laying greater stress on strict observance of such things as veiling of women, simple attire, and no divorce with the right to remarry.

The Plymouth Brethren are separated into different units, distinguished by the Roman numerals I to VIII, and divided mainly along administrative lines. In keeping with the Free Church tradition, they acknowledge no creeds, believe in the Trinity, the Virgin Birth, and Christ's premillennial coming, which, they say, is imminent. There are no specific requirements for membership except to give "satisfactory evidence of the new birth." Ministers are not ordained in the usual sense of that term, and they receive no regular salary. Churches are organized along congregational lines.

Of all the denominations in Brethren family, the Church of the Brethren (without further qualification) is both the largest and most influential.

It began in 1708 with a small covenanted group of eight persons in Schwarzenau, Germany. Two American origins are recorded: a company led by Peter Becker that settled in Germantown, Pennsylvania, in 1719; and another contingent that arrived in America in 1729, under the leadership of

Alexander Mack, to join the earlier colony. From Pennsylvania the Brethren spread across the country.

For quite some time they were mainly a rural people, whose German speech and aloofness from secular interests made them suspect and little accepted by other Protestants. As they proved their deep interior piety and willingness to co-operate in Christian unity, the Brethren achieved a prominence that few denominations of comparable size enjoy in the United States. Among their typical positions of doctrine and polity: They are opposed to war on principle and therefore are confirmed pacifists; they preach and insist on total abstinence from alcohol; they strongly recommend a simple way of life that avoids worldly amusements and luxuries; their concept of brotherhood strives to remove the barriers that divide people into classes and social divisions; and they avoid any formal creeds, while professing obedience only to the person of Jesus Christ.

Their pacifism is so characteristic that it may be taken as a dominant feature of the Church of the Brethren. With the growing tension between two different interpretations of the gospel on the matter of peace and war, their position and leadership takes on greater significance than at any other time in Brethren history. It was clearly stated by their official spokesman on the occasion of the 250th anniversary commemoration in 1958.

Our fathers regarded religious duty as entirely compatible with civil duty but not subservient to it.

The Brethren recognize the validity of civil government and have generally included in their prayers and supplications all kings and rulers and those in authority. But they established a boundary between civil and religious duty at the point where the two became irreconcilable. At that point they obey the voice of God rather than the voice of man.

The Brethren seek to be creative citizens. They are not anarchists. They support their government in loyalty but refuse to violate the commands of conscience and of religious faith at the behest of civil, political, or military power. They obey the law, they pay their taxes, they exercise the right of suffrage, and they otherwise take a constructive attitude toward government.

But in times of war Brethren seek to be removed as far as possible from violence and bloodshed. They want to serve only in those enterprises which are dedicated to the relief of suffering and which are calculated to allay the hatred and bitterness engendered by war. They are devoted to a ministry of reconciliation, believing it to be the way of Christ.[23]

Consistent with these principles, the Brethren have done outstanding work in the promotion of peace. Yet, unlike the Quakers, their stand as conscientious objectors has been denominational rather than individual.

Since coming to America, the Church of the Brethren has had two major schisms. The Brethren Church—Progressive Dunkers—started their own community in 1882 mainly because of grievances over what they considered a lack of education among the clergy and laity and a too rigid interpretation of such rules as plain dress and worship. The Progressives are actually quite conservative doctrinally, but their church structure is more congregational and less dependent on conference authority than obtains among the original Brethren.

Another break took place in 1881 for the opposite reason, that the transplanted Schwarzenau people were too liberal. Thus originated the Old German Baptist Brethren, otherwise known as Old Order Dunkers, who were against higher education, missions, church societies, and Sunday schools. While a literal adherence to these practices has been modified in recent years, the Old Order Dunkers are severely critical of any compromise with what they consider to be gospel teaching.

Mennonites in this country number less than a quarter million, yet they are divided into twelve denominations, most of which have less than ten thousand members. As a world body, the Mennonites were organized at Zurich, Switzerland, in 1525, as the Swiss Brethren or Täufer who opposed Zwingli in his readiness to unite church and state. Denying the validity of infant baptism, they were called Anabaptists because they demanded the rebaptism of all who were baptized in infancy. Their greatest leader was Menno Simons, a former priest (1496–1561) who was rebaptized in 1536 and after whom the denomination is named. The first group of Mennonites came to America from Crefeld, Germany, in 1683, and settled at Germantown, now part of Philadelphia. This was also the haven of the first Quaker, Dunker, Reformed, Lutheran, Moravian, and German Methodist congregations.

Mennonite theology is crystallized in the Confession of Dortrecht (Holland), formulated in 1632 and generally accepted by the American churches. In 1921 the Mennonite General Conference adopted a statement on the Fundamentals of the Christian Faith consisting of eighteen articles. But in recent years it was felt necessary to draw up a new confession of faith, without repudiating any earlier confession. Adopted in 1963 by the Mennonite General Conference, this latest profession of belief seeks "to restate the doctrinal position of the church in terms relevant to today's issues, and especially to incorporate the insights of the various doctrinal pronouncements of Mennonite General Conference."

In twenty articles of considerable length, the *Mennonite Confession of Faith* is a unique document that reflects a strong Anabaptist theology which faces, without compromise, the numerous pressures laid upon this church by American society. The article on "Discipleship and Nonconformity" illustrates the whole confession.

We believe that there are two opposing kingdoms to which men give their spiritual allegiance, that of Christ and that of Satan. Those who belong to Satan's kingdom live for sin and self, and refuse the obedience of faith. The kingdom of Christ is composed of those who have been born again and who have entered into a faith union with the Lord Jesus Christ. In them the fruit of the Spirit is in evidence. They recognize the lordship of Christ, perform all manner of good works. They seek for holiness of heart, life, and speech, and refuse any unequal yoke with unbelievers. They manifest only love toward those of other races, cultures, and economic levels. They regard their bodies as temples of the Holy Spirit and crucify their flesh with its affections and lusts. They therefore avoid such things as harmful drugs, beverage alcohol, and tobacco. We believe that their adornment should be a beauty of spirit, expressed in attire that is modest, economical, simple, and becoming to those professing Christian faith. They should seek to be Christian in their stewardship of money and possessions. Their recreational life should be consistent with the Christian walk. Through the Spirit they should put off the old man and put on the new.[24]

Foot washing is a sacred ordinance or sacrament, which was "instituted by the Lord Jesus."[25] Marriage is intended by God to be "a holy state, monogamous, and for life. It is also fully acceptable to God to serve Christ unmarried." Moreover, Christians "shall marry only in the Lord, and for the sake of spiritual unity in the home they should become members of the same congregation."[26]

Mennonite belief in complete non-resistance has resulted in a large number of conscientious objectors during wartime. About 50 per cent of the Mennonites drafted in World War II chose civilian service instead of combat duty.

The most distinctive teaching of the Mennonites is their ecclesiastical ban or separation from the church for recalcitrant members. Once ostracized, the excommunicate is to be shunned, without distinction. In the words of the Mennonite Confession of Faith, "If disobedience persists, the church may withhold the right to commune until the individual repents. And the church must, with a deep sense of loss, recognize that the one who goes on to full apostasy and spiritual ruin has severed his relation with Christ and His Body."[27] Though interpreted with varying degrees of severity, even at its mildest, the shunning of the separated is an effective sanction.

Amish are those Mennonites who follow a strict adherence to the ban, or exclusion of members. They take their name from Jacob Amman, a Swiss Mennonite bishop in the late seventeenth century who took literally the idea of separation from unfaithful Christians. His followers came to America in a series of emigrations and settled first in Pennsylvania, and later went to Ohio, Indiana, Illinois, Nebraska, and other Western states. A large colony also went to Canada.

Depending on how liberally they interpret plainness in clothing, food, and means of transportation, the Amish are divided into a variety of groups. Some of the most rigorous belong to the Conservative Mennonite Conference, who changed their name in 1954 from the Conservative Amish Mennonites. They practice complete non-resistance and non-conformity. Somewhat less demanding are the Beachy Amish, who withdrew from the latter denomination in 1923. They worship in meetinghouses and permit the use of modern conveniences.

Moravians, also called Unitas Fratrum and Unity of the Brethren, trace their origin to John Hus, who was burned at the stake as a Wycliffite in 1415. Their immediate foundation is dated 1467 in Bohemia, when they established their own priesthood with the help of the Waldensians. The educator, John Amos Comenius (1592–1670), was the last bishop of the Czech-Moravian branch of the Unity. They came from Germany to America in 1734, first settling in Georgia. En route, they deeply affected John Wesley by their example of "simple, courageous piety." From a few thousand adherents in the eighteenth century, the Moravians have increased tenfold in membership, divided among four denominations, of which the largest is the Moravian Church of America. Theoretically their main stress is on the love of God manifested in Christian conduct; but historically their predominant trait is Lutheran Pietism. In their teaching, the purpose of the church is to promote a "constant confidential intercourse with Christ." Great emphasis is placed on the believer's mystical union with the atoning Savior, which is to be achieved by strict observance of the church's regulations and encouraged by attractive liturgical functions.

Reformed Churches

Reformed churches are lineal descendants of John Calvin, and therefore collateral relations of the Presbyterian bodies in Europe and America. But where Presbyterianism is mainly an Anglo-Saxon development through the Scottish John Knox, the Reformed groups derive from Calvin directly. Their immediate ancestors are the Calvinists in France, Switzerland, and the Low Countries. While they are concentrated in the United States, Reformed congregations have also been established in Latin America, principally in Mexico.

History. Reformed Protestantism is commonly traced to the Synod of Dort (1619) in Holland, which adopted five articles of strict Calvinism against the Arminians, who believed in free co-operation with divine grace. According to Dort, God from eternity had chosen some persons for heaven and predistined others for damnation, irrespective of their faith or good works and dependent solely on His inscrutable will. The Arminians were condemned as heretics, and the Canons of Dort became an essential part of the Reformed doctrinal system.

The Reformed Church, in America, was a direct result of the business migration of Calvinists from Holland, sponsored by the Dutch East India Company. At first they were only scattered groups along the Hudson River, but in 1628 they organized at New Amsterdam what has become the oldest church in America with an uninterrupted ministry. In 1792 they broke away from the parent body in Holland and their first general synod was held two years later. Insistence on keeping the Dutch language in preaching and the liturgy retarded the church's growth and alienated some of its younger members, but no grave doctrinal crisis arose until the mid-nineteenth century.

To understand this crisis it is necessary briefly to retrace the European origins of the Christian Reformed Church, which, together with the Reformed Church in America, accounts for 90 per cent of the Reformed membership in the United States. After the troubles of the Napoleonic era in the Netherlands, William I reorganized the Dutch (Calvinist) Church, but in the process took over so much control that a conservative reaction set in. In 1834 a secession of strict Calvinist ministers started a church of their own. Social and economic conditions in the Netherlands forced the secessionists to migrate to the United States. One group came to Holland, Michigan, in 1846, where they were invited to enter into a loose merger with the Reformed Church in America.

Almost from the day the union was effected, some leaders in the conservative party were dissatisfied. Their basic fear was the same that had motivated those who had seceded in the Netherlands twenty years before. Believing themselves to be the true heirs of the Reformed position, they argued that continued association with the Reformed Church in America would entangle them in embarrassing alliances with churches of other beliefs. They felt that instruction in the seminary tended to weaken the Reformed tradition, and that the laity needed to be better instructed in their creedal inheritance.

But the most crucial factor was the lodge question, i.e., whether or not Reformed Church members may belong to such lodges as the Freemasons and continue in good standing in the church. The Reformed Church in America tolerated lodge membership and, in the eyes of the conservatives, belittled its significance. When the final break came during 1857, grievance over the existence of Freemasonry in the Reformed Church in America was decisive.

In 1857 four congregations with about 750 people left the Reformed Church in America to form what eventually became the Christian Reformed Church in America. A steady flow of immigrants from the Netherlands gradually swelled the membership to rival that of the parent body.

Since 1857, each of the two main branches has developed a history of its own. The Reformed Church in America remained concentrated in the East, mainly in New York and New Jersey, and in the Midwestern States of Michigan and Illinois. The General Synod meets annually, with headquarters in New York City. An elaborate missions program sponsors operations in the United States and in foreign countries, notably India, Ceylon, Indonesia, and the Near East.

The Reformed Church in America has co-operated actively with the World Council of Churches and the International Missionary Council. Its representatives have exceptional leadership in the National Council of Churches in the United States, up to the vice-presidency in the organization.

With its strong emphasis on doctrinal orthodoxy, the Christian Reformed Church developed along different lines. More concerned with integrating religion and education, and more compact in geographical distribution, the church promoted a system of Christian day schools from elementary through secondary and college grades. The Society for Christian Instruction on a Reformed Basis was organized in 1892 to federate the dozen schools in existence at that time. At its first meeting, the Society recommended that all Christian schools should be parent-society owned and operated. This departure from parochialism is generally credited with having produced the nation's most extensive program (80 per cent) of religion-centered education in the Reformed tradition.

Consistent with its stress on doctrinal integrity, the Christian Reformed Church has engaged in such projects as neighborhood evangelism, home mission work among the Jews, catechism instruction for children and adult converts, and church publications with an appeal to denominational loyalty. The preamble to the constitution of a national youth organization illustrates this emphasis on distinctively religious values: "Recognizing the desirability and necessity of uniting the youth of Calvinistic churches for service in the Kingdom of God, and the need of guidance and direction in this work in order that the youth of the church, as well-prepared servants of the Lord, may recognize Jesus Christ as King and serve Him always and everywhere, the Young Calvinist Federation of North America is established."

Doctrine and Worship. All the Reformed bodies in America subscribe to the Heidelberg Catechism (1563), the Belgic Confession of Faith (1561 and 1619), and the Canons of the Synod of Dort (1619). The guiding motif of these doctrinal standards is the affirmation of God's sovereignty. They repeatedly speak of the Glory of God which is man's universal purpose of existence. Consistent with this accent, the distance between God and man is brought out in the strongest terms.

The critical standard of doctrine is Dort, which originally met to reject the Arminian teaching on grace, and ever since this initial meeting, the Canons of Dort have been the watershed which divides orthodox from liberal Reformed believers.

Its five canons are really five chapters of numerous articles dealing, in sequence, with Divine Predestination, Redemption, the Fall and Conversion of Man, and Perseverance of the Saints. Characteristic passages exemplify the general tone:

> As all men have sinned in Adam, lie under the curse, and are obnoxious to eternal death, God would have done no injustice by leaving them all to perish, and delivering them over to condemnation on account of sin.[28]

> What peculiarly tends to illustrate and recommend to us the eternal and unmerited grace of election is the express testimony of sacred Scripture, that not all, but some only, are elected, while others are passed by in the eternal decree.[29]

> It was the will of God, that Christ by the blood of the cross . . . should effectually redeem out of every people, tribe, nation, and language, all those, and those only, who were from eternity chosen to salvation, and given to Him by the Father.[30]

The canons are differently interpreted by the two Calvinist segments. The Reformed Church in America omits the negative part condemning as heretics those who affirm the opposite. Yet both churches have the Formula of Subscription, which every minister, theological professor, elder, and deacon in the church is required to sign and promise to observe. Two sentences in the Formula summarize its substance: "We promise, that we will with all diligence and faithfulness teach the Gospel and defend the Standards of our faith, without either directly or indirectly contradicting the same by preaching or writing . . . We further promise that should we ever have any doubts . . . as to the Standards of our faith, we will neither propose nor teach the same, but will first communicate our views to the Classis to which we belong, and will subject ourselves to its counsel and decision."[31]

As a rule, preachers and writers in the Christian Reformed Church take a firm Calvinistic stand on predestination, with little or no compromise on man's ability to reject divine grace. Irresistible grace is generally professed without mitigation. The Reformed Church in America allows more latitude on the subject, and prominent churchmen do not hesitate to say that strict Calvinism is outmoded.

Both branches hold to a virtual or spiritual presence of Christ in the Eucharist, with variations that do not follow the corresponding teaching on predestination. Unlike the Lutheran position, which believes that Christ is present somehow "in, with, and under" the bread and wine, Reformed thinking avoids any kind of "localization" of the Eucharistic presence. In the words of the Heidelberg Catechism, believers asking "Do the bread and wine become the real body and blood of Christ?" are told "No; but as the water in Baptism is not changed into the blood of Christ nor becomes the washing away of sins itself, so also in the Lord's Supper the sacred bread does not become the body of Christ itself, though agreeably to the nature and usage of sacraments it is called the body of Christ."[32]

Reformed theology denies that baptism directly remits sin, either original or personal. At least this is the explicit teaching of the Heidelberg Catechism, for "only the blood of Jesus Christ and the Holy Spirit cleanse us from all sin." Baptism merely signifies that a person's sins have been remitted. It does not actually remove them.

The position of the Christian Reformed Church on absolute predestination is exemplified in a historic controversy during the mid-twenties. Three prominent ministers, Danhof, Hoeksema, and Ophoof, were censured by the Synod for protesting against the church's stand on particular election. They favored the belief that grace is given to all mankind, with men's free option to reject or co-operate with God's gift. After seceding from the denomination, they founded the Protestant Reformed Church, organized in 1926 and centered in Grand Rapids.

Consistent with their respective doctrinal differences, the churches also differ in their orders of worship. The Christian Reformed tends to be more reserved in ritual expression and less likely to make changes along the lines of the modern liturgical renewal in American Protestantism. Conversely, the Reformed Church in America for over a century has encouraged active participation in ceremonial functions, featured by its early introduction of English into church services and by its experimentation with liturgical forms drawn from other

denominations. Yet neither group is strongly orientated ritually. Until almost within living memory, there were no choirs
in any Reformed churches, and though organs are now used,
they are relative innovations in some segments of the Reformed tradition.

Organizational Structure. Church government among Reformed bodies differs widely. The Reformed Church in Hungary, for example, has bishops, and elsewhere there are superintendents. In the United States, the organization follows
the pattern set by John Knox. It is basically presbyterian,
which means that the direction and control of the church is
by a group of equals rather than by one person. At each
level of church life the directing authority is not one person
but a representative body.

As worked out in practice, the governing bodies are organized in a series of "courts" that have various names. Thus in
the Reformed Church in America, these courts are established
for a local congregation, for a number of congregations in a
locality, and finally on the national level for the whole denomination. The official terms for the governing bodies are
Provinces, corresponding to the states; Classes, which center
around municipal units as equivalent to presbyteries; and
Congregations, served by individual pastors.

In the same Calvinist tradition, the laity is given equal
authority with the clergy for directing the churches. Although
a threefold ministry is recognized (ministers, elders, and deacons), in practice the laity may exercise dominant power by
their equal representation on the governing boards. According
to the Belgic Confession of Faith, the ministers or pastors are
to preach the word of God, while elders and deacons (who
are technically laymen) "together with the pastors form the
council of the Church, that by these means the true religion
may be preserved." Moreover, each congregation, through its
lay delegates, has the right to invite clergymen to become
ministers, and to dismiss those who are not satisfactory.

A characteristic feature of Reformed Protestantism is its
attitude toward worldly amusements and luxuries. If the prevalent attitude in America is quite different from that in
Calvin's Geneva, it is still more demanding than in most
other churches stemming from the Reformation. Here, too,

the Christian Reformed Church is less compromising. A series of synodical declarations speak out against dancing, card playing, and theater attendance, although enforcement of these regulations has been extremely difficult.

Correspondingly the Christian Reformed Church has been severe in condemning divorce with the right to remarry, except on the recognized biblical grounds of infidelity. Mixed marriages with persons of another faith have also been discouraged officially. The Reformed Church in America is more lenient in making concessions, with the result that the two main bodies of Reformed thought in the United States often serve as a haven for people from the other denomination, either in the direction of more freedom or of greater Calvinist orthodoxy.

Spiritualist Churches

Spiritualism is technically defined as a belief that the spirits of the dead in various ways communicate with the living through the agency of a person called a medium. It is also a religious movement which professes to be Christian and in recent years has been organized on a national scale into several denominations, with churches, schools, and an ordained clergy.

The rise of American spiritualism is associated with the phenomena that took place at Hydesville and later at Rochester, New York, where the Fox sisters interpreted certain knockings in their home as signals from the spirit world. They worked out a system of communication. A year before, Andrew Jackson Davis had published *Nature's Divine Revelations,* which stated the basic principles that have since become the accepted philosophy of spiritualism.

At first spiritualist societies were small esoteric groups of interested persons who met regularly at séances and were united only by their common attachment to a particularly successful medium. A national society was organized in 1863, but it lasted only nine years. In 1893, the National Spiritualist

Association was established in Chicago, and is today the largest autonomous group among kindred bodies. Finally, in 1936, an International General Assembly of Spiritualists was formed, with headquarters at Norfolk, Virginia, as a co-operative federation whose primary purpose is to charter spiritualist churches throughout the world.

The doctrinal position is set forth in five propositions to which the National Spiritualist Association subscribes:

> We believe in Infinite Intelligence; and that the phenomena of nature, both physical and spiritual, are the expression of Infinite Intelligence.
>
> We affirm that a correct understanding of such expressions and living in accordance with them constitute the true religion; that the existence and personal identity of the individual continue after the change called death; and that communication with the so-called dead is a fact scientifically proved by the phenomena of Spiritualism.
>
> We believe that the highest morality is contained in the Golden Rule: "Whatsoever ye would that others should do unto you, do ye also unto them."
>
> We affirm the moral responsibility of the individual, and that he makes his own happiness or unhappiness as he obeys or disobeys Nature's physical and spiritual laws.
>
> We affirm that the doorway to reformation is never closed against any human soul, here or hereafter.[33]

In addition to the above, spiritualists believe that Christ was a medium, that the Annunciation was a message from the spirit world and the resurrection a proof that all men live on after death as disembodied spirits.

Religious services and séances are held in churches, in private homes, or in rented halls. They follow the general pattern of Protestant churches, with prayer, singing, music, reading from the *Spiritualist Manual,* a sermon or lecture, and spirit messages from the departed. Communication with the spirit world is not limited to regular church services, nor even to public assemblies of professionals.

"Making contact" with the dead is recommended at other times, even in the privacy of one's room and without the aid of a medium. The faithful are told to give a few minutes every day when they are quite peaceful and alone, to concentrate their mind on the one they wish to speak to. "Think of him or her as simply as possible . . . call them by name . . . speak to them as if they were as close to you as I fully believe they are . . . if you persevere, some realization of the presence of the beloved one will come to you." It will be so undeniable and so convincing "that a whole college of philosophers or scientists will not be able to persuade you that the one you loved and lost was not in close touch with you."

Normally, however, spirit communications require a "highly psychic" person who acts as a medium between the mortal audience and the world beyond. Mediums are not the ministers in a congregation; they are not supported by freewill offerings but through the fees that are charged for classes and séances.

Spiritualist prayers reflect a strong faith in the existence and operation of a world of intelligences that is unseen to the eye but most active on behalf of those still living in the body.

> Teach us, O Dwellers in the Land Supernal, to bear with patience and fortitude the burdens and vexations of fleeting time, and to accept all seeming disappointments as lessons in the development of our spiritual lives. May the work of bridging the chasm of death, of wiping the eyes of the mourner, be by us so faithfully done, so sweetly performed that pain may be transformed into joy, and sorrow into peace and happiness.[34]

> Help us, O Angel Loved Ones, to rise above the doubts, the fears, the pains and anguish of this life, that we may be fitting instruments to carry the word of assurance, of knowledge, of love to all who are in the shadows and have not found comfort for their souls and who are ignorant of the fact of spirit communication.[35]

The National Spiritualist Association, with a current membership of about eight thousand in some 250 churches, is the largest independent spiritualist denomination in the country. It has a seminary in Milwaukee for the training of ministers, the Morris Pratt Institute, with many of its courses offered by correspondence. A national director of education, residing in Chicago, has charge of training for the three levels of ministry in the National Spiritualist Association: ordained clergymen or ministers, licentiates who teach, and mediums.

Besides the National Spiritualist Association, there are perhaps a dozen other bodies in America that profess the same basic doctrines. They are generally short-lived, lasting a few years and then being absorbed by another society.

The Progressive Spiritual Church was founded by Rev. G. V. Cordingley in Chicago during 1907, in order to "lift spiritualism above mere psychic research, to establish it upon a sound religious basis, and to secure its recognition among other Christian denominations." Its confession of faith is substantially the same as that of the National Spiritualist Association, with some notable differences. Scriptures are recognized as the word of God and the only necessary guide for spirit communication is in the form of prophecy, palmistry, automatic writing, materialization, and spiritual healing. Thus all the preternatural phenomena in revelation are reduced to a normal operation of the spirit world, given the proper conditions of time, place, and receptive mediums. There are four sacraments: baptism, marriage, spiritual communion, and burial.

The National Christian Spiritual Alliance is another, older group, organized in 1913, which emphasizes subnormal and impersonal spirit manifestations. Mediums are allowed to baptize, but only ministers may officiate at ordination and marriage ceremonies. Main offices are located in Lake Pleasant, Massachusetts.

The Spiritualist Episcopal Church and the *Universal Psychic Science Church* came into existence in the first months after America entered the Second World War. It was occasioned by the desire of many persons to communicate with their husbands and sons who died in this war. The first group was started in 1941 by John W. Bunker, a former Methodist preacher from Grand Rapids, Michigan. Dissatisfied with the existing groups, he wanted to "provide a more churchly form of worship for spiritualism." Mr. and Mrs. J. Bertram Gerling founded the Psychic Science denomination at Rochester, New York, in 1942, where they capitalized on the city's long spiritualist tradition, going back to the Fox sisters of the last century.[36]

One evidence of the growing strength of spiritualism is the existence of an International Federation of Spiritualists, composed of representatives from forty-one nations, with which the American bodies are associated. Another sign is the number of current books by authors who may not be spiritualists themselves but who popularize the principles of spirit communication on a wide scale. Sherwood Eddy in *You Will Survive After Death,* James Crenshaw in *Telephone Between Worlds,* and Horace Westwood in *There Is a Psychic World*—all are in support of intercommunication with the dead.

REFERENCES

INTRODUCTION

1. Charles C. Morrison, *The Unfinished Reformation* (New York: Harper, 1953), pp. 29–35. [1967]
2. J. Paul Williams, *What Americans Believe and How They Worship* (New York: Harper, 1952), p. 130. [1967]
3. Morrison, op. cit., p. 190.
4. Preamble to the Constitution of the National Council of the Churches of Christ in the U.S.A., 1950.
5. Paul Tillich, *The Protestant Era* (Chicago: University of Chicago Press, 1963), pp. 56–57. [1967]

PART ONE
MAJOR PROTESTANT DENOMINATIONS

ADVENTISTS

1. James White, *Sketches of the Christian Life and Public Labors of William Miller* (Battle Creek: Seventh-Day Adventist Publishing Association, 1875), p. 279.
2. LeRoy E. Froom, *The Prophetic Faith of Our Fathers*, Vol. IV (Washington: Review and Herald, 1954), p. 992. [1967]
3. Ibid., p. 997.
4. Ibid., pp. 1000–1.
5. Emma E. Howell, *The Great Advent Movement* (Washington: Review and Herald, 1951), p. 82. [1967]
6. Ibid., p. 43.
7. Ibid., pp. 97–98.
8. Ibid., p. 108.
9. Anson P. Stokes, *Church and State in the United States*, Vol. III (New York: Harper, 1950), p. 164.
10. Howell, op. cit., p. 109.
11. *Seventh-Day Adventist Yearbook*, 1967 (Washington: Review and Herald, 1967), p. 5.

12. *Yearbook*, p. 5.
13. LeRoy E. Froom, "Seventh-Day Adventists," *The American Church*, ed. by Virgilius Ferm (New York: Philosophical Library, 1953), p. 380.
14. Ibid., pp. 377–78.
15. *Yearbook*, p. 6.
16. Ibid., p. 5.
17. Ibid., pp. 5–6.
18. Ibid.
19. Francis D. Nichol, *Answers to Objections* (Washington: Review and Herald, 1952), p. 217. [1967]
20. Ellen G. White, *The Great Controversy Between Christ and Satan* (Mountain View, California: Pacific Press, 1953), p. 53. [1967]
21. *Yearbook*, p. 5.
22. *Manual for Ministers* (Washington: General Conference of Seventh-Day Adventists, 1964), p. 85. [1967]
23. Ibid., p. 87.
24. Ibid., p. 90.
25. Ibid.
26. Ibid., p. 89.
27. Ibid., p. 92.
28. Ibid., p. 94.
29. Ibid.
30. Ellen G. White, *The Desire of the Ages* (Mountain View, California: Pacific Press, 1955), p. 661. [1967]
31. *Manual for Ministers*, pp. 93–94.
32. *Yearbook*, p. 8.
33. Howell, op. cit., p. 59.
34. Ibid., p. 36.

BAPTISTS

1. James E. Dillard, *We Southern Baptists* (Nashville: Executive Committee Southern Baptist Convention, 1949), p. 5.
2. Ibid.
3. Ibid., p. 6.
4. Robert G. Torbet, *A History of the Baptists* (Philadelphia: Judson Press), p. 62. [1967]
5. Ibid., p. 63.
6. Ibid., p. 64.
7. Ibid., p. 219.

8. Ibid., p. 309.

9. Ibid.

10. Dillard, op. cit., p. 40.

11. Edward T. Hiscox, *The New Directory for Baptist Churches* (Philadelphia: Judson Press), p. 543.

12. Ibid., p. 544.

13. Ibid., p. 552.

14. Ibid., p. 554.

15. Philip Schaff, *The Creeds of the Evangelical Protestant Churches* (London: Hodder and Stoughton, 1877), p. 738.

16. Hiscox, op. cit., p. 556.

17. Ibid.

18. Ibid., p. 87.

19. Ibid., p. 88.

20. Ibid., p. 557.

21. *Anonymous, A New Baptist Church Manual* (Valley Forge: Judson Press, 1966), pp. 31–33. [1967]

22. Ibid., p. 37.

23. *The Baptist Church Manual*, ed. by J. Newton Brown (Valley Forge: American Baptist Board of Education, 1965), pp. 11–12. [1967]

24. *The Baptist Faith and Message*, "A Statement Adopted by the Southern Baptist Convention" (Nashville, n.d.), p. 14.

25. Ralph L. Roy, *Apostles of Discord* (Boston: Beacon Press, 1953), p. 146. Cofounders with Newton of the P.O.A.U. were John A. Mackay, president of Princeton Theological Seminary; G. Bromley Oxnam, bishop of the New York area of the Methodist Church; Edwin McNeill, president of Colgate-Rochester Divinity School; and Charles C. Morrison, former editor of *The Christian Century*.

26. *The Baptist Faith and Message*, p. 14.

27. Harry E. Fosdick, *The Man from Nazareth* (New York: Harper, 1949), p. 180.

28. Billy Graham, *Christianism Versus Communism* (Minneapolis: Evangelistic Association, 1951), p. 9.

29. John A. Hardon, "Towards an American Baptist-Roman Catholic Dialogue," *Foundations* (A Baptist Journal of History and Theology, April–June 1967), pp. 150–53.

30. *Minister's Service Book for Pulpit and Parish*, ed. by Jesse Jai McNeil (Grand Rapids: Eerdmans, 1961), p. 31. [1967]

31. Ibid., p. 37.

32. Ibid., p. 41.

33. Ibid., p. 42.

34. Thomas B. McDormand, *The Art of Building Worship Services* (Nashville: Broadman Press, 1946), p. 13. [1967]

35. Hiscox, op. cit., p. 273.

36. J. M. Pendleton, *Baptist Church Manual* (Nashville: Convention Press, 1955), p. 101.

37. Ibid., p. 102.

38. Ibid.

39. Ibid.

40. Lynn Leavanworth, quoted in *Protestant Churches and Reform Today*, ed. by William J. Wolf (New York: Seabury Press, 1964), p. 43.

41. Owen D. Pelt and Ralph Lee Smith, *The Story of the National Baptists* (New York: Vantage Press, 1960), pp. 180–82.

42. Benson Y. Landis, *Yearbook of American Churches, 1956* (New York: National Council of the Churches of Christ, 1955), p. 16.

43. *The Conservative Baptist Association of America—Its History,* "Declaration of Purpose" (Chicago: 1965), p. 3. [1967]

44. Ibid., "Constitution and Declaration of Faith," p. 10.

45. Torbet, op. cit., p. 275.

46. Arminianism is opposed to Calvinism, chiefly as holding a less rigorous view of the divine sovereignty. It owes its name to Jacobus Arminius (1560–1609), a Dutch Protestant theologian.

47. Torbet, op. cit., p. 276.

48. Millennialism is now associated only with minor groups of Protestantism. But it has an impressive history which goes back to the Old Testament hopes of the Jews for a temporal Messias. As understood by Christian writers, it is a belief in the second coming of Christ before (premillennialism) or after (postmillennialism) a thousand-year period of the highest spiritual and material blessings on earth, as a prelude to the end of the world. Among the ancients, Papias, Justin, and Tertullian professed the doctrine. Even St. Augustine for a while believed in a spiritual sort of millennium. By the Middle Ages, millennialism had practically died out among Catholic writers, until revived by the sixteenth-century Protestant radicals who believed in a golden age under the scepter of Christ after the overthrow of the papacy and secular empires. Fortunately for the main body of Protestantism, this messianic complex led to such doctrinal excesses that millennialism was repudiated by the Lutheran and Reformed theologies.

49. *North American Baptist Association* (Texarkana, Arkansas: 1966), p. 142. [1967]

50. Joseph M. Stowell, *Background and History of the General Association of Regular Baptist Churches* (Hayward, California: J. F. May Press, 1949), p. 13.
51. Ibid., p. 36.
52. Ibid., p. 3.
53. Ernest A. Payne, *The Fellowship of Believers* (London: Carey Kingsgate Press, 1952), pp. 152–53.
54. George E. Levy, *The Baptists of the Maritime Provinces 1753–1946* (St. John, New Brunswick: Barnes-Hopkins 1946), p. 314.

CHRISTIAN SCIENTISTS

1. Arthur James Todd, "Christian Science," *Living Schools of Religion*, ed. by Vergilius Ferm (Paterson: Littlefield-Adams, 1961), p. 369. [1967]
2. Ibid.
3. Mark Twain, *Christian Science* (New York: Harper, 1907), p. 343.
4. Edwin F. Dakin, *Mrs. Eddy* (New York: Scribner's, 1930), p. 31.
5. Norman Beasley, *The Cross and the Crown* (New York: Duell, Sloan and Pearce, 1952), p. 5. [1967]
6. Georgine Milmine, *The Life of Mary Baker G. Eddy, and the History of Christian Science* (Garden City, New York: Doubleday Page and Co., 1909), p. 85.
7. Dakin, op. cit., p. 270.
8. Milmine, op. cit., p. 444.
9. Dakin, op. cit., p. 530.
10. Ibid., p. 521.
11. Mary Baker Eddy, *Message to the Mother Church* (Boston, 1900), p. 6. [1967]
12. Mary Baker Eddy, *Science and Health with Key to the Scriptures* (Boston: First Church of Christ, Scientist, 1934), p. 587. [1967]
13. Ibid., p. 108.
14. Ibid., p. 109.
15. Ibid., p. 116.
16. Henry W. Steiger, *Christian Science and Philosophy* (New York: Philosophical Library, 1948), p. 60.
17. *Science and Health*, p. 586.
18. Ibid., p. 592.

19. *The Christian Science Journal,* LXXII (December 1954), p. 636.
20. *Science and Health,* p. 591.
21. Ibid., pp. 582, 591.
22. Ibid., p. 466.
23. Ibid., pp. 393–94.
24. Ibid., p. 289.
25. Ibid.
26. Ibid., p. 486.
27. Ibid., p. 332.
28. Ibid., p. 324. This is a species of Docetism (from *dokein,* to appear), familiar from apostolic times. Considering matter as intrinsically evil, the Docetists held that Christ was not a man but only seemed to lead a human life.
29. Ibid., p. 583.
30. Ibid., p. 107.
31. Ibid., p. 110.
32. Ibid.
33. Ibid., p. 116. Pantheism (from *pan,* all, and *Theos,* God), which confounds the world with God, was already familiar to the ancient Greeks and Orientals. In modern times, one school of Pantheists claims that the world is absorbed by God (Spinoza); others teach that God is absorbed by the world of which He is the force and life (Goethe). Some look upon the world as a literal outpouring of the divine substance (Fichte); others, with Hegel, confound finite with infinite, being with nothing, the ego with non-ego. Christian Science is a type of Hegelianism.
34. Ibid., p. 584.
35. *McClure's Magazine,* XXXIX (May 1907), p. 109.
36. *The Christian Science Journal,* p. 663.
37. Ibid., p. 664.
38. Ibid., p. ii.
39. Quoted by Nathaniel M. Guptill, "The 'Monitor' Is Unique," *Christian Century,* LXXII (September 7, 1955), p. 1017.
40. *Manual of the Mother Church, the First Church of Christ, Scientist,* XXXIII (Boston: 1895), p. 2.
41. *Scientific American,* CLXXXVI (February 1952), pp. 40–41.
42. Ibid., (May 1952), p. 4.
43. Complete reference to this and the following statutes may be found in *Table of Statutory Provisions Favorable to Christian Science Or to Freedom Concerning Health* (Boston: First Church of Christ, Scientist, 1937).
44. *United States v. Ballard et al.,* 322 U.S. 86 (1943).

DISCIPLES AND CHRISTIANS

1. Winfred E. Garrison and Alfred T. DeGroot, *The Disciples of Christ, A History* (St. Louis: Christian Board of Publication, 1954), pp. 150–51. [1967]

2. Alonzo W. Fortune, *Origin and Development of the Disciples* (St. Louis: Christian Board of Publication, 1953), pp. 81–82. [1967]

3. Ibid., p. 101.

4. Ibid., p. 151.

5. Ibid., p. 152.

6. Winfred E. Garrison, *Religion Follows the Frontier, A History of the Disciples of Christ* (New York: Harper, 1931), pp. 297–98. [1967]

7. B. A. Abbott, *The Disciples, An Interpretation* (St. Louis: Bethany Press, 1964), p. 71. [1967] Biblical inspiration, according to the Catholic Church, is a direct, supernatural, charismatic influence on the mind, will, and executive faculties of the human writer, by which he mentally conceives, freely wills to write, and actually writes correctly all that God intends him to write and nothing else, so that God is truly the author of the sacred book produced.

8. Ibid., pp. 87, 91.

9. Ibid., pp. 86–87.

10. Ibid., pp. 88–89.

11. G. C. Brewer, *Is the Church of Christ a Denomination?* (Nashville: Gospel Advocate Co., n.d.), p. 14. [1967]

12. Leroy Brownlow, *Why I Am A Member of the Church of Christ* (Fort Worth: Brownlow Publications, 1945), p. 71.

13. Ibid., p. 72.

14. Leslie G. Thomas, *Restoration Handbook* (Nashville: Gospel Advocate Co., 1954), p. 76. [1967]

15. Abbott, op. cit., p. 117.

16. Ibid., p. 120.

17. Ibid., pp. 123, 125, 127.

18. Brownlow, op. cit., p. 168.

19. Abbott, op. cit., p. 134.

20. Ibid.

21. Ibid., p. 143.

22. Benjamin L. Smith, *Minister's Manual* (St. Louis: Christian Board of Publication, 1951), p. 7. [1967]

23. James DeForest Murch, *Christian Minister's Manual* (Cincinnati: Standard Publishing Foundation, n.d.), p. 10.
24. Alexander Campbell, *The Christian System* (Cincinnati: Standard Publishing Co., n.d.), p. 40. [1967]
25. *Christian Worship—A Service Book,* ed. by G. Edwin Osborn (St. Louis: Christian Board of Publication, 1963), p. 51. [1967]
26. Ibid., pp. 56–59.
27. Murch, op. cit., p. 47.
28. Smith, op. cit., p. 163.
29. Murch, op. cit., p. 63.
30. Ibid., p. 17.
31. Murch, op. cit., pp. 205–6.
32. Smith, op. cit., p. 179.
33. Ibid., p. 181.
34. *Christian Standard,* June 10, 1967, p. 6.

EPISCOPALIANS

1. "The Problem of Rome," *The Living Church,* August 30, 1953, p. 10.
2. Henry O. Wakeman, *The History of the Church of England* (London: Rivingtons, 1904), p. 222. [1967]
3. James T. Addison, *The Episcopal Church in the United States* (New York: Scribner, n.d.), p. 27. [1967]
4. Ibid., pp. 70–71.
5. Ibid., p. 158.
6. George E. DeMille, *The Episcopal Church Since 1900* (New York: Morehouse-Gorham, n.d.), p. 74. [1967]
7. Ibid.
8. Ibid., p. 85.
9. Powel M. Dawley, *The Episcopal Church and Its Work,* (Greenwich, Conn.: Seabury Press, 1955), p. 5.
10. *Anglican Congress, 1954: Report of Proceedings* (Greenwich, Conn.: Seabury Press, 1954), p. 195. [1967]
11. W. Norman Pittenger, "What Is an Episcopalian?" *A Guide to the Religions of America,* ed. by Leo Rosten (New York: Simon and Schuster, 1955), p. 54. [1967]
12. Ibid., p. 48.
13. "Handle with Care," *The Living Church* (Nov. 6, 1955), p. 14.

14. Ibid.

15. James A. Pike and W. Norman Pittenger, *The Faith of the Church* (Greenwich, Conn.: Seabury Press, 1951), p. 153. [1967]

16. *The People's Anglican Missal in the American Edition* (Mount Sinai, N.Y.: The Frank Gavin Liturgical Foundation, Inc., 1961), pp. 249, 150. [1967]

17. "Articles of Religion," No. 25, The Book of Common Prayer, (New York: Oxford Univ. Press, 1944), p. 607.

18. Pike, Pittenger, op. cit., p. 156.

19. Ibid., p. 158.

20. Ibid., p. 159.

21. *Constitution and Canons for the Government of the Protestant Episcopal Church in the United States of America,* Adopted in Conventions, 1789–1964. Printed for the Convention, 1964, p. 46. [1967]

22. Pike, Pittenger, op. cit., p. 160.

23. Book of Common Prayer, p. 546.

24. Wakeman, op. cit., p. 385.

25. Pike, Pittenger, op. cit., p. 161.

26. Ibid., pp. 177–78. Anglican hesitancy about the eternity of hell is answered by Anglicans in the High Church tradition, who quote the testimony of Scripture. The wicked, says Christ, "will go into everlasting (*aionios*) punishment, but the just into everlasting (*aionios*) life" (Matt. 25:46). When the Origenists (fourth century) began to teach that "the punishment of devils and wicked men is temporary and will eventually cease," they were excluded from the Church.

27. "Articles of Religion," No. 22, The Book of Common Prayer, p. 607.

28. Pike, Pittenger, op. cit., p. 173.

29. Book of Common Prayer, p. 334.

30. Ernest W. Barnes, *The Rise of Christianity* (London: Longmans-Green, 1948), p. 66. [1967]

31. Ibid., p. 93. The extent to which liberalism has penetrated the ranks of Anglicanism is revealed in a current Anglican study of the relation of Freemasonry to Christianity. Sixteen members of the Anglican hierarchy, including the Archbishop of Canterbury, and 525 clergymen were listed by name as Freemasons in Higher Degrees some years ago. "A complete list of all the (Anglican) clergy in the Craft would be many times larger." Walton Hannah, *Christian By Degrees* (London: Augustine Press, 1954), pp. 207–16. [1967]

32. George P. Atwater, *The Episcopal Church: Its Messages for Men of Today* (New York: Morehouse-Gorham, 1952), p. 74. [1967]

33. F. S. B. Gavin (Ed.), *Liberal Catholicism and the Modern World*, Vol. I (Milwaukee: Morehouse, 1934), p. vii.

34. DeMille, op. cit., p. 118.

35. Joseph Fletcher, *Situation Ethics, The New Morality* (Philadelphia: The Westminster Press, 1966), pp. 132–33. [1967]

36. *Anglican Congress*, pp. 1–2.

37. Powel M. Dawley, op. cit., p. 103. [1967]

38. Ibid., p. 141.

39. Ibid., p. 125.

40. "The Religious Life," *The Living Church*, Apr. 29, 1951, p. 14.

41. *Report of the Lambeth Conference, 1930* (London: Society for Promoting of Christian Knowledge), pp. 62, 184.

42. Peter F. Anson, *The Call of the Cloister: Religious Communities and Kindred Bodies in the Anglican Communion* (London: Society for Promoting of Christian Knowledge, 1955), pp. 594–96. The revival of religious life in the Church of England (and American Episcopalianism) began "with the dawn of the Oxford Movement and the publication of the first of the *Tracts for the Times* in 1833, (when) the 'dry bones' of Anglicanism began to stir." Ibid., p. xiii.

43. Ibid., p. 559.

44. *Constitution and Canons*, pp. 129–30.

45. Addison, op. cit., p. 275.

46. DeMille, op. cit., p. 152.

47. Ibid., p. 155.

48. Addison, op. cit., p. 278.

49. Theodore Andrews, *The Polish National Catholic Church* (London: Society for Promoting of Christian Knowledge, 1953), p. 89.

50. William A. Brown, *Toward A United Church* (New York: Scribner's, 1946), p. 58. [1967]

LUTHERANS

1. E. G. Schwiebert, *Luther and His Times* (St. Louis: Concordia, 1950), pp. 637–38. [1967]

2. *D. Martin Luthers Saemtliche Schriften*, ed. by Johann Walch (Halle, 1740 sqq.), Vol. XX, p. 223.

3. Walter A. Baepler, *A Century of Grace* (St. Louis: Concordia, 1947), pp. 5–6. [1967]

4. Philip Schaff, *The Creeds of the Evangelical Protestant Churches*, "The Augsburg Confession" (London: Hodder and Stoughton, 1877), pp. 11–12.

5. Ibid., p. 11.

6. Eric H. Wahlstrom, "Lutheran Church," *The Nature of the Church: Papers Presented to the Theological Commission of the World Conference on Faith and Order*, ed. by R. Newton Flew (London: S.C.M. Press, 1952), p. 266. [1967]

7. Francis Pieper, *Christian Dogmatics* (St. Louis: Concordia 1953), Vol. III, p. 408. [1967]

8. Schaff, op. cit., p. 10.

9. Ibid., p. 24.

10. F. E. Mayer, *The Religious Bodies of America*, "Lutheranism," (St. Louis: Concordia, 1954), p. 154. [1967] The Council of Trent condemned the notion of saving faith as a blind trust that one's sins are covered over by the merits of Christ. Salvific faith, the Council defined, is an assent of the mind to the truths of revelation, which, coupled with supernatural hope and charity, places a man on the road to heaven.

11. The letter was written to Wenceslaus Link (1530), and includes the now famous expression of Luther's attitude: *"Sic volo, sic jubeo, sit pro ratione voluntas* [I want it so, I command it so, the will must take the place of reason.]" *Luther's Saemtliche Schriften*, ed. by J. Walch, Vol. XXI, p. 314.

12. Pieper, op. cit., Vol. II, p. 533. In context, St. Paul refers to the saving power of faith in Christ independently of the detailed prescriptions of the Mosaic Law. Luther added to Paul's words by inserting "alone," so as to mean that faith, independently of good works, is sufficient for salvation.

13. Schaff, op. cit., p. 18.

14. *What Is Lutheranism?* ed. by Vergilius Ferm (New York: Macmillan, 1930), p. 215. [1967]

15. Ibid., pp. 294–95.

16. Arthur C. Piepkorn, *What the Symbolical Books of the Lutheran Church Have to Say about Worship and the Sacraments*, "Apology of the Augsburg Confession" (St. Louis: Concordia, 1952), p. 16. [1967]

17. Ibid.

18. Ibid. The Catholic doctrine on the sacraments was synthesized by the Council of Trent (A.D. 1547) in a series of propositions. Summarily, the Council defined that there are seven sacraments in the New Law, instituted by Christ; these sacraments are essentially and not only externally different than

the ritual ceremonies in the Old Testament; they are necessary for salvation and cannot be replaced by mere faith in God's promises, nor were they instituted simply to nourish faith; they contain the grace which they signify and confer grace on anyone who places no obstacle in the way; and, with the exception of baptism and matrimony, they cannot be administered by anyone, but only by those who are duly ordained to the priesthood or the episcopate.

19. Ibid., "Luther's Large Catechism," p. 17.
20. Ibid., "Apology," p. 17.
21. Ibid.
22. Ibid., p. 18.
23. Ibid.
24. Ibid.
25. Ibid. (Editor's comment).
26. Schaff, op. cit., p. 13.
27. Pieper, op. cit., Vol. III, p. 281.
28. Ibid., p. 280.
29. Ibid., p. 281.
30. Ibid., p. 261.
31. *Dr. Martin Luther's Small Catechism* (St. Louis: Concordia, 1943), p. 33. [1967]
32. Schaff, op. cit., p. 13.
33. Piepkorn, op. cit., p. 29.
34. Ibid., "Formula of Concord," p. 31.
35. Ibid.
36. Ibid.
37. Ibid. Among the original Reformers, Luther was quite singular in admitting the real presence; but unexpectedly he denied that a change of substance takes place at the Consecration. To explain this apparent contradiction, he invented the theory of "Christ's Ubiquity." Then he argued that since Christ, as God and Man, is everywhere independently of the Mass, there is no need of transubstantiation to account for His presence in the Sacrament. Catholic teaching from apostolic times held that the whole Christ, God and Man, is really and truly present in the Eucharist, *and* that this presence is effected uniquely by the words of the Consecration in the Mass.
38. Ibid., "Apology," p. 30. Besides the difference already noted, Catholic theology further denies (what many Lutherans hold) that the substance of the bread remains in the Eucharist, along with the body of Christ.

39. Piepkorn, op. cit., "Smalcald Articles," and "Apology," p. 40. When Lutherans say that the "keys remit sin," they refer to the declaration by the minister that God has forgiven a sinner; they do not mean (as Catholics do) that any words of absolution effect this forgiveness.

40. Ibid., "Augsburg Confession," p. 40.

41. Ibid., "Smalcald Articles," p. 41.

42. Ibid., "Augsburg Confession," p. 41.

43. Hjalmar Lindroth, "Confession and Absolution," *The Encyclopedia of the Lutheran Church* (Minneapolis: Augsburg Publishing House, 1965), Vol. I, p. 565. [1967]

44. *The Lutheran Agenda* (St. Louis: Concordia, n.d.), p. 64. [1967]

45. *Works of Martin Luther* (Philadelphia: Castle Press, Holman Co., 1930), Vol. III, p. 319.

46. John T. Mueller, *My Church and Others* (St. Louis: Rudolph Volkening, 1945), p. 47.

47. Pieper, op. cit., Vol. III, p. 445.

48. Ibid., p. 447.

49. Mueller, op. cit., p. 31.

50. *The Lutheran Hymnal* (Authorized by the Synods Constituting the Evangelical Lutheran Synodical Conference of North America) (St. Louis: Concordia, 1941), p. 16. [1967]

51. Ibid., p. 23.

52. Ibid., pp. 25–26.

53. Ibid., p. 27.

54. Ibid., p. 28.

55. Ibid., p. 29.

56. Ibid.

57. *Lutheran Agenda*, p. 24.

58. Ibid., p. 25.

59. *Lutheran World Federation: Constitution*, Articles II–III (*The Encyclopedia of the Lutheran Church*, Minneapolis: Augsburg Publishing House, 1965, Vol. II, p. 1430).

60. Ibid., Article II.

61. *Confirmation: A Study Document* (Minneapolis: Augsburg Publishing House, 1964), p. 46.

62. Ibid., p. 52.

MORMONS

1. William A. Linn, *The Story of the Mormons* (New York: Macmillan, 1923), p. 13.

2. Joseph F. Smith, *Essentials in Church History* (Salt Lake City: Deseret News Press, 1950), pp. 42–44. [1967]

3. Ibid., pp. 51–52.

4. Linn, op. cit., p. 39.

5. Two of the best witnesses for the influence of the Spaulding MS on the Mormon Bible are Spaulding's brother, John, and a close friend, Joseph Miller. Describing his brother's MS, John said, "It was an historical romance of the first settlers of America, endeavoring to show that the American Indians are the descendants of the Jews, or the lost tribe. It gave a detailed account of their journey from Jerusalem, by land and sea, till they arrived in America, under the command of Nephi and Lehi . . . I have recently read the 'Book of Mormon' . . . and according to the best of my recollection and belief, it is the same as my brother Solomon wrote, with the exception of the religious matter." According to Miller, "I am convinced that Spaulding's manuscript was appropriated and largely used in getting up the 'Book of Mormon.'" Ibid., pp. 53–55.

6. Ibid., p. 87.

7. *Book of Doctrine and Covenants* (Utah edition), 43:4–5; *Book of Doctrine and Covenants* (Reorganized edition), 43:2.

8. James E. Talmage, *Articles of Faith* (Salt Lake City: Church of Jesus Christ of Latter-Day Saints), p. 2. [1967]

9. *The Book of Mormon* (Salt Lake City: Church of Jesus Christ of Latter-Day Saints, 1921), p. i. [1967]

10. Talmage, op. cit., p. 311.

11. Ibid., p. 48.

12. Ibid., p. 475.

13. Ibid., p. 443.

14. Ibid., p. 445.

15. Ibid., p. 446.

16. *Book of Mormon*, p. 516.

17. *The Doctrine and Covenants* (Salt Lake City: Church of Jesus Christ of Latter-Day Saints, 1926), Chap. 20, vv. 72–74. [1967]

18. Talmage, op. cit., p. 145.

19. Ibid., p. 175.

20. Ibid., p. 176.

21. Ibid., pp. 176–77.

22. Ibid., p. 490.

23. *Doctrine and Covenants* (Salt Lake City: The Church of Jesus Christ of Latter-Day Saints, 1952), 132:61–63.

24. Linn, op. cit., p. 590.

25. Ibid., p. 595.
26. Ibid.
27. Ibid.
28. Ibid., p. 596.
29. Ibid., p. 603.
30. Ibid.
31. Ibid., p. 607.
32. Talmage, op. cit., pp. 424–25.
33. Ibid., p. 205.
34. Ibid., p. 207.
35. Ibid., p. 206.
36. Linn, op. cit., p. 194.
37. Talmage, op. cit., pp. 447–48.
38. Richard L. Evans, "What Is a 'Mormon'?" *A Guide to the Religions of America*, ed. by Leo Rosten (New York: Simon and Schuster, 1955), p. 100. [1967]

PENTECOSTALS

1. Joseph Cambell, *The Pentecostal Holiness Church* (Franklin Springs, Georgia: The Publishing House of the Pentecostal Holiness Church, 1951), p. 246.
2. Klaude Kendreick, *The Promise Fulfilled: A History of the American Pentecostal Movement* (Springfield, Missouri: Gospel Publishing House, 1961), pp. 84–86.
3. *General Council of the Assemblies of God Statement of Fundamental Truths*, "Constitution," Article V., 2, a,c,h, 1961.
4. Ibid., pp. 7, 8.
5. *Your Special Invitation* (St. Louis: Pentecostal Publishing House, n.d.) (tract)
6. *Our Gospel Message* (St. Louis: Pentecostal Publishing House, n.d.), p. 29.

PRESBYTERIANS

1. Lefferts A. Loetscher, *Brief History of the Presbyterians* (Philadelphia: Board of Christian Education of the Presbyterian Church in the U.S.A., 1938), p. 41. [1967]
2. Ibid., p. 45.
3. Cleland McAfee and Eliot Porter, *Why a Presbyterian Church?* (Philadelphia: Presbyterian Board of Christian Education, 1930), p. 12. [1967]

4. "The Westminster Confession of Faith (1646)," *Creeds of the Churches*, ed. by John H. Leith (New York: Doubleday & Co., Inc., 1963), p. 222. [1967]

5. Ibid.

6. *The Constitution of the Presbyterian Church in the United States of America* (Philadelphia: Office of the General Assembly, 1955), pp. 70–71.

7. Leith, op. cit., p. 198.

8. Ibid., p. 199.

9. *Constitution*, p. 90. Presbyterian theologians are embarrassed by the inclusion of a patent ambivalence within the same statement of doctrine. Chapter III, which quotes Calvin's predestinarianism, "is left to stand as grim as ever." One commentator admits he "has never been able to see . . . by what logic it is said to be 'in harmony with' the doctrine as given in the Declaratory Statement," adopted in 1903. (Kenneth J. Foreman, *God's Will and Ours*, Richmond, Va.: Outlook, 1954, p. 24.) In 1938–39 the U. S. Presbyterians were asked to vote on the excision of the obnoxious predestinarianism in Chapter III; two thirds wanted the doctrine eliminated, but the number was three short of the constitutional requirement; so the statement remained.

10. "The Confession of 1967," *Confessional Documents of the Presbyterian Church, U.S.A.*, pp. 178, 179, 183.

11. "The Westminster Confession of Faith (1646)," op. cit., p. 223.

12. Ibid., p. 224.

13. Ibid.

14. *Constitution*, p. 90.

15. "The Westminster Confession of Faith (1646)," op. cit., p. 226.

16. Ibid., p. 225.

17. "The Confession of 1967," op. cit., p. 186.

18. Philip Schaff, "The Westminster Confession of Faith," *The Creeds of Evangelical Protestant Churches* (London: Hodder and Stoughton, 1878), p. 655. [1967]

19. Ibid., pp. 456–57.

20. *Constitution*, pp. 68–69.

21. Ibid., pp. 242–43.

22. Ibid., p. 243. Technically the relation of elders to pastor is that of counseling assistants. "But he and they need to remember that he is responsible under God . . . not to the particular church of which he is pastor, but to the whole Church through the presbytery, which made him pastor." *Presbyte-*

rian Law for the Local Church, ed. by Eugene C. Blake (Philadelphia: Westminster, 1954), p. 66. [1967]

23. Walter L. Lingle, *Presbyterians, Their History and Beliefs* (Texarkana: Presbyterian Committee of Publication of the Presbyterian Church U.S., 1950), p. 11. [1967] One of the unsolved problems among Presbyterians is the precise status of the ruling elder. In 1943, when the Episcopalians were considering a possible merger with the Presbyterians, "They noted the grave uncertainty among Presbyterians as to whether the ruling elder is a layman or a clergyman." When the merger was voted down, this point was one of the determining factors. George E. DeMille, *The Episcopal Church Since 1900* (New York: Morehouse-Gorham, 1955), pp. 147–48.

24. *Constitution,* p. 243. There are also deaconesses in the Presbyterian Church.

25. Ibid., p. 262.

26. Ibid., p. 246.

27. Ibid.

28. Ibid., p. 248.

29. Ibid., p. 249.

30. Ibid., p. 252.

31. Ibid., p. 254.

32. Ralph L. Roy, *Apostles of Discord* (Boston: Beacon Press, 1953), p. 188. [1967]

33. "The Confession of 1967," op. cit., p. 183.

34. *Constitution,* p. 340.

35. Ibid., p. 341.

36. *The Book of Common Worship* (Philadelphia: Board of Christian Education of the Presbyterian Church in the U.S.A., 1951), p. vi. [1967]

37. Ibid., pp. 173–74.

38. Ibid., p. 175.

39. *The Book of Common Worship* (Philadelphia: Westminster Press, 1964), pp. 176–79. [1967]

QUAKERS

1. William James, *The Varieties of Religious Experience* (London: Longmans-Green, 1903), p. 7.

2. Richmond P. Miller, "What Is a Quaker?" *A Guide to the Religions of America,* ed. by Leo Rosten (New York: Simon and Schuster, 1955), p. 122. [1967]

3. Quoted in *Faith and Practice of the Philadelphia Yearly Meeting* (Philadelphia: 1955), p. 1.

4. William Penn, "Frame of Government," *The Federal and State Constitutions, Colonial Charters, and Other Organic Laws*, ed. by Francis N. Thorpe (Vol. V, Washington: 1909), pp. 3052–54.

5. *Faith and Practice of the Philadelphia Yearly Meeting*, p. 6.

6. John 1:9.

7. George Fox, *Journal*, ed. by John L. Nickalls (Cambridge Univ. Press, 1952), p. 33. [1967]

8. *Faith and Practice of the Philadelphia Yearly Meeting*, p. 11.

9. Ibid., p. 166.

10. Ibid., p. 168.

11. Robert Barclay, *An Apology For the True Christian Divinity being an Explanation and Vindication of the Principles and Doctrines of the People Called Quakers* (New York: Samuel Wood, 1832), Proposition III, pp. 2–3. [1967]

12. *Faith and Practice.* Quoted from Isaac Penington, *Works*, Part I, pp. 240–41.

13. Quoted from Barclay's *Apology*, Proposition II, in F. E. Mayer, *The Religious Bodies of America* (St. Louis: Concordia Publishing House, 1954), p. 409. [1967]

14. Howard M. Jenkins, *Religious Views of the Society of Friends*. Paper read at the World's Congress of Religions, Chicago, 1893. Quoted in *Faith and Practice*, p. 155.

15. Rufus M. Jones, *A Call to What Is Vital* (New York: Macmillan, 1948), p. 109. [1967]

16. *Faith and Practice*, p. 167.

17. Ibid., p. 168.

18. Ibid.

19. Robert Barclay, *An Apology etc.*, Proposition XIII, p. 13.

20. *Faith and Practice*, p. 78.

21. Rufus M. Jones, *The Faith and Practice of the Quakers* (New York: Harper, 1927), p. 90.

22. *Faith and Practice*, p. 24. Quaker opposition to oaths is based on the words of Christ, "Do not swear at all . . . Let what you say be simply 'Yes' or 'No'; anything more than this comes from evil" (Matt. 5:33–37).

23. *Faith and Practice*, p. 46.

24. Ibid., p. 50.

25. Ibid., p. 51.

26. Robert Barclay, *An Apology etc.*, Proposition XV, p. 14.

SALVATIONISTS

1. *The Salvation Army Year Book*, 1956 (London: Salvationist Publishing, 1956), p. 50. [1967]

2. William Booth, *In Darkest England and the Way Out* (Atlanta: Southern Territorial Headquarters, U.S.A., 1942), p. 21. [1967]

3. Ibid., p. 23.

4. Alfred J. Gilliard, *The Faith of the Salvationist* (London: Salvationist Publishing, n.d.), p. 3.

5. The periodical *Rescue Herald,* published in Philadelphia, is the principal organ of unity among the Rescue Workers on a national scale. Like the Salvationists, they are organized along territorial lines with commanders in charge of each territory.

6. *Statement of Cardinal Principles of The Volunteers of America,* received from National Headquarters, June 30, 1967.

7. *The Salvation Army Handbook of Doctrine* (London: International Headquarters, 1955), p. 1. [1967]

8. Ibid., p. 31.

9. Ibid., pp. 32–35.

10. Ibid., p. 35.

11. Ibid., p. 47.

12. Ibid., p. 49.

13. Ibid., pp. 96, 99.

14. Ibid., p. 112.

15. Ibid., p. 115.

16. Ibid., p. 118.

17. Ibid., p. 116.

18. Ibid., pp. 119, 120, 122.

19. Ibid., pp. 118–19.

20. Ibid., p. 127.

21. Ibid., pp. 131, 135.

22. Ibid., pp. 132–33.

23. Ibid., p. 160.

24. Ibid.

25. Ibid., p. 161.

26. Ibid., p. 162.

27. M. L. Carpenter, *Salvationists and the Sacraments* (London: Salvationist Publishing, 1945), p. 4. [1967]

28. Ibid., pp. 4–5.

29. Ibid.

30. *Orders and Regulations for Officers of the Salvation Army* (London: International Headquarters, 1950), pp. 121–22. [1967]

31. *Salvation Army Ceremonies* (London: Salvationist Publishing, 1947), p. 1. [1967]

32. Ibid., p. 3.

33. Ibid., pp. 6–7.

34. Ibid., p. 11.

35. Ibid., p. 16.

36. Ibid., p. 21.

37. *Orders and Regulations*, p. 279.

38. Ibid., p. 287.

39. Ibid., p. 291.

40. Ibid., p. 6.

41. Ibid., p. 11.

42. *Salvation Army Year Book*, p. 65.

43. *Orders and Regulations*, pp. 30–31.

44. Ibid., p. 12.

45. Gilliard, op. cit., p. 14.

46. Ibid., p. 18.

UNITARIANS

1. Karl M. Chworowsky, "What Is a Unitarian?" *A Guide to the Religions of America*, ed. by Leo Rosten (New York: Simon and Schuster, 1955), p. 142. [1967]

2. Ibid.

3. Harry B. Scholefield, *Guide to Unitarianism* (Boston: Beacon Press, 1955), p. 36. [1967]

4. Ralph Waldo Emerson, *Nature, Addresses and Lectures* (Boston: Houghton-Mifflin, 1883), p. 128.

5. Ibid.

6. Scholefield, op. cit., p. 53.

7. Ibid., p. 15.

8. Robert T. Weston, *Faith Without Fear* (Louisville: private printing, 1949), p. 9.

9. *Anonymous, The Free Church: Its Nature, Nurture, Character* ("Boston: Unitarian-Universalist Association, 1965), pp. 1–2. [1967]

10. Jack Mendelsohn, *Why I Am a Unitarian Universalist* (Boston: Beacon Press, 1966), p. 198. [1967]

11. Scholefield, op. cit., p. 5.

12. John H. Hershey, "The Liberal Way for Today," *Unity*, CXLI
    (May–June 1955), 31. This statement of monism is doubly
    significant; the author is minister of the First Congregational
    Church in Easton, Massachusetts, and the publication is an
    official organ of the Western Unitarian Conference, with head-
    quarters in Chicago.
13. *Services of Religion* (Boston: Beacon Press, 1953), p. vi.
    [1967]
14. Ibid.
15. Ibid., p. 6.
16. Ibid., p. 71.
17. Ibid., p. 165.
18. Ibid., p. 148.
19. Ibid., p. 152.
20. *Constitution of the Unitarian Universalist Association*, Article
    II, Section 1. [1967]
21. Ibid., Section 2.
22. Scholefield, op. cit., p. 48.
23. Ibid., p. 27.
24. Ibid.

UNITED CHURCH OF CHRIST: Congregationalists

1. Douglas Horton, "What Is a Congregationalist?" *A Guide to
   the Religions of America*, ed. by Leo Rosten (New York:
   Simon and Schuster, 1955), p. 37.
2. Oscar E. Maurer, ed., *Manual of the Congregational Christian
   Churches* (Boston: Pilgrim Press, 1951), p. 3.
3. Gaius G. Atkins and Frederick L. Fagley, *History of American
   Congregationalism* (Boston: Pilgrim Press, 1941), p. 60.
4. Ibid., p. 77.
5. Maurer, op. cit., p. 5.
6. Atkins and Fagley, op. cit., p. 108.
7. Ibid., p. 146.
8. Ibid., p. 133.
9. Maurer, op. cit., p. 29.
10. Atkins and Fagley, op. cit., p. 404.
11. Ibid., pp. 404–5.
12. Ibid., p. 405.
13. *Assembly Work Book, World Council of Churches* (Geneva,
    1954), pp. 98–99.
14. L. Wendell Fitfield, *What It Means to be a Minister of the
    Congregational Church* (Boston: Pilgrim Press, n.d.), p. 2.

15. Fitfield, op. cit., p. 3.
16. Maurer, op. cit., p. 66.
17. Fitfield, op. cit., p. 3.
18. Richard H. Bennet, *Christian Faith and Purpose, A Catechism* (Boston: Pilgrim Press, n.d.), p. 7.
19. Roy L. Minich, *What the Church Has to Offer* (Boston: Pilgrim Press, n.d.), p. 26.
20. *We Believe* (Boston: Pilgrim Press, n.d.), p. 10.
21. Ibid.
22. Fitfield, op. cit., p. 5.
23. *Manual for Church Members* (Boston: Pilgrim Press, 1952), pp. 2–3.
24. *The Congregational Christian Churches, For What They Stand* (Boston: Beacon Press, n.d.), p. 2.
25. Minich, op. cit., p. 13.
26. Ibid.
27. *Christian Teachings: A Manual for Those Preparing for Church Membership* (Boston: Pilgrim Press, n.d.), p. 9.
28. Bennet, op. cit., p. 25.
29. Ibid.
30. *My Church: Pastor's Manual* (Boston: Pilgrim Press, n.d.), p. 89.
31. Albert W. Palmer, *I Believe in Baptism* (Boston: Pilgrim Press, n.d.), p. 8.
32. Ibid., p. 7.
33. The term "transubstantiation" was first officially used by the Fourth Lateran Council in 1215. The theology of the real presence, in terms of substance and accidents, was developed mainly by St. Thomas Aquinas (1225–74). This is the reason Aquinas is sometimes credited with having coined the term. It was actually in use, however, at least a century before the Lateran Council.
34. Palmer, op. cit., pp. 8–9.
35. Ibid., p. 9.
36. Bennet, op. cit., p. 21.
37. Minich, op. cit., p. 54.
38. Ibid., pp. 54–55.
39. Ibid., p. 52.
40. Bennet, op. cit., p. 21.
41. *A Book of Worship* (New York: Oxford University Press, 1950), p. xiii. [1967]
42. Ibid., p. xxii.
43. Ibid., p. xvi.

44. Ibid.
45. Ibid., p. xix.
46. Ibid., p. xxi.
47. Ibid., p. xxiii.
48. Ibid., p. xxv.
49. Ibid., p. 109.
50. Maurer, op. cit., 210.
51. Ibid., p. 214.
52. Ibid., p. 215.
53. Ibid.
54. Ibid., p. 101.
55. *The Congregational Christian Ministry: A Handbook of Standards, Procedures and Services* (New York: Department of the Ministry, 1953), p. 7.
56. Atkins and Fagley, op. cit., p. 362. According to Catholic teaching, the priesthood imprints a permanent character on the soul and gives the power of offering Mass, forgiving sins in the name of Christ, and administering the other sacraments. Only a bishop can ordain to the priesthood.
57. Maurer, op. cit., p. 81.
58. Ibid., pp. 80–81.
59. Ralph L. Roy, *Apostles of Discord* (Boston: Beacon Press, 1953), p. 344.
60. Ibid., p. 342.
61. Atkins and Fagley, op. cit., p. 348.
62. Ibid., p. 349.
63. Ibid., p. 355.
64. Ibid., p. 351.
65. Ibid., pp. 352–53.
66. Ibid., p. 358.
67. "Movement or Machination?" *Christian Century*, LXXII (Nov. 23, 1955), 1359.
68. *Christian Century*, LXX (Dec. 16, 1953), 1444.

UNITED CHURCH OF CHRIST: Evangelical and Reformed Church

1. Oscar E. Maurer (ed.), *Manual of the Congregational Christian Churches* (Boston: Pilgrim Press, 1951), p. 30. [1967]
2. F. E. Mayer, *The Religious Bodies of America* (St. Louis: Concordia Publishing House, 1954), p. 360. [1967]

3. Julius H. Horstmann and Herbert H. Wernecke, *Through Four Centuries: The Beginnings of the Evangelical and Reformed Church* (St. Louis: Eden Publishing House, 1938), p. 113. [1967]

4. Ibid., p. 122.

5. *The Constitution and By-Laws of the Evangelical and Reformed Church*, p. 5.

6. Horstmann and Wernecke, op. cit., p. 21.

7. Ibid., p. 22.

8. *Constitution*, p. 6.

9. James I. Good, *Aid to the Heidelberg Catechism* (St. Louis: Eden Publishing House, n.d.), p. 20. [1967]

10. *My Confirmation* (Philadelphia: Christian Education Press, 1952), p. 38. [1967]

11. Oscar J. Rumpf, *Christian Faith and Life: The Meaning of Church Membership* (Philadelphia: Christian Education Press, 1952), p. 30. [1967]

12. Reinhold Niebuhr, *Beyond Tragedy* (New York: Scribner's, 1937), p. 28. [1967]

13. Reinhold Niebuhr, *Human Destiny* (New York: Scribner's, 1935), p. 70. [1967]

14. *Heidelberg Catechism*, p. 91.

15. *Constitution*, p. 6.

16. *Evangelical Catechism* (St. Louis: Eden Publishing House, 1929), p. 68. [1967]

17. Rumpf, op. cit., p. 60.

18. *Heidelberg Catechism*, p. 278.

19. *Evangelical Catechism*, p. 71.

20. *Constitution*, p. 13.

21. *Book of Worship* (Approved by the General Synod of the Evangelical and Reformed Church) (St. Louis: Eden Publishing House, 1947), p. 65. [1967]

22. *My Confirmation*, p. 2. This statement must be qualified. Confirmation still follows immediately after baptism in the Oriental Churches in union with Rome and in some Churches of the Latin Rite, e.g., in Spain. Postponement of Confirmation until the age of reason began in the West about A.D. 1000. But the administration of Confirmation without anointing with chrism was an innovation of the Protestant Reformers.

23. *Evangelical Catechism*, p. 70.

24. *Book of Worship*, p. 316.

25. *Constitution*, p. 17.

26. *Book of Worship*, p. 326.

27. Stephen Neill, *Towards Church Union* (Published on behalf of the Faith and Order Commission of the World Council of Churches) (London: Camelot Press, 1952), p. 63. [1967]
28. Ibid.
29. Ibid.
30. Ibid., p. 64.
31. Ibid.
32. Ibid.

THE UNITED METHODIST CHURCH: Methodists

1. *The Constitution for The United Methodist Church with Enabling Legislation and Other Historic Documents*, 1967, p. vii.
2. Ibid., p. 1.
3. Ibid., pp. 8–9.
4. Ibid., p. 18.
5. William W. Sweet, *Methodism in American History* (New York, Nashville: Abingdon-Cokesbury, 1933), p. 34. [1967]
6. William W. Sweet, ed. by William K. Anderson, "Methodism's Debt to the Church of England," *Methodism* (Nashville: The Methodist Publishing House, 1947), p. 50. [1967]
7. Ibid.
8. Sweet, *Methodism in American History*, p. 107.
9. Ibid., p. 105.
10. Ibid., p. 103.
11. *Doctrine and Discipline of the Methodist Church* (Nashville: The Methodist Publishing House, 1952), p. 8.
12. Ibid., pp. 25–26.
13. Ibid., p. 26.
14. Charles C. Selecman, *The Methodist Primer* (Nashville: Tidings, 1953), p. 8.
15. *Discipline*, 1952, p. 26.
16. Ibid.
17. Ibid., p. 27.
18. Ibid.
19. Ibid., p. 28.
20. Nels F. S. Ferre, "God Can Be Experienced," *Methodism*, pp. 123–24.
21. Ibid., p. 124.
22. Robert E. Cushman, "Salvation for All," *Methodism*, p. 112.
23. *Discipline*, 1952, p. 37.
24. Ibid., p. 28.

25. *Discipline*, 1952, p. 37.
26. Ibid., p. 31.
27. The Book of Common Prayer (New York: Oxford University Press, 1935), p. 610. [1967]
28. *Discipline*, 1952, p. 29.
29. Ibid.
30. Ibid., p. 30.
31. The Book of Common Prayer, p. 605.
32. *Discipline*, 1952, p. 28.
33. Ibid., p. 30.
34. Ibid., p. 120.
35. *Doctrine and Discipline*, 1964, p. 159. [1967]
36. Ibid., p. 658.
37. Ibid.
38. G. Bromley Oxnam, "Planning Our Children," *Social Problems in America* (New York: Henry Holt, 1955), p. 118. [1967]
39. *Discipline*, 1952, pp. 652–53.
40. *Doctrine and Discipline*, 1964, p. 398. [1967]
41. Ibid., p. 403.
42. Walter G. Muelder, "Methodism's Contribution to Social Reform," *Methodism*, op. cit., p. 194.
43. *Discipline*, 1952, p. 639.
44. Ibid., p. 385.
45. Sweet, *Methodism in American History*, p. 389.
46. *Discipline*, 1952, p. 494.
47. *Doctrine and Discipline*, 1964, pp. 553–54. This and the following provisions of the *Discipline* have become part of the new revised and authorized Methodist Hymnal (Nashville: The Methodist Publishing House, 1966). [1967]
48. Ibid.
49. *Discipline*, 1952, pp. 511–12.
50. *Doctrine and Discipline*, 1964, p. 572. [1967]
51. Ibid., p. 573.
52. *Discipline*, 1952, pp. 521, 523, 526.
53. Ibid., p. 523.
54. *Doctrine and Discipline*, 1964, pp. 605, 598. [1967]
55. Ibid., p. 704.
56. *Discipline*, 1952, pp. 666–67.
57. *Doctrine and Discipline*, 1964, p. 704. [1967]
58. Ibid.
59. Ibid., p. 705.
60. Ibid., p. 704.

61. Ibid., p. 705.
62. *Doctrines and Discipline of the Free Methodist Church in North America* (Winona Lake: 1952), pp. 31–34.

THE UNITED METHODIST CHURCH: Evangelical United Brethren

1. Paul W. Milhouse, *Christian Worship in Symbol and Ritual* (Harrisburg: Evangelical Press, 1953), p. 5. [1967]
2. Paul H. Eller, *These Evangelical United Brethren* (Dayton: Otterbein Press, 1950), p. 23. [1967]
3. Ibid., p. 27.
4. Ibid., p. 45. Quotation from R. Yeakel, *Geschichte der Evangelische Gemeinschaft* (Cleveland, 1890), Vol. I, p. 56. [1967]
5. Eller, op. cit., p. 75.
6. *The Discipline of the Evangelical United Brethren: 1947* (Dayton: Otterbein Press, 1947), p. 14. [1967]
7. *The Discipline of the Evangelical United Brethren: 1955* (Dayton: Otterbein Press; and Harrisburg: Evangelical Press, 1955), p. 19. [1967]
8. Ibid.
9. Ibid.
10. Ibid., pp. 27–28.
11. Ibid., p. 19.
12. Ibid., p. 25.
13. Ibid.
14. Ibid., p. 26.
15. *Discipline: 1947*, p. 439.
16. Ibid.
17. *Discipline: 1955*, p. 403.
18. *Discipline: 1947*, p. 443.
19. *Discipline: 1955*, pp. 412–13.
20. Ibid., pp. 404, 414.
21. Ibid., p. 403.
22. Ibid., pp. 364–65.
23. Ibid., p. 366.
24. Ibid., p. 365.
25. Ibid., p. 366.
26. Ibid.
27. Ibid., p. 368.
28. Ibid., p. 482.
29. Ibid., pp. 483–84.

30. *Discipline: 1955*, p. 484.
31. Eller, op. cit., p. 121.
32. Ibid., pp. 121–22.
33. *Discipline: 1955*, p. 451.
34. Ibid., p. 88.
35. Ibid., p. 100.
36. Ibid., p. 604.
37. Ibid., p. 46.
38. Eller, op. cit., p. 122.
39. *Discipline: 1955*, p. 236.
40. *Discipline: 1947*, p. 567.
41. *Discipline: 1955*, p. 210.
42. *Discipline: 1947*, p. 239.

PART TWO
MINOR PROTESTANT DENOMINATIONS

1. Declaration of Principles, I. [1967]
2. Ibid., VI.
3. Ibid., V.
4. Ibid., III.
5. Ibid., VIII.
6. Ibid., IX.
7. *Unity School of Christianity* (Lee's Summit, Mo.: 1967), p. i. [1967]
8. Ibid., p. 5.
9. *What Is Unity* (Lee's Summit, Mo.: 1967), p. 8.
10. Ibid., p. 9.
11. *Unity's Statement of Faith* (Lee's Summit, Mo.: 1967), Articles 6, 11, 24.
12. Eric Butterworth, *The Word Is Unity*, Unity School of Christianity (Lee's Summit, Mo.: 1967), pp. 3–4.
13. Ibid., p. 6.
14. *Constitution and Special Rules, Church of the Nazarene* (Kansas City, Mo.: Nazarene Publishing House, 1966), pp. 12–13. [1967]
15. Mendell Taylor, *Fifty Years of Nazarene Missions* (Kansas City, Mo.: Beacon Hill Press, 1958), p. 137. [1967]
16. John Wesley, "The Lord Our Righteousness," *Sermons* (London: 1921), Vol. II, p. 427. [1967]

17. Marley Cole, *Jehovah's Witnesses: The New World Society* (New York: Vantage Press, 1955), p. 42. [1967]

18. *Watchtower*, December 1, 1916, p. 374.

19. Joseph F. Rutherford, *Riches* (New York: Watch Tower Bible and Tract Society, 1936), p. 188.

20. Rutherford, *Salvation.* (New York: Watch Tower Bible and Tract Society, 1939), p. 199.

21. Nathan H. Knorr, *Can You Live Forever in Happiness on Earth?* (Brooklyn: Watch Tower Bible and Tract Society, 1950), p. 15.

22. Anson P. Stokes, *Church and State in the United States* Vol. II (New York: Harper, 1950), p. 615. [1967]

23. Paul H. Bowman, "Changing Principles in a Changing World," *An Adventurous Future* (Elgin: The Brethren Press, 1959), pp. 262–63. [1967]

24. *Mennonite Confession of Faith* (Scottdale, Pa.: Herald Press, 1963), pp. 21–22. [1967]

25. Ibid., p. 20.

26. Ibid., p. 21.

27. Ibid., p. 16.

28. *Canons of Dort*, Article 1, "Divine Election and Reprobation." [1967]

29. Ibid., Article 15.

30. Ibid., "The Death of Christ, and the Redemption of Men Thereby," Article 8.

31. *Reformed Standards of Unity* (Grand Rapids: Society for Reformed Publications, 1957), pp. 15–16. [1967]

32. *Heidelberg Catechism*, Question 78. [1967]

33. *Declaration of Principles*, Adopted by the National Spiritualist Association of Churches, U.S.A., Executive Offices, Milwaukee, Wisconsin. [1967]

34. *Spiritualist Manual*, National Spiritualist Association, Washington, D.C., p. 32. [1967]

35. Ibid., p. 44.

36. The first spiritualist church in Rochester, New York, is called the "International Shrine of Spiritualism." Next to it stands an obelisk with a commemorative plaque, "Erected by the Spiritualists of the World," concluding with the words: "There is no death . . . There are no dead."

PART THREE

STATISTICS ON RELIGIOUS BODIES IN THE UNITED STATES

Except where otherwise noted, the following information is from the 1968 Yearbook of American Churches, edited by Lauris B. Whitman and published by the National Council of the Churches of Christ.

Statistics are based on comprehensive data-collecting processes, most of them conducted by mail. Whenever special problems emerge, they are always discussed jointly with the churches involved and no revisions or adjustments are made without clearance from the denominations involved.

Information about the churches includes statistical data about church membership, religious education, the number of clergy, and church finances.

The method of presenting the data differs from that used in previous issues of the *Yearbook*, particularly at one point. Current reporting is separated from non-current reports. In the past, the statistical data have been published as one table. However, the individual denominational reports have covered a wide range of years. Many of them have reported for the year just past, but many failed to report each year. Where there was no current report the most recent report was used, with an indication of the date received.

This situation has created serious problems which have been pointed out in each year's *Yearbook*. However, it is a problem to which there is no easy solution. The present method of separating current and non-current statistics is a first step in creating a clearer presentation of data and, ultimately, in improving the quality of church statistics.

Several items should be noted in relation to the present statistical tables. First, twelve religious bodies have been dropped from the list. In most cases, there has been no contact with them for a number of years and repeated efforts have failed to re-establish contact. Several have been reported in terms of the 1936 Census of Religious Bodies and there are no later data for them.

The following table lists the twelve which have been

dropped. They were listed in the 1967 *Yearbook* as having 948 churches with 163,978 members. The largest single group was Federated Churches, almost all of which appear within the totals for the denominations with which they are affiliated:

Religious Bodies Not Listed in the 1968 Yearbook

Year		Members	Churches
1936	Regular Baptists	17,186	266
1945	Two-Seed-in-the-Spirit Predestinarian Baptists	201	16
1936	Old Order River Brethren	291	7
1963	Catholic Apostolic Church	—	—
1959	Church of God (Greenville, Tenn.)	30	5
1963	Federated Churches	88,411	508
1963	Central Yearly Meeting of Friends	534	12
1936	Independent Negro Churches	12,337	50
1951	Church of Jesus Christ, Cutlerites	22	1
1960	Lithuanian National Catholic	3,950	4
1940	Independent A.M.E.	1,000	12
1963	National David Spiritual Temple	40,816	66
	Totals	163,978	948

Besides the religious bodies no longer listed, there are several which did not report inclusive membership for this edition. The following table shows their inclusive membership figures as reported in *Yearbook*, 1967:

Buddhist Churches of America	92,000
National Spiritualist Association of Churches	4,962
Pentecostal Evangelical Church of God	229
Social Brethren	1,540
United Seventh-Day Brethren	125
	98,856

Current Church Statistics

TABLE 1A is the report on data received from the listed bodies for this edition. One hundred and twenty-four bodies reported their most recent statistics in one or more of the categories requested. The total current reports provide the following totals:

Number of churches	223,708
Total, inclusive membership	104,867,944
Full, communicant, or confirmed membership	47,372,058
Total clergy	264,373
Number of clergy having charges	137,626
Number of Sunday schools	219,563
Total Sunday school enrollment	40,967,187

Except in the case of the number of churches, these figures do not represent totals of all 124 bodies listed (see Table 1A). Nor do these figures include the Church of Jesus Christ of the Latter-Day Saints, since that body publishes only world-wide statistics. (In 1966, however, this church made a special analysis of its figures which indicated a total U.S. membership of 1,789,175. Comparative current data are not available.)

It should also be noted that several denominations could not report certain clergy data, thus seriously affecting the totals. There is no current information on the total number of Southern Baptist clergymen, of United Presbyterian clergymen having charges, of Methodist pastors having churches, or of Assembly of God ministers serving parishes. In 1963 the Southern Baptists reported a total of 35,000 clergymen and that figure has been repeated in *Yearbooks* since then. Last year the United Presbyterians indicated that 7800 of their clergymen served charges, while the Methodists reported 25,676. The last year's figure for the Assemblies of God was 15,669.

The following table summarizes the larger changes in the two categories relating to the clergy:

Most Recent Data on Total Clergy for Denominations Not Reporting for This Edition but Carried Previously

Baptist General Conference	700
Church of Jesus Christ of Latter-Day Saints	4,504
Southern Baptist Convention	35,000
	40,204

Most Recent Data on Pastors Having Charges for Denominations Not Reporting for This Edition but Carried Previously

Assemblies of God	15,669
Church of Jesus Christ of Latter-Day Saints	4,222
Conservative Congregational	103
Cumberland Presbyterian	615
The Methodist Church	24,676
North American Baptist Association	1,400
United Presbyterian, U.S.A.	7,800
	54,485

Non-current Church Statistics

Religious bodies not included in Table 1A are listed in Table 1B, which contains the last figures submitted. These range from reports going back to 1936 to reports that are only a year or two out of date. It is the goal and the expectation of the *Yearbook* that there will be rapid movement toward the expansion of the current table and elimination of the necessity for reporting non-current data. Until that time, however, students of the churches will have to deal with and base their generalizations on these two levels of data, recognizing the difficulties involved.

For the purposes of comparison with previous membership figures, the present total figure for current and non-current reports together with the latest data for the bodies dropped and the latest figures for the Church of Jesus Christ of the Latter-Day Saints is 125,778,656. This represents a gain of slightly less than 1 per cent over the membership figures in the 1967 *Yearbook*.

The data for this year are roughly comparable to last year's data. Readers are reminded again that the figures are not all current but are the latest available. At best this must be considered a general indication of the membership of 241 religious bodies.

TABLE 1A: *Current Church Statistics*

Religious Body	Year Reported	No. of Churches
Advent Christian Church	1967	405
Albanian Orthodox Archdiocese in America	1966	12
Amana Church Society	1966	7
American Baptist Association	1966	3,247
American Baptist Convention	1966	6,063
American Carpatho-Russian Orthodox Greek Catholic Church	1966	69
American Catholic Church (Syro-Antiochean)	1966	11
The American Lutheran Church	1966	4,899
American Rescue Workers	1967	45
Antiochean Orthodox Archdiocese of Toledo, and Dependencies in N.A.	1966	20
Apostolic Christian Churches of America	1966	72
Armenian Apostolic Church of America	1965	32
Armenian Church, Diocese of America	1966	43
Assemblies of God	1966	8,506
Associate Reformed Presbyterian Church	1966	143
Baptist General Conference	1966	573
Beachy Amish Mennonite Churches	1966	47
Berean Fundamental Church	1966	37
Bible Protestant Church	1966	43
Bible Way Churches of Our Lord Jesus Christ World Wide, Inc.	1967	343

Inclusive Membership	Full, Communicant, or Confirmed Members	No. of Pastors Having Charges	Total No. of Clergy	No. of Sunday or Sabbath Schools	Total Enrollment
29,838	29,838	333	504	381	27,659
7,000	7,000	12	15	12	710
761	761	26	xxxx	3	232
731,000	731,000	3,100	3,175	3,247	271,500
1,538,988	1,538,988	4,476	8,100	6,013	844,801
104,000	104,000	71	68	65	5,390
5,240	N.A.	10	11	6	133
2,566,581	1,732,488	3,910	5,751	5,007	908,672
5,500	5,500	45	40	47	5,268
30,000	30,000	20	27	20	N.A.
8,740	8,740	80	33	72	7,875
125,000	125,000	N.A.	34	31	2,130
136,000	N.A.	37	49	40	5,250
576,058	576,058	N.A.	11,168	9,000	1,017,000
27,758	27,758	94	131	143	17,402
91,206	91,206	508	N.A.	573	118,868
3,689	3,689	110	139	N.A.	N.A.
1,982	1,982	37	37	37	N.A.
2,610	N.A.	35	48	42	4,569
25,000	25,000	342	353	N.A.	N.A.

(*Continued*)

TABLE 1A: *Current Church Statistics (Cont'd.)*

Religious Body	Year Reported	No. of Churches
Brethren in Christ	1966	159
Buddhist Churches of America	1967	35
Christ Catholic Church of America and Europe	1966	19
Christian and Missionary Alliance	1966	1,109
Christian Church of North America General Council	1966	106
Christian Churches (Disciples of Christ), International Convention	1966	8,066
The Christian Congregation	1966	251
Christian Nation Church U.S.A.	1966	16
Christian Reformed Church	1966	629
Christian Unity Baptist Association	1966	11
The Church of God	1965	1,921
Church of God (Abrahamic Faith)	1966	119
Church of God (Anderson, Ind.)	1966	2,261
Church of God (Cleveland, Tenn.)	1966	3,727
The Church of God of Prophecy	1966	1,469
Church of Jesus Christ (Bickertonites)	1967	46
Church of Jesus Christ of Latter-Day Saints (Worldwide statistics)	1966	4,022
Church of the Lutheran Brethren of America	1966	67
The Church of Revelation	1966	1
Church of the Brethren	1966	1,056

Inclusive Membership	Full, Communicant, or Confirmed Members	No. of Pastors Having Charges	Total No. of Clergy	No. of Sunday or Sabbath Schools	Total Enrollment
8,593	8,593	156	246	156	21,349
N.A.	N.A.	45	55	44	7,095
5,737	5,737	19	19	18	702
68,829	68,829	1,109	1,104	1,106	155,889
8,000	N.A.	106	129	106	N.A.
1,894,927	1,894,927	3,157	7,540	8,066	1,095,641
44,914	44,914	253	258	237	29,523
3,300	N.A.	17	21	19	96
275,530	145,472	544	843	669	74,804
617	617	4	15	6	N.A.
73,868	73,868	1,891	2,529	2,024	98,606
6,200	6,200	91	99	110	8,000
143,364	143,364	1,798	2,780	2,000	247,358
220,405	220,405	3,400	2,597	3,561	355,000
43,441	N.A.	1,365	3,314	1,458	90,000
2,309	2,309	60	209	0	xxxx
2,480,899	2,480,899	N.A.	xxxx	4,022	N.A.
5,795	5,795	77	95	67	5,817
750	750	7	33	0	xxxx
191,402	191,402	813	2,089	1,054	147,257

(*Continued*)

TABLE 1A: *Current Church Statistics* (*Cont'd.*)

Religious Body	Year Reported	No. Churc
Church of the Nazarene	1966	4,6.
Congregational Christian Churches, National Association of	1966	3.
Congregational Holiness Church	1966	1.
Conservative Congregational Christian Conference	1966	ε
Cumberland Presbyterian Church	1966	9ε
Duck River (and Kindred) Associations of Baptists	1966	7
Eastern Orthodox Catholic Church in America	1966	
Elim Missionary Assemblies	1966	7
Ethical Culture Movement	1966	3
Evangelical Congregational Church	1966	16
Evangelical Covenant Church of America	1966	52
Evangelical Free Church of America	1966	51
Evangelical Lutheran Synod	1966	8
Evangelical Methodist Church	1965	15
Evangelical United Brethren Church	1966	3,97
Free Christian Zion Church of Christ	1966	74
Free Methodist of N.A.	1966	1,14
Free Will Baptists	1966	2,10
Friends United Meeting (The Five Years Meeting of Friends)	1966	50
General Association of Regular Baptist Churches	1966	1,24

nclusive mbership	Full, Communicant, or Confirmed Members	No. of Pastors Having Charges	Total No. of Clergy	No. of Sunday or Sabbath Schools	Total Enroll-ment
350,882	350,882	4,310	6,273	4,849	871,331
110,000	N.A.	266	N.A.	N.A.	N.A.
4,859	4,859	146	302	N.A.	N.A.
13,513	13,513	N.A.	170	80	12,096
88,248	59,057	N.A.	743	757	56,206
8,316	8,316	122	152	N.A.	N.A.
160	160	3	5	2	134
4,000	4,000	85	85	80	N.A.
5,500	5,500	18	38	20	1,785
29,744	29,744	136	156	163	31,733
64,950	64,950	492	665	517	74,133
50,312	50,312	579	746	528	72,375
15,798	10,606	43	54	77	4,566
9,311	9,311	140	239	150	14,273
732,377	732,377	2,889	3,628	3,970	555,085
22,260	N.A.	321	340	119	4,195
60,175	60,175	1,064	1,517	1,146	137,355
178,450	178,450	2,109	3,310	2,109	146,900
70,673	70,673	367	508	327	46,812
170,299	170,299	1,112	1,556	1,244	N.A.

(Continued)

TABLE 1A: *Current Church Statistics (Cont'd.)*

Religious Body	Year Reported	No. Churc.
General Baptists	1966	84
General Church of the New Jerusalem	1966	3
General Conference, Mennonite Church	1966	18
General Convention of the New Jerusalem in the U.S.A.	1966	5
Hutterian Brethren (South Dakota)	1966	2
Independent Baptist Church of America	1966	
Independent Fundamental Churches of America	1966	86
International Pentecostal Assemblies	1966	6
Jewish Congregations	1965	4,70
Lutheran Church in America	1966	5,86
Lutheran Church—Missouri Synod	1966	5,64
Mennonite Church	1966	94
The Methodist Church	1966	37,60
Missionary Church Association	1966	13
Moravian Church in America (Unitas Fratrum)		
(Northern Province)	1966	11
(Southern Province)	1967	4
National Fellowship of Brethren Churches	1966	20
National Primitive Baptist Convention in the U.S.A.	1966	1,87
National Spiritual Alliance of the U.S.A.	1966	2
National Spiritualist Association of Churches	1966	18

Inclusive Membership	Full, Communicant, or Confirmed Members	No. of Pastors Having Charges	Total No. of Clergy	No. of Sunday or Sabbath Schools	Total Enrollment
64,498	64,498	814	1,231	844	82,500
2,028	2,028	15	31	N.A.	N.A.
35,841	35,841	205	416	188	37,086
3,743	3,743	50	55	35	1,903
2,835	2,835	35	29	28	1,100
25	25	2	2	0	xxxx
101,435	101,435	749	1,185	864	176,088
7,500	7,500	60	150	60	9,125
5,725,000	N.A.	4,300	5,800	N.A.	N.A.
3,147,959	2,167,277	4,979	7,016	5,707	1,126,249
2,729,897	1,806,187	4,522	6,469	5,567	961,958
81,248	81,248	1,397	1,754	882	124,172
10,310,619	10,310,619	N.A.	29,287	N.A.	6,758,905
9,475	9,475	144	195	132	19,075
38,270	27,717	92	112	100	14,385
22,373	22,373	46	60	48	12,409
29,563	29,563	208	307	208	40,226
1,225,000	1,225,000	565	587	1,800	168,200
3,162	N.A.	50	68	0	xxxx
N.A.	N.A.	59	174	N.A.	490

(Continued)

TABLE 1A: *Current Church Statistics (Cont'd.)*

Religious Body	Year Reported	No. Churc
New Apostolic Church of N.A., Inc.	1966	1(
North American Baptist Association	1966	1,5(
North American Baptist General Conference	1966	3:
North American Old Roman Catholic Church	1967	:
Old Order Amish Mennonite Church	1966	3(
Old Order (Wisler) Mennonite Church	1966	!
Open Bible Standard Churches, Inc.	1967	25
Oregon Yearly Meeting of Friends Church	1966	(
The Orthodox Catholic Patriarchate of America	1966	:
Pacific Yearly Meeting of Friends	1966	:
Pentecostal Church of God of America, Inc.	1967	97
Pentecostal Evangelical Church of God, National and International, Inc.	1966	
Pentecostal Holiness Church, Inc.	1966	1,38
Pilgrim Holiness Church	1966	95
Presbyterian Church in the U.S.	1966	4,00
Progressive National Baptist Convention, Inc.	1966	65
Protestant Conference (Lutheran)	1966	
Protestant Episcopal Church	1966	7,56
Protestant Reformed Churches of America	1966	1!
Reformed Church in America	1966	90:

nclusive mbership	Full, Communicant, or Confirmed Members	No. of Pastors Having Charges	Total No. of Clergy	No. of Sunday or Sabbath Schools	Total Enrollment
18,567	18,567	169	207	164	5,703
200,000	200,000	N.A.	3,000	N.A.	N.A.
53,742	53,742	295	419	335	57,493
18,954	17,774	32	54	31	2,945
21,023	21,023	851	1,083	N.A.	N.A.
7,512	7,512	74	118	N.A.	N.A.
27,000	27,000	259	553	259	N.A.
6,055	6,055	63	159	63	5,836
2,850	2,850	25	25	2	65
2,227	1,486	0	0	29	N.A.
115,000	N.A.	975	1,325	975	N.A.
N.A.	N.A.	2	10	0	xxxx
65,040	65,040	1,206	1,953	1,300	140,001
32,814	32,814	882	1,662	957	109,038
955,402	955,402	2,681	4,223	4,149	661,648
521,581	521,581	653	857	650	754,353
1,435	1,435	7	14	8	377
3,429,153	2,267,372	7,353	10,719	7,063	935,695
3,061	1,598	13	15	11	645
377,671	228,987	819	1,212	879	137,014

(Continued)

TABLE 1A: *Current Church Statistics (Cont'd.)*

Religious Body	Year Reported	No. Church
Reformed Mennonite Church	1966	?
Reformed Presbyterian Church of N.A.	1966	6
Religious Society of Friends (General Conference)	1965	29
Reorganized Church of Jesus Christ of Latter-Day Saints	1966	1,09
Roman Catholic Church	1967	23,73
Romanian Orthodox Episcopate of America	1966	4
The Russian Orthodox Greek Catholic Church of America	1966	30
Salvation Army	1966	1,21
Serbian Orthodox Church in the U.S.A. and Canada	1967	5
Seventh-Day Adventists	1966	3,16
Social Brethren	1966	3
Southern Baptist Convention	1966	33,92?
Synod of Evangelical Lutheran Churches	1964	6?
Ukrainian Orthodox Church of U.S.A.	1966	10?
Unaffiliated Conservative and Amish Mennonite Churches	1966	4?
United Brethren in Christ	1966	30?
United Christian Church	1967	1?
United Church of Christ	1966	6,94?
United Missionary Church	1966	21?
The United Presbyterian Church in the U.S.A.	1966	8,96?

Inclusive Membership	Full, Communicant, or Confirmed Members	No. of Pastors Having Charges	Total No. of Clergy	No. of Sunday or Sabbath Schools	Total Enrollment
500	500	20	35	N.A.	N.A.
5,535	5,535	55	95	69	5,031
31,670	N.A.	23	N.A.	N.A.	N.A.
182,251	182,251	1,093	16,303	1,200	91,300
46,864,910	N.A.	17,375	59,979	14,266	6,155,742
50,000	50,000	33	42	38	1,423
56,549	43,536	270	337	N.A.	N.A.
294,201	125,021	1,125	3,889	61,704	3,857,093
65,000	65,000	56	64	52	5,450
374,433	374,433	1,877	2,315	3,234	388,451
N.A.	1,623	31	42	28	1,407
10,947,389	10,947,389	30,278	N.A.	33,062	7,601,095
21,656	15,435	52	63	62	6,978
87,475	87,475	107	131	107	918
1,840	1,840	70	91	N.A.	N.A.
22,658	22,658	276	278	298	34,659
600	600	11	8	8	1,138
2,063,481	2,063,481	5,973	8,774	N.A.	1,015,418
11,733	11,733	200	286	216	31,168
3,298,583	3,298,583	N.A.	12,850	8,968	1,686,950

(Continued)

TABLE 1A: *Current Church Statistics (Cont'd.)*

Religious Body	Year Reported	No. o Churcl
United Seventh-Day Brethren	1967	
The United Wesleyan Methodist Church of America	1966	
United Zion Church	1966	1
Vedanta Society	1966	1
Volunteers of America	1966	9
Wesleyan Methodist Church of America	1966	1,17
Number of Bodies Reporting	xxxx	12.
Totals Reported	xxxx	223,70
The Anglican Church of Canada	1966	3,53
Baptist Union of Western Canada	1966	15
Evangelical United Brethren Church	1966	11
Jewish Congregations	1961	N.A
Presbyterian Church in Canada	1966	1,13
United Baptist Convention of the Atlantic Provinces	1966	60
United Church of Canada	1966	5,21
United Missionary Church of Canada	1966	7
Number of Bodies Reporting	xxxx	7
Totals Reported	xxxx	10,82

Inclusive membership	Full, Communicant, or Confirmed Members	No. of Pastors Having Charges	Total No. of Clergy	No. of Sunday or Sabbath Schools	Total Enrollment
N.A.	N.A.	4	N.A.	N.A.	N.A.
550	550	5	12	4	310
880	880	16	17	13	1,547
1,000	N.A.	19	N.A.	N.A.	N.A.
31,140	31,140	352	338	180	12,190
49,593	39,419	1,294	1,743	1,138	120,660
119	106	117	118	106	99
4,867,944	47,372,058	137,626	264,373	219,563	40,967,187
1,292,762	671,410	1,800	2,647	2,386	240,896
17,504	17,504	126	161	176	18,122
13,722	13,722	78	92	113	11,543
254,368	N.A.	N.A.	N.A.	N.A.	N.A.
200,125	200,125	N.A.	836	1,064	N.A.
68,951	68,951	237	308	515	41,854
1,062,006	1,062,006	N.A.	3,480	4,544	585,654
3,458	3,458	60	93	70	8,740
8	7	5	7	7	6
2,912,896	2,037,176	2,301	7,617	8,868	906,809

N.A.—Not available, not reported

xxxx—Not applicable

The Church of Jesus Christ of Latter-Day Saints collects statistics only on a worldwide basis. Their figures therefore are not included in the U.S. Totals shown in Table 1A, above.

Official figures published by the Reformed Church in America include data from outside the United States, but under U.S. judicatories, as follows: Number of Churches 32; Inclusive Membership 9,164; Communicant Membership 4,033; Number of Pastors Having Charges 32; Total Number of Clergy 35; Number of Sunday or Sabbath Schools 32; Total Enrollment 2,592; in addition to the figures shown in Table 1A, above.

TABLE 1B: *Non-current Statistics*

Religious Body	Year Reported	No. of Churches	Inclusive Membership	No. of Pastors Having Charges	Total No. of Clergy
African Methodist Episcopal Church	1951	5,878	1,166,301	5,878	7,089
African Methodist Episcopal Zion Church	1965	4,583	1,100,000	2,850	2,983
African Orthodox Church	1957	24	6,000	24	50
African Union First Colored Methodist Protestant Church Inc.	1953	33	5,000	33	40
American Catholic Church, Archdiocese of N.Y.	1961	18	4,369	12	18
Apostolic Christian Church (Nazarean)	1960	51	2,347	15	147
The Apostolic Faith	1965	43	4,678	43	75
Apostolic Lutheran Church of America	1961	58	6,994	24	28
Apostolic Overcoming Holy Church of God	1956	300	75,000	300	350
Associate Presbyterian Church of N.A.	1965	4	650	2	3
Bethel Baptist Assembly, Inc.	1965	22	5,147	22	31
Brethren Church (Ashland, Ohio)	1964	120	18,013	96	149
Bulgarian Eastern Orthodox Church	1962	23	86,000	10	13
Calvary Pentecostal Church, Inc.	1960	22	8,000	22	141
Christadelphians	1964	850	15,800	xxx	xxx
Christian Catholic Church	1965	5	1,555	5	10
Christian Methodist Episcopal Church	1965	2,598	466,718	2,214	2,259
Christian Union	1965	130	5,821	80	80
Christ's Sanctified Holy Church	1957	30	600	19	30
Church of Christ	1956	12	3,000	42	211
Church of Christ (Holiness) U.S.A.	1965	159	9,280	76	76

Denomination	Year				
Church of God (Apostolic)	1954	7			9
Church of God (Seventh-Day)	1960	7	2,000	7	76
The Church of God (Seventh-Day), Denver, Colo.	1964	56	5,500	46	N.A.
Church of God and Saints of Christ	1959	217	38,127	N.A.	112
Church of God by Faith	1965	105	3,470	97	6,000
Church of God in Christ	1965	4,500	425,500	4,000	86
Church of God in Christ (Mennonite)	1961	38	5,000	80	60
Church of God of Illumination	1963	14	9,000	60	
Church of Our Lord Jesus Christ of the Apostolic Faith, Inc.	1954	155	45,000	150	165
Church of the East and of the Assyrians	1952	10	3,200	8	38
Church of the Gospel	1965	4	42	3	2
Church of the Living God	1964	276	45,320	332	376
Churches of Christ	1965	18,500	2,350,000	4,300	7,000
Churches of Christ in Christian Union	1965	228	7,514	220	285
Churches of God, Holiness	1965	32	25,600	16	29
Churches of God in N.A. (General Eldership)	1965	374	36,550	277	379
Conference of the Evangelical Mennonite Church	1965	21	2,516	20	46
Congregational Methodist Church	1957	223	14,274	169	308
Congregational Methodist Church of U.S.A.	1954	100	7,500	100	120
Conservative Baptist Association of America	1965	1,500	325,000	1,422	2,500
Cumberland Methodist Church	1954	4	65	2	6
Emmanuel Holiness Church	1955	56	1,200	55	90
Evangelical Lutheran Church in America (Eielsen Synod)	1957	44	4,220	3	3

(*Continued*)

TABLE 1B: *Non-current Statistics (Cont'd.)*

Religious Body	Year Reported	No. of Churches	Inclusive Membership	No. of Pastors Having Charges	Total No. of Clergy
Evangelical Mennonite Brethren	1964	16	1,644	16	33
Fire-Baptized Holiness Church	1958	53	988	N.A.	N.A.
Fire-Baptized Holiness Church (Wesleyan)	1957	53	1,007	52	82
Fundamental Methodist Church, Inc.	1965	12	574	12	12
General Conference of the Evangelical Baptist Church, Inc.	1952	31	2,200	22	37
General Six-Principle Baptists	1965	3	125	3	3
Gospel Mission Corps	1965	6	200	4	N.A.
Greek Orthodox Archdiocese of North and South America	1965	443	1,770,000	468	567
Holiness Church of God, Inc.	1965	26	884	24	32
Holiness Methodist Church	1965	23	1,000	23	35
Holy Orthodox Church in America (Eastern Catholic and Apostolic)	1965	4	260	4	10
Holy Ukrainian Autocephalic Orthodox Church in Exile	1965	15	4,800	15	24
House of God, Which Is the Church of the Living God, the Pillar and Ground of the Truth, Inc.	1956	107	2,350	80	170
Hungarian Reformed Church in America	1959	40	11,110	26	36
Independent Assemblies of God, International	1962	136	N.A.	136	367
Independent Churches	1936	384	40,276	N.A.	N.A.
International Church of the Foursquare Gospel	1963	741	89,215	741	2,690
International General Assembly of Spiritualists	1956	209	164,072	221	190
Jehovah's Witnesses	1965	5,141	330,358	N.A.	N.A.

Liberal Catholic Church	1956	8	4,000	6	33
Lumber River Annual Conference of the Holiness Methodist Church	1959	7	360	5	5
Mennonite Brethren Church of N.A.	1965	81	13,171	111	173
The Metropolitan Church Association	1958	15	443	13	62
National Baptist Convention of America	1956	11,398	2,668,799	7,598	28,574
National Baptist Convention, U.S.A., Inc.	1958	26,000	5,500,000	26,000	27,500
National Baptist Evangelical Life and Soul Saving Assembly of U.S.A.	1951	264	57,674	128	137
Netherlands Reformed Congregations	1960	14	2,500	4	4
New Congregational Methodist Church	1958	11	518	6	11
North American Old Roman Catholic Church	1965	30	18,500	30	45
Ohio Yearly Meeting of Friends Church (Evangelical Friends Alliance)	1965	87	7,059	93	157
Old German Baptist Brethren	1965	54	4,225	46	130
The (Original) Church of God, Inc.	1965	75	18,000	50	60
Orthodox Presbyterian Church	1965	110	12,867	86	150
Pentecostal Assemblies of the World, Inc.	1960	550	45,000	450	600
Pentecostal Church of Christ	1965	41	1,158	40	65
Pentecostal Fire-Baptized Holiness Church	1965	41	500	46	38
Pentecostal Free-Will Baptist Church, Inc.	1965	176	10,000	112	210
Pillar of Fire	1949	61	5,100	N.A.	N.A.
Plymouth Brethren	1960	665	33,250	xxxx	xxxx

(Continued)

TABLE 1B: *Non-current Statistics (Cont'd.)*

Religious Body	Year Reported	No. of Churches	Inclusive Membership	No. of Pastors Having Charges	Total No. of Clergy
Polish National Catholic Church of America	1960	162	282,411	151	144
Primitive Advent Christian Church	1965	10	597	8	29
Primitive Baptists	1950	1,000	72,000	N.A.	N.A.
Primitive Methodist Church, U.S.A.	1965	86	11,945	71	60
The Reformed Catholic Church (Utrecht Confession) Province of N.A.	1957	20	2,217	18	21
Reformed Church in the United States	1965	20	2,554	14	18
Reformed Episcopal Church	1963	64	7,007	54	81
Reformed Methodist Union Episcopal Church	1965	21	16,198	22	31
Reformed Presbyterian Church, Evangelical Synod	1965	109	10,400	112	247
Reformed Zion Union Apostolic Church	1965	50	16,000	23	4
Religious Society of Friends (Conservative)	1961	21	1,696	xxxx	xxxx
Religious Society of Friends (Kansas Yearly Meeting)	1965	89	8,227	89	160
Russian Orthodox Catholic Church in America Patriarchal Exarchate	1965	67	152,973	61	98
The Russian Orthodox Church Outside Russia	1955	81	55,000	92	168
The Schwenkfelder Church	1962	5	2,300	4	4
Second Cumberland Presbyterian Church in U.S.	1959	121	30,000	121	125
Separate Baptists in Christ	1962	84	7,496	65	106
Seventh-Day Baptists (German, 1728)	1951	3	150	2	4
Seventh-Day Baptist General Conference	1964	65	5,773	47	73
Southern Methodist Church	196?				

	Year				
Syrian Antiochian Orthodox Church					
Syrian Orthodox Church of Antioch (Archdiocese of the U.S.A. and Canada)	1963	7	25,000	7	77
Triumph the Church and Kingdom of God in Christ	1965	420	43,500	420	1,200
Ukrainian Orthodox Church of America (Ecumenical Patriarchate)	1959	37	40,250	43	52
Union American Methodist Episcopal Church	1957	256	27,560	240	276
Unitarian Universalist Association	1965	1,044	166,622	568	863
United Baptists	1955	586	63,641	415	1,100
United Free Will Baptist Church	1952	836	100,000	915	784
United Holy Church of America, Inc.	1960	470	28,980	379	400
United Pentecostal Church, Inc.	1965	2,000	125,000	2,000	2,061
Unity of the Brethren	1964	32	6,142	13	13
Wisconsin Evangelical Lutheran Synod	1964	869	358,466	629	789

N.A.—Not available, not reported
xxxx—Not applicable
For further data, and for bodies not listed above, see other editions of YBAC, especially editions 1967 and 1965.

Constituency of the National Council of the Churches of Christ in the U.S.A.

A separate tabulation has been made of the constituent bodies of the National Council of the Churches of Christ in the U.S.A., and is given below:

Constituent Body	Year	Number of Churches	Inclusive Membership	Pastors with Charges
Armenian Church, Diocese of America	1966	43	136,000	37
Baptist				
American Baptist Convention	1966	6,063	1,538,988	4,476
National Baptist Convention of America	1956	11,398	2,668,799	7,598
National Baptist Convention, U.S.A., Inc.	1958	26,000	5,500,000	26,000
Progressive National Baptist Convention, Inc.	1966	650	521,581	653
Seventh-Day Baptist General Conference	1964	65	5,773	47
Brethren, Church of the	1966	1,056	191,402	813
Christian Churches (Disciples of Christ), International Convention	1966	8,066	1,894,927	3,157
Eastern Orthodox				
Antiochean Orthodox Archdiocese of Toledo, and Dependencies in N.A.	1966	20	30,000	20
Greek Orthodox Archdiocese of North and South America	1965	443	1,770,000	468
Romanian Orthodox Episcopate of America	1966	44	50,000	33
Russian Orthodox Catholic Church in America Patriarchal Exarchate	1965	67	152,973	61

The Russian Orthodox Greek Catholic Church of America	1966	309	56,549	270
Serbian Orthodox Church in the U.S.A. and Canada	1967	52	65,000	56
Syrian Antiochian Orthodox Church	1963	81	110,000	81
Syrian Orthodox Church of Antioch	1963	7	25,000	7
Ukrainian Orthodox Church of America	1959	37	40,250	43
Evangelical United Brethren Church	1966	3,970	732,377	2,889
Friends				
Friends United Meeting (The Five Years Meeting of Friends)	1966	502	70,673	367
Philadelphia Yearly Meeting of the Religious Society of Friends	1965	292	17,159	23
General Convention of the New Jerusalem in the U.S.A.	1966	56	3,743	50
Lutheran Church in America	1966	5,860	3,147,959	4,979
Methodist				
African Methodist Episcopal Church	1951	5,878	1,166,301	5,878
African Methodist Episcopal Zion Church	1965	4,583	1,100,000	2,850
Christian Methodist Episcopal Church	1965	2,598	466,718	2,214
The Methodist Church	1966	37,603	10,310,619	N.A.
Moravian Church in America (Unitas Fratrum)				
Northern Province	1966	113	38,270	92
Southern Province	1967	49	22,373	46
Polish National Catholic Church of America	1960	162	282,411	151
Presbyterian				
Presbyterian Church in the U.S.	1966	4,002	955,402	2,681
The United Presbyterian Church in the U.S.A.	1966	8,968	3,298,583	N.A.

Constituent Body	Year	Number of Churches	Inclusive Membership	Pastors with Charge
Protestant Episcopal Church	1966	7,562	3,429,153	7,353
Reformed				
Hungarian Reformed				
Church in America	1959	40	11,110	26
Reformed Church in				
America	1966	902	377,671	819
United Church of Christ	1966	6,945	2,063,481	5,973
TOTAL (34 bodies)		144,486	42,251,245	80,211

N.A.—not available, not reported

Unlike tables shown elsewhere in this section, the totals above combine both current and non-current (but last-reported) components.

Statistics on Church Finances

For this edition of the *Yearbook* seventy-one United States religious bodies supplied some or all of the information requested concerning financial contributions. Sixty were able to provide either total contributions only, or total contributions distributed by benevolences and congregational expenses. The total dollars thus represented were $3,266,533,260.

Table 2 details some of the statistics of church finances, computed per capita, furnished by the responding bodies.

In terms of the per member contributions shown, the median total contribution is $111.02, generally for the year ending in 1966. The mean average for the same figures is noticeably higher, at $127.09.

As a guideline in analyzing church expenditures, the first statistical column of Table 2 shows contributions for benevolence purposes as a percentage of total contributions. Because of incomplete data, this could be computed for only fifty-nine of the seventy-one bodies reporting. Among these, however, the median contribution for benevolences is 20.7 per cent of all contributions, and the mean average is 25.3 per cent.

TABLE 2: *Some Statistics of Church Finances*

Religious Body	Benevolences as Percentage of Total Contributions	Total Benevolences	PER MEMBER REPORTS Congregational Expenses	Total Contributions	Fiscal Year Reported
	%				
Advent Christian Church	20.2	$ 15.48	$ 61.06	$ 76.54	1967
American Baptist Association	NA	.29	NA	NA	1966
American Baptist Convention	15.4	11.40	62.45	73.85	1966
American Lutheran Church	18.0	16.34	74.58	90.92	1966
Assemblies of God	NA	19.71	NA	NA	1966
Associate Reformed Presbyterian Church	26.0	24.81	70.48	95.29	1966
Baptist General Conference	20.3	42.14	165.05	207.19	1966
Berean Fundamental Church	27.2	69.68	186.14	255.82	1966
Bible Way Churches of Our Lord Jesus Christ World Wide, Inc.	NA	1.12	NA	NA	1967
The Christian and Missionary Alliance	NA	83.63	NA	NA	1966
Christian Churches (Disciples of Christ), International Convention	16.1	9.25	48.36	57.61	1966
Church of God (Abrahamic Faith)	11.7	15.97	120.97	136.94	1966
Church of God (Anderson, Ind.)	14.7	25.11	146.17	171.28	1966
Church of God (Cleveland, Tenn.)	22.1	49.60	175.30	224.90	1966
					(*Continued*)

TABLE 2: *Some Statistics of Church Finances* (*Cont'd.*)

Religious Body	Benevolences as Percentage of Total Contributions	Total Benevolences	Congregational Expenses	Total Contributions	Fiscal Year Reported
	%	PER MEMBER REPORTS			
The Church of Jesus Christ (Bickertonites)	59.4	17.08	11.66	28.74	1967
Church of the Brethren	27.7	24.12	63.11	87.23	1966
Church of the Lutheran Brethren of America	NA	72.13	NA	NA	1966
Church of the Nazarene	19.8	35.76	144.61	180.37	1966
Congregational Christian Churches, National Association of	NA	4.67	NA	NA	1966
Conservative Congregational Christian Conference	43.0	49.26	65.28	114.54	1966
Cumberland Presbyterian Church	14.4	15.71	93.70	109.41	1966
Eastern Orthodox Catholic Church in America	25.0	31.25	93.75	125.00	1966
Elim Missionary Assemblies	NA	43.75	NA	NA	1966
Ethical Culture Movement	13.1	20.64	136.36	157.00	1966
Evangelical Congregational Church	19.3	18.56	77.85	96.41	1966
Evangelical Covenant Church of America	23.0	48.73	163.10	211.82	1966

Evangelical Free Church of America	29.1			83.63	1966
Evangelical Lutheran Synod	23.0	19.21	64.42	148.77	1965
Evangelical Methodist Church	8.0	11.96	136.81	79.69	1966
Evangelical United Brethren Church	19.7	15.71	63.98	.12	1966
Free Christian Zion Church of Christ	23.2	.03	.09	NA	1966
Free Will Baptists	NA	NA	31.26	NA	1966
Friends United Meeting (The Five Years Meeting of Friends)	28.0	17.40	44.79	62.19	1966
The General Association of Regular Baptist Churches	41.1	59.53	85.47	145.00	1966
General Baptists	6.0	3.96	62.18	66.14	1966
The General Conference Mennonite Church	44.2	65.11	82.36	147.47	1966
General Convention of the New Jerusalem in the U.S.A.	NA	28.21	NA	NA	1966
Hutterian Brethren	67.7	.22	.11	.33	1966
Independent Baptist Church of America	98.9	181.00	2.00	183.00	1966
Independent Fundamental Churches of America	38.9	72.14	113.48	185.62	1966
Lutheran Church in America	21.4	17.82	65.56	83.38	1966
The Lutheran Church—Missouri Synod	21.7	24.08	86.94	111.02	1966
Mennonite Church	48.2	34.19	36.80	70.99	1966
The Methodist Church	10.9	4.33	35.49	39.82	1966
Missionary Church Association	20.6	44.70	172.03	216.73	1966

(Continued)

TABLE 2: *Some Statistics of Church Finances (Cont'd.)*

Religious Body	Benevolences as Percentage of Total Contributions	PER MEMBER REPORTS			Fiscal Year Reported
	%	Total Benevolences	Congregational Expenses	Total Contributions	
Moravian Church in America (Unitas Fratrum)	12.9	15.14	102.33	117.47	1966
National Fellowship of Brethren Churches	14.9	36.14	206.89	243.03	1966
North American Baptist Association	13.5	5.85	37.59	43.44	1966
North American Baptist General Conference	21.7	31.24	112.82	144.06	1966
North American Old Roman Catholic Church	22.7	2.28	7.76	10.04	1967
Oregon Yearly Meeting of Friends Church	19.8	29.02	117.47	146.49	1966
Pentecostal Holiness Church, Inc.	9.0	13.34	134.82	148.16	1966
Pilgrim Holiness Church	13.3	32.90	214.22	247.12	1966
Presbyterian Church in the U.S.	24.7	30.56	93.23	123.79	1966
The Protestant Conference (Lutheran)	8.0	2.54	29.13	31.67	1966
The Protestant Episcopal Church	18.0	18.39	83.81	102.20	1966
Reformed Church in America	25.2				

Reformed Presbyterian Church of North America	NA	164.55	NA	NA	1966
Reorganized Church of Jesus Christ of Latter-Day Saints	51.0	22.85	21.95	44.80	1966
The Romanian Orthodox Episcopate of America	NA	.12	NA	NA	1966
Serbian Orthodox Church in the U.S.A. and Canada	40.2	31.08	46.15	77.23	1967
Seventh-Day Adventists	72.0	219.18	85.20	304.38	1966
Social Brethren	3.1	1.71	53.37	55.08	1966
Southern Baptist Convention	17.2	10.52	50.64	61.16	1966
Synod of Evangelical Lutheran Churches	12.2	11.72	84.34	96.06	1964
United Brethren in Christ	21.0	28.36	106.79	135.15	1966
United Church of Christ	14.3	12.17	72.94	85.11	1966
United Missionary Church	NA	NA	NA	245.18	1966
United Presbyterian Church in the U.S.A.	20.2	20.17	79.79	99.96	1966
United Zion Church	30.4	73.34	168.01	241.35	1966
Wesleyan Methodist Church of America	20.7	64.73	247.92	312.65	1966
Number of Bodies Reporting	xxxx	69	60	60	xxxx
Total Amounts Reported	xxxx	$676,420,421	$2,612,297,386	$3,266,533,260	xxxx
The Anglican Church of Canada	20.4	$ 10.89	$ 42.49	$ 53.38	1966
Baptist Union of Western Canada	16.8	24.69	122.03	146.72	1966
The Evangelical United Brethren Church	27.6	33.22	87.19	120.41	1966

(Continued)

TABLE 2: *Some Statistics of Church Finances (Cont'd.)*

Religious Body	Benevolences as Percentage of Total Contributions	Total Benevolences	Congregational Expenses	PER MEMBER REPORTS Total Contributions	Fiscal Year Reported
	%				
United Church of Canada	23.2	10.66	35.32	45.98	1966
United Missionary Church of Canada	NA	NA	NA	239.67	1966
Number of Bodies Reporting	xxxx	4	4	5	xxxx
Total Amounts Reported	xxxx	$ 19,186,172	$ 68,487,049	$ 88,502,007	xxxx

NA—Not available, not reported
xxxx—Not applicable
Reformed Church in America figures include reports from thirty-two churches outside the United States, but under U.S. judicatories.

Value of New Construction of Religious Buildings

Estimates of the annual value of new construction of religious buildings, 1925–66, inclusive, indicate that a new high was reached in 1966, according to a statistical table entitled "Value of New Construction Put in Place in the United States, 1966" appearing in the *Construction Review*, U. S. Department of Commerce, issue of March 1967.

The published figures at five-year intervals and for 1966 follow:

Year	Value	Year	Value
1925	$165,000,000	1950	$ 409,000,000
1930	135,000,000	1955	736,000,000
1935	28,000,000	1960	1,016,000,000
1940	59,000,000	1965	985,000,000
1945	26,000,000	1966	1,174,000,000

Ministers Report Total Compensation

A sample of 2201 ministers in nine denominations reported in 1956 the following figures with respect to their *total compensation:*

Average total compensation (cash salary, allowance, fee, perquisite [including rental allowance or an estimate of the rental value of dwelling furnished]) $5827

(Of this amount the average cash salary was $4436)

The denominations represented were The Methodist Church; Congregational Christian; Presbyterian, U.S.A.; United Lutheran; American Baptist; Church of the Brethren; Disciples of Christ; Evangelical and Reformed; Protestant Episcopal. (From *The Church as Employer, Money Raiser, and Investor,* by F. Ernest Johnson and J. Emory Ackerman. New York, Harper and Brothers, 1959.)

A sample of 5623 ministers of fifteen Protestant denominations revealed a median cash salary of $5158 in 1963. To total income was added $1300 as value of housing furnished; $459 for utilities furnished; and $89 in fees. (From this about $600 should be deducted for "unreimbursed loss" for professional auto expenses.) "The larger the church membership, the larger the median salary." There was relatively little variation region by region. The median cash salary varied, from denomination to denomination sampled, from $3750 to $5669. (*Information Service*, National Council of Churches, Dec. 5, 1964, a report prepared by Ross P. Scherer, for the Department of Research, National Council of Churches.)

Christian Day Schools Under Protestant Auspices

Statistics are for the academic year, 1967–68, and cover all schools directly under Protestant auspices. Elementary schools exclude kindergarten. Secondary schools include the upper grades up to the twelfth.

	ELEMENTARY		
	Schools	*Teachers*	*Enrollment*
Lutheran Churches	1,648	7,869	192,717
Other Protestant Churches	1,868	9,989	187,431
Total	3,516	17,858	380,148
	SECONDARY		
Lutheran Churches	32	782	14,554
Other Protestant Churches	160	1,880	20,699
Total	192	2,662	35,253
Grand Total	3,708	20,520	415,401

INDEX